THE POSTSECULAR RESTORATION AND THE MAKING OF LITERARY CONSERVATISM

This book reveals a synergy between postsecularity – as a critique of emergent liberal secular ideals and practices – and the modern literary sphere, in which conservative writers feature prominently. Corrinne Harol argues boldly yet compellingly that influential literary forms and practices including fiction, mental freedom, worlding, reading, narration, and historical fiction are in fact derived from these writers' responses to secularization. Interrogating a series of concepts – faith, indulgence, figuring, reading, passivity, revolution, and nostalgia – central to secular culture, this study also engages with works by Aphra Behn, John Dryden, Margaret Cavendish, and Walter Scott, as well as attending to the philosophies of Thomas Hobbes, David Hume, and Edmund Burke. Countering eighteenth-century studies' current overreliance on the secularization narrative (as content and method, fact and norm), this book models how a postsecular approach can help us to understand this period, and secularization itself, more fully.

CORRINNE HAROL is Professor of English and Film Studies at the University of Alberta. She is the author of *Enlightened Virginity in Eighteenth-Century Literature* (2006) and co-editor of *Literary/Liberal Entanglements* (2017). Her work explores the impact of secularization on eighteenth-century literature.

THE POSTSECULAR RESTORATION AND THE MAKING OF LITERARY CONSERVATISM

CORRINNE HAROL
University of Alberta

Shaftesbury Road, Cambridge CB2 8EA, United Kingdom

One Liberty Plaza, 20th Floor, New York, NY 10006, USA

477 Williamstown Road, Port Melbourne, VIC 3207, Australia

314–321, 3rd Floor, Plot 3, Splendor Forum, Jasola District Centre, New Delhi – 110025, India

103 Penang Road, #05–06/07, Visioncrest Commercial, Singapore 238467

Cambridge University Press is part of Cambridge University Press & Assessment, a department of the University of Cambridge.

We share the University's mission to contribute to society through the pursuit of education, learning and research at the highest international levels of excellence.

www.cambridge.org
Information on this title: www.cambridge.org/9781009273480

DOI: 10.1017/9781009273497

© Corrinne Harol 2023

This publication is in copyright. Subject to statutory exception and to the provisions of relevant collective licensing agreements, no reproduction of any part may take place without the written permission of Cambridge University Press & Assessment.

First published 2023

A catalogue record for this publication is available from the British Library.

Library of Congress Cataloging-in-Publication Data
NAMES: Harol, Corrinne, 1963- author.
TITLE: The postsecular restoration and the making of literary conservatism / Corrinne Harol.
DESCRIPTION: New York : Cambridge University Press, 2023. | Includes bibliographical references and index.
IDENTIFIERS: LCCN 2022030703 (print) | LCCN 2022030704 (ebook) | ISBN 9781009273480 (hardback) | ISBN 9781009273459 (paperback) | ISBN 9781009273497 (epub)
SUBJECTS: LCSH: English literature–Early modern, 1500-1700–History and criticism. | Conservatism–Great Britain–History–17th century. | Politics and literature–England–History–17th century. | Great Britain–History–Restoration, 1660-1688.
CLASSIFICATION: LCC PR437 .H37 2023 (print) | LCC PR437 (ebook) | DDC 820.9/004–dc23/eng/20220930
LC record available at https://lccn.loc.gov/2022030703
LC ebook record available at https://lccn.loc.gov/2022030704

ISBN 978-1-009-27348-0 Hardback

Cambridge University Press & Assessment has no responsibility for the persistence or accuracy of URLs for external or third-party internet websites referred to in this publication and does not guarantee that any content on such websites is, or will remain, accurate or appropriate.

Contents

Acknowledgments — *page* vi

Introduction — 1

PART I POLITICAL AND FICTIONAL RELATIONS

1 Faith: Impersonating Faith, or How We Came to Have Faith in Fictions — 27

2 Indulgence: The Stuart Declarations of Indulgence and Their Afterlives — 67

PART II POSTSECULAR LITERARY EXPERIENCES: WORLDS AND TIME

3 Figuring: Margaret Cavendish's Critique of Imagining and Worlding — 103

4 Reading: John Dryden's Postsecular Apostolic and the Time of Literary History — 134

PART III POLITICAL AGENTS AND NOVEL FORMS

5 Passivity: The Passion of *Oroonoko* and the Ethics of Narration — 177

6 Revolution and Nostalgia: Walter Scott and the Forms of Jacobite Nostalgia — 211

Coda: On Literary Conservatism as a Formal Category — 243

Bibliography — 248
Index — 275

Acknowledgments

This book has taken so long to complete that its supporters and collaborators are so varied that it is impossible to do them justice. For generous financial support, thanks to the University of Alberta Faculty of Arts, the Kule Institute, and the Killam Foundation as well as the Social Sciences and Humanities Research Council of Canada. Thanks to the scholarly communities that have listened to and responded to various presentations of work in progress, especially at the Canadian Society for Eighteenth-Century Studies, the American Society for Eighteenth-Century Studies, Western University, the Folger Library, and the University of Alberta. The Department of English and Film Studies at the University of Alberta provided many thoughtful interlocutors for my work, but thanks especially to Katherine Binhammer, Pat Demers, David Gay, Isobel Grundy, Gary Kelly, Eddy Kent, Mike O'Driscoll, Mark Simpson, Peter Sinnema, and Christine Stewart. For scholarly comradery regarding secularization, thanks to David Alvarez, Matthew Augustine, Alison Conway, Sarah Ellenzweig, Howard Horwitz, Mary Helen McMurran, and Helen Thompson. Research and editorial support was provided by Caroline Jennings, Jessica MacQueen, Katherine O'Briain, and Kit Rhem. Thanks to librarians at the University of Alberta, the British Library, the Lewis Walpole Library, and, especially, the William Andrews Clark Memorial Library. For reading, listening, and responding to me over many years of thinking through this book, thanks to Helen Deutsch, Jayne Lewis, Julie Rak, Teresa Zackodnik, and Subhash Lele. Thanks to my siblings, Michael, Kim, and Kristen Harol, for always believing in me. And thanks to my canine companions for many walks and reminders to relax. Special thanks to the anonymous readers for uncommonly generous and rigorous readings and to the editorial team at Cambridge University Press, especially Bethany Thomas.

An earlier version of Chapter 3 appeared as "Imagining Worlds and Figuring Toleration: Freedom, Diversity, and Violence in *A Description of a New World, Called the Blazing-World.*" In Alison Conway and David Alvarez, eds., *Imagining Religious Toleration*, University of Toronto Press, 2019, 97–118. An earlier version of Chapter 5 appeared as "The Passion of *Oroonoko*: Passive Obedience, The Royal Slave, and Aphra Behn's Baroque Realism." *ELH* 79.2 (2012): 447–475.

Introduction

The Postsecular Restoration undertakes an exploration of a phenomenon that is often remarked upon but frequently disavowed: that many of the writers of the Restoration period who are considered innovators in the literary field – in particular Margaret Cavendish, Aphra Behn, and John Dryden – were politically conservative, in that they supported monarchy, they were Catholic, they were intolerant, or they were antidemocratic. This book makes the case for the synergistic relationship between a nascent postsecular worldview – one based not on clinging to tradition but in a thoughtful response to emergent liberal secular ideals and practices – and the emergence of the modern sphere of literature, in which conservative writers play a prominent role. Thus, it addresses a critical blind spot: The conservative political orientation of these writers has typically been treated as separate from their literary contributions, leveraged against their literary contributions, explained away as a function of their historical conditions, or ignored altogether. One reason for this may be that literary scholars tend to identify with liberal or progressive politics, and, as a result, our means of seeing connections between literature and politics have tended to obscure questions of how conservative political orientation and literary innovations relate.

Restoration literature – fondly characterized by its comedy, obscenity, sectarianism, and sophisticated linguistic ambiguity – has received significant scholarly attention, but in literary studies the Restoration has been often treated as a literary orphan or as an atavistic and exuberant interlude between early modern and modern, attached to the eighteenth century but ideologically and aesthetically distinct. Its denouement in 1688–89 has represented, in the eighteenth century and well beyond, a model of secular reform, the glorious flagship of Whig historiography. As the centerpiece of England's process of secularization, 1688–89 is credited with the separation of religious and political realms via religious toleration, the privatization of religiosity, the defeat of Catholicism, and an incremental process shifting authority from monarchy to parliament. More broadly, these processes of secularization have been tied to England's commercial and colonial ascendency of the eighteenth century and the triumph of liberalism more generally. For these reasons, historians and political theorists have long been interested in 1688–89. In literary studies, however, it has been largely ignored, and its legacies on the literary field have largely been obscured by literary critics. This study asks us to rethink Restoration literature and its legacies alongside a reconsideration of the legacy of 1688–89 in the literary field.

Recent literary and cultural studies have brought new attention to secularization. In eighteenth-century studies, this has mainly resulted in challenging the facts of secularization, but its norms and forms, and thus our methods for studying the period, have persisted. Secularization refers narrowly to the separation of politics and religion, the disenchantment (or de-transcendentalization) of the world, and the replacement of religious authority with reason in order to pave the way for modernization. Typical accounts of secularization have focused on its impacts on politics or religion. But secularization impacted the fully array of human experiences, habits, feelings, and aspirations. The postsecular lens adopted in this study makes visible the ways that secularization transformed not only religion, politics, or literary themes but also such things as human relationships, theories of mentation and imagination, methods of reading, and literary forms themselves. This is why the writers treated here are not those (for the most part) who attend specifically to religion or politics but rather those who explore the ways that secularization impacted other areas of life. Beginning with insights and tools from postsecular theory, this study ultimately offers its own theory of the postsecular, in which these more subtle transformations, in realms that fall between the chasm that is supposed to segregate secular from religious (and public from private), are made visible – or even made possible – by writers aligned with conservative causes. Literary conservatism on this account begins with a conservative political orientation but takes place in the literary realm and reveals impacts of secularization in realms well beyond religion or politics.

The book uses case studies as a lens into how a postsecular ethos and literature are related. Each chapter centers on a keyword or concept, some of which (faith, indulgence, and passive obedience) were presecular but transformed by secularization and which are obviously tied to a conservative worldview, while others (figuring, reading, revolution, and nostalgia) are more aligned with secularization and liberalization but are revealed to be central to this study's account of literary conservatism. Together, these concepts begin to show how comprehensive the conservative response to secularization was and how significant to culture broadly. Each chapter also focuses on one or two writers and one or more aspects of literary history or form: the fictional imagination, the novelistic narrator, literary history, and historical fiction. Although mainly centered on Restoration writers, the texts span the very long eighteenth century, from Thomas Hobbes' *Leviathan* (1651) through Walter Scott's *Waverley* (1814), thus participating in a nascent scholarly idea of a long Restoration.[1] The methods of the chapters differ, but what they have in common is the effort to understand a secular or postsecular ethos or concept and to connect it to developments in literary history. In so doing, they demonstrate that conservatism's roots are postsecular: that is, they entail a comprehensive response to secularization in all aspects of culture. This book thus traces part of the prehistories of both conservatism and postsecularism, arguing that their affects, commitments, fears, and modes of life show up in literary forms before conservatism is formulated fully as a political ideology in the nineteenth century and before what we now call postsecular culture and critique.

Secularization, 1688–1689, and the Long Restoration

The characterization of England's culture, including its literary history, in the eighteenth century cannot be separated from accounts of secularization, which we may begin by defining as the association of Protestant culture with modernization. In so defining secularization, I follow critics such as Max Weber, Talal Asad, and Gil Anidjar, who have equated secularization not with the decline of religion in general but with the global ascendance of Christianity.[2] While Weber identifies this process as specifically Calvinist, and Asad locates its current meaning in mainstream Protestantism, Anidjar suggests a longer history: "Secularism is a name Christianity gave itself when it invented religion, when it named its other or others as religions."[3] In this study, secularization is highly associated with the events of 1688–89 and thus with the Whig account of Protestant/progressive history, and the defeat of Catholicism, that is its legacy. Since the eighteenth century, the secularization narrative has functioned as both fact and norm. The triumph of reason over superstition, the freedom to think (about religion and anything else) for oneself, the coincidence of secular societies (such as England) with economic success, all of these things have made it difficult to rethink the triumph of secularization: what Philip Nord refers to as the "[t]he secularizing juggernaut – so certain of itself, so tempting, so imposing."[4] I align the writers studied here as well as my methods for studying them with postsecularism insofar as they register – and register skepticism about – the far-reaching effects of secularization and thus offer a wedge into rethinking this juggernaut. A postsecular critique of secularization takes the position, in Ernst-Wolfgang Böckenförde's well-known formulation, that "the liberal secular state lives on premises that it is not able to guarantee by itself," which suggests that secularization as the theoretical separation of religion from politics masks the impossibility (it cannot be guaranteed "by itself") of such separation in practice.[5] For Michael Kaufmann, postsecular criticism destabilizes "certitudes about what counts as 'religious' and 'secular'" (69).[6] This is because secularization impacts not just the distinction between politics and religion but disciplinary disarticulation more generally, and this has limited our understanding of its impacts in other domains, something that postsecular critics call attention to. Saba Mahmood calls secularization a "totalizing project" that has "sought not so much to banish religion from the public domain but to reshape the form it takes, the subjectivities it endorses, and the epistemological claims it can make," and she adds that its force resides in how it produces "a particular kind of religious subject who is compatible with the rationality and exercise of liberal political rule."[7] Secularization is thus a larger category, in which Anglicanism, official tolerance for certain other religions, as well as non-religious cultural and political institutions – and people's experiences of them – take shape. This is a process that takes many centuries, yet the premise of the book – and indeed the evidence offered by the chapters – is that the Restoration was not just a catalyst for this process but also a locus of early concerns about it. The postsecular orientation of this study rejects the secularization narrative's periodization, arguing instead that the secular and the postsecular are coterminous.[8] This is the case for the writers I treat as being postsecular: They are not simply reacting to secularization in retrograde ways but innovating in literary forms as they consider its multifarious implications. In this sense, as Allen Dunn argues, "the postsecular may be less a new phase of cultural development than it is a working through of the problems and contradictions in the secularization process itself."[9] Secularization is a total system that is underpinned by Protestant epistemology, economics, politics, and eschatology, and yet it endeavors to go unnoticed.[10] Reformation theologians made invisibility key to Protestantism (no one can tell who is saved or what happens in the afterlife); this invisibility is central both to its ability to be, at least aspirationally, universal and to its perception as secular rather than religious.[11] The writers studied here, at this particular moment in the development of the secularization juggernaut, had a privileged perspective to make visible questions about the premises of the liberal secular state, the impacts of secularization across the sphere of culture, and the incoherence of (liberal) theory and reality.

The key conservative political event of this period is the Restoration of the monarchy in 1660, which sets in motion the literary and political events analyzed here. In this study, the Restoration is taken more broadly as an ongoing conservative response to secularization and to revolution – to the Puritan revolution that preceded the Restoration and especially to the events of 1688–89, which has been seen as a triumph for secularization: settling the question of religious freedom, inaugurating an era of stable parliamentary rule, strengthening the constitution, increasing liberty, and setting the stage for England's financial and cultural growth of the eighteenth and nineteenth centuries.[12] The way one chooses a name for any event reflects a certain bias and the event under consideration here proves – perhaps even invented or at least epitomizes – that rule. Whig historians have deemed the events of 1688–89 "the glorious revolution" or the "bloodless revolution."[13] "Glorious" and "bloodless" are ways to celebrate this moment as a watershed of modernity, both because the monarchy was weakened and because it was ostensibly nonviolent. Calling the event "glorious" can be seen as an early, paradigmatic, strategy of secularization (in Carl Schmitt's formulation) because it re-signifies a religious term into a secular system of meaning and value.[14] Indeed it uses a religious term of idealized spirituality, "glorious," to celebrate a seminal event of secularity, "revolution." Revisionist historians who wish to counter this whiggish narrative of progress have commonly referred to the events with the adjective "bourgeois," suggesting it simply replaced one ruling class for another, without disrupting the class system.[15] In naming this event, it is not just the modifiers that are debated but also the nouns: "revolution" celebrates the event as a foundational act of political agency, emphasizing human intentionality, the ability to remake the political world according to a group's interest or values. While most historians have used "revolution," the event is alternately called by quite the opposite terms, "invasion" or "abdication."[16] Despite these debates, in which nomenclature is a proxy for politics, the significance of 1688–89 has persisted in narratives of the triumph of secularization, and the political events and political writings of 1688–89 have loomed large in accounts of English history and politics and in narrations of liberalism and modernity. These events have been seen as foundational to the emergence of secular liberal modernity and have placed England at the center of that story.

While the Whig perspective sees 1688–89 as a definitive punctum – ending the Restoration and beginning secular liberalism – and while Marxist historians belittle its significance, this book centers it, providing a different lens for thinking about how the Restoration set the stage for a long postsecular, and literary, response to liberalization. It treats the two bookends of the Restoration (1660 and 1688–89) not as events wholly separated by ideology and historical periodization, but rather as exemplary of the tensions and ambiguities that would dominate eighteenth-century culture. It also fills a scholarly gap, in that literary critics have neglected this area, treating the literature of the Restoration as separate from the political events of 1688–89. Recently, historical interest in 1688–89 has enjoyed yet another renaissance, with books by Tim Harris, Lisa Jardine, Steve Pincus, and Kevin Sharpe mining the archive of both historical and cultural documents about this period.[17] These historical studies have tended to reinforce the long-standing Whig/Marxist debate and in that sense have not offered literary scholars new approaches to the literature of this period. Some historians have explored the connection between these events and literary history. For Mark Knights, the political crisis that built up during the late Restoration left a significant legacy on literature: "[T]he contest over meaning necessarily produced by public political strife was a key element of later Stuart political culture and hence an important element in preparing and stimulating a public appetite for prose fiction."[18] Howard Nenner focuses more narrowly on 1688–89, arguing that "the political nation began by embracing the warming pan myth and then moved on to further flights of political imagination."[19] By contrast, for literary critics, 1688–89 has not been seen as a significant event, except to the extent that it has been an important strategy for periodization, where it has sometimes served to mark the end of the Restoration and sometimes served as the beginning of a story about the history of the novel or the emergence of the distinction between public and private that is central to secularization.[20] Literary scholars have tended to downplay its other literary productions and significance. According to Steven Zwicker, 1688–89 is distinguished, as far as a political event, by the fact that no great works of literature resulted from it, excepting John Dryden's *Don Sebastian*.[21] Few critics today write about *Don Sebastian*, never mind the broader field of literature related to 1688–89. There are significant exceptions, scholars who accord 1688–89, if not its literature, significance. Anthony Jarrells uses 1688–89 as a lens to challenge the periodization, nationalization, and institutionalization of literature that scholars have associated with the long eighteenth century and its culmination in the conservatism of romanticism.[22] And Michael McKeon's account of the ways that progressive and conservative ideologies share motivations but achieve "oppositional coherence as rival interpretations" and how this led to changes in the concept of genre is an important inspiration for this book.[23]

The goal of this book is not to rehearse the Whig/Marxist debate about the revolutionary bona fides of 1688–89, to side ultimately with the critics who see the event as bourgeois or conservative. Rather, I build on these critics who have linked literary and political developments, and I take seriously the idea that 1688–89 is not a beginning nor an ending but rather a watershed – an extremely complex one – in both secular liberalism and literary history. I also explore why, given our collective ambivalence about its revolutionary aspects and the fact that so many subsequent literary developments would come from the conservative opposition, this is so. Thus, the events of 1688–89 – so crucial to liberal political narratives and historiographical theory but under-examined in literary studies – are the historical center of this book, but more broadly it considers the larger questions raised by what we might call the long Restoration, which sees both the 1660 Restoration and the 1689 settlement as unstable and formative of eighteenth-century culture. It explores the ways that the political events and ideas of the long Restoration appeared in – or did not – and shaped the literary field.

In focusing on formal responses to Restoration politics, I am following a line of inquiry long established. Michael McKeon's approach to the literature of this time period is especially compelling. For McKeon, the Restoration is marked by its formal experimentation and genre-defying (or genre-bending) results.[24] In many ways, this book builds on McKeon's work, though it focuses more narrowly on the formal experimentation and genre-innovation in this set of writers who did not support the liberalizing efforts of 1688–89; it is also less interested in finding close corollaries between form and political ideology. In fact, I set aside the main ways that the conservative world view has been tied to form in the long eighteenth century: The Augustan neoclassical mode, with its love of order and rules, and the Tory satirists, with their vexatious tone, have stood as the emblems of conservatism; these areas have been well explored by other critics.[25] I have chosen different texts because I focus not on literature as political (as in satire) nor on form as a corollary of politics (as in the couplet) but rather on literature as experimental, a way of thinking and shaping, one that might have been especially appealing to these conservative writers and might explain the generic innovations that this period is known for. While my intentions are literary rather than historical or political, I take inspiration from Roland Barthes statement that "A little formalism takes one away from history, but ... a lot brings one back to it."[26] This contention maybe especially relevant when trying to recover critiques of secularism because as Laura Levitt argues, an overemphasis on content or theme is a sign of "the 'invisible hand' of Protestantism" in which belief trumps practices, rituals, and other formal elements of culture.[27] Thus, I focus on literary form in order to uncover aspects of the postsecular orientations of these writers in their historical specificity.

While Restoration literature is fondly characterized by its comedy, obscenity, sectarianism, and sophisticated linguistic ambiguity, and while the early eighteenth century is lionized as the great age of satire as well as the beginnings of the rise novel and the age of sensibility, the literature studied here is less categorizable, both in terms of period and genre. "Generically unstable" does not even begin to do justice to the myriad of ways that writers used the occasion of the Restoration and its denouement to experiment with literary forms. From this generic experimentation emerges – and we might see this as an effect of secularization – an increasing distinction between literature and politics. Political forms and modes like allegory, masque, and the occasional poems lose prominence in the literary sphere. Satire, of course, enjoys a heyday in the eighteenth century, especially in the great Tory satirists, but this has mainly been seen as intellectual opposition or expression rather than direct political production or intervention.[28] In the novel, the arena where Whig influence, as writers, readers, and inspiration for thematics, is strongest, politics and religion, narrowly defined, are virtually banished, in favor of ideology and virtue. At least, this is the way that the methods of literary critics of the last couple of decades have tended to frame things.[29] In order to challenge these narratives and this periodization, I analyze writers for whom the liberalizing turn of 1688–89 was neither salutary nor permanent. They were not convinced that monarchy, Catholicism, or the Stuarts should be consigned to the dustbin of history, and they innovated in literary forms as a response. They take up a series of questions – about state violence, rebellion, religion, tradition, personal agency and collectivity – that are still vital to today's political discourse and especially to both conservatism and postsecular politics and culture. They also reveal a deep ambivalence about imaginative transformation as political. In other words, they are ambivalent about both liberalism and the political potential of literature. The specificity of this ambivalence spans a wide range, including Aphra Behn's exploration of the passivity of novelistic narration, Dryden's retreat from political allegory to literary interpretation, and Margaret Cavendish's wholesale rejection of the utopian possibilities of the imagination. Analysis of these phenomena leads the book to argue for the intertwining of conservatism and literature, including literary forms, literary histories, and literary methods. In writing a book that centers 1688–89, I am implicitly staking a claim for modernity that follows a well-worn path of locating the beginnings of modernity in the political events of this time, seeing in the decline of sovereign monarchy and the emergence of liberal political theory an epistemic historical break. And yet I will also be challenging narratives of modernity, progress, and secularization, offering a different perspective on the narratives about modernity that we take for granted.

This book follows historical events only in a broadly schematic way, including literature written from the Restoration through the early nineteenth century. In answering one of the questions that the project started with – why are literary representations of 1688–89 either impoverished or underappreciated – the surprising answer rests on the fact that it was conservative writers who offered some of the most significant responses and because their responses were not representational but formal, or we might say not political but literary. Even texts, such as Dryden's *Don Sebastian* and Behn's *Oroonoko*, which are representational of the dynastic change of 1688–89, are allegorizations, moving the revolutionary scene out of England, and they are approached here not as political acts but as experiments in reading and literary narration, respectively. Still, the overarching commonality in these writings, as far as politics goes, is an antirevolutionary – which is related to an antitheoretical – stance. This strain runs so deep, and not only in conservative writers, that 1688–89 is denied to be a revolution, and only represented allegorically, as if revolution cannot take place in England. *The Postsecular Restoration* connects this conservative stance to the literary formations of these writers.

Making Literary Conservatism

The central literary figures in this study are conservative, and for a number of reasons, that means that this is a book about conservatism, both literary and political, and that it may itself be a conservative book. In focusing on avowedly conservative writers working in the mainstream of political and literary life (this is more true for Dryden and Scott, but it has been a long time since anyone working on Behn or Cavendish can be seen to be doing groundbreaking literary history), this book is vulnerable to the charge of perpetuating a conservative political and literary agenda. In one sense it is, because it is not defensive about the politics of these writers; it does not argue for the radical potential of the literary realm or the latent progressivity of monarchism, Catholicism, or conservatism. It is not interested in uncovering the political goals (whether conservative or progressive) of literary texts because it does not take the position that literature and literary critique are fundamentally political. Rather than trying to defend the literary sphere by linking it to politics, this project explores how literature emerges in relation to modern ideas of politics. It treats seriously the conservative concerns of these authors whose literary achievements have been celebrated, but the goal is understanding of the literary sphere not advocacy or judgment, of either politics or literature. I have been influenced by and persuaded by Jacques Rancière's analysis of the literary field, finding affinities with both his attraction for novels as a locus of modern political consciousness and his conviction that they can only go so far as political action. Rancière defines political action as the bringing to consciousness those anonymous people taken for granted by societal institutions of meaning and action; literature "loosens bodies from the meanings that people want them to take on."[30] Defined this way, politics can only be liberal or progressive politics – that is, based on principles of formal equality and the expansion of the political community by detaching subjects from their culturally defined roles. The political projects of literary historians have often had this implicit liberalizing bent: we turn to the archive in order to uncover the perspectives (of women, lower classes, and political or religious minorities) that mainstream literature and politics have ignored; this is one way to maintain a liberalizing worldview while legitimating literary history and criticism. But for Rancière, the literary realm always, in the end, privileges its own aesthetic coherence, preferring its own "luminous halo" over the "equality of democratic subjects."[31] Literature thus for Rancière can at best be only an epiphenomenon of the political.

Rancière's career has run parallel to his former colleagues in the Frankfurt school, the Althusser/Adorno strand of critique that has been even more influential on English Studies in determining our ideas about how literature and politics relate, by privileging critique that focuses on uncovering the ideological orientation of literary texts. Where such critique admits that conservatism permeates literature, it posits literary critique as the necessary corollary to literature's reactionary tendencies; ideological analysis is the salve that justifies the continuation of both literature and literary critique.[32] Ideological or symptomatic analysis based on the Althusserian lineage and projects of recovery based in Rancière have formed the two most important ways – ideological and archival – that literary historians of the past couple of generations have framed their work as political. Although I am just as disappointed as any progressive with the failure of the political realm to reform into a more egalitarian, democratic, or postcapitalist form, I do not think literature can be blamed for this failure or expected to remediate it. Nor do I think that repeatedly measuring literature by this standard of judgment is a necessary orientation or a necessarily productive line of critique. In going back to a moment when the modern regimes of literature and politics were not yet determined – before that is the novel that Rancière takes as the exemplar of modern literary culture and before the full flowering of the enlightenment, which is both the straw man and the condition of possibility of ideological critique – and in taking up conservative writers without the goal of ideological critique, this project endeavors to explore a different way of thinking about literature and politics, one in which literature stands not merely as an epiphenomenon of the political nor as unconscious of its own ideology but rather one in which literature is a complex field of formal experimentation for political and cultural transformations. In taking this approach and in taking seriously the conservatism of these writers, I follow the insights of Simon During, who argues that literature is "against democracy" and that its value is that it can be mined as a resource for understanding why democracy, and the liberal project more generally, has faltered.[33] But I take a more reparative (in Eve Sedgwick terms) approach, recovering the things threatened by secular culture that these writers valued and endeavored to transform in ways useful to them, and thus perhaps to us.[34]

One way that the secularization narrative has persisted is that scholarly accounts of eighteenth-century literature have tended to overstate the importance of epistemology, progress (and thus narrative), and individual subjectivity or agency – centerpieces of the secularization narrative. Instead, in order to explore the ways that these writers might have already been postsecular, I investigate a series of concepts whose influence seems to wane under secularism – that are associated with the perseverance of mystical or presecular modes of thought – or that are emergent liberal concepts which are treated differently by these writers and texts.[35] The method in each case is to uncover a more nuanced sense of the concepts' historical meanings. The intent is not to point out how (to invoke Bruno Latour) "we have never been" secular but rather to complicate a narrative of secularization.[36] Part of the goal is simply to show that secularism has assumed a certain meaning for these terms, which has limited our investigations of the commitments, the meanings, and the historical processes behind them, as well as, most importantly for this project, their influence in literature. In refusing to accept secularized histories, definitions, and norms, the goal is not to challenge the facts of the secularization thesis but rather to understand the ways that these writers were offering a critique of the process of secularization, by pointing out its unresolved tensions and their implications in areas of culture within and beyond politics and religion. The writers analyzed here assume that the ideology and the project of secularization impacted many areas of life and that its project was (and still is) alive and unsettled in ways that provide an opportunity for experimentation, critique, and innovation. This book shows how that process unfolded in the literary field and indeed why the literary field is centrally connected to that project. The central concerns of secularization, that is toleration and religious freedom, figure prominently in several chapters, but in the endeavor to take conservatism and postsecularity more broadly as worldviews, the lines of inquiry extend well beyond religion and politics.

In focusing on the literary responses of conservative writers to the Restoration, I do not claim exclusivity about the quality of their response nor the priority of conservatism in the literary field – or the political one. I also do not think that this book works to entrench distinctions between liberal and conservative politics and worldviews. In fact, I think it does the opposite: in finding so many contradictions and nuances in the thinking and writing of these conservative writers, and in reading their writing as a response to liberal developments rather than as a clinging to tradition – as postsecular rather than presecular and anti-ideological rather than traditionalist – this book provides evidence for the interdependence of liberal and conservative strains of thinking. Conservatism can be subsumed under the larger category of liberal modernity, a phenomenon that becomes more obvious in neoliberalism but that scholars working on this period have already identified: Steve Pincus' account of James II's politics as not retrograde traditionalism but a rival vision of modernity is one example and Michael McKeon's concept of "oppositional coherence" is another.[37] This perspective on liberal/conservative dynamics parallels the postsecular perspective on the religious/secular as being a "conscious contemporarily/co-existence of religious and secular worldviews."[38]

Ironically, conservatism is largely anachronistic to this period and to most of these writers who seem so easily to fit its criteria. The French revolution, and in particular Edmund Burke's criticism of it, is often considered the major impetus for the articulation of modern political conservatism, defined broadly as prioritizing lived experience, communal authority, and incremental change over individualism, revolution, and theoretical reason in politics.[39] While liberalism will need to await the nineteenth-century for some of its key developments, its central concepts (rights, freedom, and individualism) and key terms (especially liberal) are already central to political debate during the Restoration. One consequence of this uneven development is that literature that takes up liberal questions may have a more mimetic aesthetic and a more clearly ideological intent, while proto-conservative literature is more opaque (or more formalized) and less obviously political, a distinction that makes sense not only historically but also formally, given that conservatism is committed to incremental (not revolutionary or imaginary) transformation and to practice preceding theory. This is perhaps why it has been difficult for scholars, most of us more identified with a liberal orientation (whether as commitment or antagonist), to grapple with the conservative ideas and commitments of this literature and also perhaps why it has been tempting to overlook or explain away this conservatism. Rather than trying to reverse-engineer an account of early conservatism in the grammar of contemporary conservatism, which would necessarily be anachronistic, I take these writers on their own terms, focusing on the concepts they deploy and the formal experiments they undertake. To the extent that I try to draw a line from these writers to full-fledged conservatism, I do so speculatively and via methodology rather than ideology. In so doing, I build on some classic accounts of conservatism. Karl Mannheim's idea of a "style of thought" influences the choice to orient around questions of form, not just literary forms but also forms of mentation such as indulgence and nostalgia.[40] Mannheim's description of conservatism as an "intuitive, qualitative, concrete form of thought" provides inspiration for linking these forms of mentation and the kinds of literary experiences modeled by these writers to conservatism and for arguing that literature more broadly is also fundamentally "intuitive, qualitative, concrete" and therefore maybe conservative.[41] This is why conservatism is "made" out of a literary response to secularism. From Mannheim, I also borrow the idea that the basic intention of conservatism must be lived as the authentic experience of a group, and I focus on Jacobitism as the authentic group experience (albeit retroactively, as I explain in the final chapter). This emphasis on both groups and lived experience provides a counterpoint to liberalism's emphasis on individuals and ideologies. Edmund Burke provides the inspiration for several lines of inquiry about how writers were using the past – what J. G. A. Pocock call a "common law mind" – to ground not just politics (as incremental change versus liberal abstraction) but also literature and literary forms of mentation and genres.[42] From George Lakoff, I draw upon the notion of a conservative worldview, one available in metaphors, and this is why I put so much focus on language and concepts in relation to form.[43] For the purposes of this book, I approach conservatism as: anti-revolution; as an ongoing ambivalence about some of the modernizing trends undertaken during and especially as a consequence of the long Restoration; and also as an anti-foundationalist, anti-ideological and anti-theoretical practice.[44] As such, conservatism shares a number of features with the literary practices (figuration, indulgence, narration, reading) explored in this book, and therefore with the modern literary sphere more generally. Thus, in arguing for the "making of literary conservatism," I focus on formal experiments (as making) and on the connections between conservatism and modern forms of literature and thinking. The concept of "making literary conservatism" gets at what I take to be the way conservative writers engaged with aspirational liberal transformations via literary form, and in this sense form is inherent to the manifestation of their postsecular conservatism.

Chapter Summaries

The following six chapters, grouped into pairs, take up these writers in ways that reconcile their conservative, postsecular orientations with their literary innovations. The first two chapters, grouped together as "Political and Fictional Relations" (Part I), address the ways that two key concepts of England's presecular political theology – faith and indulgence – were transformed during the Restoration and how they in turn influenced the nascent literary culture's conceptions of both itself and of human relationships. In other words, they analyze how the politico-theological concepts of faith and indulgence persisted in social and affective relations and influenced the literary field. Chapter 1, "Faith: Impersonating Faith, or How We Came to Have Faith in Fictions," explores the secularization of the concept of faith. Over three sections it offers a sense of how faith was taken up by Reformation theologians, by political theorist Thomas Hobbes, and by Aphra Behn in her earliest prose fiction. The chapter takes up "faith" at a key point in its history, in order to account for what it meant before secularization and for what its role would be in a secular epistemology, politics, and culture. It reads two conservative writers, Thomas Hobbes and Aphra Behn, in order to see how they link the idea of faith to the emergent category of fiction: in Hobbes, the political project of contract relies on fictionality for its form, while in Behn, the fictional project of the nascent novel relies on faith for its form. Hobbes' *Leviathan* denies (or does not anticipate) a secular idea of faith as necessary to the political commonwealth, but his suturing of the Christian commonwealth to the political body politic is necessitated by this disavowal: lack of faith constitutes the anxious void around which Hobbes' social contract is fictionalized. In Aphra Behn's early prose fiction *Love Letters Between a Nobleman and His Sister*, which offers a proleptic and microcosmic history of the novel, a secular concept of faith – with its demand to disarticulate faith from both epistemological and political concerns and to locate it in the realm of sexual relations – accounts for the text's generic instability and innovations: its move over the course of three books from epistolary and allegory to omniscient narration and finally to limited omniscience. As a whole, this chapter explores how the secularization of faith radiated into the formal concerns of politics and literature and the social concerns of human relations.

The second chapter, "Indulgence: The Stuart Declarations of Indulgence and Their Afterlives," analyzes the concept and procedure of indulgence during the Restoration and its persistence in the eighteenth century. It argues that the Stuart Declarations of Indulgence as mechanisms of religious liberty were not superseded by toleration; rather, they articulated a formal and affective structure for political and personal relations that persisted as a minor form in the eighteenth century, as exemplified in the writing of David Hume, Edmund Burke, Samuel Richardson, and Olaudah Equiano. While tolerance is a policy and a practice grounded in a theory of formal equality, indulgence persists as a way to imagine relationships with women, with children, and with enslaved and colonized people. In the work of David Hume, indulgence also persists as a method of skepticism, a theory of mental freedom that is the corollary of political freedoms (of religion and speech in particular). But indulgence is also the form in which Hume's racism appears. Questions about mental and physical freedom are thus addressed not only via the indulgence/toleration distinction but also in terms of slavery and racism. Both chapters in this first part take presecular concepts that would seem to be left behind by liberal secularism and demonstrate their persistence, or even centrality, not just to conservatism but to literature and to liberal secularity more generally.

The next two chapters, comprising a part called "Postsecular Literary Experiences: Worlds and Time" (Part II), investigate how Margaret

Cavendish and John Dryden explore two foundational secular concepts: worlds (spatiality) and time (history or temporality). Cavendish focuses on the possibilities of the fictional imagination, which she calls "figuring," as a means of imagining alternative worlds, while Dryden theorizes a reading practice that is based on religious experience, both mystical and embodied, that is founded on a theory of literary temporality. Both authors explore the interaction between literary experience and the immanence (the place and time) of secular society, but while Cavendish's response is rather pessimistic, Dryden offers literary experience as a consolation and possible remediation of secular experience. Chapter 3, "Figuring: Margaret Cavendish's Critique of Imagining and Worlding" undertakes a case study of Cavendish's foray into a favored intellectual strategy of modernity: to imagine a world (and therefore a politics) that follows the laws of the natural world as discovered by science. Such projects, in ways that Cavendish reveals, rely on the assumption that politics, science, and literature have an inextricable relationship; this view itself is what constitutes a secular "worldview." While both liberal and conservative orientations require a worldview, a conservative worldview has been seen as at once more limiting and more violent, a worldview that insists that others shares one's worldview if they share one's world, while the worldview of liberalism is grounded in ideas of diversity and tolerance, the possibility of an ever-expanding, cosmopolitan world.[45] This is the proto-liberal view that Cavendish's proto-conservatism and theory of the literary imagination finds untenable. Cavendish's conservatism is manifested explicitly in the representations of sovereign violence that seem necessary to protect worlds and implicitly in the significance of a method of "figuration" that Cavendish theorizes – and practices – as the foundation of form in the natural world, the social world, and the literary imagination. Such figuration cannot escape the violent reality of secular nationalism inherent in the notion of "worlds."

Chapter 4, "Reading: John Dryden's Postsecular Apostolic and the Time of Literary History," analyzes John Dryden's writings of the 1680s, tracking his move (his literary conversion if you will) from allegory and allegoresis to new concepts of literary history and literary hermeneutics that demand new reading practices. It analyzes Dryden's mid-career allegories as investigations into how conservative theories of temporality, figured here as the possibility of understanding across time, produce theories of literature and theories of reading that are oriented toward the future but that are necessarily grounded in the past and in material bodies. It focuses on the shift in Dryden's career from *Absalom and Achitophel* and

The Hind and Panther, as occasional poems meant to influence an ongoing political situation, to *Don Sebastian*, a play meant to be read in the future. Dryden's mid-career conversion moves from literature as politics to literature as literary history; as such, this chapter is a case study of the way that the shift from allegory to novel in the literary realm is connected to the shift from early modern politics (as state craft or theology) to modern politics as grounded in ideology. This chapter argues that Dryden's writings from the 1680s secularize a ritualized, affective, transformative, and Catholic reading practice. It accounts for the fundamental conservatism of literary history in terms of its attachment to the past, but it also shows how central the future is to Dryden's literary history. It speculates that a literary conservatism – literary temporality as communion and literary interpretation as committed to a hermeneutics of immanence – constitutes a conservatively based idea of reading that resonates once again in the twenty-first century critical turn to post-critical and post-nationalistic methods.

The final part, "Political Agents and Literary Forms" (Part III), explores the ways that writers used the figure of the counterrevolutionary to explore the possibilities of human political agency and to manage concerns about colonization and rebellion. Chapter 5, "Passivity: The Passion of *Oroonoko* and the Ethics of Narration," builds on the argument about Aphra Behn's generic innovations initiated in Chapter 2. It recovers a historical meaning of "passive obedience," a precursor to modern theories of civil disobedience, and it uses this concept to read both the protagonist, an African prince enslaved in a new world colony, and the narrator, a colonial woman writer, of *Oroonoko*. It argues that the narrator of *Oroonoko*, and by inference novelistic narration in general, is based on assumptions about the ethics of individual detachment (or ironic distance) from political action. In recovering the idea of passive obedience and the figure of Christ's passion as a model for novelistic narration and a conservative ethics of citizenship under liberalism, this chapter offers a critique (in the sense of alternative meant to expand our understanding of the concept) of liberal theories of political action as well as an argument against the novel's foundation in liberal theories of individualization and agency. It also takes up the problems of racism and slavery as central to understanding both the liberal/conservative dynamic and the development of the novel form.

The final chapter, "Revolution and Nostalgia: Walter Scott, and the Forms of Jacobite Nostalgia," takes up two concepts, revolution and nostalgia, central to the Restoration and its literary representations and also central to the periodization of the eighteenth century. The shifting meaning of "revolution" (as return versus break with the past) registers both the ambitions of secular modernity to be historical and the way that such secularity at once celebrates and circumscribes human agency. I take up the term revolution in relation to the events of 1688–89 by way of thinking about why this paradigmatic event of modernity – the first "modern" revolution on some accounts – only very hesitantly embraces the idea of revolution. I then move to the very end of the story (the beginning of the nineteenth century), with an analysis of the figure of the Jacobite in Walter Scott's *Waverley*, in order to argue that historical fiction works by a logic of nostalgia, structuring the past as the place of the fantasies of the present. One of the great ironies of 1688–89 is that the figure of the revolutionary that it bequeaths to literary history is a Jacobite not a Whig and a British national not a colonized or enslaved person. This strategy embraces, albeit nostalgically, both the revolutionary project and the restorative (or counterrevolutionary) one. In this chapter, I endeavor to consider why revolution becomes the central if disavowed political fantasy of secular modernity; why nostalgia, a word invented in 1688 and reaching its apotheosis and its formal incarnation as historical fiction over a hundred years later, haunts the project of secularity; and why the Jacobite is at once the exemplary revolutionary, the prototypical nostalgic, and the object of nostalgic investment. This chapter also explains why representations of the "revolution" of 1688–89 tend to allegorize it in terms of racial or colonial conflict and thus how the invention of the Highland rebel managed England's ambivalence about its own experience with revolution and its colonization projects. The overarching idea of this chapter is that the dynamic between revolution and nostalgia animates both a conservative worldview – a postsecular politics of restoration – and literary history.

Notes

1 See, for example, Elaine Hobby, "Introduction: Prose of the Long Restoration (1650–1737)," *Prose Studies* 29 (2007): 1–3; David A. Brewer, "The Even Longer Restoration," *Restoration: Studies in English Literary Culture, 1660–1700* 40, no. 2 (2016): 96–104; Blair Hoxby and Ann Baynes Coiro, eds., *Milton in the Long Restoration* (Oxford: Oxford University Press, 2016); and Michael McKeon, "Paradise Lost, Poem of the Restoration Period," *Eighteenth-Century Life* 41, no. 2 (April 22, 2017): 9–27.
2 Max Weber, *The Protestant Ethic and the Spirit of Capitalism*, trans. Talcott Parsons (New York: Charles Scribner's Sons, 1958); Talal Asad, *Formations of the Secular* (Stanford, CA: Stanford University Press, 2003); Gil Anidjar, "Secularism," *New German Critique* 33 (2006): 52–77.

3 Anidjar, "Secularism," 62.
4 Philip Nord, "Introduction," in *Formations of Belief: Historical Approaches to Religion and the Secular*, eds. Philip Nord, Katja Guenther, and Max Weiss (Princeton, NJ: Princeton University Press, 2019), 1–10, 2.
5 Ernst-Wolfgang Böckenförde, *Staat, Gesellschaft* (Berlin: Suhrkamp, 1976) [English translation: *State, Society and Liberty: Studies in Political Theory and Constitutional Law*, Oxford: Berg, 1991], 60.
6 Michael Kaufmann, "Locating the Postsecular," *Religion & Literature* 41, no. 3 (2009): 69.
7 Saba Mahmood, "Secularism, Hermeneutics, and Empire: The Politics of Islamic Reformation," *Public Culture* 18, no. 2 (2006): 326, 344.
8 Early modern scholars, especially those working on John Milton, have made inroads in this direction, arguing from according to Lee Morrissey "a history of literature and the postsecular [that] is older than might otherwise be expected"; "Literature and the Postsecular: *Paradise Lost?*," *Religion & Literature* 41, no. 3 (2009): 100. See also Feisel G. Mohamed, *Milton and the Post-Secular Present: Ethics, Politics, Terrorism* (Stanford, CA: Stanford University Press, 2011).
9 Allen Dunn, "The Precarious Integrity of the Postsecular," *boundary 2* 37, no. 3 (2010): 92.
10 In the US context, Tracy Fessenden has called Protestantism an "unmarked category." *Culture and Redemption: Religion, the Secular, and American Literature* (Princeton, NJ: Princeton University Press, 2007), 6.
11 Martin Luther, John Calvin, and – in the English context – Richard Hooker all emphasized this invisibility. For an overview of this see P. D. L. Avis, *The Church in the Theology of the Reformers* (London: Marshall, Morgan, & Scott, 1982), 5–7.
12 Well-known articulations of this perspective include Gilbert Burnet, *Bishop Burnet's History of His Own Time* (London: printed for Thomas Ward, 1724); Thomas Babington Macaulay, and C. H. Firth, *The History of England from the Accession of James II* (London: Folio Press, 1985); and George Macaulay Trevelyan, *The English Revolution, 1688–1689* (London; Oxford: Oxford University Press), 1938.
13 Herbert Butterfield is credited with the phrase "Whig interpretation of history," a derogatory term insofar as it suggests that the event was not liberal or revolutionary enough; instead it promoted the interests of the bourgeois class; *The Whig Interpretation of History* (New York; London: W. W. Norton, 1931). For an overview of when these adjectives ("glorious" and "bloodless") appeared, and also when and who called it a "revolution," see James R. Hertzler, "Who Dubbed It 'The Glorious Revolution?'," *Albion* 19, no. 4 (1987): 579–85. He argues that Protestant preachers were referring to the event as the "glorious revolution" within twenty years of the event, and perhaps this was due to Gilbert Burnet's influence (582).
14 According to Schmitt, modern political concepts are "secularized theological concepts." Carl Schmitt and George Schwab, *Political Theology: Four Chapters on the Concept of Sovereignty* (Chicago: University of Chicago Press, 1985), 36.

15 In the wake of Butterfield, the Whig interpretation of history, tied closely to the secularization thesis that this book tracks, fell out of favor. Revisionist historians began to challenge both the factual basis of the Whig interpretation as well as its value system. See J. C. D. Clark, *English Society 1688–1832: Ideology, Social Structure and Political Practice during the Ancien Regime* (Cambridge: Cambridge University Press, 1985); J. P. Kenyon, *Revolution Principles: The Politics of Party, 1689–1720* (Cambridge; New York: Cambridge University Press, 1977); David Ogg, *England in the Reigns of James II and William III* (Oxford: Clarendon, 1957); Lucile Pinkham, *William III and the Respectable Revolution* (Cambridge, MA: Harvard University Press, 1954); J. H. Plumb, *The Origins of Political Stability, England, 1675–1725* (Boston: Houghton Mifflin, 1967); J. G. A. Pocock, *Three British Revolutions, 1641, 1688, 1776* (Princeton, NJ: Princeton University Press, 1980); Lois G. Schwoerer, ed., *The Revolution of 1688–1689: Changing Perspectives* (Cambridge: Cambridge University Press, 1992); W. A. Speck, *Reluctant Revolutionaries: Englishmen and the Revolution of 1688* (Oxford, England; New York: Oxford University Press, 1988). Particularly influential in this revisionist approach to the Whig interpretation has been the work of Marxist historians, especially Christopher Hill, *The Century of Revolution, 1603–1714* (New York; London: Routledge, 2014). See also Richard Ashcraft, *Revolutionary Politics & Locke's Two Treatises of Government* (Princeton, NJ: Princeton University Press, 1986), and Shelley G. Burtt, *Virtue Transformed: Political Argument in England, 1688–1740* (Cambridge; New York: Cambridge University Press, 1992); J. R. Jones, ed., *Liberty Secured?: Britain before and after 1688* (Stanford, CA: Stanford University Press, 1992). Despite the derogatory nature of the term "Whig history," this book contends that we are far from abandoning the norm (if not the fact) of the Whig interpretation, insofar as we frame history as a struggle between those in favor of progress and those against it.

16 J. P. Kenyon is one of the most prominent advocates of this revisionary view, especially in *Revolution Principles*, 12–13. Jonathan Israel makes the case for "invasion"; "Introduction," *The Anglo-Dutch Moment: Essays on the Glorious Revolution and Its World Impact* (Cambridge: Cambridge University Press, 2003), 4.

17 Tim Harris, *Revolution: The Great Crisis of the British Monarchy, 1685–1720* (London: Penguin, 2007); Jardine Lisa, *Going Dutch: How England Plundered Holland's Glory*, Reprint edition (New York: Harper Perennial, 2009); Steve Pincus, *1688: The First Modern Revolution* (New Haven, CT: Yale University Press, 2009); Kevin Sharpe, *Rebranding Rule: The Restoration and Revolution Monarchy, 1660–1714* (New Haven, CT: Yale University Press, 2013).

18 Mark Knights, *Representation and Misrepresentation* (Oxford: Oxford University Press, 2005), 63.

19 Howard Nenner, *The Right to Be King: The Succession to the Crown of England, 1603–1714* (Chapel Hill: University of North Carolina, 1995), 86.

20 The year 1689 is implicated in an invigoration of philosophical discourses of rights, subjectivity, and empiricism central to the novel, in classic literary

histories of the novel such as Ian Watt, *The Rise of the Novel* (Berkeley: University of California, 1967); Michael McKeon, *The Origins of the English Novel, 1600–1740* (Baltimore: Johns Hopkins University Press, 1987); and Nancy Armstrong, *Desire and Domestic Fiction: A Political History of the Novel* (Oxford: Oxford University Press, 1987). It has also been seen as a turning point in the emergent disarticulation of public and private spheres that will be played out in the novel, in critics who are responding to Jürgen Habermas, *The Structural Transformation of the Public Sphere: An Inquiry into a Category of Bourgeois Society* (Cambridge, MA: MIT Press, 1989). See, for example, Katharine Gillespie, *Domesticity and Dissent in the Seventeenth-Century* (Cambridge: Cambridge University Press, 2004); Diane E. Boyd and Marta Kvande, *Everyday Revolutions: Eighteenth-Century Women Transforming Public and Private* (Newark: University of Delaware Press, 2008); John Richetti, "The Public Sphere and the Eighteenth-Century Novel: Social Criticism and Narrative Enactment," *Eighteenth-Century Life* 16, no. 3 (1992): 114–29; Amanda Vickery, *The Gentleman's Daughter: Women's Lives in Georgian England* (New Haven, CT: Yale University Press, 1998).
21 Steven N. Zwicker, *Lines of Authority: Politics and English Literary Culture, 1649–1689* (Ithaca, NY: Cornell University Press, 1993), 173–74.
22 Anthony Jarrells, *Britain's Bloodless Revolutions: 1688 and the Romantic Reform of Literature* (New York: Palgrave Macmillan, 2005).
23 McKeon, *The Origins of the English Novel, 1600–1740*, 171.
24 Ibid.
25 A case could be made for including Alexander Pope and Jonathan Swift in this study as proto-conservative writers responding to 1688–89. But I set aside from this study both Pope's poetic forms and Swift's satire, because they have received significant critical attention linking their politics and form. While there is certainly more to say about how they might relate to both earlier (Behn, Cavendish, and Dryden) and later (Hume, Burke, and Scott) writers in this study, in terms of how their conservatism and form relate to 1688–89, I do not develop that line of inquiry.
26 Roland Barthes, *Mythologies*, trans. Annette Lavers (New York: The Noonday Press, 1957/1972), 112.
27 Laura Levitt. "What Is Religion, Anyway? Rereading the Postsecular from an American Jewish Perspective," *Religion & Literature* 41, no. 3 (2009): 107.
28 See, for example, Howard Erskine-Hill, *Poetry of Opposition and Revolution: Dryden to Wordsworth* (Oxford; New York: Clarendon Press, 1996); Ronald Paulson, *The Fictions of Satire* (Baltimore: Johns Hopkins University Press, 1967); Claude Julien Rawson, *Satire and Sentiment, 1660–1830* (Cambridge: Cambridge University Press, 1994); Michael Seidel, *Satiric Inheritance: Rabelais to Sterne* (Princeton, NJ: Princeton University Press, 1979); and Howard D. Weinbrot, *Eighteenth-Century Satire: Essays on Text and Context from Dryden to Peter Pindar* (Cambridge: Cambridge University Press, 1988). Abigail Williams' more recent study makes the case challenging these narratives by taking more seriously the impact of Tory writers on eighteenth-

century literature; *Poetry and the Creation of a Whig Literary Culture 1681–1714* (Oxford: Oxford University Press, 2005).

29 Influential accounts of the novel in this vein include Armstrong, *Desire and Domestic Fiction*; McKeon, *The Origins of the English Novel, 1600–1740*; and Rachel Carnell, *Partisan Politics, Narrative Realism, and the Rise of the British Novel* (New York: Palgrave Macmillan), 2006.

30 Jacques Rancière, *Politics of Literature*, Jacqueline Rose, trans. (Cambridge, UK: Polity Press, 2011), 44.

31 Quoted in Jacques Rancière, "Writing, Repetition, Displacement: An Interview with Jacques Rancière," *Novel* 47, no. 2 (2014): 306.

32 The concept of symptomatic reading was developed in Louis Althusser and Étienne Balibar, *Reading Capital*, trans. Ben Brewster (London: New Left Books, 1970). Fredric Jameson's work *was influential in enco*uraging a generation of scholars to search for "a latent meaning behind a manifest one." Fredric Jameson, *The Political Unconscious: Narrative as a Socially Symbolic Act* (Ithaca, NY: Cornell University Press, 1982), 59.

33 Simon During, *Against Democracy: Literary Experience in the Era of Emancipation* (New York: Fordham University Press, 2012), vii.

34 Eve Kosofsky Sedgwick, "Paranoid Reading and Reparative Reading, or, You're So Paranoid, You Probably Think This Essay Is About You," in *Touching Feeling* (Durham, NC: Duke University Press, 2003), 123–52. For Sedgewick, reparative reading counteracts the "strong theory" of paranoid reading with the local and the specific. As such, and ironically perhaps, it thus fits with my theory of literary conservatism.

35 I considered thinking about these terms as "keywords" in the tradition of Raymond Williams, and indeed I have come to think that such a method is uniquely suited to the eighteenth century, when writers thought and wrote in terms of keywords, when words were alive and complex in ways that exceeded definition. Raymond Williams, *Keywords: A Vocabulary of Culture and Society* (New York; Oxford: Oxford University Press), 1985. Williams' keyword approach is derived from his study of the idea of "culture," and as such is an inherently conservative method, tied to a conservative, antitheoretical ethos and politics, and hence keywords may be seen as a conservative form taken up by the book. Yet I am interested in how particular writers deploy these terms rather than being committed to a longer trajectory of a word (though I do try to suggest such trajectories with "faith" and "indulgence").

36 Bruno Latour, *We Have Never Been Modern* (Cambridge, MA: Harvard University Press), 1993.

37 McKeon, *The Origins of the English Novel, 1600–1740*, 171. Pincus aligns James with a "Catholic modernity" *1688: The First Modern Revolution*, 143–78. Both of these scholars' work are influential in my approach to this time period and this literature, although I am much less interested in categorizing political ideology.

38 Kristina Stoeckl, "Defining the Postsecular," Paper presented at the seminar of Prof. Khoruzhij at the Academy of Sciences in Moscow in February 2011, viewed May 5, 2022, from Stoeckl_enpost secular.pdf.

39 On this history see Karl Mannheim, "Conservative Thought," in *From Karl Mannheim*, ed. Kurt H. Wolff (New York: Oxford University Press, 1971), 260–350. Roger Scruton, whose promotion of conservatism rests on its historical links to the eighteenth century, characterizes conservatism as a "specifically modern reaction to the vast changes unleashed by the Reformation and the Enlightenment," *How to Be a Conservative*, Reprint ed. (London: Bloomsbury Continuum, 2015), viii. I use the term "conservative" (as opposed to more historically grounded alternatives, such as counter-enlightenment) because I intend to be anachronistic in the spirit of what Victoria Kahn calls "reverse anachronism" that facilitates a "genuine dialogue between the early modern and modern periods"; *Wayward Contracts: The Crisis of Political Obligation in England, 1640–1674* (Princeton, NJ: Princeton University Press, 2009), 22. Also, I intend the term to encompass a range of more specific and historically grounded terms (royalist, Catholic, Jacobite, common law) that I address, and name, more specifically as appropriate.

40 Karl Mannheim opposes "capitalist bourgeois consciousness [which] … knows no bounds to the process of rationalization" with the "intuitive, qualitative, concrete forms of thought" characteristic of conservative style of thought ("Conservative Thought," 271, 273). In this sense I am arguing that literary style might be inherently conservative, and so too might my methods in this book.

41 Mannheim, "Conservative Thought," 273.

42 J. G. A. Pocock, *The Ancient Constitution and the Feudal Law: A Study of English Historical Thought in the Seventeenth Century*, 2nd ed. (Cambridge: Cambridge University Press, 1987).

43 George Lakoff, *Moral Politics: How Liberals and Conservatives Think*, 2nd ed. (Chicago: University of Chicago Press, 2010).

44 This view of conservatism is not without critics. See, for example, Corey Robbins, who argues that the perpetuation of social stratification is the defining feature of conservatism. *Reactionary Mind: Conservatism from Edmond Burke to Sarah Palin* (Oxford: Oxford University Press, 2011), 3–40. Because I am less interested in politics than in the ways that secularization was responded to by conservatives in literature, this book does not stake a claim to a new viewpoint on this debate. I accept the antitheoretical definition of conservatism because, even if it is not the purpose of conservatism, it is one of the main ways that literary writers responded to secularization. Their politics of hierarchy is, in most cases, well established, but I am interested in ways their postsecular response turns up in other areas of culture.

45 Lakoff, *Moral Politics*, 24–40.

PART I

Political and Fictional Relations

CHAPTER I

Faith
Impersonating Faith, or How We Came to Have Faith in Fictions

> Faith ... consisteth not in our Opinion, but in our Submission
> —Hobbes, *Leviathan*

> And reason saw not, til faith sprung the light
> —Dryden, "*Religio Laici*"

> Faith does not demand that dogmas should be true as that they should be pious ... philosophy has no end in view save truth: faith, as we have abundantly proved, looks for nothing but obedience and piety.
> —Spinoza, *A Theologico-Political Treatise*

When scholars working from the perspective of the secularization thesis – that is most of us working in eighteenth-century studies – talk about the meaning of "faith," it is typically opposed to reason. This is because the secularizing force of the Enlightenment endeavored to define religion as a matter of subjective, unsubstantiated belief, or "faith," and it developed epistemological methods and criteria that defined ultimate religious truth as unavailable to human modes of reason. Humans might discover that (Christian) religious practice was reasonable (as for example John Locke argues) and even morally necessary (according to Immanuel Kant), but beginning in the seventeenth century, religious truth was increasingly defined as transcendent and subjective and therefore as separate from the immanent and objective modes of human knowledge prioritized in enlightenment modernity.[1] That is, under secularization, epistemological categorization tautologically determines the religious/secular divide, with faith as religious and reason as secular. The other secular meaning of faith – specifically in its iteration as "fidelity" – involves sexual relations. During the eighteenth century, the word "fidelity" was increasingly used in reference to monogamy rather than to monarchy or monotheism. In other words, "faith" was secularized by increasingly deploying it, with a negative connotation, in the realms of epistemology and sexual relations. Under the episteme of enlightenment secularism, "faith" came to be defined as religious, private, and opposed to evidence-based modes of knowledge and understanding. Faith came to be the realm of that which is set aside from the secular sphere of reason and science, that which is taken to be true without evidence or logic – a category that includes privatized religion and romantic commitment. By the late eighteenth century, religion was largely transformed from being primarily a guide to activity (obedience) to a subjective condition connected to epistemology (belief). Accordingly, Thomas Hobbes' view that faith provides a model for political obedience would seem rigid and conservative; John Dryden's view that reason depends on faith's "light" would seem quaint; whereas Benedict Spinoza's view that philosophy and religious faith belong to profoundly distinct realms would prove to have been prophetic of the long arc of the secular enlightenment.

Scholarship on the eighteenth century has often taken these secular assumptions about the meaning of faith as a guide to inquiry and method. Historians and theorists of secularization have focused – and not without legitimate reason, as it was a key philosophical debate – on the epistemological status of faith, that is, on sorting out the distinction between enlightenment (especially empirical) modes of reason and religious belief. This critical project has influenced literary scholars in terms of how we approach both eighteenth-century literature and religion via epistemological questions.[2] The significance of sexuality to eighteenth-century literary critics might be seen as another way that the secularization thesis has influenced the methods and assumptions of literary scholars, given our – and I include myself here – pervasive interest in the period's sexual and romantic content and how this has typically been segregated from studies of religion. This is perhaps because we have tended to align sexual asceticism and sexual hypocrisy with Catholicism and thus sexual expression with secularization and Protestantization.[3] In short, as scholars of Restoration and eighteenth-century literature, our objects of study, disciplinary orientation, and methods derive from secularism, creating blind spots about "faith."

This chapter begins by explaining how this formulation of faith – one that prioritizes epistemology and sexuality – is historically specific and ideologically foundational to secularization, and it recovers a moment in the late seventeenth century when this formulation was emergent but was not yet a foregone conclusion, in order to understand the significance of this transformation in the meaning of faith for the literary field.[4] In what follows, I outline the landscape of faith in the late seventeenth century, teasing out the contours of its various social, political, epistemological, theological, and sectarian meanings and uses, in order to contextualize the importance of faith first to Thomas Hobbes' political philosophy in *Leviathan* and then to Aphra Behn's fictionalization of sexual politics in her early prose fiction *Love Letters between a Nobleman and His Sister*. I trace the ways that faith, which I show to have been historically central to personal relations, lost its grounding in personal relations, in order to understand how this transformation relates to Hobbes' political theory and Behn's techniques of prose fiction. The more general purposes of this chapter are to understand why and how the redefinition (or secularization) of faith related to what we might call the relationship between politics and the imagination in the projects of Hobbes and Behn and therefore how it relates to their conservatism.

In broad terms, I argue that before the secularization (and in particular that secular watershed of 1688–89), faith was not private and not exclusively about religion and it was not primarily (or at least exclusively) an epistemological category. Rather, faith was seen as, among other things, a motivator for action, and it was opposed not to truth but to law, compulsion, and obedience. It was also a category dependent on interpersonal relations: faith, unlike truth, could typically only attach to persons. My readings of Hobbes and Behn explore this question of how faith relates to personhood and interpersonal relationships via analysis of their uses of impersonation, personification, and narration. As such, this chapter endeavors to uncover the seventeenth-century use of the word "faith" as a place where political, religious, and sexual relationships – and their relationship to one another – are worked out. It argues that the late seventeenth-century crisis of faith was a political and social problem, one that was not so much solved as sublimated by segregating faith into the realms of religion and sexual relations. It suggests that redefining "faith" – as religious epistemology and sexual fidelity – was not an effect of secularization but rather an agent of it, a key to how writers conceptualized the late seventeenth-century crisis in political theology and thus paved the way for its resolution. In excavating the late-seventeenth-century political meaning of faith, this chapter shows how it came to play a role in the increasing disciplinary distinctions not only between religious and secular but also between literature and politics, and it argues that this crisis of faith was one of the impetuses for emerging techniques of prose fiction.

"Faith" in the Seventeenth Century

The OED suggests some useful points about the history of the word faith and how it relates to secularization and especially to the later seventeenth century. The original meaning of "faith" was not exclusively or even particularly religious: It originally meant to keep ones promises, and it developed from there to explain the personal and contractual aspects (not necessarily the epistemological ones) of Christian religion. Its most common grammatical forms are as an adjective or adverb, although it also appears frequently (especially in Restoration drama) as an interjection ("Faith!").[5] Its use as a verb is quite infrequent and interestingly distributed: there is, according to the OED, "no evidence" of its use as a verb "between the mid-seventeenth century and late nineteenth century."[6] That is, during the time of the ascendance of enlightenment secularism, you could not enact faith or have faith enacted upon you. Rather, faith typically appears as an adjective to describe people or actions, a quality possessed by people, or an injunction to this quality. This aspect of "faith" marks an important distinction from "belief," which appears more frequently as verb (to believe), a phenomenon that may be an outcome of the linguistic structure of English but that is nonetheless consequential for how the concepts of faith and belief developed in England.[7] "Faith's" first appearance as a non-religious "system of belief" emerges in the mid-seventeenth century, in a derogatory sense: "mere political faith" was not considered real faith. Following soon after this historical redefinition, in the late seventeenth century, came another significant one: The term "fidelity" came to be associated with sexuality and marriage.[8] Finally, it is not until the late nineteenth century, according to the OED, that faith came to have our modern meaning, as belief without evidence or investigation. The reasons for this little excursion into the OED are not only to support the point that the epistemological aspect of faith is historically specific to secularity and merely emergent in the late seventeenth century. It also shows that faith has traditionally, at least until the nineteenth century, been primarily a way of describing trust in interpersonal relations: that is, faith belonged to social or political domains more so than to epistemological or religious domains. The historical definitions of faith show that domains of faith – religion, politics, and romantic relations – are connected and have a complex history in which the late seventeenth century plays an important role.[9]

Google's NGram viewer supports the argument that the latter half of the seventeenth century was a key moment in the history of "faith," and it even offers clues as to why that might be so. Between 1500 and 2008, the use of the word faith peaks in 1673, with subsidiary summits in 1652, 1686–88, and 1719.[10] The reasons that "faith" is so prominent in the seventeenth century seem obvious. For one, publication in 1611 of the

King James Bible (KJB), where "faith" appears frequently, especially in the New Testament, and the Protestant emphasis on bible reading (especially new testament reading) would have made the word and the concept of faith central to theologico-political debates, as indeed it was. A major theological issue was *sola fide* – justification by faith alone, which was hotly contested throughout the seventeenth century and, according to J. Wayne Baker, effectively resolved by the end of it.[11] But in addition, the other domains of faith – political and sexual – and their relation to religion were likewise hotly contested and perhaps just as important to the seventeenth-century interest in faith as the theological debates about *sola fide* were. Although the statistical validity of NGram has not been fully (or even preliminarily) studied, and thus one hesitates to make fine distinctions, the specific peaks in the incidence of "faith" indicate that "faith" appears in moments of crisis for political theology – during the interregnum, during debates over the Test Act, and during James II's reign (1719 is a bit more difficult to explain). This distribution suggests that writing about "faith" in the late seventeenth century was often motivated by (and thus an attempt to solve) a crisis of faith – and its related terms of law and obedience – in the political realm. This crisis of "faith" manifests in literature and especially drama around questions of sexual (in)fidelity, which is of course something that scholars of Restoration literature have always noticed.[12]

Analysis of seventeenth-century theological/sectarian writers who endeavored to articulate the meaning of "faith" fleshes out the above contention. Within the context of the larger Reformation, their work shows the ways that for English Protestant writers, the religious, political, and social aspects of faith were intertwined in complex and diverse ways. I make no attempt to tell a cohesive story about their secularization (Protestantization) of faith, given the unevenness of the process of secularization, the volatility of the political situation, and the diverse theological and political spectrum that these writers represent. Rather, I try to represent that diversity within a broader picture of the process of the secularization of faith and the way its central domain shifted from social relations to epistemology. These writers do share a broad approach to faith, which I try to outline. For example, they repeatedly argue for the sufficiency of scripture to Christian faith, and given that the nature of religious truth is one of the central sectarian debates, they focus on certain scriptural verses. By far the most common verses quoted from the *KJB* are "faith cometh by hearing" (Romans 10:17) and "faith is the substance of things hoped for, the evidence of things not seen" (Hebrews 11:1). These two verses emphasize the social and habitual aspects of faith (it "cometh by hearing," that is in social or pedagogical settings) as well as the affective ("hope") and epistemological ("evidence") aspects of its meaning. These two verses are not necessarily exemplary of the variety of ways "faith" appears in the *KJB*, and their prominence in these writings is thus significant, indicating the extent to which these writers emphasized these two aspects of "faith" and their relationship.[13]

Faith in its most general/traditional definition is central to how these writers conceptualize the central religious relationship, that between God and humans. As Church of England clergyman and poet Barten Holyday (1593–1661) puts it, "Of all virtues faith is most acceptable to God because God is most honoured by faith, for by faith we trust God, we take God's word."[14] This linkage of truth and trust in humans' relationship with God suggests why faith might have become such an important Christian concept during the Reformation. Scholars have already made the point, which I build upon here, that "faith" pertains to the social and interpersonal aspects of religion, because Christianity is a religion that figures what it calls faith as contractual and interpersonal: God and humans keep faith with each other by keeping promises. Slavoj Žižek, drawing on the work of Octave Mannoni and Jacques Lacan, makes such a point: in a Christian context, faith is a symbolic pact, and, as such, it differs from "belief," which can exist outside of interpersonal relations. Faith and belief are thus distinguished not by epistemology but by sociability.[15] For Lacan, the symbolic order is something we have faith in without the necessity of "belief" but with the necessity of an "Other," importantly for Lacan (and Žižek) a fictionalized one.[16] Along a similar line, Paul Griffiths and Reinhard Hütter argue that for Christians faith is "never merely an assent to truth. It is also a disposition to trust and the activity of trusting ... Faith understood in this way is not principally cognitive, but rather constitutive of a relation that could not otherwise be entered into."[17] This dual nature of faith became, according to Griffiths and Hütter, "constitutive of the Reformation tradition such that faith has an intellectual as well as an affective component: assent to truth and trust in God's promises."[18] Thus, the original meaning of faith, as trust in persons, does not disappear with the Reformation; rather faith becomes a central concept for explaining the relationship of God and humans, even as it declines as a way of conceptualizing other kinds of relationships.

The distinction between the kind of relationship one has with God and the kind one has with other humans hinges upon the distinction between faith and law. Some early Reformers articulate a line of thinking whereby the priority of faith over law means that faith encompasses law, rather than (as would later be the case) being set aside from it, and what we might now see as sacred and secular functions, including social and personal ones, are intertwined. For example, the early Scottish Reformer and Protestant martyr Patrick Hamilton (1504?–28), in saying "Fayth maketh god & man good freindes/Incredulyte maketh them foes," figures the relationship of God and man as a social arrangement (friendship), but then goes on to clearly assert the superiority of religious relations over secular ones, saying, "It is good to trust in god & not in man" and "it is good to trust in god and not in prynces."[19] Because the language of sacred and secular relations – faith, friends, trust – is the same, human relations are essentially a degraded form of sacred relations, rather than being something completely different. Hamilton opposes faith with "incredulity," with the former productive of social relations and the latter destructive. Disbelief or "incredulity" leads to a state of social and political discord (foes) while its opposite, faith, is the foundation of stable relations (friends). So while the epistemological sense of faith is clearly in evidence in the early Reformation, it is not the primary meaning of faith nor the primary end of faith, nor is faith a degraded form of belief but rather an exalted one. In its relation to law, faith is a category of political and social relations, and the primacy of religion, at least to theologians, means that both secular law and order – the political and social relations among humans – and epistemology are based on and subordinate to the relationship God establishes with humans.

As the Reformation developed, theologico-political writers increasingly endeavored to make faith a sacred category quite separate from its colloquial or secular meanings. Their articulation of a religious meaning for faith – its segregation from what would come to be seen as secular realms – was anchored in the theory of two kingdoms and in the doctrine of *sola fide*.[20] For Luther and other Reformers, the two kingdoms theory was a means of asserting the priority of the spiritual over the temporal – the kingdom of God was sovereign.[21] It was also a primary ground upon which theories of secularization developed, in particular the privacy and primacy of interiorized subjectivity.[22] The implications of this were worked out in the Reformation – especially in its Lutheran strains – prioritization of faith over works. The doctrine of *sola fide* – or justification by faith alone – argued that salvation can never be deserved but rather comes by God's grace alone. The segregation of law from grace and thus of moral or secular actions (including good works and obedience to laws) from the sacred process of salvation can be seen as a strong instrument of secularization, in its most narrow sense of the strict separation of the political and religious realms. *Sola fide*, though a highly contested concept especially between Lutheran and Calvinist strains of reform, was nonetheless a central tenet of all Protestant doctrine.[23]

The doctrine of *sola fide* made faith central to theology and thus, at least to some extent, a theological concept: In other words, *sola fide*, or faith alone, also promoted what we might call *sola fide theologico*, or faith as a purely theological (and thus secularizing) concept. In some cases, this sacralization of faith was quite explicit. For example, the nonconforming minister John Rogers (1610–80) endeavors to limit the meaning of faith to its theological role in justification of the elect and thus to stress its opposition both to good works and to what we might call secular meanings of the term.[24] Rogers separates faith not only from colloquial uses of the term but even from those uses in the Bible that are not related to justification of the elect. Thus, faith is not, according to Rogers, "our beleeving any mans word, or promise to us, or mans writing, which is a faith and confidence in him" nor is it "keeping our promises," "the doctrine of the Gospell," a determination of "the lawfulness of this or that," the "historical faith" of believing the bible to be true, "temporary" faith, nor Faith in miracles.[25] By clearing the ground summarily from these broad and diverse meanings of faith, Rogers follows a line of segregating (thus secularizing) the social and political spheres from the religious, with real faith applicable only in the spiritual realm.

For many Reformers, faith did have a central epistemological mandate and was foundational to one's identity as a Christian. Faith came to mean a belief in the factual truth of the bible and especially of Jesus' life. Repeatedly, Reformation theologians rehearse the central tenets of Protestant belief: that Christ was born, he was risen, and he will come again. As William Jackson (1636 or 7–80) puts it, "the chief contents, and matter of it, are the conception, birth, speeches, actions and sufferings of this *Great One*."[26] Faith became a theological concept grounded in a rather mundane epistemological mandate: to believe in a certain limited narrative of facts about Christian history.[27] Holyday argues that faith is "more properly grounded" in the "sufficiency" of God's acts than in the specification of them."[28] While these Reformers thus contract the realm of faith to be believed, they emphasize the effects and affects of such belief, a distinction often characterized as the difference between historical belief and "general faith." The conforming (Presbyterian) Francis Fuller (1636–1701), for example argues that true faith is not in "the understanding only" but rather it is "particular and appropriating" and has a "quickening influence on the will."[29] In such accounts, faith exceeds belief, rather than merely being a debased version of it. Still, this is a secularizing view of faith, because it internalizes faith and distinguishes it from belief. It is also a way of distinguishing Protestant from Catholic faith, which for Jackson is "implicit," versus the "absolute rule" provided by reformed faith.

On one hand, *sola fide* restricted faith to a limited, religious, realm. But it also made faith – with its grounding in limited belief – the central quality of identity: those with true faith were the elect and election was the central question of identity. It thus meant that the subjective states encompassed by faith – including belief, hope, love, and trust as well as doubt – were often prioritized, in theology and especially in its Lutheran strains, over action. In the Calvinist strains of reform, moral and obedient actions provided evidence of faith but were not fully convincing: faith was always a matter of some doubt. Max Weber's account of Calvinism hinges on this point: *sola fide* led to the mandate of "proving one's faith in worldly activity," proof that manifested in actions but whose primary sensory manifestations were in "consciousness" and "attitude."[30] Hence material actions were subordinated to both faith and to the interiorized orientations that were at once the effect of faith and the evidence for it, and the epistemological problem of faith centered on Christians' doubt about their own faith, not on God or other people. As Holyday puts it: "God's art means that because we doubt we fear the strength of our faith, and this then increases our faith."[31] *Sola fide* did several things concurrently: it defined faith as an epistemological category and as a theological category, and it defined religion as subjectivity (faith or belief) not actions. This would mean that other forms of subjective cognition (and affect) could be deployed, destroyed, or repurposed for secular, and postsecular, purposes.

I have been outlining the ways that the relationship between the two meanings of faith – as trust in persons and religious truth – was under contestation by Reformation theologians and in particular by writers in England during the late-seventeenth-century political crises, with trust in persons declining as mode of legitimate religious experience. This phenomenon is exemplified by Reformation attacks on the Catholic papacy. Seventeenth-century Protestant theologians talked about faith in order to refute Catholicism, especially the formulations from the Council of Trent, with a particular focus on Cardinal Bellarmine (1542–1621), the influential counterreformation theologian. Anglican theologians tried to stake out a middle ground on many theological issues, but infallibility presented a particular problem. At issue in the infallibility debates were questions of obedience and individual freedom and judgment as well as questions about national autonomy. Anglicans tried to navigate between the "liberty of private judgment" asserted by radical Protestants and the slavish following of papal authority, which was problematic not only to emergent theories of individual political, moral, and epistemological agency but also to English sovereignty.[32] In this debate over infallibility, we see the cleaving of faith's two central domains of meaning: personal relations and epistemology. As William Jackson puts it, believing in an infallible judge makes it "as if a person and a proposition were the same thing." In Jackson, the secularization of faith (into epistemology) is related to the reformation critique of papal authority, where faith should be taken as "Objective, for the matter or things to be believed," not "the arguments and motives that persuade us" or the "arguments from reason or authority why we believe." Faith as belief does not depend on a person to be believed or in whom one trusts. We see here a shearing off of the two colloquial meanings (trust in a person and belief in a proposition) of faith. In devout writers, such as Fuller, faith is connected to the personhood of God, insofar as God creates faith: "faith is sometimes taken for the Doctrine and sometimes for the Grace of Faith, viz. the Things to be believed, and the Grace by which we believe."[33] Still, this distinction between person and doctrine, with persons (with the exception of God) being cast as illegitimate objects of belief, is a hallmark of Reformation theology as it is of enlightenment epistemology.

These seventeenth-century English theological writers understand faith not mainly as an epistemological concept, but far from evidencing a pre-enlightenment epistemological deficit or naiveté, their writings on faith often display a sophisticated concern about the connections among epistemological, social, and theological realms. Holyday, for example, says,

> there is not any action in man's life performed without a kinde of beliefe; no man of a rectified reason undertaking any business, but with a belief both of the possibility of it, and the benefit. Which as it is true even of civil faith in outwards life, so is it much more true of the true faith in the inward life.[34]

Instead of a degraded form of knowledge or epistemology, faith was thus sometimes seen as something related to or prioritized over reason: "whatsoever creature is indued with reason, the same is thereby also made capable of a faith; all faith presupposing reason, in which it is implanted, in which it is employed" (Holyday). For Fuller, faith goes "in time and nature before assurance" – so faith is a precursor to and the foundation of knowledge.

I do not want to suggest that anything like a resolution, a fully secularized faith, was reached during this period. While I began with a broad-stroked claim about faith under the secular enlightenment, the nature of faith was far from a settled question by the end of the Restoration (or ever). While figures like John Locke and John Toland made the case for a radically epistemological (or demystified) approach to religion, there were at the end of the seventeenth century both more radically mystical and more moderate positions available. Still we might see that with the political settlement of 1688–89, the volatile question of Protestant (at least Church of England) faith settled down. The erudite and voluminous writings of Bishop and theologian Edward Stillingfleet (1635–99) and Archbishop of Canterbury John Tillotson (1630–94) represent this mainstream position.[35] Beginning in the 1660s they wrote, mainly against Roman Catholic writer John Sergeant (1623–1707) and in response to each other, a series of exchanges about the nature of Protestant faith.[36] These writings were extremely influential and were republished during the 1688–89 events. Stillingfleet had a series of well-known exchanges with Locke over the dangers of "scepticism and infidelity" and the importance of the "mysteries of faith."[37] But he also makes the most fully articulated argument about Anglican faith, which we might take to be the liberal secularized view. His arguments can be summarized as: scripture provides a "rule" which allows one to determine belief; general points of faith (the rule of faith) differ from particular points (articles of faith); and the purpose of faith is salvation, not certainty. In short, he separates scripture, which is true and infallible, from the application of it, which, as it is conducted by fallible mortals, is not. While admitting the truth of scripture, he also insists that this is not its purpose, because the purpose of scripture is nothing other than salvation. He distinguishes the kind of "absolute certainty" that one may have about "matters of fact" (50) from religious issues, which, guided by the rule of scripture, involve judgment and therefore error. To the extent, then, that "persons" or "meer creatures" are involved in questions of faith, their involvement raises questions about epistemology (questions of judgment, belief, and application of rules) not trust (45). Tillotson simplifies this position further, repeatedly arguing that the rule of faith consists of two tenets: that the "Scripture be ... sufficiently plain" that it provides a rule of faith if men use it "*sensibly and discreetly*" (without a "*rigorous balancing of every word and syllable*").[38] He argues against the idea that reason is "*dim-sighted ... hoodwinkt* and *blind*" and for the ability of mere humans to make appropriate use of scripture (154). One of the main arguments in the Protestant/Catholic debates about faith relates to the unreliable nature of oral tradition, and hence the fallibility of humans is central to the Protestant cause. These writers must then resolve the fallibility of (Catholic) interpretation of scripture while also validating its efficacy (for Protestants) as a guide to faith. Tillotson addresses the inadequacy of oral tradition by arguing that it "depends upon the certainty of mens senses, and an assurance of the ability and integrity of those who were dead 1500 years before we were born," a set of assumptions that Tillotson, although known as a liberalizer and for making arguments in favor of a reasonable faith, cannot make (83). Stillingfleet puts it thus: "Absolute Certainty there cannot be where Person are left uncertain" (85). Hence the emerging consensus about faith emphasizes both human reason and its limits. Faith is a function of how well people apply the rules of scripture, not about keeping promises with or believing other people, and this leaves faith epistemologically fragile, subject to the vagaries of human judgment. Paradoxically, this rather fragile religious belief is the foundation of a modern liberal secular view of human liberty: the freedom to think for oneself, even if erroneously (a point I will develop in the next chapter). And this ideal is figured in emergent liberal political terms as a right, not an obligation or an occasion for obedience. As Stillingfleet puts it "when any thing is offer'd as necessary to be believed in order to Salvation, every Christian hath a Right as Liberty of Judging" (71).

While the seclusion of faith into privatized, subjective arenas and therefore the project to make it a realm of epistemological frailty was just beginning at this time, nonetheless these discourses reveal a complicated sense of what is at stake in this project, of how significant secularized (or reformed) ideas of faith are to liberal modernity. Our modern understanding of faith as epistemology (belief) is not a rejection of these theological discourses but rather a derivation of them. These writers, *en media res* of the seventeenth-century debates about political theology, reveal what a secular view of faith (as degraded knowledge) tends to obscure: that is, faith's importance, at this time and thus to the secular project more generally, to knowledge and to political and interpersonal relations and to theories of liberal freedom. This brief analysis of the history of faith suggests that the secularization of faith depersonalized the concept and severed a relationship between trust and truth. The rest of this chapter analyzes how Hobbes and Behn responded to this redefinition, and how they used imaginary constructs – the *ex nihilo* creation of the state and the techniques of prose fiction – to allow for the imaginative reconnection of trust and truth, at least to some (postsecular) extent.

Impersonating Faith in Hobbes' Body Politic

Although he was an important theologian and secularizer of the late seventeenth century, although "faith" appears frequently in his writings, and although many critics have analyzed his attitude toward religion – in fact it is a growing concern – few have thought about what Thomas Hobbes might mean by faith itself, and his treatment of the word and concept of faith has received little attention. Joshua Mitchell hits upon the problem when he connects the problem of faith in Hobbes to his personification of the Leviathan as a figure for governmental sovereignty: "The Leviathan is a figure for whom faith is a stumbling block" (71).[39] This image of an amalgamated and impersonated political figure physically stumbling over faith suggests something crucial about what I want to address here: how important and vexed faith is to Hobbes' theory of impersonated religious and political authority.

In Carl Schmitt's influential formulation of the secularization narrative, religious forms and concepts precede secular political formulations and provide the foundation for them. "All significant concepts of the modern theory of the state," Schmitt argues in a much-cited passage, "are secularized theological concepts."[40] Hobbes himself suggests such a formulation for his political theory in many places, for example at the beginning of *The Leviathan* where he states that political structures follow God's natural law: "NATURE (whereby God hath made and governed the world) is by the Art of man, as in many other things, so in this also imitated, that it can make an Artificial Animal."[41] From the perspective of the secularization thesis, which is how I first read Hobbes, one might conjecture that Hobbes is going to argue that the structure and functions of faith in God are somehow – via man's imagination or "art" – transferred to faith in a secular sovereign. If faith – in its central definition of keeping one's promises – is what makes men keep their covenant with God, based on their belief that he has the power to punish infractions, then the powerful Leviathan, erected in fear, could inspire a secularized form of faith and obedience to authority. But this is not the path that Hobbes' argument takes. This is at least partially because Hobbes' whole project is to eliminate immaterial things (including the emotions, imaginations, and beliefs related to faith) from the political realm. Thus, his project is not to figure out how or why we have faith in secular things but rather to argue that secular politics does not need faith, or at least that it is not fundamentally based on faith. This turns out to be a very tricky problem for Hobbes, a stumbling block that the Leviathan – a fictionalized, abstract, and divided figure of sovereignty – resolves rather tenuously. Perhaps this is why the Leviathan is figured by Hobbes here, at the beginning of his treatise, as an "animal" not a person. If faith attaches only to persons, Hobbes' Leviathan seems less available for such a relationship than the Christian God, or a human. But then of course Hobbes' problem becomes the actual person of the king and what kind of relationship subjects may have with the sovereign.

"Faith" takes us to a number of problems at the heart of Hobbes, including the relationship between multitudes and persons. In a religious realm, the relation is sutured by faith: "All formed religion," Hobbes claims, "is founded at the first from the faith which a multitude hath in some one person" (*Lev* 1. 12. 24). But in the political realm, the process is more complicated. As a materialist endeavoring to systematize a secular sovereignty, Hobbes has a problem: how, as he puts it, can "A multitude of men" be "by one man, or one Person, Represented" (*Lev* 1.16.13). Although the political problem replicates the structure of the religious one, Hobbes' political philosophy would seem to be dependent on eliminating faith from the equation. Hobbes' ingenuous solution, of course, is that this multitude be "made *one* Person": the artificial persona of the state (*Lev* 1.16.13). The frontispiece to the *Leviathan* is the most famous representation of this process, but this figure or fable of the Leviathan both belies Hobbes' initial animal metaphor and also does not manage to capture the way that Hobbes actually resolves this particular problematic. For Hobbes' sovereignty involves a double impersonation: The state is the first person, an artificial one with authority, but the persona of the state is abstract (imaginary or animalistic) and therefore cannot "do" anything. A natural – that is an actual embodied – person, who is the figure and the embodiment of sovereignty, then represents the state, wields power and takes actions on its behalf. The natural person retains elements not encompassed by his role as sovereign.[42] Both this duality and this excess are central to the problem of faith in Hobbes. Hobbes' two theories of multitudes and monisms – in religion and politics – are thus neither fully analogous nor opposites, and the path of secularization that Hobbes takes in order to connect secular and sacred sovereignty, via impersonation and faith, turns out to be quite complex.

Hobbes' two assertions about multitudes and persons establish important things about the similarities and the differences between religion and politics: Both religion and politics rely on Hobbes' theory of personhood and his monism; in both cases, the problem of the multitude is solved – or at least seems to be solved – by the unification under one persona (albeit a doubled one in civil politics and a tripled and apostolic one in

Christianity). Otherwise, such an institution has no authority at all, because authority for Hobbes is inherently connected to personhood: An entity without personhood "can neither command, nor do any action at all; nor is capable of having any power, or right to any things; nor has any will, reason, nor voice; for all these qualities are personal" (*Lev* 3.34.24). Hobbes' theory of power is inseparable from his materialism and from his theory of personal authority, and this is why and how religious and political authority are similarly structured around persons. But I am more interested in the differences for Hobbes in the domains of religion and politics. Ideal political sovereignty for Hobbes entails an impersonation of the multitude, which allows for representation, but this is not the case for religion: The religious leader is not a representative and therefore cannot be an amalgamated person with authority in the way the Leviathan is.[43] More to the point, while religion involves faith, political sovereignty, precisely because of its different approach to multitudes and persons, does not, at least primarily. Hobbes argues at length that political commonwealths – including Christian commonwealths – are not secured by faith but by power. He will come to argue that faith has a supportive role in commonwealths – that Christian commonwealths are the ideal form of government because faith in God is synergistic with obedience to a political sovereign – but at a foundational level, faith is a key difference between spiritual and civil sovereignty.

As explained earlier, in the context of secularization faith is as an epistemological category. Hobbes does articulate a version of the distinction between belief and faith that will come to be crucial to the secularization thesis, but he does so in a way that is quite particular to the issues raised by seventeenth-century political theology and thus shows how the former (or at least Hobbes' version of the former) was a resolution to the latter: that is, how the secularization of faith into belief solved a problem in political theology. Belief, according to Hobbes, pertains to "saying[s]" or "doctrine[s]" while faith pertains to "persons" (*Lev* 1.7.5-6). Even when we say we "believe *in*" (emphasis mine), which Hobbes claims is a singularly ecclesiastical phrasing, we are expressing a belief in the doctrine of God or the creed of a religion, not the person (*Lev* 1.7.7). "Faith" pertains, in both secular and sacred spheres, to the fact that belief in a doctrine comes from recognition of the authority of the person who speaks, not from any evidence or reasoning about "the thing itself" (*Lev* 1.7.7). Faith here is not about what we believe, but whom and why we believe: "[W]hatsoever we believe ... is faith in men only" (*Lev* 1.7.7). Significantly, and although God is also an impersonation, God cannot be an object of faith in this way: We do not believe God, but believe in God.[44] Hobbes' emphasis on faith as being invested in persons is a key to his political theory: the way that faith seems at first to be categorically excluded and yet winds up being important.

Hobbes' definition of faith is somewhat vague, but by his use of it, along with a sense of how it was used in the seventeenth century, we can say that faith for Hobbes is an affective inclination and habitual orientation that can be trained, that it is found only in interpersonal/social relations and thus is consequential to the realm of politics, and that its antagonists are not facts or truth but rather law and works. Where faith conflicts with law, and this is the place where it most commonly makes its appearance in seventeenth-century political theology, it becomes (as will be discussed further in Chapter 5) a theological justification for political disobedience or ethical disregard. Thus, obviously, in the debate of faith versus law, Hobbes is clearly on the side of law.[45] Hobbes' deployment and partial definitions of the word faith in his discussion of religion reveal several reasons for how and why faith must be excluded from politics, at least at the level of the artificial person of the state.

First, where law applies to bodies, faith is an accident (an attribute or perhaps an affect) not a substance, and therefore it is fundamentally different from the material bodies that matter to politics.[46] Hobbes implies that to believe that faith can be "infused or inspired" into bodies is analogous to the philosophically ridiculous belief in transubstantiation, wherein Catholics "make those *Nesses, Tudes and Ties*" to be so many spirits possessing the body (*Lev.* 1.5.10, Lev 1.8.27).[47] We might say that Hobbes does not believe in the politics of adverbs, that he is afraid of adverbs, or more simply, that adverbs are not secular: They imply a possession, modification, or explanation of the body and its motions.[48] By aligning faith with spiritual possession, and thus positing it as a threat to the materialist destiny of bodies, Hobbes participates in secularizing faith, delegitimating it both as epistemology and as politics.

Second, faith is unreliable. In political situations where men are "not subject to civil power" (i.e., in formulations that precede the kind of Christian Commonwealth for which Hobbes advocates) faith in God – and the consequent fear of punishment in the next world – helps to ensure that men keep a "covenant of peace" (*Lev* 1.14.31). But such faith is fragile, subject to support as miracles, justice, and virtue can provide, and thus vulnerable to failing when these things do. In a string of almost parallel clauses in Chapter 12, Hobbes articulates how dependent religious faith is on these supports: "So that miracles failing, faith also failed" …

"So that Justice Failing, faith also failed" ... "the failing of virtue in the pastors, maketh faith fail in the people" (*Lev* 1. 12. 29, 30, 31). This depiction of faith as unreliable advocates for a political system not subject to its vagaries, that is, for excluding faith from a foundational role in Hobbes' project of imagining a fully systematized and stable political order.

Finally, despite or perhaps because of these frailties of faith, frailties fully grounded in Hobbes' materialist commitments, faith is dangerous, a powerful force (mainly for evil) in a commonwealth. A natural person can produce faith (that is faith in himself) when he "procureth credit with the rest" (*Lev* 2. 31. 3). This process of producing faith in people happened with the apostles because of revelation, but in seventeenth-century England such supernatural forms of procuring faith are necessarily, for Hobbes, both faked and prejudicial to government. The law of nature forbids the "violation of faith" that would lead to rebellion, but "potent" subjects who lack "fidelity" are dangerous and susceptible to such violations against the law of nature. A "popular, ambitious man" can start rebellion as if by "witchcraft" (*Lev* 2.29. 20). Hobbes' critique of faith can thus be encapsulated as: Faith has no substance and is thus not properly the domain of politics; faith is too vulnerable to be the foundation of politics; and if faith is directed to natural faithless persons, it subjects the commonwealth to rebellion. Hobbes is fearful of the faith that subjects have in the sovereign and also of the possibility that subjects might invest faith in each other and thereby "procureth credit" that is proper to the sovereign. This is why Hobbes' political theory necessarily disavows the social and communal ties that we might see as secured by faith.[49]

This view of faith accounts, to some extent, for Hobbes' double impersonation. The process whereby the sovereign represents the state and not the people acts as a way to insulate the state from the vagaries of faith: We may lose faith in the natural person representing the state, but faith makes no sense with regard to the state. The artificial person of the state, like "children, fooles and madmen" (*Lev* I,12.16) cannot represent itself and likewise cannot be a subject of faith. It cannot engage in actions and thus cannot be modified by adverbs such as willful, intentional, or faithful, nor can it be the object of such orientations. We can have no feelings and therefore no recourse against the state.[50] This double impersonation is also what allows the state to be insulated from punishment under the law: Without a natural persona, without the ability to "act," the state has authority but not responsibility. As an artificial person, it can covenant with the sovereign to be represented by it, but it is a covenant that, unlike the Christian covenant with God, does not rely on faith and punishment as the means for enforcing it.[51] The sovereign, in his manifestation as a natural person, can be the subject and the object of faith, but this is not his role as representer of the state. People can have faith in him, although that faith is not fundamental to his role as sovereign but rather adjunctive to it. This is why the Christian commonwealth, in which people have faith in the natural sovereign but not in the artificial persona of the state, is the ideal form of government for Hobbes.

And so the duality in the persona of sovereignty is replicated, by the end of *Leviathan*, in the duality of the Christian commonwealth – this is what critics call Hobbes' dual separation. Hobbes' problem of the multitude is thus not solved by singularity but by duality: two figures of sovereignty, artificial and natural, and two aspects of government, political commonwealth and Christian. Faith is the key to both of these separations – to what distinguishes them and what makes them work synergistically. When a Christian sovereign represents the state, the vagaries of faith are solved: The multitude unifies into the authority of a state that cannot be subject to the dangers of faith, and the impersonated sovereign, in whom the multitude has invested faith, can harness the positive aspects of faith for the state. This is the way in which I read Hobbes as postsecular (in Schmitt's sense of the term): He first secularizes (depersonalizes) the state and sovereignty, and then reinjects faith. Secularization and the social contract are not fully worked out in Hobbes. Faith as a realm of interpersonal relations and therefore sociability is something that Hobbes worries about, that provides a stumbling block for his theories. He can eliminate it from the state, via the dual and separated personas of state and sovereign, and he sutures Christian faith to the civil commonwealth, but Hobbes fears a kind of extra-Christian, postsecular faith, seeing it as an ongoing threat to the state. This is why he wants to materialize it, habituate it, and suture it to politics and why he invents the artificial and fictional persona of the state, a being immunized from faith and at the same time, at least ideally, supported by it.[52]

Finding Faith in Fiction

A scene toward the end of Aphra Behn's *Love Letters between a Nobleman and His Sister* illustrates the non-secular heart of what we have come to call secularity. In this scene, the narrator recounts watching the ordination of the text's most romantic and faithful character, Octavio. "Never was any thing so magnificent as this Ceremony," reports the narrator, "a most magnificent Scene of Glory." "I swear," she recounts "I was never so affected in my Life with any thing."[53] She describes the scene almost as a baroque painting, with the handsome young male novitiates appearing as "a hundred little Angels" all dressed in white and the "Clouds most rarely and Artificially set off" "so bright and dazzling (sic)" that "their lustre was hardly able to be look'd on" (380). She repeatedly claims that the scene exceeds her ability to describe it: "no Fancy, no Imagination" could faithfully represent its "Charms" (382). Witnessing this religious ritual that marks the limits of her powers of description is a religious experience for the narrator. "I confess, I thought myself no longer on Earth," she says, and " a thousand times I have wish'd to Die," and "I fancied myself no longer on Earth, but absolutely ascended up to the Regions of the Sky" (381, 382).

Two things in this scene are relevant for this chapter's genealogy of faith as well as for a possible alternative history of secularization and the novel. First, it is the moment where the narrator becomes involved in the story as a character (she "went among the rest" to the event) and emerges as the complex, ironic, narrator upon which Behn's stake as an innovator in the novel, that most secular of genres, rests, a narrator who is emotionally and ethically invested in – though always at one step removed from – the characters and events she represents, a point that will be developed more in Chapter 5 (379). Second, this is a Catholic ceremony and a postsecular conversion narrative, where the nephew of the Prince of Orange (soon to become England's icon of Protestantism) renounces the secular world, the world of political intrigue and sexual romance that dominates the text and where his love for and faith in the beautiful and fickle Sylvia is doomed to be betrayed. This scene occurs toward the end of the three-part prose fiction, and it resolves, at least temporarily and symbolically, the crisis of faith that the text has been dramatizing. That crisis is figured in this text, as it is in much Restoration literature, as the fallout from the decline in Stuart divine right political theology: Once the sacred bond of king and God is shaken, self-interested, faithless libertinism – both political and sexual – becomes a focus of literary interest. Published separately in three volumes over the course of James II's tumultuous ascension and reign (1684, 1685, and 1687) and mixing political events, a real amorous scandal, and emergent techniques of fictionalization, *Love Letters* offers a unique window into an early moment in the relationship of faith (as politics, religion, and love) and fiction. Later novels will resolve this crisis of faith via monogamy; They will make a kind of political theology of monogamy to replace the political theology based on a link between monotheism and monarchy; that is, a couple's faith in each other will come to supersede their faith in God or monarch – this is one way to read the plots of many later novels, including Behn's *Oroonoko*. But here, both the narrator and Octavio explain the scene as a "sacrifice" for Sylvia's infidelity: Octavio intends this sacrifice to redeem Sylvia, and the narrator experiences it as her own redemption (382).

Sylvia begins *Love Letters* as politically loyal to James II, whereas her libertine brother-in-law and soon-to-be faithless lover Philander is a rebellious supporter of the Protestant upstart Duke of Monmouth. Before the consummation of their affair, Sylvia intuits the connection between political rebellion and romantic faithlessness, and she tries to retrieve her lover's loyalism, and thus proleptically to ensure his romantic fidelity, with a description of what it feels like to be in the presence of the King: "'[T]is impossible to look," she explains at the "awful face" of the "Sacred Person" of the king "without that reverence wherewith one wou'd behold a God!"; "'tis most certain," she exclaims, "that every glance from his piercing, wondrous eyes, begets a trembling Adoration" (40). Such a look, Sylvia is certain, would retrieve the loyalty of the "most harden'd of your Bloody Rebels" (41). Like the narrator's description of her own experience of the ordination, Sylvia describes such moments of faith as an aesthetic experience with physical effects, in other words or in the grammar of the baroque, as experiences of faith that are embodied in materialized persons and thoroughly compelling. Infidelity is impossible in the face (literally) of such a person, whose image disables human agency.

These two moments of faith are anomalies in a text that is mainly concerned with mundane if well-plotted sexual and political intrigue – that is, with secular things. I take secularity here as the mandate that meaning be found in immanent, human things, not in transcendent ones, and I see Behn as working out how such secularization produces a crisis of faith over whether it is possible to have faith and to find meaning in mundane humans. Behn is interested in what it is like to live without an entity in which faith can be anchored – whether a God, a political sovereign, or a romantic partner – and in what happens when the connections among faith's three realms – religion, politics, and love – shift or disarticulate. In this way, faith, for Behn, offers a means to examine the process we call secularization, which is responsible for this disarticulation.

In order to make the case that faith is at stake in *Love Letters*, I analyzed the occurrence of the term "faith" in the text, and a few things stand out. First, "faith" (which occurs seventy-nine times, with another eighteen occurrences of "fidelity") is almost always used negatively or subjunctively: characters confess a lack of faith, they accuse a lack faith in others, and they sometimes speculate about what the presence of actual faith might make possible, but they very rarely assert faith positively about themselves or others. The most common construction by far is "faithless" (thirty times), which is importantly distinct from (though a precursor to) the key action in the plot: romantic "unfaithful"-ness. I would argue that the crisis of faith is a main theme – if not the main theme – in all of Behn's prose fictions and much of her writing around the political crisis of the late 1680s. For example, in her congratulatory poem to Queen Mary (after the regime change of 1688–89 that Behn, of course, did not support) Behn welcomes the new Queen to "Britain's Faithless Shore."[54] In another example, among Oroonoko's last words to the "faithless Governor" and "faithless crew" whipping him are "you will ... no more find Faith in me."[55]

Behn uses prose fiction, even invents techniques of prose fiction, as a means for grappling with this crisis of faith. Behn's experiments in fictional form, beginning with *Love Letters*, explore the vicissitudes of human emotion and action in the absence of a religious or political sovereign who gives meaning to human relations via a foundational pact of faith. The literary form that a world of faith takes is allegory, where faith in one realm is the same thing as faith in the others. Loyalty as Sylvia describes it is an allegorical form of faith in which religious belief, political loyalty, and romantic love are vertically integrated, mutually reinforcing, and interchangeable faiths that produce similar affects. Leaving such allegory behind with Sylvia's failed attempt to retain her lover by yoking their affair to political loyalty, *Love Letters* moves, over its three parts, through other ways of formally organizing relationships of faith and showing how the three domains of faith relate, or fail to relate.

In what follows, I argue that in the three-part structure of Behn's first prose fiction, form follows faith: The experiments in narrative form, which conspire to make the text generically innovative, are produced by Behn's investigation into and critique of the secularization of faith. Her political and religious conservatism leads to these innovations and thus to making new forms of literary conservatism. The shifts in point of view over the three parts, from epistolary to omniscient to limited omniscience, are modes of grappling with the secularization of faith. Moreover, insofar as this movement predicts a history of the novel, *Love Letters* predicts the ways that this genre will work out a relationship to the secularization of faith.

Part One is an epistolary *roman à clef*. Epistolarity, an early form of the novel, is often seen as giving priority to individual feeling, choice, and desire, while the genre *roman à clef* is a frail (or secular) allegory linking the political realm with the personal but not typically the religious realm. *Love Letters'* generic and formal features thus participate in the late-seventeenth-century reconfiguration of political and familial relations and the questions this raised about the possibility of human faithfulness. Part One pursues this question via personification, which animates the epistolary form and the allegory. In the letters, the two lovers are ostensibly negotiating the terms of their affair (as if working out a contract to which they could consent), but each assumes the other to be faithless and each describes their own agency as under the control of personifications both semi-sacred and mundane.[56] The narrative covers a mundane series of actions: waiting, longing, the consummation of a trivial love affair, and the lack of political action. But the letters are uncommonly animated via personification. "Love" and "Honour" – those ubiquitous Restoration demi-gods – play key roles here, as God and tyrant (respectively) vying for sovereignty over the two lovers: honour is a "Tyrant," and love is a "God" who "banish[es]" honour (11).[57] These abstract qualities not only play political roles but also exhibit bodily affects; for example, honour "blushes" (17). This first part of *Love Letters* thus explores the notion of being in a relation of political and physical subordination – even a "slave" to – personified ideas such as love and honour (31). But a host of other lesser abstractions and mundane materialities are personified too and vie for the fickle attention of the two lovers. These less esteemed and more immanent personas also emote, persuade, have material impacts and exert narrative agency: body parts have feelings (eyes "languish," 9) learn things (Sylvia's tongue and heart learn politics and business), have free will (lips are "unwilling," 16), and take action (hands "wander," and "rov[e]" 22, 37). Sometimes even interior furnishings are personified (the curtains in Sylvia's bedroom are "conscious," 88). These personifications have relations with humans and each other that are perhaps more compelling and certainly more abundant, complex, and material than the relations between the two main human characters: passions can "claim Passion" and beauty can become "indebted" (31). Thus, these personifications are allegorically represented as having a narrative, and they allow us to read the first part of *Love Letters* as a specific and complex allegory for human political relations (beyond merely sex is an allegory for politics), that is, an allegory for the complexity and chaos of human agency and for the ways that humans may or may not be controlled.

Samuel Johnson (1709–84) defined personification as "the change of things to persons," a line of thought that has allowed critics interested in thing theory, ecopoetics, and animal studies to examine personification in terms of how it challenges a thesis of human exceptionality.[58] But Behn approaches the possibilities of personification and the ontology of humanity from a different perspective, one that does not assume a norm of human agency. To the extent that *Love Letters* is about human agency, the most agential human-like things are personifications, and the human characters are fully effects of these conflicted and capricious impersonations. As an experiment in what we might call reverse personification, the text does not so much deploy personification as a poetic trope but instead depicts characters in the grip of a mania of personification, apersonal because possessed by personifications. This argument does not rest on a claim for any aesthetic or formal innovation, as personification was a baroque technique suitable to a worldview in which human behavior is subordinated to cosmic forces: the animation of personification goes hand in hand with subordination (and death) in much baroque art.[59] But Behn situates this ambivalently animate force within a narrative that does not concern spirituality but instead revolves around mundane political questions about rebellion, and thus these personifications tell us about Behn's response to the secularization of politics and love and particularly about her response to Hobbes. Personifications such as Hobbes' Leviathan are related to how an individual becomes generalized and thus how a body politic can be formed.[60] *Love Letters*' personifications may thus be read as doubly allegorical of personhood: both about how individuals may be constituted (as consistent or not) by a heterogeneous set of values, body parts, and passions and about how a body politic may (or may not) be formed out of a heterogeneous group of persons.

These possibilities about the effects of personification are played out differently with the two protagonists: The confusion in which Sylvia finds herself in Part One as a result of this riot of personifications causes her to make, rather late in the affair, the assertion of her royalism, while Philander's similar experience of personification, by contrast, makes him revel in the capriciousness of unmarried love and rebellious politics. That is, while Sylvia's experience of inconsistency promotes a desire for and a political case for a royal sovereign, Philander's results in infidelity and political rebellion. While a rabble of persons (like a rabble of personifications) produces "change and inconstancy," the King – for Sylvia and other royalists – can mitigate the confusion (caused by personifications) both within and among persons (45). If *Love Letters* ended here and if we took

Sylvia's situation as providing the moral of the story, we would have an allegory of the need for sovereign fictions, an allegory synergistic with the figure of Hobbes' Leviathan, based on a similar concern for the effects of secular human faithlessness. In short, Part One reveals the two protagonists to be faithless because driven by so many contradictory forces, and their chaotic emotional experiences mirror the political situation – they narrate themselves as if each is a sovereign state experiencing political unrest. Sylvia's sister expresses (and Sylvia later repeats) what we might take to be the moral of this part of the story "believe me, there is no lasting faith in sin" (74).[61]

After the consummation of the affair, at the end of Part One, Sylvia reports: "the mystery's now reveal'd, the mighty secret's known, and now will be no wonder or suprize," signaling a shift in both theme and form (89). In Part Two, the characters shift from the immediacy of letters and the drama of hyperbolic personification to express their passion to the expediency of disguise to effect their elopement, estrangement, and infidelities. That is, the text shifts from representing and formalizing an ontological state of faithlessness to undertaking a similar project for the activities of unfaithfulness. With this shift from instability to disguise and from uncertainty about faith to willful unfaithfulness, new techniques of narration emerge. If Part One utilized epistolarity and personification to impart vitality and immediacy to the central action, which is as mundane as it is predictable, Part Two uses omniscient narration to explain and contextualize a nonstop series of disguises, betrayals, misdirected and misleading letters, and violence that are part and parcel of infidelity. This Part is the most fully fictional of the three Parts, and it is the most secular in the sense that there is no mystery whatsoever, no outside the characters' shenanigans, nothing factual, normative, symbolic, or aesthetic that transcends the omnisciently narrated fictional infidelities. There are only human beings negotiating with each other in a faithless world. The relationships among love, religion, and politics are no longer allegorical but rather merely rhetorical or metaphorical. Sylvia for example is a "deceiving Idol" who appears to Octavio alternately like a divinity or a tyrant. Any connection to power or spirituality resides only in the false perspective of humans enthralled by her superficial beauty (and in the absence of anything else with which to be enthralled). So in return for his idolatry, Octavio too becomes mere simile: "like a Martyr," "like a false Worshipper," and "like a tame ignoble sufferer" (226). The omniscient narrator provides the factual information needed to understand the plot and also provides the normative judgments on the faithlessness of humans.

The form thus dramatizes the desire for secrets and the need for objective truth in a world where the allegorical connections of God, monarch, and lover are shorn apart – that is, it offers a different way to understand the reason that faith and epistemology are connected in secular modernity. Octavio and his sister Calista are the exceptions, faithful characters in a faithless world whose function is to call into relief the aesthetic, personal, and narrative implications of faithlessness.

The other possible late blooming exception to the faithlessness that drives Part Two is the narrator, who at the end of Part Two promises that Part Three "shall most Faithfully relate" the rest of the story (252). We might assume that this is a rhetorical move meant to entice continued readership, and so it probably is, but I want to suggest that this promise from the narrator might also suggest that the omniscient narration lacks fidelity in some ways, that the narrator of part Two, almost completely detached from the characters, is not in a relation of faith to the characters or the readers, and she promises a different relationship in Part Three. Indeed, a very different narrator emerges in Part Three.

In Part Three, we find a nearly complete formal separation of politics from personal relations and a separation of fact (or reality) from both faith and fiction: Brilliard narrates the political plot – the part of the story that is based on the historical facts – while the narrator recounts the romantic and fictional plot. We also find this separation of the personal, the political (and the religious) at the level of content: Monmouth and Octavio must take vows of celibacy in order to pursue their political and religious ambitions. Part Three thus offers a microcosmic case study of the emerging categorical distinctions between politics and fiction and between political, religious, and amorous faith. The narrator explicitly distances herself from the political events and invests her narrative role and her faith, in terms of a promise and in terms of an ethic, in the fictional story. There are several ways that she invites us to see this faith as being unstable or a matter of doubt: For example, the poetic justice she promises Sylvia never comes, and, as noted before, she admits that her powers of description are inadequate to the ordination scene. But as a narrator, she assumes she is in a relationship of faith with the reader. Her compact with the reader is merely to "Faithfully relate" a world that is fictional but quite a bit more mysterious and enchanted than the real/political world (252). The text ends by juxtaposing two postsecular tableaus: Monmouth's belief in oracles and fake charms, which presages his fall, is outside the narrator's bailiwick and beneath her interest, while Octavio's ordination elicits what seems to be a record of the narrator's conversion, if not to religious faith than at least from narrator to character and thus to a different form of narration and a new compact of faith.

Love Letters offers us insight into a possible way to re-narrate the secularization of the novel. We might even say you can read the three parts as predicting the history of the novel, with each part relating to a major moment in the literary history of the novel: the early epistolary novel in Part One, nineteenth-century realism/omniscience in Part Two, and a kind of postmodern irony or postsecular baroque in Part Three. The main point here is that *Love Letters* reveals the relationship of the novel and secularity to be how human beings can find "faith" in one another being worked out at the level of narrative form. Faith acts as part of the mechanism that determines the difference between the domains of fiction, religion, and politics. Fictional faith is not religious covenant nor political contract. Moreover, as we saw with Hobbes, what seems to be a radical reckoning with secularization turns postsecular very quickly.

This reading of Behn can help us to begin to imagine how literary histories of the eighteenth century might change if we set aside the secularization thesis: the commonplace that religion is separated from other realms of life, including politics, and that this historical shift is consequential for all areas of culture. The holy trinity of twenty-first-century critical trends – the religious turn, the theological turn, and the postsecular turn – have made slow inroads in challenging the secularization thesis and eighteenth-century literary history; however, as scholars of the eighteenth century, and as part of a larger discipline of literary studies, the secularization thesis is deeply embedded in our methods and values, and this is especially true for historians of the novel.[62] Literary history is itself a secular, enlightened mode of critique, and the novel is the most important genre in our secular literary histories. This is because the novel, literary history, and secularism are historically coincident, and the novel is often seen as giving form to the intellectual and ideological values of secularism: as dialogic, nonhierarchical, and committed to plurality and immanence, the novel opposes the monotheism, monolinguism, and transcendence central to Judeo-Christian religious and literary culture. Hence, most historians of the eighteenth-century novel (including me) have given secularism a key role. For Ian Watt, the novel is immersed in secular culture, and unlike allegory, which relies upon a "transcendental scheme of things," the novel's worldview concerns itself with human social relationships, and "a measure of secularization was an indispensable condition for the rise of the new genre."[63] Michael McKeon brings the novel and the secularization thesis even closer, arguing that the novel mediates the early modern secularization crisis, which pitted scientific against religious truth. For McKeon, the novel allows religion to be about belief and faith; it thus contributes to the spiritualization and thus the secularization of religion. György Lukács defines the novel as "the epic of a world that has been abandoned by God."[64] And James Wood calls the novel the "slayer of religions."[65] Together, these critics suggest an irony in our secular literary history: We define the novel as imminent, interested in the realities of the world, and we define religion as belief, thus making immanent religious practices ipso facto not novelistic (not even religious) and thus making both a non-secular novel and a religious social relation category errors. Kevin Seidel has provided one account of how limited this account of the novel is (both in terms of content and reading practices) and thus how we might challenge the seemingly natural connection between secularity and novels, and Lisa O'Connell has urged us to consider seriously what it means to say that the novel constructed a "secular virtue," but more work needs to be done to revise this account of literary history.[66]

So as part of challenging this literary history, I have gone back to the beginning of the novel, to a key moment in the political history of secularization, in order to excavate how the novel and the project we now call secularization were entwined, or *how we began to have faith in fiction*. What are the implications of this for challenging the axiomatic connection of novels and secularity? If *Love Letters* serves as an allegory for the history of the novel (and I am not the only critic to suggest this: William Warner and Ros Ballaster have argued something similar), then the progress of the three parts and the importance of the ordination scene in particular challenge the idea that novels are about demystification.[67] Instead, the narrator/character/reader trinity may constitute a kind of mystical/allegorical structure of postsecular faith. Thus, novels may not be secular in the ways we think. They may not follow a subtraction, replacement, or expropriation thesis. Rather, novels may be a kind of ceremony for the theology of secular culture, a ritual that bonds humans, where humans find faith in each other via narration and fiction. Above all, this analysis of Behn reminds us of something that has always been paradoxical about eighteenth-century literary history: that conservative writers are so influential in what we take to be a secularization narrative, even in that most secular form, the novel. What would a literary history look like that linked the conservative and postsecular concerns and the formal innovations of writers? This is an unresolved problematic in eighteenth-century literary history that this book begins to address.

Conservative Faith

Over the long arc of conservatism, faith becomes a central defining feature of its worldview. In analyzing how conservative writers took up the problem of faith at a key moment in its secular redefinition, this chapter offers some insight into the prehistory of this aspect of conservatism. It shows that concern about faith as depicted by Hobbes and Behn – and indeed perhaps even for the theological writers of the seventeenth century – was not driven by religious, political, or sexual traditionalism. Rather, they seem concerned with the secularization of faith: with what the implications are for separating faith, in a religious sense, from trust in political and romantic relations. While Hobbes' project seems founded on the importance of separating politics from personal relations, its dual separations suggest the dangers of that project. Behn's *Love Letters* is more forthright about its concerns about the secularization of faith – its plot premise begins by linking the dangers of sexual infidelity and political rebellion. Its moments of religiosity, such as they are, stand only as unrealistic counterpoints to this dangerous secularity. I will develop the analysis of Behn's prose fictions more in Chapter 5, but the point here is that the secularization of faith is related to the conservative projects of Hobbes and Behn, insofar as they worry about how faith can be removed from political and social life without negative effects. They are concerned not about the loss of religion from public life but about the loss of the nonreligious structures of faith – trust in people – to political and social life. As writers concerned with the central politic dramas of the late seventeenth century – the Puritan Revolution, the Restoration, and the Exclusion Crisis – they offer insight into the key questions that would inform the path of secularization. Their postsecular responses inhere not only in their loyalism but also in their concern about how the secularization of faith would influence personal relations, in both politics and romance. They might even provide insight into why conservatism's influence in areas of culture outside of politics and religion has been so strong: in, for example, the ongoing culture wars in the United States and the complex relation between politician's personal lives and their work. The fact that both writers turn to fiction to restore faith – or to make it postsecular – tells us something about the disciplinary relationship between literature and politics that would obtain after the Restoration: Secularization would assume a separation between them, but this masks a deep synergy, in which the forms of each are responses to secularization, and secularization of faith in particular.

Critics have noted the centrality of fiction to secularity, including Hobbes' political theory and the novel form. Victoria Kahn has shown how fictions about the state of nature and the social contract were central to Hobbes, and Jonathan Lamb has argued that Hobbes' political science depends upon separating good from bad fictions.[68] For such critics, fiction is the necessary mental process that allows for the kind of human agency central to secular political history. If fiction is central to secularity, so too is faith. Lamb seems to say something similar in his rhetorical flourish that "faith in fiction" is the foundation of historical action.[69] But in this account "faith" is secular, a habit of mind and theory of relationality that makes secular history possible. Catherine Gallagher argues most forcefully for the connection of secularity and fiction, saying "all of the developments we associate with modernity – from greater religious toleration to scientific discovery – required the kind of cognitive provisionality one practices in reading fiction."[70] For Gallagher, developments central to secular modernity – toleration and science – depend upon a secularized notion of faith that this chapter has been endeavoring to nuance and revise. One way to put it might be that instead of needing to have "faith" (in its secularized meaning of belief) in "fiction" (because it is necessary to politics), the secularization of faith in Hobbes causes the need for political fiction, which disavows its dependence on faith. The dynamic between faith and fiction works a bit differently in Behn who, by grappling with the changes in faith and politics intensified by the exclusion crisis, invents techniques of prose fiction. In both cases, faith and fiction are centrally connected. George Lakoff's account of the contemporary conservative worldview finds a morality rooted in family values to be at its heart (and also, though disavowed, at the heart of liberalism).[71] The late seventeenth-century was the moment when the allegorical connection between family structure and politics was shorn apart, an historical phenomenon that has been well explicated by other scholars.[72] For Lakoff, understanding a political worldview requires understanding the connections among its parts. What I offer here is an account of the ways that faith connected family values (in terms of romantic fidelity) to politics and religion, and how two writers with proto-conservative leanings imagined the consequences and possible modes of remediation of the emergent consensus about these relations, or lack thereof. Hobbes and Behn are not conservative in the sense of wanting to maintain traditional structures of politics and family, nor are they religious. Rather, they are modern conservatives, concerned about the secularization of faith and inventing modern forms of politics and fiction in order to grapple with this process. As such, this account of the connection between faith and fiction differs from accounts such as those of Kahn, Lamb, and Gallagher, which take the secularization thesis at face value. Whereas they tend to posit fiction (and its habits of mind) as central to modernity, with "faith" surviving as a fully secularized way of describing the relationship between agents and fictions, in Hobbes and Behn faith itself is being preserved in these fictions. So we might say that Hobbes and Behn teach us to have faith in fiction as a way of preserving the various functions of faith in the secularized realms of politics, romance, and novels.

Notes

1. John Locke, *The Clarendon Edition of the Works of John Locke: The Reasonableness of Christianity: As Delivered in the Scriptures*, ed. John C. Higgins-Biddle (New York: Oxford University Press, 2000). The transformation (of religion into faith) that Locke represents makes possible Kant's efforts to erect a moral system based on secular reason, to define the human as one who is free but who "binds himself through his reason to unconditional laws." Immanuel Kant, *Religion within the Boundaries of Mere Reason*, trans. Allen Wood and George Di Giovanni (Cambridge: Cambridge University Press, 1998), 33. In Kant's famous formulation, reason and faith are ontologically distinct but structurally dependent on one another in terms of developing the moral and social laws foundations of modernity: one has to "deny knowledge, in order to make room for *faith*." *Critique of Pure Reason*, trans. Paul Guyer and Allen Wood (Cambridge: Cambridge University Press, 1997), 117, Bxxx. For a helpful discussion of this aspect of Kant, see Richard J. Bernstein, "The Secular-Religious Divide: Kant's Legacy," *Social Research* 76, no. 4 (Winter 2009): 1035–48. Building on Kant, the nineteenth-century secularization project increasingly denied the links between faith and knowledge as well as faith and morality: the sense that faith was a theological notion separate from human notions of truth makes possible the nineteenth-century "death of God" in Hegel and Nietzsche. Both Locke and Kant are trying to offer a nuanced relationship between faith and reason, and obviously I cannot do their arguments justice here. I am merely suggesting that their long discourses that attempt to establish a relationship between faith and reason, however nuanced, suggest that the distinction between them is central to the secular project.
2. Catherine Gallagher both summarizes and exemplifies this trend, in "The Rise of Fictionality," in *The Novel: Volume 1: History, Geography, and Culture*, ed. Franco Moretti (Princeton, NJ: Princeton University Press, 2006), 336–63. Gallagher argues that the point of the fictionality of novels is to discourage the habit of mind she calls "faith" and to install instead an "attitude of disbelief" (346). While Gallagher's argument, like much other scholarship in this line of

argumentation – which takes epistemological issues to be central to the novel and to faith – is compelling, this chapter endeavors to uncover a different meaning of faith and thus a different impetus for fictionality.

3 My previous book *Enlightened Virginity in Eighteenth-Century Literature* (New York: Palgrave, 2006) was in dialogue with a number of books about eighteenth-century literature sexuality, domesticity, and romance, which often connected such issues with both politics and epistemology. Other examples include Nancy Armstrong, *Desire and Domestic Fiction: A Political History of the Novel* (Oxford: Oxford University Press, 1987); Rosalind Ballaster, *Seductive Forms: Women's Amatory Fiction from 1684 to 1740* (Oxford: Oxford University Press, 1998); Katherine Binhammer, *The Seduction Narrative in Britain, 1747–1800* (Cambridge: Cambridge University Press, 2009); Michael McKeon, *The Origins of the English Novel, 1600–1740* (Baltimore: Johns Hopkins University Press, 2002); Ann Jessie Van Sant, *Eighteenth-Century Sensibility and the Novel: The Senses in Social Context* (Cambridge: Cambridge University Press, 2004). The point of this chapter is not to renounce this interest in such topics, but rather to suggest that they may benefit from an orientation that takes the history of secularization into account.

4 I take secularization to be both a historical fact and one that has been overemphasized by critics. For more on its impact in eighteenth-century studies, see my essay (with Alison Conway), "Toward a Postsecular Eighteenth Century," *Literature Compass* 12, no. 11 (November 2015): 565–74. Some work in postsecularism takes faith to be epistemological, but other work is recognizing the connection of this meaning to secularism itself. For a sense of the zeitgeist about this from a theistic postsecularism, see Karen Armstrong, "Let's Revive the Golden Rule," July 2009, TED video, 9:38, www.ted.com/talks/karen_armstrong_let_s_revive_the_golden_rule.

5 *Oxford English Dictionary Online*, s.v. "faith, n. and int.," March 2022, www-oed-com.login.ezproxy.library.ualberta.ca/view/Entry/67760?rskey=kSpxsy&result=1&isAdvanced=false.

6 *Oxford English Dictionary Online*, s.v. "faith, v.," March 2022, www-oed-com.login.ezproxy.library.ualberta.ca/view/Entry/67761?rskey=kSpxsy&result=2&isAdvanced=false.

7 Griffiths and Hütter point out that Greek has both noun (*pistis*) and verb (*pisteuō*) forms of "faith," while the Latin *fides*, like the English "faith" which derives from it, has no corresponding verb. Griffiths and Hütter surmise that this lexical issue contributes to the distinction between "an act of faith and an act of belief" in English that this chapter is discussing (11). Paul J. Griffiths and Reinhard Hütter, eds., *Reason and the Reasons of Faith* (New York: Bloomsbury, 2005).

8 The OED's first citation of the meaning of fidelity as "conjugal faithfulness" is 1694. But of course the meaning was in play before, though its entanglement with religious or political meanings might account for this separate meaning making such a late entrance. One historically fascinating use is John Milton

proclaiming, in relation to his support of divorce, his "addicted fidelity" to the Parliament. John Milton, "Tetrachordon," in *The Essential Prose of John Milton*, eds. William Kerrigan, John Rumrich, and Stephen M. Fallon (New York: Random House Publishing Group, 2013), 236. Another interesting example is the way that Francis Fuller refers to religious faith as an "act of affiance," in *A Treatise of Faith and Repentance* (London, 1684), 13.

9 In a related vein, "faith" now also means the particular religion you subscribe to: "Protestant faith," "Catholic faith," "Jewish faith," etc. As a noun that suggests belief and that can take different adjectives (in fact that makes religious commitment an adjective), this use of faith reinforces its epistemological frailty.

10 https://books.google.com/ngrams/graph?content=Faith&case_insensitive=on&year_start=1300&year_end=2015&corpus=15&smoothing=3&share=&direct_url=t4%3B%2CFaith%3B%2Cco%3B%2Cs0%3B%3Bfaith%3B%2Cco%3B%3BFaith%3B%2Cco#t4%3B%2CFaith%3B%2Cco%3B%2Cs1%3B%3Bfaith%3B%2Cco%3B%3BFaith%3B%2Cco. Derivatives of faith such as fidelity, fiancé, and affiance follow a similar pattern. I am aware of some of the serious limitations of relying on Google Ngram data. My point is not that it alone proves anything about the history of the term faith but rather that it confirms what primary and scholarly sources also reveal, which is a historically specific concern with faith in its political, religious, and romantic senses during the late seventeenth century. Perhaps one interesting point of contrast is that "loyalty" has a very different history from faith: peaking around 1650, it seems almost unaffected by 1688–89: in fact, the 1690s is one of the nadirs in "loyalty's" history. One explanation is that loyalty does not have the interdisciplinary flexibility of "faith" (loyalty does, however, enjoy a resurgence in the late 1710, presumably for political reasons). Interestingly, "false" follows a similar trajectory to "faith"; while this might seem to contradict my point, in fact I would argue that "false" itself is not an epistemological category at this time either. Like "faith" it indexes social trust and reliability, not belief.

11 J. Wayne Baker, "Sola Fide, Sola Gratia: The Battle for Luther in Seventeenth-Century England," *The Sixteenth Century Journal* 13, no. 1 (Spring 1985): 115–33. Baker traces, from a purely theological standpoint, the course of this debate, which he situates in the context of the reception of Luther in England, showing that by the end of the seventeenth century, it was mostly resolved against *sola fide*. My purpose is to link the story Baker tells so well to the political history of late seventeenth-century England. For a discussion of Hobbes' interpretation of *sola fide*, see Perez Zagorin, *Hobbes and the Law of Nature* (Princeton, NJ: Princeton University Press, 2009), 127.

12 For scholarship on this phenomenon, see, e.g., Carole Pateman, *The Sexual Contract* (Cambridge: Polity, 1988); and Susan Staves, *Players' Scepters: Fictions of Authority in the Restoration* (Omaha: University of Nebraska Press, 1979).

13 A search on www.kingjamesbibleonline.org/ finds 338 total instances of "faith" in the *KJB*. "Faith" is much more of a theme in the New

Testament – it appears about six times more frequently in the New Testament than in the Old Testament, which is longer. In the Old Testament, faith refers more often to God: he keeps the covenant and therefore is faithful. Humans are less reliably faithful, and God despairs of finding a "faithful man" (Proverbs 20:6) and a "faithful priest" (Deuteronomy 32:20 1 Samuel 2:35). Faith in the *KJB* is about character, not epistemology. But faith also has a full range of meaning in the Old Testament – it refers to work and business transactions (2 Kings 12:15, 22:7, 2 Chronicles 34:12), to political appointments and standards (Nehemiah 7:2, Nehemiah 13:13, Proverbs 29:14, Hosea 11:12), to honesty and testimony (Psalms 5:9, Proverbs 14:5, Psalms 89:1), and to romantic commitment (Hosea 2:20). The key general distinction between Old and New Testament is that faith in the New Testament focuses more exclusively on the faith of humans (subjects) not of rulers or God (see, e.g., Romans 14:22) and that faith is opposed to law rather than the fulfilment of law. Faithfulness is not a characteristic of power but that which power rewards, with power (Matthew 25:21, Luke 12:42) health (Mark 2:5, Mark 5:34, Mark 10:52), and forgiveness (Luke 5:20). "O Ye of little faith" is a sentiment repeatedly expressed about humans (Matthew 6:30, Matthew 8:10, Matthew 8:26, Matthew 14:31, Luke 12:28). Although the Old Testament God of covenant is frequently figured as a partner in a relationship of faith, seventeenth-century writers often made the case that faith was a New Testament phenomenon. Francis Fuller for example says, "[T]here was never but two ways to Life, viz, That of the Old Covenant and this of the New; that by Works and this by Faith; and both as the Condition, not as the Cause of Life" (*A Treatise of Faith and Repentance*, 3). This emphasis on the New Testament version of faith – and even selective aspects of it – is part of what I am calling the secularization of faith.

14 Barten Holyday, *Of the Nature of Faith: A Sermon* (London, 1654). For biographical information, see the *ODNB*. F. D. A. Burns, "Holyday, Barten (1593–1661)," in *Oxford Dictionary of National Biography* (Oxford University Press, September 23, 2004), https://doi.org/10.1093/ref:odnb/13625.
15 Slavoj Žižek, *On Belief* (London; New York: Routledge, 2003), 108–9. Žižek's reading of Christianity is explicitly political, discerning in the Pauline community of believers the first version of a revolutionary collective.
16 For a more extended analysis of Lacan on faith, see Robert Pfaller, *On the Pleasure Principle, In Culture: Illusions without Owners* (London: Verso, 2014). Pfaller argues that Lacan's "symbolic" is also the "order of fictions," which are always the others' fictions, and he shows that faith is really the realm of the imaginary (55).
17 Griffiths and Hütter, *Reason and the Reasons of Faith*, 6.
18 Ibid., 6.
19 *A most excellent and fruitful treatise, called Patericks Places concerning the doctrine of fayth, and the doctrine of the law: which being knowen, you haue the pith of all diuinitie. With a briefe collection or exposition of a summe of S. Pauls doctrine touching iustification by fayth, in Iesus Christ: which is the only*

marke to shoote at, and the only meanes to obtaine saluation. (London: Printed by William White dwelling in Cow-lane neare Holborne Condite, and are there to be solde, 1598). The ODNB credits Hamilton with a "pivotal role" ... "in the focusing and application of Lutheran theology in Scotland" especially with regard to the question of faith versus works. Iain Torrance, "Hamilton, Patrick (1504?–1528)," in *Oxford Dictionary of National Biography* (Oxford: Oxford University Press, September 23, 2004), https://doi.org/10.1093/ref:odnb/12116.

20 The two kingdoms or "two governments" theory developed during the Reformation by Martin Luther and Phillip Melancthon was modeled on Augustine's city of God. Luther put it thus: "God has ordained the two governments: the spiritual, which by the Holy Spirit under Christ makes Christians and pious people; and the secular, which restrains the unchristian and wicked so that they are obliged to keep the peace outwardly." Martin Luther, "Secular Authority: To What Extent It Should Be Obeyed," in *Martin Luther: Selections from His Writings*, ed. John Dillenberger (Garden City, NJ: Anchor/Doubleday, 1961), 363–402.

21 This doctrine of two governments (or two kingdoms) was taken up by Puritan writers like John Milton and John Locke as well as adversaries like Thomas Hobbes: All three seemed to accept the premise that the two kingdoms meant that civil government could not dictate matters of conscience, although the implications of this insight were quite different for each of them. John Milton, *A Treatise of Civil Power in Ecclesiastical Causes Shewing That It Is Not Lawfull for Any Power on Earth to Compell in Matters of Religion* (London: Printed by Tho. Newcomb, 1659); John Locke, "Civil and Ecclesiastical Power," in *Locke: Political Essays*, ed. Mark Goldie (Cambridge: Cambridge University Press, 1997).

22 One major impact of the two governments theory has been to make freedom of conscience the foundation of secular modernity. But the structure of the two governments also means that this central concept of secularity can be figured (as it will be in Hobbes) as irrelevant to secular society. In other words, secular society is based on a kind of sanctification of liberty of conscience, which thus means that liberty of conscience is not to be deployed (in a strict interpretation of two governments) in secular society. This is a point that Wendy Brown has developed regarding tolerance, in *Regulating Aversion: Tolerance in the Age of Identity and Empire* (Princeton, NJ: Princeton University Press, 2009).

23 Baker makes this point ("Sola Fide," 115). Baker offers a fuller elaboration of these debates in England; he traces how works-righteousness "crept back into Protestant theology" via an emphasis on its role as "assurance," if never the cause, of grace ("Sola Fide," 125). Baker's research shows how works became evidence for faith, and thus how faith became in need of evidence; further, his analysis shows that predestination could be seen as predating faith, thus making faith itself merely a sign or evidence of grace. He thus concurs with Max Weber's thesis that Luther's influence eroded over the course of the

seventeenth century. Weber argues in his seminal book on *The Protestant Ethic and the Spirit of Capitalism*, trans. Talcott Parsons (New York: Charles Scribner's Sons, 1958) that economic prosperity can be attributed especially to Calvin's theological doctrine of work as God's chosen duty. In this interpretation of the Calvinist strain of theology that comes to dominate England, works are relevant, but as not the "cause" but only the "means" of "knowledge of a state of grace" (*The Protestant Ethic*, 141). Weber contrasts the Lutheran emphasis on "emotionalism" with Calvinistic "ascetic action," in which conduct and works (*fides efficax*) are "indispensable as signs of election" (*The Protestant Ethic*, 114–15), and recounts the Lutheran critique of Calvinism as a reversion to works. Still, most scholars, Weber included, distinguish a Catholic theology of incremental good works from a Reformed (or for my purposes secular) emphasis on internality, even if it is expressed as "systematic self control" (*The Protestant Ethic*, 115).

24 John Rogers, *The Doctrine of Faith: wherein are practically handled ten principall points, which explain the nature and vse of it* (London, 1627; reprinted many times through 1640). Rogers (1610–80) was a clergyman and ejected minister, probably with connections to English Protestant martyr John Rogers (1500–55). See Stephen Wright, "Rogers, John (1610–1680)," *Oxford Dictionary of National Biography* (Oxford: Oxford University Press, September 23, 2004), https://doi.org/10.1093/ref:odnb/23984.

25 *The Doctrine of Faith*, 3–15.

26 *Of the rule of faith a sermon at the visitation of the Right Reverend Father in God, William Lord Bishop of Lincolne, holden at Bedford August 5, 1674* (Cambridge, 1675). Jackson does not appear in the ODNB. OCLC lists three titles for Jackson, with *The Rule of Faith* printed five times. Biographical dates are from *Early English Books on Line*.

27 This is not to dismiss the Reformation emphasis on faith, which is absolutely central. My point here is that it becomes focused on Christ not on the believer.

28 Holyday, *Of the Nature of Faith*, 23.

29 Fuller, *A Treatise of Faith and Repentance*, 7. For biographical information see M. J. Mercer, "Fuller, Francis (1636?–1701)," *Oxford Dictionary of National Biography* (Oxford: Oxford University Press, September 23, 2004), https://doi.org/10.1093/ref:odnb/10228.

30 Weber, *The Protestant Ethic*, 121.

31 For Weber this Calvinist "sort of feeling" also organized social and political life (*The Protestant Ethic*, 122). R. T. Kendall argues that Calvin's conception of faith transformed, as later Calvinist theologians separated faith and knowledge, *Calvin and English Calvinism to 1649*, rev. ed. (Eugene, OR: Wipf & Stock, 2011). Although *sola fide* is not as central to theological debates now as it was in the seventeenth century, contemporary theologian Peter Berger, among other faithful writers, argues for its ongoing importance with his claims that Protestantism is centered on this distinction between faith and knowledge and that *sola fide* acknowledges uncertainty as a good. Peter Berger,

"Protestantism and the Quest for Certainty," *Religion Online*, accessed June 20, 2017. www.religion-online.org/showarticle.asp?title=239&gt.
32 C. Hutchinson, *Of the Authority of Councils and Rule of Faith* (London: Printed for R. Clavel, W. Rogers, and S. Smith, 1687). Hutchinson's solution rested on the argument that a council of people would be less fallible than an individual, an argument with obvious implications for the political debates of the late seventeenth century, and one that makes sense in terms of attacking the pope's infallibility. But the argument founders a bit on the logic that it was a council (Trent) that asserted this infallibility.
33 Fuller, *A Treatise of Faith and Repentance*, 1.
34 Holyday, *Of the Nature of Faith*.
35 The ODNB calls Stillingfleet "the leading theologian and apologist of the Church of England." Barry Till, "Stillingfleet, Edward (1635–1699)," in *Oxford Dictionary of National Biography* (Oxford: Oxford University Press published September 23, 2004; last modified January 3, 2008), https://doi.org/10.1093/ref:odnb/26526. As one of the key figures in the resistance to James II, he can be seen as an important liberal theorist and an important architect of the modern political consciousness.
36 Beverley Southgate, "Sergeant, John (1623–1707)," in *Oxford Dictionary of National Biography* (Oxford: Oxford University Press, September 23, 2004), https://doi.org/10.1093/ref:odnb/25095.
37 (*Works*, 3.530) cited in *ODNB*.
38 John Tillotson, *THE Rule of Faith: or an ANSWER to the TREATISE of Mr. I. S. entituled, Sure-footing, &c. By JOHN TILLOTSON, D.D. Preacher to the Honourable Society of Lincolns-Inn. To which is Adjoined A REPLY TO Mr. I.S. his 3^d APPENDIX, &c. By EDW. STILLINGFLEET D. D. One of His Majesties Chaplains in Ordinary*, 2nd ed. (London: Printed by H.C. for O. Gellibrand, at the Golden-Ball in St. Paul's Church-yard, 1676), 93.
39 Joshua Mitchell, "Hobbes and the Equality of All under the One," *Political Theory* 21, no. 1 (1993): 78–100. Mitchell's account suggests that Hobbes redefines faith as not interior, in order to establish continuity between the New and the Old Testaments and thus the legitimacy of a Christian Commonwealth.
40 Carl Schmitt and George Schwab, *Political Theology: Four Chapters on the Concept of Sovereignty* (Chicago: University of Chicago Press, 1985).
41 Thomas Hobbes *Leviathan*, ed. J. C. A. Gaskin (Oxford: Oxford University Press, 1996), Introduction, para. 1 (Following convention, further citations to Hobbes will be by section and paragraph number).
42 I am following Quentin Skinner's account here. The state is an abstract person and needs a representer (the sovereign) but this means that the sovereign does not represent the people. Quentin Skinner, "Hobbes and the Purely Artificial Person of the State," *Journal of Political Philosophy* 7, no. 1 (March 1999): 1. On dual separation and its relevance for the corporate from of capital, see Mark Neocleous, "Staging Power: Marx, Hobbes and the Personification of Capital," *Law and Critique* 14, no. 2 (2003): 147–65.

43 Neither is God's impersonation exactly the same as the political amalgamation because God is unified in himself (the trinity does not amalgamate nor represent and is not an entity that can wield power in this world).
44 "But by believing, as it is in the Creed, is meant, not trust in the Person; but confession and acknowledgement of the doctrine. For not only Christians, but all manner of men do so believe in God, as to hold all for truth they hear him say, whether they understand it, or not; which is all the faith and trust can possibly be had in any person whatsoever: but they do not all believe the doctrine of the creed." (*Lev* 1.7.6).
45 According to Alan Ryan, for Hobbes, religion is a matter of law not truth, "Hobbes, Toleration, and the Inner Life," in *The Nature of Political Theory*, eds. David Miller and Larry Siendentop (Oxford: Clarendon, 1983) 197–218.
46 I take Hobbes' use of "attribute" and "accident" as interchangeable: anything not substantial or essential to the thing or person. Affect, in this sense, is a subcategory of attribute. As an affect, faith is a quality a human may have, but it is not foundational or essential. At times, faith operates as affect, though Hobbes would prefer that it comes to act as habit. Another way to put is that if affect theory categorizes affects (spontaneously and subjectively experienced feelings in the body) and connects each to a predictable response, then Hobbes, in addition to wanting faith attached only to Christianity, wants to move faith from affect into predictable response (habit). Insofar as affect theory treats affect as the biological or physiological part of emotion I am not using the theory strictly, but I do think that Hobbes treats faith as something that mysteriously straddles the mind/body connection, so I am using "affect" here to express that orientation. The connection of Hobbes and Spinoza (who claims to be highly influenced by Hobbes but who articulates his influential theory of affect in the wake of Hobbes) on this is probably significant but beyond what I can really develop here. For Benedictus de Spinoza, the term affect is the modification or variation produced in a body (including the mind) by an interaction with another body which increases or diminishes the body's power of activity (potentia agendi), *Ethics*, Part 3: *The Collected Works of Spinoza*, vol. 1, ed. and trans. Edwin Curley (Princeton, NJ: Princeton University Press, 1985). Hence, Spinoza connects interpersonality and power in a way that deviates quite a bit from Hobbes. Whereas Spinoza wants to find ways that feelings can radiate out to actions, Hobbes wants to foreclose that possibility. My argument in this chapter is that "faith" is a place where Hobbes' argument frays a bit and that later developments of secularization, which insist on faith as an epistemological category not a feeling or an action, develop this line of thinking. Recent interest in affect is thus part and parcel of a postsecular turn, an interest in how interpersonal experiences (including between God and humans) function outside of belief and political action and especially outside what we typically see as a secular liberal subjects (because according to Deleuze and Guattari, affects are not connected to subjects). Gilles Deleuze and Félix Guattari, *A Thousand Plateaus: Capitalism and Schizophrenia* (London: Bloomsbury, 1988).

47 It comes not via "inspiration or infusion" but rather by hearing and education (and here revelation is included, though considered irrelevant for seventeenth-century England).
48 See for example Saba Mahmood on the exemplary and adverbial character of Egyptian Muslim women's piety, *Politics of Piety: The Islamic Revival and the Feminist Subject* (Princeton, NJ: Princeton University Press, 2011). See also Ronald Dworkin, who argues that the "final value of our lives is adverbial, not adjectival, a matter of how we lived, not the final result" (In "What is a Good Life" quoted in *The New Yorker*, September 14, 2015). He develops this idea of "secular sacredness" in *Religion without God* (Cambridge, MA: Harvard University Press, 2013).
49 See Sheldon Wolin's lucid discussion of this "power without community" aspect of Hobbes' thought, in *Politics and Vision: Continuity and Innovation in Western Political Thought* (Princeton, NJ: Princeton University Press, 2009), 243–56.
50 Edmund Burke referred to the formation of government as necessarily covered by a "secret veil." *The Writings and Speeches of Edmund Burke*, ed. P. J. Marshall (Oxford: Clarendon Press, 1981), VI: 316–17. I am arguing that in Hobbes' theory the veil is thrown over the artificial person – it is a veil that makes the persona of the state incapable of the personal relations of faith.
51 The only punishment that may happen to a state, like a corporation, is dissolution, an outcome that Hobbes precludes. On this reading, the replacement of a sovereign does nothing to the artificial person of the state.
52 The language of immunity has become central to contemporary scholarship on politics and sovereignty. Robert Esposito characterizes modern political thought, as inaugurated by Hobbes, as centering immunity; *Bios: Biopolitics and Philosophy*, trans. Timothy Campbell (Minneapolis: University of Minnesota Press, 2008), 46–59. Jacques Derrida argues that the sovereign's "absolute power" is also their "vulnerability" (the attempt to protect from contagion is what threatens their sovereignty and thus functions like an autoimmune disorder); *The Beast and the Sovereign*, trans. Geoffrey Bennington, 2 vols. (Chicago: University of Chicago Press, 2009), 2: 7.
53 *The Works of Aphra Behn. Vol. 2, Love-Letters between a Nobleman and His Sister (1684–7)*, ed. Janet Todd (Charlottesville, VA: InteLex, 2004 and London: Pickering & Chatto, 2000–1), 379–80, 383. All subsequent references will be to this version.
54 Aphra Behn, *A Congratulatory Poem to Her Sacred Majesty, Queen Mary upon Her Arrival in England by Mrs. A.* Behn (London: Printed by R. E. for R. Bentley ... and W. Canning ..., 1689).
55 Aphra Behn, *Oroonoko and Other Writings* (Oxford: Oxford University Press, 2009).
56 See Elizabeth Cook for a discussion of how family relations differed from political relations (as affective rather than political) and thus how the decline of patriarchal theory left the domestic sphere "dangerously unregulated," *Epistolary Bodies: Gender and Genre in the Eighteenth-Century Republic of*

Letters (Stanford, CA: Stanford University Press, 1996), 15. She reads late seventeenth- and early eighteenth-century literature as an effort to compensate for the death of the father and epistolary fiction as a social contract for family relations.
57 Later love too becomes a tyrant, from Sylvia's perspective (*The Works of Aphra Behn*, 146).
58 Samuel Johnson, "Personification," in *A Dictionary of the English Language in Which the Words Are Deduced from Their Originals, and Illustrated in Their Different Significations by Examples from the Best Writers*, 4th ed., revised by author (Dublin: printed for Thomas Ewing, 1775).
59 See, e.g., Walter Benjamin's classic argument on the baroque, *The Origin of German Tragic Drama*, trans. John Osborne (repr. London; New York: Verso, 2009).
60 On the centrality of generalization and social cohesion to personification, see Earl Wasserman, who locates the impetus for neoclassical personification in man's "natural preoccupation with the genus to which he belongs" and in the "innate sense of benevolence which binds man together into a society." Earl Wasserman, "The Inherent Values of Eighteenth-Century Personification," *PMLA* 65, no. 4 (1950): 456. Clifford Siskin develops this idea; in examining how Augustan writers link uses of language and configuration of communities; he argues that personification provides a "syncecdochic affirmation of community." Clifford Siskin, "Personification and Community: Literary Change in the Mid- and Late Eighteenth Century," *Eighteenth-Century Studies* 15, no. 4 (1982): 376–77.
61 Behn is of course a storyteller and not a moralist; the faithless world of Part One of *Love Letters* may produce personal and political unrest, but at the same time, the animation of the personifications, the immediacy of the epistolary form, and the touch of celebrity mystique afforded by the *roman à clef* genre do give faithlessness a good deal of narrative excitement.
62 Back in 2008, Gauri Viswanathan suggested that literary studies, because of its historical connection to religion, has been slow to take up the challenges of postsecularism; Gauri Viswanathan, "Secularism in the Framework of Heterodoxy," *PMLA* 123, no. 2 (2008): 466–76. I have argued, with Alison Conway, that eighteenth-century studies have been particularly recalcitrant because of the close connection of enlightenment and secularism. Conway and Harol, "Toward a Postsecular Eighteenth Century."
63 *The Rise of the Novel* (Berkeley: University of California Press, 1967), 80, 84.
64 György Lukács, *The Theory of the Novel*, trans. Anna Bosock (Berlin: Merlin Press, 1971), 88.
65 James Wood, *The Broken Estate: Essay on Literature and Belief* (London: Jonathan Cape, 2000), xi–xii.
66 Kevin Seidel, *Rethinking the Secular Origins of the Novel: The Bible in English Fiction 1678–1767* (Cambridge: Cambridge University Press, 2021); Lisa O'Connell, "Literary Sentimentalism and Post-Secular Virtue," *Eighteenth-Century Life* 41, no. 2 (2017): 28–42.

67 Rosalind Ballaster, "'The Story of the Heart': *Love-Letters between a Noble-Man and His Sister*," in *The Cambridge Companion to Aphra Behn*, eds. Derek Hughes and Janet Todd, Cambridge Companions to Literature (Cambridge: Cambridge University Press, 2004), 135–50; William B. Warner, "Licensed by the Market: *Behn's Love Letters* as Serial Entertainment," in his *Licensing Entertainment: The Elevation of Novel Reading in Britain, 1684–1750* (Berkeley: University of California Press, 1998), 45–87.
68 Victoria Kahn, *Wayward Contracts: The Crisis of Political Obligation in England, 1640–1674* (Princeton, NJ: Princeton University Press, 2004); Johnathan Lamb, "Imagination, Conjecture, and Disorder," *Eighteenth-Century Studies* 45, no. 1 (October 14, 2011): 53–69.
69 Lamb, "Imagination," 59.
70 Gallagher, "The Rise of Fictionality," 347.
71 George Lakoff, *Moral Politics: How Liberals and Conservatives Think*, 3rd ed. (Chicago: University of Chicago Press, 2016).
72 Carole Pateman's compelling feminist account of the shift from compact to contract has explored this phenomenon from a feminist, and critical, perspective, which has been influential in literary studies of the marriage plot (*The Sexual Contract*). Regarding the history of the novel, the most thoroughgoing account may be Michael McKeon's in *Origins of the English Novel* and in "Historicizing Patriarchy: The Emergence of Gender Difference in England, 1660–1760," *Eighteenth-Century Studies* 28, no. 3 (Spring 1995): 295–322.

CHAPTER 2

Indulgence
The Stuart Declarations of Indulgence and Their Afterlives

In 1660, following the radical changes of the Puritan Revolution, England restored the monarchy. Then, in 1688–89, England exchanged monarchs: from the Catholic James II, who threatened, according to some detractors, to return England to sectarian strife at best or medieval Catholicism at worst, to William of Orange, who would become a Protestant hero, still celebrated every July 12 by the Orange Order. The period 1688–89 is often described as a watershed moment for religious freedom in England, although not of course in Ireland, and its spirit is exemplified in John Locke's *Letter Concerning Toleration*, which argues that belief cannot be coerced and that the state should not be involved in spiritual salvation and thus argues for tolerating religious difference as a part of a larger argument about the separation of religious and political functions.[1] I do not intend to dispute the claims that the restored Stuarts were crypto Catholics or that 1688–89 is a watershed for secularization and toleration but rather to tell a part of the story often glossed over: the way that religious liberty – what was called toleration and came to be considered a foundational right of democracy – was advocated for by the Restoration Stuart Kings via the logic, the language, and the sovereign procedure of Royal Indulgence.[2] Charles II and James II were not against religious liberty. In fact, they staked their sovereignty on settling the religious conflict of the civil wars by extending religious freedom in the form of Declarations of Indulgence, which would suspend penal laws about religious conformity. As Catholics, crypto or avowed, the Stuarts tried, via these measures, to align with dissenting Protestants against mandated conformity to the Church of England, a project that unraveled in 1688–89. In other words, the Restoration settlement lived and died on the fig leaf of religious liberty, granted by and figured as indulgence. This chapter will explore the fate of indulgence, arguing for its significance not just to religious freedom but also to mental freedom, including the freedoms of error and fiction; to emotions; to authorship; and to the management of racial, colonial, and gender inequalities. It also helps to shed light on the logic and limitations of its shadow concept of toleration.

Charles' efforts to solve sectarian conflict by suspension of the penal laws regarding religious conformity were a central issue in his twenty-five-year reign. As part of his bid to be restored in 1660, Charles issued the Declaration of Breda, which promised pardon for those involved in the civil wars.[3] While the Clarendon Code laws of the 1660s would go against this spirit by attempting to coerce religious conformity, the 1672 Declaration of Indulgence admits that such forcible measures were "fruitless" and a "sad experience."[4] The Declaration of Breda, issued before Charles was restored, promises to call upon Parliament to issue pardons, but the Declarations of Indulgence are instead based on the king's authority to suspend the laws. The Indulgence of 1672 claims the king's power to suspend "hath been declared and recognised to be so, by several statutes and acts of Parliament," and thus Charles claims performativity for his Declaration, relying on his "will and pleasure" as having legal standing.[5] The late Stuart claim to absolute power was thus, ironically, invoked in these declarations as the right to suspend laws rather than to enforce them, to indulge their subjects rather than to claim obedience.[6] Commenting on this irony, the Whig historian Thomas Babington Macaulay would express surprise that "an act so liberal" would be done "in a manner so despotic."[7] The laws at issue were the penal laws regarding religious conformity, and suspending them was thus the mechanism for religious freedom.

James II's fragile three-year reign was even more closely aligned with the question of indulgence, and he took a more aggressive path to asserting the validity of his power of Indulgence, a path that shows how freedom of religion was entangled (at this time as it would be later, for example in the US Constitution) with the freedoms most central to liberal political theory – freedom of speech, freedom of the press, freedom of assembly – as well as with issues of nondiscrimination in employment.[8] Before issuing his first declaration, James attempted to shore up his right to suspend laws by packing the Supreme Court for the case of *Godden* v. *Hales*.[9] That case made an argument about legal qualifications for jobs: James wanted to hire Godden, so the story goes, because he was the best person for the job, and the nation's peace and prosperity were best served by not discriminating for employment based on religious affiliation. With a win in this case, James tested this power of suspension in 1687, when he issued his first Declaration of Indulgence. James' Indulgence was more far-reaching than Charles', not only extending liberty to dissenters or even Catholics but rather encompassing "all our loving subjects" as if "every individual person" were named.[10] James involved freedom of the press and speech in his Indulgence by requiring it to be published and to be read aloud in Anglican churches. The resistance to these requirements by seven prominent Anglican bishops was followed by their imprisonment and their acquittal at trial, an event that catalyzed the end of James' rule. William was invited by a group including those same bishops to invade England; William issued his Act of Toleration, formally separating indulgence and religious liberty and granting toleration to limited populations – dissenters but not Catholics; and the 1689 Bill of Rights declared the king's power of suspension illegal.

So what differences obtained between indulgence and toleration as modes of religious liberty? This is a complex and tricky question, as the two terms were often conflated and as toleration has come to encompass a wide range of behaviors and institutions. On one level, I am making a distinction between indulgence and toleration that did not obtain at the time: people used the terms interchangeably. James, for example, issued a "Toleration" in Scotland before his 1687 Indulgence in England, though they functioned similarly.[11] For his part, William used the language of indulgence in his Toleration Act. One can distinguish indulgence and toleration by separating procedure (or form) and substance: During the Restoration, indulgence is based on the king's prerogative to suspend laws, and toleration speaks to religion as the content addressed in that royal procedure.[12] Later, toleration would separate almost completely from sovereign mandate, to be conceived of as a right to be protected rather than a privilege granted by the government.[13] The story usually told about this shift to toleration, in the service of the history of liberalism and for the claim that 1688–89 was a watershed moment in that history, is that toleration established religious freedom as the foundation of all other liberal rights.[14] But the story has many more nuances than a straight line from indulgence to toleration and from absolutism to modern liberalism, with 1688–89 as the dividing line. The fact that so many writers in the seventeenth and eighteenth centuries conflated indulgence and toleration – and the fact that freedom of religion is founded in this procedure, this conflation, and this historical moment – bears consideration.

Indulgence as practiced by the Stuarts differs in several respects from classical liberal statements of religious freedom such as Locke's *Letter* and the first amendment to the US Constitution. Epistemology is one key difference, especially in relation to legal and social functions: The royal prerogative to indulge is based in the recognition of the limits of human knowledge and human institutions. The declarations frame conscience as "tender" – that is, in need of protection, and easily influenced – and as such issue pardon for those "how faulty so ever."[15] According to Charles, the sectarian strife of the Civil Wars – not the faulty conscience of any individual – was responsible for differences of opinion in religion: "the passion and uncharitableness of the times" having itself "produced several opinions in religion"; as such, the individual believer was not to be held accountable for erroneous religious beliefs and practices.[16] What is more, indulgence challenges the truth of law itself, as its authority is based on the assumption that common law and natural law or God's law will be out of sync – that common law is inevitably flawed and sometimes dramatically so – and thus it affords the sovereign the right to dispense with the laws in individual or specific cases or to suspend them. Because of this distinction between common law and God's law, it is not surprising that religion would be the test case for the limits of the law.[17] In short, the Declarations of Indulgence extended permission to be wrong based on both the inherent fragility of human conscience and knowledge and the practical flaws of law and society.

Toleration takes a rather different approach to epistemology and human institutions. Tolerance assumes that one party, the tolerator, knows better, and believes themselves to be right, more reasonable, and so on, but tolerance acknowledges, albeit reluctantly, that truth cannot be coerced. Tolerance in this sense is granted only to people whose behavior is held to be objectively wrong but not illegal, erring but eligible for remediation, by a tolerator who is more enlightened. In other words, in toleration, the error and the illegality are distinct issues. Toleration consists of a shift in focus from the actor to the act – we do not tolerate people but actions and ideas – and from an indulgent and charitable perspective to a judgmental orientation.[18] For example, instead of "tender," William's toleration describes the conscience as "scrupulous."[19] Where indulgence admits the fragility of human conscience, human laws, and human society, toleration offers itself as a force of correction for individual human error. Such correction works, however, first on the tolerators themselves (in this sense it shifts focus back on the actor, but on the tolerator not the recipient of toleration): The tolerator comes to make, in Adam Wolfson's account of Lockean toleration, a kind of "fundamental inner adjustment" that allows them to see religious belief as "opinion."[20] The mental procedure of toleration produces an orientation toward religious truth as opinion (or faith, as explored in Chapter 1) not fact and thus as incapable of proof. So it is not just the content of religious belief that is at stake in toleration but the epistemological method of such belief: We may disagree as long as we agree that our beliefs are opinion. Thus, Catholicism is not tolerated because its belief in transubstantiation is not only theologically but epistemologically – or not only substantively but formally – wrong. Locke thought the reasonableness of Christianity – its belief about belief – would mean that a tolerant society would be a Christian one. As Robert Kraynak puts it in his analysis of Lockean toleration, "toleration is always based on an exclusive moral choice and an ultimate moral uniformity of opinion."[21] Toleration, moreover, is itself the procedure for achieving such ultimate morality. Lars Tønder explains this activist force of toleration thus: "[T]olerance exceeds self-restraint and repressive benevolence" and allows for the possibility of a more active tolerance in which tolerators are motivated by the desire to experiment and "become otherwise."[22] This formulation may seem to leave open the question of which party will "become otherwise," but under toleration as secularization such "becoming otherwise" is assumed to mean becoming Christian and thereby the tolerator, not the tolerated. Toleration is a technique of the Christian, enlightened subject that is based in questioning the legitimacy not of the civil law or society but of the individual conscience and reason, and its force of correction is not the authority of the sovereign or the magistrate but the persuasive and tolerant force of the (Christian and secular) social world.[23]

A second constellation of differences between indulgence and toleration involves emotions and reciprocity. The rhetoric of the Stuart's Declarations of Indulgence is based in the "loving" relationship between a sovereign and his subjects: James claims to issue his Indulgence "out of our princely care and affection unto all our loving subjects" and leaves room for even further dispensation according to James' own "pleasure." In framing indulgence thus, the Stuarts assume the position of a priest absolving sin via an infusion of love, which is modeled on and derived from God's love for humans, figured as *agape* or (in Latin) *charitas*. This princely affection also models parental relations, with indulgence flowing from the parent's love for their children, who are assumed to be in need of indulging – they are inherently sinful and erring. The affect of indulgence extends beyond love: Charles' Indulgence flows not just from his love for his subjects but also from his "little liking" of penal laws, from his "dislike" of bloodshed, and because it would be "grievous" to him to enforce such laws.[24] Indulgence is based in a sovereignty that relies, in ways fairly illegible to a liberal politics founded in toleration, on the sovereign's feelings: his "marks of distinction or displeasure."[25] Toleration by contrast is about repressing feelings. Its affects orient (as critics such as David Alvarez and Lars Tønder have argued) around the management of unpleasant feelings among formal equals, not the loving and indulgent feelings of a parent or a deity.[26] Tolerance does not express any consent to or empathy with the tolerated ideas or behavior. On the contrary, it implies a negative judgment accompanied by negative feelings, which are to be managed rather than indulged or allowed to determine state policy.

Indulgence is based not just on feelings but also on reciprocity: The sovereign grants indulgence even as they petition for it. James II said, "as he expected the free liberty of his owne [conscience] soe he desired not to abridge that of another's."[27] Charles said his motivation for his Indulgence was because "we desire more to enjoy what is ours, than that all our subjects may enjoy what by law is theirs" and also that it was founded upon his own "true tenderness of conscience."[28] Indulgence is part, as R. N. Swanson has argued, of a "spiritual economy of gift exchange and reciprocal action."[29] Tolerance by contrast flows only in one direction and is based in a formal structure wherein the state or sovereign is viewed procedurally: William's Act of Toleration makes mention of neither his own feelings nor his own need for toleration.[30] In fact, scholars suggest that William's official Act of Toleration was also a tolerant act (small caps), in that it went against William's own inclinations, his much more liberal orientation toward religious freedom.[31] Still, William's toleration retains the political and interpersonal aspects of indulgence, in that it is something one person grants to another, as opposed to an inherent or inalienable individual right. This is perhaps why Immanuel Kant calls tolerator a "haughty title."[32] In sum, the difference between toleration and indulgence shows that indulgence is a practice (not a theory or a law) that entails making exceptions to the abstractions of rules or laws. As such, indulgence (like faith in Chapter 1) is grounded in personal, emotional, and contingent experiences that take place under differential power relations, and this is how it eschews rationality, abstraction, and equality. In other words, although they share a history and set of concerns, toleration fits with a liberal worldview, while indulgence violates its basic premises.

When William issued the Toleration Act, it did not wholly distinguish itself from the Stuart Acts of Indulgence. Like those Acts, it works by a logic of sovereign prerogative: It begins by asserting, in quite a lot of detail, all the previous sovereign laws that would no longer apply to dissenters, including all penal provisions of the 1559 Act of Uniformity as well as the 1581 statute making conversion to Catholicism treasonous and therefore punishable by death.[33] But it frames its logic not as suspension or dispensation of the law but rather as interpretation of the law: such laws, the act asserts, shall not "be construed to extend to any person or persons dissenting from the Church of England." In other words, over a century of laws about religious conformity were interpreted, post hoc, to have only ever meant to be applied to Catholics, Jews, Muslims, and atheists, not to the many strains of dissent that would develop between 1559 and 1689. As such, the Act of Toleration frames itself as tolerant: as a force and a method of truth, not politics; as knowing more than the sovereigns of the past; and as reinterpreting (rather than suspending) the laws and how they are to be enforced.

Another crucial difference between the Stuart Indulgences and the 1689 Toleration was that the authority to make such interpretation is not the king's alone but rather is shared with "the advice and consent of the Lords Spiritual and Temporal, and the Commons." In framing his Toleration, and his royal authority, in such a way, William was in accordance with Bill of Rights, which the Parliament had already drafted and read to him and which would be ratified a few months later.[34] The first provision of the Bill was that the king did not have powers of suspension. This limitation of the sovereign power of suspension – aimed mainly at the Stuart Declarations of Indulgence – was the centerpiece of political reforms of 1688–89.

The larger and long-term implications of this Restoration process that moved from indulgence to toleration are important and have been articulated by various scholars: First, in shifting from temporary but robust indulgence to permanent and limited toleration, England abandoned comprehension or unity, the project to bring all English people into the Anglican church, giving up on the dream of an institutionally unified society.[35] It eliminated the suspension power, leaving the executive with much more limited powers of pardon.[36] It also, as Laura Zwicker has argued, pushed religious dispute into the political sphere, protecting, at least on some accounts, the church at the expense of the state, and thereby all but assuring ongoing sectarian strife in the political sphere (not the religious).[37] But this is the story of the triumph of tolerance, while I am trying to tell the story in the minor key of indulgence. To do so, I want to first back up a bit, to briefly explore the history of indulgence.

Why did the Stuarts use the language of indulgence instead of say suspension or dispensation? In so doing, they linked religious freedom with the Catholic practices of selling indulgences, so criticized by reformers such as Martin Luther, who began his career by denouncing what he saw as the corruptions of indulgence and then went on to condemn the practice itself and whose *Disputation on the Power and Efficacy of Indulgences*, more commonly known as the 95 Theses, is seen as the catalyst for the Reformation. And where did this practice of indulgence originate, but in the granting of pardons to Christian warriors fighting Muslims in the Crusades? The original Indulgence was granted by Urban II in the Clermont decree in 1095, given to those who go "to Jerusalem to liberate the Church of God."[38] These Indulgences were a theological innovation at the time because they remitted not just the penalties for sins but in fact the sins themselves. In so doing – that is, in remitting sins in exchange for service in a holy war – the practice of indulgence activated, and remained the locus for, a centuries-long academic project for the justification of war.[39] More to the point, indulgence was an original form of religious liberty, figured as a mode of freeing people from penalty for religious errors or failures.[40] As the system of medieval Catholic indulgences developed, both sides of the transaction – those who could offer them and what kinds of practices and currencies could be exchanged for remission of sins – expanded. The system developed into an elaborate medium of exchange between sins and worldly practices, one based on a combination of official sanction and informal administration, and it conflated financial, religious, military, and affective practices. The opponents of the Stuart Declarations of Indulgence saw this connection to medieval Catholicism, steeping their rhetoric in reforming passion: one for example arguing against the Indulgence based on its "odious" origins in "the sulphureous Fountain of Rome."[41] In short, procedural questions about religious liberty that were central to the revolution of 1688–89 had been circulating since not just the Protestant Reformation but indeed since the Crusades and the system of indulgences they initiated. The Stuart choice to invoke this controversial language and the history of indulgence thus must have been significant to their cause, perhaps in ways that its afterlife can make clear.

"Indulgence" persists as a model, in minor key, for liberty and its limitation throughout the eighteenth century. It is one of the ways that a presecular model of relationships and of thinking persists and transforms into a postsecular one. In what follows, I trace a bit of the afterlife of indulgence in the eighteenth century: first by showing how indulgence travels between David Hume's historical account of indulgences, both medieval and Stuart, and his more colloquial uses of indulgence in his theory of mind. I then go on to suggest that indulgence persists in eighteenth-century literature and political theory as a way of thinking about those people – children, females, enslaved persons, and colonial subjects – left out of a rights-based political discourse or those, like enslaved people, whose lack of freedom is the very foundation of the rights of others. Indulgence, I am suggesting, is a concept and a formal mechanism – a habit of mind, an affect of governing and being governed, a theory of liberty – whereby a postsecular mentality is sustained alongside the development of tolerance and modern ideas of religious and political freedom.

David Hume, the Ambivalence of Indulgence, and the Lessons of 1688–1689

David Hume's writings on indulgence reveal a profound ambivalence about the practice. On the one hand, as a supporter of the Reformation and a critic of James II, Hume writes passionately against the history of the use of indulgence as a formal religious and political mechanism: Popes who sold indulgences and the Stuarts who declared them were similarly abusing their authority. But indulgence is also important for Hume, in the political sphere as well as the mental; in both arenas, indulgence is a force of liberty. In politics, indulgence is on the side of innovation, advancing liberties not yet codified in law and tradition. In his theory of mind, Hume defends indulgence as a skeptical practice: By indulging in thoughts that are not certain or that are against one's beliefs, one contributes both to belief and to understanding one's belief (as if not "true" at least "satisfactory").[42] Indulgence also has parallel disadvantages: When used as a way of disrupting the balance of power in a mixed government by reducing the authority of law, indulgence is dangerous; when used as an excuse for laziness of thought (or a "warm imagination" T 1.4.7), indulgence is not philosophy. In both spheres, that is, indulgence is a force that can serve to achieve balance or to disrupt it. Overall, indulgence is figured in Hume as part of the practice of cultivating mixed government and skeptical reasoning, and thus indulgence is central to Hume's epistemology, his politics, and his ethics. It may also be related to his racism.

Hume's thesis in *The History of England* rests on the superiority of mixed and established governments for balancing authority and the principle of liberty.[43] This is the measuring stick of history, and England's progress is tracked, over six volumes, as the slow but sure development of this governmental system and principle.[44] For Hume, 1688–89 is a culmination of this process, when James' Indulgence – the epitome of his bid for absolute power in a moment when the balance between monarchy and Parliament should have been reaching equilibrium – was defeated. Hume wrote the last volume of his *History* first, and then backed up to track England's mixed constitution forward to 1688–89. In order to set up his case against the late Stuarts and their practice of indulgence, Hume's history of the Reformation makes a case against medieval indulgences based on their being an illegitimate and immoral exchange, in which "devout" people defer money from their "usual expenses" in order to contribute to "the grandeur and riches of the court of Rome" (H 3.29, 138). The problem is not only the unfairness of this exchange from poor people to rich institution but also that the riches are purchased by selling something that should be outside the system of exchange. In order to justify selling indulgences, that is in order to have something to exchange, the Catholic Church pretends to be entitled to the "great stock of merit" from the "good works" of the saints and even to "the unexhausted treasury" of the merits of Christ himself (H 3.29, 137). The concept of a "treasury of merits" and the use of money and contractual language for indulgence was long-standing in the Catholic tradition.[45] Hume imports this monetary metaphor in order to critique indulgence, downgrading the granting of indulgence to mere "traffic," "retail," and a worldly system of accounting that supports "licentious lives," (H 3.29, 137–38). In so doing, Hume distances indulgence from grace and liberty, which are figured as non-exchangeable. Protestant faith-based theology posits that Christ's grace can never be earned and therefore is not subject to exchange, because sinfulness will always exceed human morality and good works.[46] Salvation thus cannot be involved in arithmetical or contractual transactions. Martin Luther used the language of rights (*ius*) with respect to remission of sins, in a logic that counters the traffic in indulgences: Religious freedom, including remission of sin, is not something to be granted (via indulgence) by the pope but rather something outside the system of exchange, a right granted by God.[47] To the extent that civil liberties are built upon the foundation of religious liberty, then the liberal theory of inalienable rights (including religious freedom) shares this logic: faith and rights cannot be exchanged but works and indulgences can be, and this is why indulgence is justly left behind as liberal politics moves toward a rights-based theory of liberty.[48]

Hume of course does not support a natural rights-based theory of liberty. Rather, his principle of liberty depends upon the accretion of liberty over centuries, supported by the indulgence of monarchs who worked (in the large scheme of things) toward England's mixed constitution and its balance of liberty and authority. In "On the Liberty of the Press" (1742), Hume celebrates England's tradition of freedom, which includes "censuring every measure entered into by the king or his ministers," and he claims that such liberty is not "indulged in any other government."[49] Importantly for Hume, indulgence in this sense is a function of law, not a deviation from law, and it is made possible by the mixed form of government that England's long history has developed: "The reason why the laws indulge us in such a liberty, seems to be derived from our mixed form of government."[50] Hume credits the monarchical part of the mix with promoting such indulgence and therefore liberty: A secure monarch cannot feel jealous of his subjects and is therefore "apt to indulge them in great liberties, both of speech and action."[51] Hume thus rests his case on what might seem ironic: Indulgence produces liberty in monarchies but arbitrary power in republics. Hume verges on making a case for freedom of the press as a right, but only because it is "attended with so few inconveniences"; as such, according to Hume, "it may be claimed as the common right of mankind, and ought to be indulged them almost in every government except the ecclesiastical, to which, indeed, it would be fatal."[52] In mixing up the language of indulgence and rights, Hume is consistent with his own thinking that mixed governments could potentially (though unlikely in reality) achieve a perfect balance of powers, so that the distinction between law and dispensation (and thus the salutary function of indulgence) would disappear. This is the trajectory he is tracking in order to account for the events of 1688–89, the culmination, though written first, of his *History*.

Hume's account of 1688–89 depends upon walking a fine line between his Tory and Whig sensibilities, on criticizing the actions of the late Stuarts – as overstepping their authority – without discounting the political traditions and customs that support their authority and his theory of government. Hume's critique of their practices of rule is centered on their Declarations of Indulgence. With respect to Charles II, Hume asserts that no grievance against him was more alarming than the Declaration (H 6.65, 274), which was tolerance in an "illegal manner" (H 6.65, 276), part and parcel of Charles' "love of ease" (H 6.65, 275). When he turns to James II, his criticisms of indulgence are yet more barbed. Hume refers to this Indulgence as a "scheme" (H 6.70, 482) based on James' idea that the "people enjoyed no liberties, but by his royal concession and indulgence" (H 6.70, 482). Regarding events of 1688–89, Hume suggests that James' downfall was a function of a highly developed system of mixed government. In declaring his Indulgence, James surely overstepped the bounds of his authority and upset this balance, and thus the bishops were justified in withholding their active obedience (H 6.71, 492–93). Despite his "lofty ideas" about his power of prerogative, James' Indulgence lacked the "authority of laws" that only an act of parliament could bestow (H 6.71, 497). At times, Hume conflates toleration and indulgence, but he also reveals the split between them that would come to see toleration as consonant with modern liberal theories of governance: "[S]imple toleration" is opposed to the kind of "absolute superiority" (H 6.71, 500) on which a king's right to grant indulgence is based. While Hume's account sometimes suggests that England's mixed monarchy itself assured the defeat of James' scheme of indulgence, he also credits the fact that William, who had been "educated in those principles and accustomed to that practice" of toleration, was able to advance the development of England's mixed monarchy via toleration (H 6.71, 503). Hume, like other writers, credits William with a salutary disconnect between his private personality and his public actions. While other writers, as mentioned earlier, see William as being more tolerant than his Act of Toleration, Hume's way of splitting person and politics credits the political over the personal: He confesses that William's "virtue" is "not the purest" (H 6.71, 504). Nonetheless, William's role is so central to England's progress, Hume claims, that it would be difficult to find another person "whose action and conduct have contributed more eminently to the general interests of society and mankind" (H 6.71, 504). Such disconnect between person and politics can be seen as sign of William's tolerance, for tolerance, in contrast to indulgence, proceeds from a discipline of the individual passions and prejudices, from a separation of the personal and the political.

Hume's distinction between toleration and indulgence is central to understanding how indulgence travels between Hume's political discussions in the *History* and his theory of mind in both *A Treatise of Human Nature* and *An Enquiry Concerning Human Understanding*.[53] Hume's longest discussion of toleration occurs in Volume III of the *History*, where indulgence functions as an important precondition of toleration. Intolerance characterizes people who due to "stupid ignorance and barbarism ... never indulge themselves in any speculation or enquiry" and "never were allowed to imagine that their principles could be contested" (H 3.37, 432). Indulgence is thus a precursor to and necessary condition of toleration, a habit of mind that makes toleration, as a social virtue, possible. In this discussion, as elsewhere in Hume, indulgence is not all to the good, as too much indulgence also precludes toleration: "delicate" people whose beliefs are never challenged are "indulged" in a "false tranquility" (H 3.37, 432). Given this distinction between toleration and indulgence, it is significant although not surprising that in Hume's theory of mind, in both the *Treatise* and the *Enquiry*, the language of indulgence, not toleration, figures importantly as a mental action that is necessary to pursuing truth. Toleration is a social and political good, but it has little place in Hume's theory of mind. Indulgence, by contrast, is repeatedly invoked, and it functions, formally or structurally, in a way analogous to its role in the *History*.[54] I have been describing the ambivalence of indulgence in Hume's *History*, where indulgence is on the side of liberty and monarchy and must be balanced by the authority of Parliament. In Hume's theory of mind, indulgence plays a formally similar role, where it is a force of liberty and imagination that allows for authority – in this case the authority of reason, facts, and ignorance – to be contested.

Just as governments are best when mixed, humans are best suited to a "mixed kind of life," one that balances the difficult work of attending to the social world (those issues that bear upon "action and society") with philosophical reflection (E 1, 4). Indulgence can function in multiple ways to promote or retard true philosophy. Reason would like a "full and uncontrolled indulgence," but skeptical philosophy will insist on checks to such indulgence via, strangely enough, more indulgence. Indulgence is central to skeptical philosophy, for it is via the mechanisms of indulgence that we conjecture about the identity and persistence (the "fiction of continued existence") of phenomena (T 1.4.2).[55] Hume uses the term "indulgence" to describe the formal process connected to the "license" or "liberty" of "conjecture," linking indulgence with the mental freedom that, if balanced, allows for inference about causation (E 11, 105 and 107). Indulgence is thus, in a way that Hume avers is counterintuitive, central to skepticism:

> A true sceptic will be diffident of his philosophical doubts, as well as of his philosophical conviction; and will never refuse any innocent satisfaction, which offers itself, upon account of either of them. Nor is it only proper we should in general indulge our inclination in the most elaborate philosophical researches, notwithstanding our sceptical principles. (T 1.6.7)

In this account, indulgence functions both as a source of pleasure rooted in the imagination and also as a kind of inner toleration, or a way of internalizing (or at least entertaining) difference of opinion: It is thus an ambivalent force, which for Hume is all to the good. Indulgence for Hume bears key differences from toleration, because it is not based on exclusive or preferential opinion, because it is pleasurable, and because it can function positively or negatively. Indulgence is bad when it is on the side of "ease" but good when it demands that we entertain opinions or ideas that we do not (yet) believe. Indulgence is also something to be guarded against, especially by philosophers, who are apt to be so enamored with complex, counterintuitive, or "vulgar" ideas that they embrace with "surprize and admiration" anything that challenges ideas (T 2.1.1). In such cases, the "pleasure," "agreeable emotions," and "satisfaction" that indulgence of contrary ideas provides is in danger of convincing the philosophers that such ideas have a legitimate foundation (T 2.1.1).

Indulgence is a concept that travels between Hume's use of the term in his writing about the official mechanisms of Indulgence (where it is a proper noun) to the more expansive (or colloquial) uses in his history of mind (where it is a verb), in ways that Hume himself has not made intelligible. Indulgence functions in Hume both as a fully formed idea and as a way of describing the process by which we come to have ideas. Indulgence as a verb is thus a precursor to nominal ideas: When we "indulge our inclination" to suppositions about identity and continued existence, the practice of indulgence fills the interval between perception and the moment when we "preserve a perfect and entire identity to our perceptions." (T 1.4.2). Donald Livingston's account of Hume's participatory method for concepts explains it thus: "Ideas are not timeless (except as abstractions) and do not constitute reality. They function more as historical mirrors that reflect and make us self-conscious of experiences that were lived through in ignorance of the ideas that now render them intelligible."[56] Given his rigorous account of the way we come to have ideas, it may be a bit perverse to read Hume as making a clear argument about indulgence in his account of the Reformation and of 1688–89 and to suggest that his use of indulgence is less self-conscious in his theory of mind. As the *History* was written after the *Treatise* and the *Enquiry*, one might be tempted to conclude that Hume has not yet made an intelligible idea of indulgence. But that ignores the fact that he consistently uses the two meanings of indulgence – as royal decree ("Indulgence") and mental process ("indulgence") – in concert and that he regularly connects them. The second meaning appears as well in the *History*, in ways consistent with his theory of mind in the two earlier texts. Moreover, indulgence is central to Hume's thinking about 1688–89 ("Indulgence") as well as his thinking about thinking ("indulgence"), as this account of 1688–89 in the *Treatise* shows:

> I am better pleased to leave this controverted subject, if it really admits of controversy; and to indulge myself in some philosophical reflections, which naturally arise from that important event. (T3.2.10)

Hume shifts his focus here from the facts of James' rule and its demise to the seemingly remarkable fact that people easily accepted the new line of monarchical succession. The events of 1688–89 – including James' Indulgence – are thus the occasion to indulge in thinking about thinking more broadly. The disruption of the monarchical line, he argues, was accepted because it was "founded on a very singular quality of our thought and imagination" (T 3.2.10), which is that "the mind naturally runs on with any train of action, which it has begun; nor do we commonly make any scruple concerning our duty, after the first action of any kind, which we perform" (T. 3.2.10). So once James had forfeited his authority, people ascribed the power to have done so to Parliament. This is how an event that was beyond "all common authority" came to be ascribed to authority: Because people had no conceptual framework for something so "illegal," they defaulted to the usual mechanisms of the mind (running in a straight line) to accept the succession (T 3.2.10). Peoples' minds run along such linear tracks both backward and forward in time, so that predecessors and ancestors may be granted rights by their posterity. This is why when writing in the mid-eighteenth century, Hume can say that William's authority was derived from the princes who succeeded him.

In deflecting the question of the subject's right to rebel against James and shifting it to a question of how people came to accept the new line of succession, Hume suggests why 1688–89 could be taken up by both liberal and conservative commentators, why 1688–89 could be called a revolution (of which more in the last chapter) and also seen as a culmination of England's long tradition of mixed government. Indulgence is central to Hume's postsecular conservatism: His antidogmatic, anti-ideological, and antitheoretical approach to history and to philosophy. He views Cromwell and James similarly with "indulgence," and he makes the case (for indulging Cromwell as well as implicitly for his general approach) based on the "blindness and infirmities of the human species" (6.61, 109). For Hume, 1688–89 is such an interesting case because it would seem to controvert all his own principles about tradition and authority (in 1688 he would not have been in favor of removing the King), but he uses it as a case study for how authority is constituted over time and as a result of the general ways that our minds work. The period 1688–89 is both the example of the official Indulgences that went too far and the occasion for Hume's own mental indulgence – that is, his ability to think philosophically about how the mind thinks – and thus it produces a theory of how the authority of government relates to the authority of reason. He will later write six volumes on the subject of the authority of government – with James'

Indulgence of 1687 as the counterintuitive example that confirms the principle that governmental authority should be not rebelled against – but the kernel of this connection between the two kinds of indulgence is quite clear already in the *Treatise*.

The Afterlives of Indulgence

My analysis of Hume demonstrates that indulgence as a mechanism of both political and mental freedom was central to 1688–89 and persisted after it, albeit in realms outside of religion and government. "Indulgence," that centerpiece of the Restoration and its demise, perseveres over the long eighteenth century in at least three ways. First, Indulgence persists as way of framing relations to categories of people left out of a logic of rights, toleration, or mental freedom. Women, children, enslaved persons, and colonial subjects are often depicted as being indulged or desiring indulgence. Secondly, and in a related vein, indulgence persists in relation to feelings. In the late-eighteenth-century discourse about reason and feelings, indulgence persists mostly in the realm of feeling, not (contra Hume's use in theory of mind) thinking. And finally, in an example that may counter that general rule, indulgence is a term that authors often use to express their relation to readers: They petition their readers – as dissenters and Catholics once petitioned their kings – for indulgence. Indulgence persists overall as an indispensable subsidiary to a culture of toleration and civil rights. It obtains in relations of power but also in realms of feelings and error. It haunts the liberal project – as slavery and colonization do more generally – with a form of power that is intimate and potentially lenient but also condescending and authoritative.[57]

Of course, as a model of governance, indulgence is rejected in 1688–89. That moment is often considered (from our distant perspective) one in which the theory of patriarchy, which connected the rule of fathers over the family to the sovereignty of kings, begins to be dismantled at last by a liberal theory of the origins of governmental authority. Robert Filmer's *Patriarcha* articulated the conservative position that there is a seamless chain of authority from God through the king to fathers.[58] John Locke's *Second Treatise on Government* repudiated the natural authority of kings and fathers, investing the power of consent in the governed.[59] Carole Pateman argues that this shift to social contract theory depended upon repressing the contracts that kept women, servants, and enslaved people oppressed, participating in contracts that precede and exclude them or that are implicit or disavowed.[60] Locke himself did not seem interested in indulgence, and this chapter adds nothing new to the work done on Locke's ideas of consent and how it figures domestic or colonial relations.[61] Rather, indulgence persists in the eighteenth century as a means of theorizing various relations of unequal power and as such provides an indication of how unsettled questions about the relations of liberal freedom and power remained in eighteenth century culture and thus why the metaphor and the mechanism of indulgence lived on after the Restoration.[62]

Prose fiction and novels in particular – as a place where female obedience and freedom are mediated – are replete with indulgence. Many of Aphra Behn's late prose fictions invoke this trope with respect to relations between sovereign and subject or parent and child.[63] This trope of indulgence also figures prominently in Samuel Richardson's *Clarissa* (1748), the eighteenth century's longest and most celebrated novel, whose heroine is a crypto-Jacobite in her embrace of indulgence.[64] Clarissa repeatedly frames her relations to her parents, and especially to her mother, as indulgence. Her parents have indulged her until the ripe old age of eighteen in refusing the suitors for her hand in marriage. But the novel opens, and continues for what many readers consider an excessively long time, because her parents refuse to indulge her in refusing Mr. Solmes, an "odious" man, one eminently ill-suited to be the husband of the exemplary Clarissa Harlowe, as her friend Anna Howe repeatedly asserts.[65] But instead of making her case based on these reasons – on her own reasons, or on objective standards of value, or on her own rights, which she legally has based on an inheritance from her grandfather – Clarissa repeatedly pleads for indulgence.[66] She desires that her family recognize (or indulge) her feelings and that her family's feelings for her, especially her mother's feelings, should supersede their reasons (which are monetary) for marrying Solmes. Her relationship with Lovelace – the aristocratic libertine who will eventually rape her – centers, at least to some extent, on their shared affinity for models of indulgence. The novel *Clarissa* figures indulgence negatively overall – as part of a system whereby obedience is expected and indulgence unreliable – but the character Clarissa, an icon of female virtue, clings to a nostalgic notion of indulgence, even as she persistently claims the right to refuse consent. *Clarissa* provides an example the feminization of indulgence, which may be part of the larger feminization of Catholicism that Frances Dolan (and other critics, including me) have described.[67] Like Catholic practices overall, indulgence persists in representations of women as a way of precluding their full participation in a rights-based liberalism by depicting them as desirous of – or suited to – a system that works by indulgence.

Edmund Burke, often considered the first major conservative thinker, offers some insight into this persistence of indulgence in the feminine and domestic realm and beyond. Burke does not write extensively about the Stuart Indulgences or medieval Catholic indulgence, but the concept of indulgence is nonetheless central to his conservatism, insofar as it is linked to a traditionalist view of the origin of rights and freedoms of subjects.[68] As a privilege of power, indulgence is a mechanism of condescension regarding those left out of official rights. Indulgence is the purview of the weak, the feminine and the beautiful, and it is the proper recompense for the patience and obedience of such subjects. According to Burke, "the subordinate turn on reliefs, gratifications, and indulgences"; such indulgence means that subordinates are "more lovely, though inferior in dignity."[69] Indulgence for Burke (as for the Stuarts before him) operates in the realm of love, not that of respect, virtue, or power. Indulgence functions, in a way that can be salutary, to dilute authority due to affection for the weak. Parental authority, for example is "almost melted down into the mother's fondness and indulgence," whereas the stronger authority of the father precludes both love and indulgence.[70] In this way, Burke is building upon the idea of indulgence as a dispensation, offered by one with authority, out of affection for those weaker, in mind or body. One should, he argues, show a "degree of indulgence towards human frailty."[71] For Burke, indulgence is thus a mechanism, as it was for Hume, for tempering the authority of the state, a portal whereby human affection and female softness, as well as tradition, can check the sublime power of male authority. The kind of condescension figured in indulgence is also an effective governmental strategy, even with, or perhaps especially with, subjects who resist authority. In such cases, indulgence from the powerful can induce the affections that make governance possible.

In his writing on England's relationship to the American colonies, Burke repeatedly pleads for indulgence as a mechanism of government, one that will create ties of affection between England and its colonies. When indulged in "acts of lenity," according to Burke, even a "rugged people" can be conciliated."[72] He furthers this argument by reporting that the American colonialists – freedom-loving and indulgent – are also more indulgent to their slaves than the English are, which is a political good, for theirs slaves, who are "indulged with greater liberty," are also "more faithful than ours."[73] Burke repeatedly invokes indulgence as a model for relations with women, children, colonials and enslaved people: those left out of the "ancient constitution." And yet as part of his case for arguing that the "people of the colonies" should be admitted into an "interest in the Constitution," Burke invokes what he calls "Ancient indulgences" arguing that precedent exists for "indulging" the illegal actions of the colonialists based on a paternal relationship to them and that England should codify such precedent via a "solemn declaration of systematic indulgence."[74] "Our ancient indulgence" Burke says, may have been pursued to a fault with the colonies, but "our fault was more tolerable than our attempt to mend it, and our sin far more salutary than our penitence."[75] This rhetoric, which connects indulgence, toleration, sins, and penance, suggests that Burke is able to transpose the historical meaning of indulgence onto his conservative political argument: Indulgence is a formal mechanism to avoid revolution via maintaining emotional relations in the absence of political rights (Chapter 5 argues that novelistic narration is another such formal mechanism and Chapter 6 argues that nostalgia fulfills a similar role). For Burke, indulgence is part of a common law system whereby the Ancient constitution protects the heritable rights and property of the "kingdom." Indulgence is a mechanism of England's salutary habit, as Burke puts it "of adopting our fundamental laws into the bosom of our family affections."[76]

Indulgence can also be abused. Burke recognizes that indulgence is extra-legal and therefore unpredictable and subject to abuse. In calling out the hypocrisy of England's dealing with the colonies, Burke writes:

> I know it is said, that your kindness is only alienated on account of their resistance, and therefore, if the colonies surrender at discretion, all sort of regard, and even much indulgence, is meant towards them in future. But can those who are partisans for continuing a war to enforce such a surrender be responsible (after all that has passed) for such a future use of a power that is bound by no compacts and restrained by no terror? Will they tell us what they call indulgences? Do they not at this instant call the present war and all its horrors a lenient and merciful proceeding?[77]

In opposing here "compacts" with "indulgence" Burke offers a prescription for good governance, in which indulgence sets the conditions for compacts of obedience while "terror" negates the kind of trust needed for both indulgence and obedience. In order to remediate their poor governance of the colonies, Burke intimates, England cannot demand obedience with the promise of future indulgence but must instead begin anew with an indulgence not based on guaranteed obedience. Indulgence, in other words, is the foundation of both governmental authority and personal freedom. It must be used carefully by governments wishing to inculcate obedience. In a related argument, Burke argues against England's overly strict control of Catholicism in Ireland, calling the penal laws there a "scheme of indulgence, grounded at once on contempt and jealousy."[78] Burke also offers the East India Company, and its management by Warren Hastings, as examples of corrupt practices of indulgence. At times in his speeches to Parliament during Hasting's impeachment trial, Burke's descriptions of the East India Company could be taken from reformation critique of the medieval system of indulgences, whereby extra-governmental power is exercised with tyranny, corruption, bribes, and fraud. In this context, indulgences are promised in bad faith by an illegitimate authority, and they operate as a mechanism of a multilevel corrupt system. The company and its agents, he says, "indulged themselves in the most extravagant speculations of plunder," and Hastings himself is one who "cannot commit a robbery without indulging himself at the same time in the practice of his favorite arts of fraud and falsehood."[79] The East India Company represents for Burke the corruptions that happen when business acts as a quasi-governmental force and thus where indulgence can be abused, because businesses, unlike governments, do not temper their power and authority with personal relations and affection.

In Burke's writing and his speeches to Parliament, he not only descries this misuse of indulgence by the East India Company and petitions for indulgence of the colonials and other weak subjects. He also repeatedly invokes a common rhetorical device of eighteenth-century speakers and authors: petitioning his audience for indulgence. Burke uses this formula frequently, and in ways telling of his ambivalence about the practice and his (relative) confidence as an author. He avers, for example, on publication of the second edition of *A Philosophical Enquiry into the Origin of Our Ideas of the Sublime and Beautiful* that the book may require "yet [a] greater share of indulgence" than "at its first appearance."[80] Here Burke does not so much petition for indulgence as describe the audience as needing to provide it. Burke's supplications for indulgence are often somewhat ironic or seemingly disingenuous, for example when he says, "I claim for myself the necessary indulgence that must be given to all weakness."[81] And in a metaphor revealing of the reciprocity and ambiguity of indulgence and also of the rhetoric and facts of freedom at this time, Burke positions himself, metaphorically, as both an enslaved person in need of indulgence and the person who can grant such indulgence, "I lengthened my chain a link or two, and, in an age of relaxed discipline, gave a trifling indulgence to my own notions."[82] In this example, the slavery metaphor is telling of Burke's ambivalence toward the subjects of indulgence, including him – the slavery metaphor tests the limits of indulgence, as does actual slavery.[83] The ambivalence arises because Burke both receives and dispenses indulgence, and it reveals a structural ambivalence: The freedom that indulgence offers as well as the power to dispense it depends upon the unfreedom of others. Moreover, as indulgence is reciprocal (kings themselves desire it and even Edmund Burke), it also implies the ability to change categories: If the king needs indulgence, then the enslaved person may become free. This is perhaps why Burke, who in general argues for indulgence of the less powerful, makes distinctions among the various objects of indulgence. Because "slaves" are "stubborn and intractable" he stops short of arguing for an "effeminate indulgence" of them.[84] Enslaved people test the limits of indulgence in Burke's theories.

The problematic connection of indulgence to slavery is also evident in a very different type of text, Olaudah Equiano's autobiography, which exhibits many of the uses of indulgence that this chapter has been tracking: He begs the reader's indulgence at both the beginning of the narrative and the end (42, 252); he refers to emotions as being indulged (71); and he exemplifies its significance to family relations (47, 66).[85] He also, in describing a slave owner, reveals (in a way that responds to Burke) the complex logic of indulgence:

> He allows them two hours for refreshment at mid-day; and many other indulgencies and comforts, particularly in their lying; and, besides this, he raises more provisions on his estate than they can destroy; so that by these attentions he saves the lives of his negroes, and keeps them healthy, and as happy as the condition of slavery can admit. (122)

Equiano mastered eighteenth-century rhetoric regarding both slavery and authorship as well as the eighteenth-century use of irony. The use of indulgence as a technique to perpetuate a more just version of slavery in this example repeats Burke's logic. But Equiano's *Narrative* overall betrays no ambivalence about its wholesale rejection of the system of slavery. As such, this passage must be read ironically, showing how indulgence actually supports slavery and therefore is part of its evil: The master "saves the lives" of the slaves from whom he profits not because of the loving or familial affect of indulgence but in order to profit. In Burke, we saw that slavery travels what seems to be a long distance from actual slavery (which he does not descry and in which indulgence is central) to its ironic and metaphorical uses with respect to himself. This range is telling of Burke's attitude not just toward himself as a petitioner, speaker, and author but more so toward indulgence: It is the purview of the weak, which includes, however nuanced or insincerely, Burke himself as an author as well as colonized people and enslaved people. Burke's invocation of slavery regarding himself is rhetorical and hyperbolic, but the connection between indulgence and slavery is significant. For Burke, indulgence is the liberty that allows authorship and freedom more broadly: it is a historically necessary precursor to liberty as a right. In other words, the concept of indulgence reveals that slavery is conceptually linked to liberty and liberalism just as it is literally linked to colonialism and capitalism. In this sense, actual chattel slavery and Burke's ability to be an author are linked, something that is revealed in Burke's ambivalence about both indulgence and his own literary endeavors. Equiano's critique of indulgence as both the foundation of freedom and of slavery reveals this connection. This is a connection that must be buried or denied in theories that aspire to universal claims about humanity or politics.

Hume makes one such argument about humanity and politics. In *Of National Character*, Hume argues against the idea of a "national character," something similar to, but not synonymous with, race or ethnicity. For Hume, neither environment nor biology (that is, race) can account for differences in people from different countries; rather society and political structure are the foremost influence on national character. In order to make his case, he purports to "run over the globe" and "revolve the annals of history," and indeed his examples reach as far away as China and as far back as ancient Greece.[86] But then in a footnote, Hume writes, completely counterintuitively, that notwithstanding his entire argument still he is "apt to suspect the negroes to be naturally inferior to the whites" (FN 10). Hume's racism was further confirmed by the discovery of a letter urging the purchase of an enslaved person.[87] Hume was not otherwise known to have participated in the slave trade or to have articulated the racist ideologies on which it was perpetuated. It is thus ironic, or we might say indulgent, that Hume's racism appears in a footnote to an essay dedicated to debunking the idea of a national character and the idea that morality is inherent or attributable to environment. In a telling use of slavery as metaphor, John Stuart Mill argues that Hume was "completely enslaved by a taste for literature" by which Mill meant that Hume had no "regard for truth or utility."[88] For Mill, Hume's taste for literature, which is linked to his skepticism and thus (on my account) his affinity for indulgence, serves only to "excite emotion."[89] In short, Mills' quip connects Hume's mental freedom, his literary bent, and, in those moments in which Hume's logic fails or exceeds his rationality, his prejudices. So how then can we read this footnote that appears to counteract Hume's larger thesis? We might see certain kinds of footnotes as themselves a locus of indulgence (one this writer also indulges in): They cannot be fully justified and may even counteract rational argument, and they may be places where emotions or prejudice can be indulged in an essay otherwise written with academic rationality. Indulgence, as Hume knows and Mills implies, is related to the imaginative power and to literature, and it can either challenge or support ones prejudices. It is a place where rationality and monolithic theories (about, for example, freedom or humanity) may be contested. This footnote, alongside Burke's seemingly disingenuous petition for indulgence for himself and Equiano's ironic representation about how it functions in slavery, shows how quickly a mechanism of indulgence can turn into a sense of entitlement (to an extra degree of freedom) for those in power, one whose logic is antithetical to theoretical or universal accounts of freedom and equality and thus that must be buried in footnotes. Thus, indulgence permits Hume's anti-foundationalist conservatism; his mental freedom; and, in moments of emotion or freedom from rules of logic, his racism and sense of superiority over others. These things are indelibly connected. In Hume, mental freedom depends on the tropes of slavery and indulgence, revealing their inseparability, which is also true in the economy: The freedom of white British men depends on the racialized slavery of black people. Scholars of race such as Charles Mills in fact argue that modern conception of race develop in response to the need to distinguish who has power and freedom and who does not, manifesting first in chattel slavery of Africans and persisting in modern forms of racial liberalism, which must necessarily deny the ambivalence and the persistence of indulgence as well as the unfreedom of those upon whose bodies and labor the freedom of some depends.[90] As Hume puts it: "a true observation in politics: the two extremes in government, liberty and slavery, commonly approach nearest to each other" ("Liberty of the Press"). He might have added that the ground on which they meet is often indulgent and racist, as well as literary.

This chapter has shed light on why indulgence and literary modes of mentation are central to Hume and Burke and therefore to the longer eighteenth-century philosophy of mind and philosophy of history as well as to the literary field. One asks indulgence of an interlocutor for thinking that is speculative and not subject to proof, for anything that might be not true or not conducive to peace. In this sense, indulgence as a formal dispensation from the law provides a model for skepticism, for philosophical speculation, for literature, and for slavery. The uses of indulgence in Hume and Burke partake of both their conservatism and their orientation toward literature: They provide a link between the history of freedom of conscience and the freedoms of speech and press that underpin literature, which are in turn dependent on both the kind of mental freedom for which Hume advocates and the racist speculation in which he indulges. This chapter has been tracking a fundamental ambivalence in indulgence between weakness or dependency (including slavery) and freedom. As such, it reveals something about how the trope of slavery and its actual use in Equiano and in capitalism more generally developed alongside liberalism's (and conservatism's) rhetoric of freedom. Indulgence shows that liberal rights cannot be separated from slavery, that liberalism is a system that depends upon exceptions and upon the unfreedom of enslaved people.[91] It reveals why the postsecular has always lived alongside the secular and the conservative alongside the liberal. All of these examples – from *Clarissa* to Burke and Hume to Equiano, reveal, from their differently entitled relationship to freedom, that liberalism cannot (as Böckenförde says) make good on its promises of equality and freedom, that its premises depend upon exceptions, indulgences, and unfreedom.[92]

In historicizing the concepts of faith and indulgence and in exploring their connection to liberal values and to fictionality, the first two chapters of this book have been arguing against the kind of oppositional thinking – faith is the opposite of fact, indulgence is the opposite of absolute power, and conservative is the opposite of liberal – that structure our modern secular and sectarian world view. In so doing, I am not advocating for faith or indulgence (instead of truth or tolerance) but rather showing their function within the liberal systems that they seem to oppose. The conservatism of these writers – Hobbes, Behn, Hume, and Burke – inheres not in their resistance to modernity, and therefore to secularity and fictionality, but rather in their modernization of the concepts of faith and indulgence, a process that depends on linking them to fictionality and literary experimentation and that allows these writers to leverage a critique of liberalism. For Catherine Gallagher, fictionality is inherently modern, because it inculcates an attitude of incredulity that provides a bulwark against the kind of naïve gullibility that she characterizes as faith.[93] Both faith and indulgence would seem to be opposed, in secular modernity, to the kind of "superior discernment" and "cognitive provisionality" that Gallagher links to fiction and that she sees as central to the secularization project.[94] But faith and indulgence, once modernized and attached to fiction, require an intellectual complexity that is antidogmatic, antitheoretical, and anti-foundationalist, even if it is at the same time subject to intolerable abuse; the invocation of tolerance here is deliberate, because tolerance needs to rationalize itself, while indulgence flows from feeling. In Gallagher's secular account of the rise of fiction, the presecular concept of faith – and so too, I am extrapolating, indulgence – should be left behind.

But this chapter shows that these concepts are inherently connected not only to liberalism but also to fictionality and the modern literary field.[95] I have also been showing how both concepts – faith and indulgence – are ways of imagining relationships among people. Faith secures relations between sovereigns and subjects, between lovers, and between narrators and readers, while indulgence underpins relations not only between powerful and weak (and between truth and speculation) but also between authors and readers. Both concepts are aligned with human emotions and human relations, against (at least in theory) politics, and thus they provide insight into the postsecularity, and thus the politics, of the literary field.

Notes

1. John Locke, "A Letter Concerning Toleration," in *Second Treatise of Government and a Letter Concerning Toleration*, ed. Mark Goldie (Oxford: Oxford University Press, 2016).
2. I capitalize indulgence when it refers to a specific royal decree and use the uncapitalized form for other uses.
3. King Charles II, *His Declaration to All His Loving Subjects of the Kingdom of England*. Dated from his Court at Breda in Holland, the 4/14 of April 1660 ("Declaration of Breda").
4. Charles II, *His Majesty's Declaration to All His Loving Subjects*, March 15, 1672, quoted in J. P. Kenyon, *The Stuart Constitution* (Cambridge: Cambridge University Press, 1986), 382.
5. Ibid.
6. This is of course only part of the story, which is not to undermine the vast absolutist powers the Stuarts claimed, nor the brutal enforcement of penal laws at times, especially for example in the case of Quakers.
7. Thomas Babington Macaulay, *The History of England from the Accession of James II*, vol. 1 (New York: Harper, 1849), chapter 2. For Macauley, the Indulgence epitomizes Stuart absolutism: "a monarch who is competent to issue such a declaration is nothing less than an absolute monarch," ibid., vol. 2, chapter 7.
8. The US Bill of Rights demonstrates this entanglement of freedom of religion with other freedoms central to liberalism: "Congress shall make no law respecting an establishment of religion, or prohibiting the free exercise thereof; or abridging the freedom of speech, or of the press; or the right of the people peaceably to assemble, and to petition the government for a redress of grievances." The Constitution of the United States, amend. I.
9. Hales was a close associate of James whose avowed Catholicism would have made him ineligible for public office. The case was brought deliberately in order to challenge the Test Act (the accuser, Godden, was acting on instructions from Hales and presumably James). The decision asserted the

sovereignty of the king: his power to make, and therefore dispense with, laws. For a discussion of this case, see Dennis Dixon, "Godden v Hales Revisited – James II and the Dispensing Power," *The Journal of Legal History* 27, no. 2 (2006): 129–52.

10 James II, *King James the Second His Gracious Declaration to All His Loving Subjects for Liberty of Conscience* [4 April 1687], quoted in Kenyon, *The Stuart Constitution*, 389.

11 James II, *Scottish Declaration of Toleration*, February 12, 1687.

12 On the substance/procedure distinction, see Andrew R. Murphy, *Conscience and Community: Revisiting Toleration and Religious Dissent in Early Modern England and America* (University Park: Penn State Press, 2001), 137–42. As Murphy puts it, toleration is the freedom to worship outside the Anglican Church and Indulgence is the sovereign action that would make it legal to do so.

13 Gordon Schochet distinguishes between liberty as a right and toleration as *grans* or privilege. In this account, toleration still bears the trace of its roots in Indulgence, but it moves toward liberty and rights. Indulgence did not immediately turn into rights, and toleration can be seen as a transitional term, between indulgence and a full theory of rights, "toward an entitlement that is antithetical to the idea of a grantor and is itself a standard by which political agencies are to be judged." Gordon Schochet, "John *Locke and Religious Toleration*," in *The Revolution of 1688–89: Changing Perspectives*, ed. Lois G. Schwoerer (Cambridge: Cambridge University Press, 1992), 150. Locke is key for developing this theory of "toleration" as right: He argues that it need not be defended on utilitarian or practical grounds, but rather he argues that intolerant practices by governments or individuals are an abuse of power which the rights-bearing subject has the right to resist.

14 José Casanova makes the case for the centrality of religious freedom to other liberal ideas: "[R]eligious freedom, in the sense of freedom of conscience, is chronologically the first freedom as well as the precondition of all modern freedoms … and inasmuch as the right to privacy serves as the very foundation of modern liberalism and of modern individualism, then indeed the privatization of religion is essential to modernity." José Casanova, *Public Religions in the Modern World* (Chicago: University of Chicago Press, 1994), 40. On the significance of Locke's theory of toleration as a natural right and as the foundation for modern ideas of freedom as grounded in the individual, broadly conceived, see Owen Chadwick, *The Secularization of the European Mind in the Nineteenth Century* (Cambridge: Cambridge University Press, 1990), 25. On the significance of the Act of Toleration to the long history of religious liberty, see Anthony Gill, *The Political Origins of Religious Liberty* (Cambridge: Cambridge University Press, 2007), 1–3. For the claim that religious liberty as theorized by Locke mandated the principles of government – formal equality and government neutrality – central to liberal democracy, see Elissa B. Alzate, *Religious Liberty in a Lockean Society* (New York: Palgrave, 2017). On the conflation of indulgence and toleration around the

Sacheverell trial and the Schism Act debates, see Nicholas Tyacke, "The 'Rise of Puritanism' and the Legalizing of Dissent, 1571–1719," in *From Persecution to Toleration: The Glorious Revolution and Religion in England*, eds. Ole Peter Grell, Jonathan I. Israel, and Nicholas Tyacke (Oxford: Oxford University Press, 1991), 47. The key distinction in that case was not toleration versus indulgence but rather either one versus comprehension.

15 "Tender conscience" appears in the "Declaration of Breda" (see fn 3) and *The Scottish Declaration of Toleration*. "How faulty so ever" appears in the "Declaration of Breda." According to Teresa Bejan, "tender conscience" referred mainly to dissenters and nonconformist. *Mere Civility: Disagreement and the Limits of Toleration* (Cambridge, MA: Harvard University Press, 2017), 181n26.

16 "Declaration of Breda."

17 On the history of suspension and dispensation, including their conflation and their relevance to Charles I, see Jacqueline Rose, *Godly Kingship in Restoration England: The Politics of the Royal Supremacy, 1660–1688* (Cambridge: Cambridge University Press, 2011), 90–91.

18 Hagit Benbaji and David Heyd, "The Charitable Perspective: Forgiveness and Toleration as Supererogatory," *Canadian Journal of Philosophy* 31, no. 4 (2001): 567–86.

19 The Toleration Act is geared toward "scrupulous consciences"; Charles' "Declaration of Breda" is offered as "a liberty to tender consciences"; and his 1672 Indulgence says "we are indulgent to truly tender consciences." James also addressed his Indulgence to tender consciences. But this distinction is not complete: Henry Sacheverell for example referred to the toleration act as "an indulgence the government has condescended to give to consciences truly scrupulous," *The Perils of False Brethren, Both in Church and State* (London, 1710), quoted in Tyacke, "The 'Rise of Puritanism'," 46.

20 Adam Wolfson, *Persecution or Toleration: An Explication of the Locke-Proast Quarrel, 1689–1704* (Lanham, MD: Lexington Books, 2010), xvi.

21 Robert P. Kraynak, "John Locke: From Absolutism to Toleration," *American Political Science Review* 74, no. 1 (1980): 53–69.

22 Lars Tønder, *Tolerance: A Sensorial Orientation to Politics* (Oxford: Oxford University Press, 2013), 3.

23 On this view, the roots of religious freedom are located in the restrictions on the power and force of the magistrate (or sovereign) even as it conjures, as William Walker argues, the force of persuasion – toleration replaces the power and force of magistrate with persuasive force of polity, "Force, Metaphor, and Persuasion in Locke's a Letter Concerning Toleration," in *Difference & Dissent: Theories of Tolerance in Medieval and Early Modern Europe*, eds. Cary J. Nederman and John Christian Laursen (Lanham, MD: Rowman & Littlefield, 1996).

24 *His Majesty's Declaration to All His Loving Subjects, 26 December 1662*, quoted in Kenyon, *The Stuart Constitution*, 381.

25 Ibid.

26 David Alvarez, "Reading Locke after Shaftesbury: Feeling Our Way towards a Postsecular Genealogy of Religious Tolerance," in *Mind, Body, Motion, Matter: Eighteenth-Century British and French Literary Perspectives*, eds. Mary Helen McMurran and Alison Conway (Toronto: University of Toronto Press, 2016), and Tønder, *Tolerance*.

27 James II, *Speech by James II to an Assembly of Lords and Privy Councilors, Reported in BPL*, Ms AM. 1502, vol. 7 no. 49, October 23, 1688, quoted in Scott Sowerby, *Making Toleration: The Repealers and the Glorious Revolution* (Cambridge, MA: Harvard University Press, 2013), 290n3.

28 "Declaration of Breda." The second quotation is from *His Majesty's Declaration to All His Loving Subjects, 26 December 1662*, quoted in Kenyon, *The Stuart Constitution*, 378.

29 R. N. Swanson, *Indulgences in Late Medieval England: Passports to Paradise?* (Cambridge: Cambridge University Press, 2007), 60.

30 Where William's Toleration Act invoke feelings, they pertain only to the subjects of the crown. Its stated goal is to "to unite their Majesties Protestant subjects in interest and affection."

31 On William's own orientation – his "personal inclination" toward toleration, and also on how the Dutch strategy was to promote a difference between William and James on toleration, see Jonathan Israel, "William III and Toleration," in *From Persecution to Toleration: The Glorious Revolution and Religion in England*, eds. Ole Peter Grell, Jonathan I. Israel, and Nicholas Tyacke (Oxford: Oxford University Press, 1991), 135.

32 Immanuel Kant, "An Answer to the Question: What Is Enlightenment?" in *What Is Enlightenment?: Eighteenth-Century Answers and Twentieth-Century Questions*, trans. and ed. James Schmidt (Berkeley: University of California Press, 1996), 62.

33 Parliament of England. *An Act to Retain Queen's Majesty's Subjects in Their due Obedience*, 1580/1. 23 Eliz. I. c.1

34 The Declaration of Right was read to William and Mary in February 1689. The Bill of Rights was ratified in December 1689.

35 For Roger Thomas, "indulgence" is not clearly distinguished form comprehension. So The "Declaration of Breda," for example, could have meant comprehension. "Comprehension and Indulgence," in *From Uniformity to Unity, 1662–1962*, eds. Geoffrey F. Nuttall and Owen Chadwick (London, 1962).

36 On Charles' experience with Parliament and the powers of suspension versus pardon, see Rose, *Godly Kingship*, 103–4.

37 Laura Zwicker, "The Politics of Toleration: The Establishment Clause and the Act of Toleration Examined," *Indiana Law Journal* 66, no. 3 (1991): 773–99.

38 Christopher Tyerman, *God's War: A New History of the Crusades* (Cambridge, MA: Harvard University Press, 2006), 67.

39 It is ironic that according to Tyerman crusades were a way to develop a shared sense of identity and purpose that were not based on ethnicity and language,

but as they evolved, they offered justification for a nationalist "defense of the homeland," a way of throwing a "crusading mantle over secular warfare." Tyerman, *God's War*, 911.

40 They were as such a model of religious freedom based on freeing the sinner from religious law not, as the Stuart Indulgences would be, from common law, an important distinction that I cannot develop here.

41 "Sulphureous Fountain" is from John Speed, *The History of Great Britaine* (1614), quoted in Jacqueline Rose, *Godly Kingship*, 93n14.

42 *A Treatise of Human Nature*, eds. L. A. Selby-Bigge and P. H. Nidditch, 2nd ed. (Oxford: Oxford University Press, 1978). All subsequent references will be to this edition, by book, chapter, and paragraph, using the abbreviation "T."

43 *History of England: From the Invasion of Julius Caesar to the Revolution of 1688*, foreword by William B. Todd, 6 vols. (Indianapolis, IN: Liberty Fund, 1985). All subsequent references will be to this edition, by volume, chapter, and page, using the abbreviation "H."

44 For a thorough treatment of this topic, see Nicholas Capaldi and Donald W. Livingston, eds., *Liberty in Hume's History of England* (Dordrecht: Springer Netherlands, 1990), especially the Introduction, and Donald W. Livingston, "Hume's Historical Conception of Liberty," in *Liberty in Hume's History of England*, 102–53.

45 This idea of a "treasury of merit" has a long tradition in Catholic theology. For a discussion of the use of monetary metaphors for atonement, see Robert W. Shaffern, "Images, Jurisdiction, and the Treasury of Merit," *Journal of Medieval History* 22, no. 3 (January 1, 1996): 237–47. Shaffern argues that "the arithmetical and contractual language and imagery" developed not for theological reasons but as a means to manage popular religious practice, and it culminated with Thomas Aquinas whose formalism was based on the idea that "contractual requirements and jurisdictional propriety determined whether and how much remission was received" (243). Shaffern's larger point, relevant to Hume's critique of James, is that indulgences were a way to promote the pope's sovereignty over the Church, based on his "plenitude of power" (244).

46 According to R. N. Swanson, indulgences were an "appendage" of the theological debate about purgatory, sin, and forgiveness. *Promissory Notes on the Treasury of Merits: Indulgences in Late Medieval Europe* (Leiden: Brill, 2006), 4.

47 Though translations differ, several of the theses, in most translations, use the language of rights to argue that remission of sins is a right, not something to be granted (via indulgence) by the pope. In Timothy Wengert's translation these appear as "in that by right" (thesis 13) or "has a right" (thesis 36) and "have a right to full remission" (thesis 87). *Martin Luther's Ninety-Five Theses*, trans. Timothy Wengert (Minneapolis, MN: Fortress Press, 2015).

48 The central question of rights, as with the question of grace, is who has access to them. Universal rights, unlike grace, are possible in theory. My point in linking them here is just to show how they function similarly outside the system of exchange and how they are linked in the history of religious

freedom. They are compatible also to the extent that they can be seen to have been granted (by a god or monarch) without payment or earning.
49 David Hume, "Of the Liberty of the Press," in *The Complete Works and Correspondence of David Hume*, Electronic Edition, *Essays Moral, Political, and Literary*, Part 1 (Charlottesville, VA: InteLex, 2000), para. 1.
50 Ibid., para. 2.
51 Ibid.
52 This sentence does not occur in all versions. See ibid., note d. Hume did not believe in natural or inalienable rights, but rather rights accreted over time by tradition: a "common right" is a corollary of common law, where rights as well as law first pertain to property. For a discussion of Hume's theory of property rights – and against equality – based on utilitarianism, see Neil MacCormick, "Legal Right and Social Democracy," *Queen's Quarterly; Kingston, Ont.* 89, no. 2 (Summer 1982): 291–92.
53 David Hume, *Enquiries Concerning the Human Understanding and Concerning the Principles of Morals*, ed. L. A. Selby-Bigge, 2nd ed. (Oxford: Clarendon Press, 1902/1963). All subsequent references will be to this edition, by section and page, using the abbreviation "E."
54 Hume does not always distinguish between the terms, though he uses indulgence much more frequently, leaving toleration to refer to a formal governmental function. He does make the connection between philosophical indulgence and governmental tolerance in the following: "I think, that the state ought to tolerate every principle of philosophy; nor is there an instance, that any government has suffered in its political interests by such indulgence" (E 11.114).
55 "The supposition of the continu'd existence of sensible objects or perceptions involves no contradiction. We may easily indulge our inclination to that supposition. When the exact resemblance of our perceptions makes us ascribe to them an identity, we may remove the seeming interruption by feigning a continu'd being, which may fill those intervals, and preserve a perfect and entire identity to our perceptions" (T 1.4. 2).
56 Livingston, "Hume's Historical Conception of Liberty," 109.
57 *Avery Gordon described haunting as* "when the over-and-done-with comes alive"; this applies to slavery but also to the mechanism of indulgence, which allows slavery to persist. "Some Thoughts on Haunting and Futurity," *Borderlands* 10, vol. 2 (2011): 2. This haunting may be seen as a larger sense of how slavery haunts liberalism: Because indulgence persists, slavery persists, and indeed the lack of freedom of enslaved people is the very foundation of liberalism. I am grateful to Teresa Zackodnik for suggesting this idea of slavery as haunting the liberal project via the mechanism of indulgence, even as I cannot begin to do justice to it here. The concept of slavery haunting liberalism has been discussed in relation to Toni Morrison's *Beloved* (New York: Plume, 1987). Scholars who have developed this line of inquiry include, among many others: Ian Baucom, *Specters of the Atlantic: Finance Capital, Slavery, and the Philosophy of History* (Durham, NC: Duke University Press,

2005); Avery F. Gordon, *Ghostly Matters: Haunting and the Sociological Imagination* (Minneapolis: University of Minnesota Press, 2008); Saidiya Hartman, "The Time of Slavery," *South Atlantic Quarterly* 101, no. 4 (Fall 2002): 757–77; Tia Miles, *Tales of the Haunted South: Dark Tourism and Memories of Slavery from the Civil War Era* (Chapel Hill: University of North Carolina Press, 2015); Hershini Bhana Young, *Haunting Capital: Memory, Text and the Black Diasporic Body* (Hanover, NH: University Press of New England, 2006).

58 Robert Filmer, *Patriarcha: Or, the Natural Power of Kings* (London, 1680).
59 [John Locke], *Second Treatise on Government* (London, 1689/90).
60 Carole Pateman, *The Sexual Contract* (Cambridge: Polity, 1988) 116–53. For Pateman, women and enslaved people share status as property in persons, but the analogy or logic connecting marriage and slavery is problematic, as there are significant differences. Charles Mills offers one account of how the racial contract differs from the sexual contract, though his support of contract overall differs from Pateman. *Racial Contract* (Ithaca, NY: Cornell University Press, 2014). They collaborated on these issues in Carole Pateman and Charles Mills, *Contract and Domination* (Cambridge: Polity, 2007).
61 See, for example, Gillian Brown, *The Consent of the Governed* (Cambridge, MA: Harvard University Press, 2001), who argues that Lockean consent is worked out via figuring the colonies as children.
62 Such a position on indulgence can also be seen in Hume, who depicts Anne Boleyn as using both indulgence and severity (the twin tools of absolutism) to manage the "intractable spirit" of Henry (H 3.30, 200). And Henry is seen as improperly refusing indulgence to Anne Ascue, to whom he should have, according to Hume, shown indulgence due to "the weakness of her sex and age" (3.33, 314). In Hume, as elsewhere in the eighteenth century, indulgence is a process linked to women and weakness. But this gendered nature of indulgence is subordinate, in Hume, to the way that indulgence can function to tip the balance (in either direction) of liberty and authority: When indulgence is issued by a monarch as a means of increasing liberty, it is positive and when it is used as a mental process to combat bigotry and overzealousness and to increase skepticism it is good. So when Mary refuses any "indulgence to the opinions of others," it is a sign of her "extreme ignorance" and productive of persecution (3.36, 407).
63 See *The History of Agnes De Castro, The Unfortunate Bride: Or, The Blind Lady a Beauty: The Wandering Beauty;* and *The Unhappy Mistake; Or, The Impious Vow Punish'd.* In *The Project Gutenberg EBook of The Works of Aphra Behn*, Montague Summers, ed., 2009.
64 Samuel Richardson, *Clarissa: Or the History of a Young Lady*, ed. Angus Ross (Reprint, New York: Penguin 1986).
65 Solmes is called "odious" in letters XV, XVI, XXVII, and XLIII. Richardson, *Clarissa*.

66 See, for example, the letters: IX "Here is clemency! Here is indulgence!"; XVII "All your scruples, you see, have met with an indulgence truly maternal from me"; XIX "To take all that good-nature, or indulgence, or good opinion confers, shews a want of moderation, and a graspingness that is unworthy of that indulgence; and are bad indications of the use that may be made of the power bequeathed"; XXV "I presume not, I say, to argue with my Papa; I only beg his mercy and indulgence"; XXIX "when I recollect my father's indulgence to me"; XXXIX, "I depended, they said, upon their indulgence, and my own power over them." Richardson, *Clarissa*.

67 Francis Dolan, *Whores of Babylon: Catholicism, Gender, and Seventeenth-Century Print Culture* (Ithaca, NY: Cornell University Press, 1999); Corrinne Harol, *Enlightened Virginity in Eighteenth-Century Literature* (New York: Palgrave, 2006).

68 In his speech on the Toleration Bill, Burke argues for extending toleration and refers to it as indulgence ("if you do not grant this indulgence ..."). *The Writings and Speeches of Edmund Burke, Volume II: Party, Parliament and the American Crisis*, ed. Paul Langford (Oxford: Clarendon 1981), 370.

69 Edmund Burke, *A Philosophical Enquiry into the Origin of Our Ideas of the Sublime and the Beautiful* [1757], in *The Writings and Speeches of Edmund Burke*, vol. 1, *The Early Writings*, ed. Paul Langford (Oxford: Clarendon 1997), 271.

70 Ibid., 272.

71 Edmund Burke, "Speech on Moving His Resolutions for Conciliation with The Colonies. March 22, 1775," in *The Writings and Speeches of Edmund Burke*, vol. 3, *Party, Parliament, and the American War*, ed. Paul Langford (Oxford: Clarendon 1996), 105.

72 Edmund Burke, "Speech on American Taxation. April 19, 1774," in *The Writings and Speeches of Edmund Burke*, vol. 2, *Party, Parliament, and the American Crisis*, ed. Paul Langford (Oxford: Clarendon 1981), 449.

73 Edmund Burke, *An Account of The European Settlements in America: In Six Parts: Each Part Contains An Accurate Description of The Settlements*, vol. 1 (London, 1757), 234.

74 Burke, "Speech on Moving," 136.

75 Ibid., 119.

76 In elaborating on this later he says,

> In this choice of inheritance we have given to our frame of polity the image of a relation in blood; binding up the constitution of our country with our dearest domestic ties; adopting our fundamental laws into the bosom of our family affections; keeping inseparable, and cherishing with the warmth of all their combined and mutually reflected charities, our state, our hearths, our sepulchres, and our altars.
> (Edmund Burke, *Reflections on the Revolution in France*, ed. Frank M. Turner [New Haven, CT: Yale University Press, 2003], 30.)

77 Edmund Burke, "Letters to the Sheriffs of Bristol," in *The Writings and Speeches of Edmund Burke*, vol. 3, *Party, Parliament, and the American War*, ed. Paul Langford (Oxford: Clarendon 1996), 306.

78 Edmund Burke, "A Letter to a Peer of England on the Penal Laws Against Irish Catholics," in *The Works and Correspondence of ... Edmund Burke* (F. & J. Rivington, 1852), 494.
79 Edmund Burke, "Speech in General Reply June 7, 1794 ...," in *The Works of the Right Honorable Edmund Burke* (Little, Brown, 1881), 13.
80 Burke, *A Philosophical Enquiry*, 189.
81 Edmund Burke, "Speech on the sixth Article of Charge. May 5, 1789."
82 Edmund Burke, "A Letter to William Elliot, Esq., Occasioned by The Account Given in A Newspaper of The Speech Made in the House of Lords by the **** Of ******* in the Debate Concerning Lord Fitzwilliam," 1795.
83 Ibid., n73.
84 Burke, "Speech on Moving," 123.
85 Olaudah Equiano, *The Interesting Narrative of the Life of Olaudah Equiano* (Peterborough: Broadview, 2001).
86 David Hume, "Of National Character," in *Essays Moral, Political, Literary (LF ed.)* (Liberty Fund, 1777).
87 David Hume, "Further Letters of David Hume," ed. Felix Waldmann (Edinburgh: Edinburgh Bibliographical Society, 2014), 65–69.
88 John Stuart Mill, Review of Brodie, *History of the British Empire*, in *The Westminster Review* 2 (1824): 34, cited in Livingston, "Hume's Historical Conception of Liberty," 152n1.
89 Ibid.
90 Charles Mills, *Black Rights/White Wrongs: The Critique of Racial Liberalism* (Oxford: Oxford University Press, 2017), 4–9.
91 On the idea of the exception, see Carl Schmitt and George Schwab, *Political Theology: Four Chapters on the Concept of Sovereignty* (Chicago: University of Chicago Press, 1985) and Giorgio Agamben, *Homo Sacer: Sovereign Power and Bare Life*, trans. Daniel Heller-Roazen (Stanford, CA: Stanford University Press, 1998).
92 Ernst-Wolfgang Böckenförde, *Staat, Gesellschaft* (Suhrkamp, 1976) [English translation: *State, Society and Liberty: Studies in Political Theory and Constitutional Law*, trans. James Amery Underwood (Oxford: Berg, 1991)], 60.
93 Catherine Gallagher, "The Rise of Fictionality," in *The Novel: Volume 1: History, Geography, and Culture*, ed. Franco Moretti (Princeton, NJ: Princeton University Press), 336–63, 345.
94 Ibid., 347.
95 Gallagher's claim that fictionality "rises" in the eighteenth-century realist novel has been contested. See, for example, Monika Fludernik, "The Fiction of the Rise of Fictionality," *Poetics Today* 39, no. 1 (February 1, 2018): 67–92; and Simona Zetterberg Gjerlevsen, "A Novel History of Fictionality," *Narrative* 24, no. 2 (May 2016): 174–89. I am not taking a side on the historicity or the ontology of fiction. I see Gallagher's argument as an example of how secular our arguments about eighteenth-century literature tend to be, and I am offering these chapters as interventions in that scholarly trajectory.

PART II

Postsecular Literary Experiences
Worlds and Time

CHAPTER 3

Figuring
Margaret Cavendish's Critique of Imagining and Worlding

The first two chapters explored how key ideas of political theology (faith and indulgence) were transformed in response to the secularizing impulses of the Restoration and how the literary field became a means for preserving and redeploying these concepts in secularizing political and social realms. Another way to put it is that the first two chapters tracked how faith and indulgence remained central to secularity and help us to understand the fissures in secular culture, with literature and fiction as the mediums for that process. The next two chapters, "Postsecular Literary Experiences: Worlds and Time" (Part II), explore a different process, whereby resolutely secular concepts of spatiality and temporality are approached in proto-postsecular ways, via new forms of literary experience, which are made possible by these secular concepts and which in turn critique them. Cavendish's method of figuring worlds and Dryden's method of reading across time may appear to be retreats from the secular world of politics, insofar as they can be seen as a methods of purging the political of religious, emotional and antirational influence by segregating those realms within the literary. But in these writers, literary experience provides a means to explore the complexity of the material and political world – as both space and time – as well as to explore the limits of human reason (the ability to understand the world) and political agency (the ability to make or remake the world). Such literary experiences reveal a liberal view of politics and secularization to be both simplistic and dangerous. Margaret Cavendish Newcastle's representation of the literary imagination as figuration and John Dryden's invention of literary history as a mode of reading – both of which seem to rest on the power of humans – are found to be rooted in their writers' presecular commitments that subordinate individual reason, imagination, and agency: to the vitalistic and monistic laws of nature in the case of Cavendish and to Catholic ritual in the case of Dryden.[1] In both, literary experience tempers human political agency via experiences of complexity, temporality, and error. These two chapters thus provide case studies of the ways that traditionalist (Catholic, Royalist, bound to the past) thinking transformed into forms of mentation and writing important to the modern literary sphere as well as to modern conservatism and postsecularism.

By way of understanding the significance of Cavendish's view of literary experience – as figuration – this chapter explores how Cavendish responds to two related trends in seventeenth-century thinking: theories that connect the natural world and the political world, and theories of possible/alternate worlds. We might see both of these theories as ways of constituting arguments for how human society works. My argument about Cavendish begins with an analysis of the first possibility: the intellectual strategy, a favored one of modernity, to imagine a world (and therefore a politics) that follows the laws of the natural world as discovered by science. Such projects, in ways that Cavendish makes clear, rely on the assumption that politics, science, and literature have an inextricable relationship; this view itself is what constitutes a modern worldview. While both liberal and conservative orientations require a worldview, a conservative worldview has been seen as at once more limiting and more violent, a worldview that insists that others shares one's worldview if they share one's world, while the worldview of liberalism is grounded in ideas of diversity and tolerance, the possibility of an ever-expanding, cosmopolitan world that is peaceful because of reason and toleration.[2] This is the proto-liberal view that Cavendish's proto-conservatism and theory of the literary imagination finds untenable. Cavendish's conservatism is manifested explicitly in the representations of sovereign violence that seem necessary to protect worlds and implicitly in the significance of a method of "figuration" that Cavendish theorizes, and practices, as the foundation of form in the natural world, the social world, and the literary imagination.

The title of Cavendish's prose fiction *A Description of a New World, Called the Blazing-World* (1666) suggests several things about the way I want to read its investigation into the literary imagination.[3] The title gestures to the "New World," that destination, in the Restoration period, of pilgrims fleeing religious persecution in England, as well as the locus of indigenous pagan cultures that shadow Europe's Protestant/Catholic sectarianism. The title also invokes seventeenth-century philosophical debates about the nature of "worlds," which revolved around how the particularity of the material world relates to the nature of the larger physical whole. Although the two "worlds" in the title reference the same world (the Blazing one), the repetition suggests both the text's doubling techniques and its fictional thought experiment, which rests on a Galilean understanding of the universe wherein the earth, shaped like a globe, is just one

Figuring: Margaret Cavendish's Critique of Imagining

of many such worlds in the universe but also the only one we have to live in. "World" is a secular concept insofar as it restricts human experience to the immanent frame (there is nothing beyond worlds) but also insofar as it suggests a project of universality (humans must share the world or the universe). Cavendish's emphasis on "world" gestures to the extent that the understanding of our world, earth, as a globe in a universe allows for both the reality and the imagination of other worlds and an understanding of the connections among them – the impossibility of full separation.[4] This is a phenomenon that turns out to be scientific, political, and aesthetic. *The Blazing World* was appended to Cavendish's *Observations on Experimental Philosophy*, a configuration that indicates that together the texts will investigate the relationship between the literary imagination and philosophical or scientific truth, expressed in the titles as the difference between description and observation.[5] Cavendish describes the two texts as having "Sympathy and Coherence with each other," and she uses a simile to express this relation: the two texts "were joyned together as Two several Worlds, at their Two Poles."[6] The textual configuration is thus analogous to the thought experiment, and together they suggest that Cavendish is engaged in thinking about the relationship between science and literature as a way of thinking about the nature of worlds, including new worlds, real worlds, and fictional worlds. This chapter will argue that in *The Blazing World*, the literary imagination, as a world-creating faculty that shares attributes with politics and science, necessitates an engagement with questions about secularization, and in particular about toleration and the state-sanctioned violence that toleration seeks to manage.[7]

The connection between the literary imagination and political power is a prominent theme of *The Blazing World*. Though she "cannot be Henry the Fifth, or Charles the Second" Cavendish announces (in her preface "To the Reader"), she will, via her literary imagination, "endeavour to be, Margaret the First," and as she has "neither Power, Time nor Occasion, to be a great Conqueror" rather than "not be Mistress of a World" she has made "One of [her] own" (*BW*, 124). Later in the text, the immaterial creatures of the Blazing World suggest that everyone has such power: "[E]very human Creature can create an Immaterial World fully inhabited by Immaterial Creatures, and populous of Immaterial subjects [...] all this within the compass of the head or scull" (*BW*, 185). The epilogue continues this theme, inviting readers to imagine themselves as subjects of the Blazing World "in their minds, fancies or imaginations" or, if they prefer, to "create worlds of their own, and govern them as they please" (*BW*, 225). These testimonies to the world-creating powers of the literary imagination have been read by critics as an assertion of the sovereignty of the individual artistic subject, incidentally female, a paean to the potency of the imagination to promote both female empowerment and peace – or we might say the power of the literary to be political.[8] In such readings, the text's reactionary and violent elements, along with Cavendish's own well-known conservative politics, must be explained away or segregated from her literary and intellectual accomplishments.[9] This chapter instead sees these aspects of Cavendish's project as inherently connected. It argues that Cavendish rejects the idea of the imagination, which produces violence, in favor of "figuring."

The Blazing World was written in a crucial time for the history of toleration, a history that reveals the close connection between toleration and state violence. As discussed in Chapter 2, the Restoration began and ended with crises around the issues of how peace and freedom of conscience could coexist. *The Declaration of Breda* (1660) promises to replace the "distraction," "confusion," "bleeding," and "wounds" that characterized the Civil Wars and interregnum with "quiet and peaceable" rule.[10] Its logic is that political peace depends upon religious toleration. But still, it prioritizes peace, and therefore the state, over religious freedom, with Charles promising that under his rule "no man shall be disquieted or called in question for differences of opinion in matter of religion, *which do not disturb the peace of the kingdom*" (emphasis mine).[11] This Declaration – and especially the religious freedom that it promised – proved to be one of the most contentious aspects of Charles' rule. During the 1660s, while Cavendish was writing and publishing *The Blazing World*, Charles's efforts to instantiate religious freedom in the name of political peace were stymied by Parliament.[12] The problem that Cavendish and Charles were grappling with in the 1660s has been central to the question of toleration throughout its history. Put broadly, the issue is that the more one embraces diversity as either a fact or an ideal of social or religious existence, the more difficult it becomes to imagine a form of government, other than absolutism, that can manage this diversity.[13] A central paradox in the history of toleration is that it is a liberal and secular ideal that, at least when Cavendish was writing, seemed more compatible with (and was advocated for on behalf of) Catholic monarchists.[14] Liberal theorists of the generation after Hobbes and Cavendish continued to struggle, as liberal theorists still do, to resolve this problem. John Locke can imagine common ground in religion and politics, but only by becoming more normative around forms of sociability and morality. Pierre Bayle is more inclusive of religious difference than Locke, but he does not seem to be able to imagine a form of government that can formally manage this diversity. As Elena Russo puts it, in the "beauty contest" (i.e., in the contest to be more liberal and modern) between Bayle and Locke, Bayle is credited with being more "far-reaching and robust" but also with being both more "ambiguous" and less hopeful about the possibility of toleration outside of a "strong state" that is "willing to assume the responsibility of enforcing the peace."[15] This question of civil peace extends toleration further into international politics, and theorists of toleration posed the related question of whether the relations that obtained between people in a nation (which were ideally, in tolerationist theory, freedom and peace) could obtain between nations. The Restoration problem of the violence of sectarian conflict and civil war – and the role of sovereignty in managing it – was thus analogous to questions about violence across sovereign nations and thus whether the world can be tolerant.

One prominent way that theories of the Enlightenment, and indeed of the long arc of modernity more broadly, attempted to resolve such dilemmas in political philosophy was to turn to the natural sciences, to ground political ideas in theories of nature.[16] Materialist philosophy was revived and renovated in the seventeenth century in tandem with the emergence of new political theories and realities. Enlightenment thinkers – Thomas Hobbes and Locke exemplify this trend in England – posited that humans are entities that are subject, like atoms, to the physical laws of matter and motion, a move that makes possible a science of politics that can (theoretically) manage humans just as a science of nature can (theoretically) manage the natural world.[17] In other words, political science was founded in natural science, with many thinkers believing that if they could just formulate or understand the laws of the natural world adequately, then they could solve the problem of human political organization, including diversity, freedom, and violence.[18] When grounded as such in science, questions of politics and toleration can be approached in a variety of registers – from atoms, to humans, to the world, to worlds, and to the universe or the divine cosmos – with each point a possible analogy for the other. This is where Cavendish's world-figuring imagination merges with her monism, which is grounded in the assumption that universal laws of nature are founded in God's creation. But this strain of thinking ran into much theological controversy, with the charge of atheism inevitably invoked against such theories, because they could be seen as threatening to both human exceptionality and divine creation.

Margaret Cavendish occupied a singular position in seventeenth-century England, one that set the stage for her entry into these debates.

As a young member of the court in exile with her influential husband William Cavendish, the Duke of Newcastle, Cavendish was exposed to the leading political, philosophical, scientific, and aesthetic theories of day; she was conversant with controversies between rationalist and empiricist epistemologies as well as among monistic, dualistic, and pluralist theories of matter. Cavendish's husband was a patron of Hobbes – her marriage took place a few months after a dinner party her husband hosted, at which Hobbes and John Bramhall famously debated liberty of conscience – and Hobbes is generally considered to be a major intellectual influence on her long writing career. Certainly, they ruminated on the same topics, including materialism, political power, violence, the nature of political and cultural systems, and the faculty of the imagination. While her intellectual affinities with Hobbes are complex, her relation to the Royal Society is more straightforward: having satirized the new science in *The Blazing World*, she was in turn mocked when she visited the academy the following year, an event memorialized in Samuel Pepys's account in his diary.[19] Known in her day for dressing up in outlandish clothes, including male ones, and for refusing the rules of spelling and grammar in the service of literary invention and originality, Cavendish is most commonly modified by the adjective singular. And it is a word that captures how her legacy has been explored: She is remembered both as a unique figure – one specifically important to women's literary history – and as someone, who, for better and for worse, was committed to ideals of singularity.[20] On the worse side, her royalism, monotheism, and theocracy have proved (in, for example, Catherine Gallagher's influential reading as well as in Rachel Trubowitz's account of the "female monarchical self") a stumbling block for critics who do not share her political orientation – although, in a move whereby the critical problem becomes its own solution, her feminism is often considered inextricable from her monarchism.[21] On the better side, perhaps, stand both the way her singularity is seen as related to her literary invention and accomplishment and the way her commitment to singularity informs her vitalism: In the literary realm, being singular means being original, unique, and thereby proliferating variety – and modernity, in the sense of pluralism – in literary forms and genres, while from a vitalist standpoint singularity challenges both mind/body and subject/object dualism and human exceptionalism and thus is amenable to critical trends in antihumanist thinking.[22] Cavendish's singularity thus stands politically on the side of tradition, while philosophically, scientifically, and aesthetically it sides with originality and therefore multiplicity and difference – in short, modernity. I start with Cavendish's singularity (or its flip side: what

Figuring: Margaret Cavendish's Critique of Imagining

Alexandra Bennet calls her "often contradictory self representation") and her position in relation to Hobbes and the Royal Society as a way into thinking about how her self-presentation and her scholarly reception are related to her political and philosophical positions.[23]

In order to explore how Cavendish connects science, the literary imagination, and the politics of toleration in *The Blazing World*, I analyze the text's engagement with the problem of "parts," "particulars," "variety," and "division" in natural philosophy as offering a corollary to religio-political questions about difference of opinion. I read *The Blazing World* as a thought experiment in whether a fully vitalistic universe can peacefully support "division" of opinions as well as matter – and thus in how "opinion" in science is related to opinion in religion and to the governmental structures that manage both. Through this approach, I endeavor to reconcile what seem to be two opposing aspects of Cavendish's thought: the thoroughgoing vitalism that sees substance (including rational thought) as both self-moving and infinitely various and her commitment to absolute monarchy and state-sponsored violence in the political realm. Unfortunately, Cavendish does not offer any particularly useful – to our twenty-first-century perspective – solutions, for *The Blazing World* ends with a revocation of the sovereign's decree of toleration and with the invasion and conquest of another sovereign world. *The Blazing World* tries to imagine how freedom of conscience, academic freedom, and biological diversity can peacefully coexist. It suggests that they can and do coexist in the individual but not in what Cavendish calls the world, which is at once a product of human (sometimes literary) culture, a self-enclosed totality that must be managed by power and violence, as well as inevitably just one world among many. Thus, I read *The Blazing World* as an engagement with the failure of both the literary imagination and the liberal project of secularization via toleration, precisely because of their relation to each other.

Figuring Parts and Wholes

The world that Cavendish's imagination creates, the Blazing World, is notable, insofar as it is different from seventeenth-century England, both for its diversity and for its peacefulness: the Blazing World is full of a variety of what we call species – bear men, lice men, men like foxes, etc. – as well as a variety of what could be seen as races: In the Imperial city, the creatures are not morphologically distinct but they are of different colors, some "azure, some of a deep purple, some of a grass-green, some of a scarlet, some of an orange-colour, &c." (*BW*, 133) An ethos of "neighbors" informs relations among these different populations. The bear and fox men, for example, treat each other with "civility and courtship" (*BW*, 127). The narrator and the inhabitants of the Blazing World attribute this peaceful coexistence of difference to the facts that they have but one language, one Emperor, and "one opinion concerning the worship and adoration of God" (*BW*, 135). Note, however, that it does not call for one truth, about God or anything else.

The geography of the Blazing World supports both this diversity and this peacefulness – the topography is dominated by islands separated by bodies of water, with long passages over water necessary to traverse the lands of the different species. As citizens of island communities, the hybrid animal men of Blazing World have "no other enemies but the winds" (*BW*, 129).[24] The seat of the Blazing World is called Paradise, and its geography affords even more protection; with only one entry via a barely visible cleft in a wall of high rocks, it is then approached via a labyrinth "so winding and turning" that only small boats could pass (*BW*, 131). The Imperial City itself is like an island within an island within this natural fortress: It appears "in form like several islands; for rivers did flow betwixt every street," with a series of gates, so artfully placed that "a stranger would lose himself" (*BW*, 131). So the geography and architecture of the Blazing World exclude the category of strangers and thereby make the category of enemies impossible. The Blazing World is a "world" because its diverse parts are unified culturally and politically and perhaps because physical difference, and therefore difference of opinion, is mediated by geography: It is configured for peace. Following the travelogue of the Blazing World that brings the protagonist to the Imperial city, she is made Empress of this Blazing World, and she must consider how to govern it, a question that the text pursues, obliquely, via the question of parts and wholes in nature.

This philosophical question of the relationship of parts and wholes is the central concern of the *Observations on Experimental Philosophy* – the textual world attached to *The Blazing World*. The *Observations*' critique of experimental science rests largely on the analytic method of the Royal Society, which assumes a discoverable relation between parts and wholes. "Nature cannot be known by any of her parts," Cavendish asserts repeatedly (*OEP*, 200). For example, the five human senses, she argues, each provide a "perfect knowledge in each part" and yet are "ignorant of each other" (*OEP*, 46). This example of the human senses serves as a microcosm of the way all of nature works. All matter is "self-moving" and "self-knowing" but – or because of this – there can be no extrapolation

Figuring: Margaret Cavendish's Critique of Imagining

from parts to wholes (*OEP*, 30). If this is true for bodies, it is even more true for Nature: "Now if there be such variety of several knowledges, not only in one creature [...] what may there be in all the parts of nature?" (*OEP*, 47). As Deborah Boyle explains, an observer cannot know matter as well as the matter knows itself, and thus Cavendish's vitalism and her critique of experimentalism rest on the fact that difference of opinion derives from the nature of matter as self-knowing.[25] Whereas Descartes distinguishes truth (*sciencia*) from opinion, Cavendish thinks all knowledge is opinion, derived from one's situation in a particular body, place, and time. Peter Dear has argued that the experimentalist community focused on description rather than causation, as a means to avoid "socially disruptive disagreements."[26] Cavendish's vitalism, by contrast, finds disagreements inevitable, fundamental to the nature of matter, a proposition that the "description" of the Blazing World, which occupies most of the first half of the text, supports.

This diversity in nature raises the problem of how these self-knowing and self-moving parts can be unified into a whole, natural or political. Many critics want to see in vitalism a liberatory, tolerationist vision that science might offer to politics, a model for managing difference or for balancing freedom and restrictions on freedom: If self-knowing and self-moving entities can coexist in nature then why not in society? (This of course begs the questions of how peaceful nature is and whether ontology can be the grounds of politics or ethics.)[27] Critics have tended to read a liberal/feminist strain in Cavendish and in vitalism more generally.[28] But the corollaries between nature and politics in Cavendish are quite complicated. She will argue, in the *Observations*, and demonstrate, in *The Blazing World*, that parts can be "figured" into wholes but that these figures are not stable, they are not based on mutually accepted truths, and they do not supersede the nature of the parts from which they are formed.

The inherent divisiveness of nature and thus of knowledge, for Cavendish, cannot be rectified by "Art" (by which Cavendish means science). As she explains, "Art, which is but a particular creature, cannot inform us of the truth of the infinite parts of nature, being but finite itself" (*OEP*, 48). There is thus no possible knowledge of wholes. What there is, instead, is "figuration" – the unifying or reconfiguration of parts into new holistic formations: Nature is "infinitely various in her works – and subject to infinite changes" (*BW*, 148). The question is not whether there can be universal knowledge – Cavendish dismisses this possibility – but rather how parts "ignorant of each other" can "agree in the production of a figure" (*OEP*, 159). This is a question for both scientific knowledge and governance. In an analogy between science and religion that is telling for my argument about how her natural philosophy relates to her politics of toleration – and thus how figuration relates to parts – Cavendish explains:

> Although every part hath its own knowledge and perception; yet, when many parts are conjoined into one figure, then, by reason of that twofold relation of their actions and near neighbourhood, they become better acquainted. And, as many men assembled in a church, make but one congregation, and all agree to worship one God, in one and the same manner or way; so, many parts conjoined in one figure, are, as it were, so many communicants, all agreeing, and being united in one body. (*OEP*, 159)

This passage suggests that vitalistic nature and religious communion work by a similar process of figuration, whereby participation in the figure promotes peaceful relations – not via knowledge but neighborly acquaintance based on proximity.[29] Thus, the two worlds of Cavendish's text – the scientific and the literary – explore the relations between particular knowledge and unifying figuration in the related spheres of science and religion (or culture more broadly). The analogies between these two spheres – explicit and implied – transmute across the two texts as Cavendish explores what diversity of opinion means in each sphere. For example, at the level of nature as well as, implicitly, geopolitics, there are "factions and quarrels" that produce "mixed species," which then has the effect of driving other species out of their habitation. Cavendish sees such struggle as inevitable and morally neutral, a function of the self-moving, self-knowing nature of matter. Of hybrid invasive species, for example, the Empress learns from the worm men: "[T]heir life [...] is their own, and not their Parents; for no part or creature of Nature can either give or take away life, but parts do onely assist and join with parts, either in dissolution or production of other Parts and Creatures" (*BW*, 153).

Cavendish's solution to how a body politic can be unified out of such diversity of form, opinion, and intention is in conversation with both Hobbes and the Royal Society, as Anna Battigelli has argued.[30] Hobbes' famous solution to this problem, the Leviathan, is a process of amalgamation whereby the unruly multitude is unified into a singular sovereign. It is an artificial process that produces an artificial, that is, cultural, entity; unity is produced *ex nihilo*, sharing no substance with that which it unifies.[31] The Royal Society's analytic method works differently, by producing difference or disfiguration out of unity and purpose: The louse that the Empress sees as a pest to humans while recognizing its own incontrovertible destiny to be louse-like, is disarticulated from its nature – made "strangely shaped" – by the analytical machine of the microscope, which produces information so "tedious" that the narrator forebears relation of it (*BW*, 144) . Cavendish's thought process, by contrast, is synthetic and figurative rather than analytical or accretive: from parts and divisions she conceptualizes a singularity that is of the same substance, though a different figuration, as the parts, and she imagines that by nature of participating in the same figure, parts develop affinities.[32] Cavendish does not take the natural world as a metaphor, cause, or measuring stick for politics. Instead, when it comes to representing how science relates to politics and how parts unify into wholes, Cavendish relies on simile. A literary figure that resists abstraction, simile expresses both the relationship between science and culture and the fundamental way that each works on its own; simile is used by Cavendish to explore how entities in nature and politics are configured and thus can be reconfigured. In short, Cavendish's philosophical commitments explain the inevitability of division of opinion, locating it at the most basic level of matter. Opinion, as a function of matter, cannot be unified or a force of unification, but it can, over time, be figured and reconfigured. The role of governance is a similar process of figuration, which should seek not to rectify or exacerbate divisions, but rather to shape them into a connected whole, a world.

The Politics of Difference

When the protagonist is made Empress of the Blazing World, she bases her theory, as well as her initial practice, of political rule on vitalism (all substance is self-moving), monism (one religion, one sovereign, one substance), and what we might now call a very liberal approach to difference: The Empress at first allows her subjects – who are variously colored, diversely speciated, and differently abled – the liberty to pursue erroneous beliefs and specialized experience. In other words, the Empress shares philosophical positions about nature that reflect the *Observations*, and she tries to base a politics and a government – like so many seventeenth-century thinkers did – on these scientific principles. The first sovereign action of the Empress is to create schools, which are the means whereby difference, inherent in the material reality (which is in turn connected to the geographical arrangement) of her subjects, becomes manifest in opinion. The bear men take the position of the Royal Society regarding the world-uniting potential of scientific knowledge: without microscopes, they say, "the world ... would be but blind" (*BW, 143)*. But the telescopes and microscopes so beloved by the bear-men do nothing to settle the "differences and divisions" over cosmology (*BW*, 140); rather, they fracture their users' opinion even more. The Empress' proposed solution – the dissolution of the schools and the instruments which multiply opinion – is countered by the bear-men's argument that arguing is their "only delight" and "dear to [them] as [their] lives" (*BW*, 142), and the Empress agrees to let them have their debates in their school as long as they do not cause "factions or disturbances in state, or government" (*BW*, 142). The problem the Empress is addressing – as was Charles II at the same time and as was explained in Chapter 2 – is explicitly the one of what "the world" believes and what kind of belief can be tolerated – or indulged – by a government committed to peace (*BW*, 145).[33]

While there is no difference of opinion about religion in the Blazing World before the Empress arrives, she, finding its inhabitants ignorant of religious truth, introduces the potential of such difference by converting her subjects to her own religion. Although conversion is easy enough (apparently one just needs to utter the religious truth to make people believe), maintaining religious conformity requires a spectacular display, one that is managed by the Empress' scientific knowledge, which she has gained by her travels and inquiries. There may be only one religious truth, but Cavendish knows full well that there is more than one way to worship, just as there are multiple possible sovereignties, languages, and worlds. To manage this, the Empress builds two chapels: one for preaching sermons of terror and one for sermons of comfort. These chapels are separate from the religious truth she, and now her subjects, believe. They are not about truth or salvation but rather about the pragmatic management of her subjects as a community; these places of religious practice function as a kind of figuration or world-remaking made possible by the Empress' sovereignty and her scientific knowledge. The key to the Empress' problem – that is, what causes the need for a management strategy – is that she transports the truth of God to a different world, that her notion of religious truth transcends worlds and thus threatens them. Not so for organized religion, which is for Cavendish something very different from religious truth and is related to the sovereign's role in maintaining peace. This is why the Empress' preaching and her religious rituals bear almost no relation (except causal) to each other, with the former a matter of simple truth and the latter reliant on conjuring the power and the protection of a godlike figure in the form of the Empress' sovereignty. Truth is one thing, and the figuring and reconfiguring power of religion, politics, and culture another (this indirectly supports the thesis in the first chapter, which showed how truth was not as consequential for religion as secularization would have it). The Blazing World is peaceful when it has only one language, one religion and one sovereign, a configuration that is restored via the Empress' spectacular religious practices.

This is all well and good for the majority of the first part of *The Blazing World* – the introduction of divisive scientific opinion, religious truth, and religious ritual and conformity seem to have no political or cultural ramifications that cannot be reversed (as in the case of her schools) or managed (as in the case of her religious practices). Well, except that the Empress is lonely and a bit bored, which results in her inviting a "scribe" in the form of a fictional Margaret Cavendish, to join her in the Blazing World. So now in addition to an imaginary world having been paired with a "real" one and a philosophical text with a literary one, we have a fictional character, based on a real one, who provides a double for the imaginary character. This imaginative process is repeated – doubled again – when Margaret Cavendish, who is envious of the Empress' sovereignty and her world, desires to learn how to make her own world. Even before she begins to practise this world-imagining skill, the initially doubled world has proliferated: first by the revelation that the fictional Cavendish hails not from the same world as the Empress nor from the world of the readers but from yet a third world, and second by the immaterial spirits' revelation that there are "infinite" worlds already existing (*BW*, 184).[34] Alas, none of these infinite worlds are available to the characters' imaginative desire for sovereignty because, the spirits inform us, "none [. . .] is without government" (*BW*, 185). This suggests that worlds and governments are synonymous or at least coexistent. Indeed, this seems to be one of the points that the characters learn by their imaginative world-making. The character Margaret Cavendish tries to "imagine" a world based on the "opinions" of a variety of philosophers, both ancient and modern: Thales, Pythagoras, Plato, Epicurus, Aristotle, Descartes, and Hobbes. These attempts to imagine a world abstracted from material reality – imagination working on opinion – all founder by tormenting her mind with monsters, puzzles, puppets, and other unpleasant mental experiences (*BW*, 187–88). This experience is not only mentally unpleasant, but it also defies the logic of figuration and the configuration of parts and wholes upon which her science depends, for "all the parts of this Imaginary World came to press and drive each other" (*BW*, 188). That is, imagination based on opinion is both scientifically wrong and violent. In a scene that acts as an account of conversion to a conservative worldview insofar as they reject theory and imagination as a way to account for worlds and governance, the two women discover that neither "opinion" nor "pattern" can provide the basis for a world – or a government (*BW*, 189). Instead, they allow the "rational matter" in their minds to "move to the creation" of imaginary worlds, which turn out to be so "full of variety" and "so [...] wisely governed" that they are beyond the capacity of human language to describe (*BW*, 188). In other words, the rational matter of the mind, via its capacity for figuration, produces at once the variety and the coherence characteristic of worlds, at least of peaceful ones, even as such worlds exceed the rational mind's ability to conceptualize them rationally. Thus, although the text may seem to celebrate imagination and reason, it actually takes a critical view of them throughout. The Empress, for example, finds mathematics with its "imaginary points and lines" to be entertaining, but ultimately irrelevant to governance, a mere dalliance with "Non-beings" (*BW*, 159). Similarly, in the well-known quotation from the epilogue that seems to suggest subjects can become sovereigns via the imagination, Cavendish qualifies this, suggesting that people imagining worlds and their own sovereignty need to be cautious: "But yet let them have a care, not to prove unjust Usurper" (*BW*, 225). As such, the *Blazing World* provides not a celebration of pure imagination or opinion but a warning about their dangers. Instead of these mental processes, it offers figuration as the proper model of the world, of politics, and of literature.

The text's doublings and its world-imagining exercise are both an allegory for how literary figuration works and a justification for a conservative worldview: not theory, opinion, or imagination, but rather reconfiguration. By reformulating materials and ideas already existing, the literary imagination produces figuration that proliferates versions (new configurations) of reality.[35] This is why the figure of two worlds is both the text's thought experiment and form and why simile is its fundamental trope: The fictional Blazing World, indeed, any fictional world, will be produced out of the matter already existing – in this case, the philosophical truths explicated in the "Observations" and the life experience of Margaret Cavendish. Along similar lines, just as worlds cannot be successfully figured from opinion, so too should art not be formed "methodically and artificially" from rules. For example, theatrical plays in the world of Margaret Cavendish are properly "composed of old stories, either Greek or Roman or some new-found world" (*BW*, 192). The literary imagination, like singular models of sovereignty, is a method of synthesis via figuration; it produces similitude and unity from experience rather than from theorization or analysis. For Cavendish, the literary imagination is world-creating, not a means of understanding or creating *ex nihilo* but rather a process of figuring and synthesizing various preexisting parts.[36]

These processes of figuration and refiguration, of doubling and simile, mean that worlds are not isolated. We see this in the ways that the imaginary world-creating exercises of the Empress and the fictional Margaret Cavendish redound to the political situations of the worlds of both. First the Empress decides, based on her imaginative world-creation, that the differences of opinion produced by her schools threaten the Blazing World with "rebellion," and hence she dissolves them (201). And so goes the world of academic freedom monitored by a sovereign who cares about the pleasures and honours the differences of her subjects. With its mandated and manipulated religious conformity and its restriction on intellectual debate, the Empress' Blazing World turns out to be rather intolerant. To the extent that this revocation of liberty of conscience represents a change of mind, it is fully consistent with Cavendish's philosophical commitments – the mind as matter is subject to reconfiguring change just as all matter is – as well as with her literary method. One of Cavendish's most common literary strategies involves arguing with herself – changing her mind and changing it again.[37] It is another of her techniques for doubling and a way in particular of figuring – as well as addressing directly – questions of toleration in literary forms. In her *Orations of Divers Sorts* (1662), for example, she writes three orations about liberty of conscience. One oration argues for such liberty under the conditions where subjects already have a religion, because trying to change their religion will threaten peace; the second oration argues against liberty of conscience because it leads to liberty in the state, which threatens peace and safety; and the third – where she attempts to find a mean between a "furious" and a "factious" people – argues that liberty of conscience is acceptable with respect to private devotion as long as it does not impact the public (in other words, she makes an argument for toleration based on secularization).[38] The Orations, and indeed the rest of Cavendish's oeuvre, is replete with such internal difference of opinion – she sometimes takes six or seven positions on the same topic. This plastic ability of the mind is ultimately what allows it to be world-figuring and reconfiguring, because minds, like worlds, are united not by opinion but by form and figuration. And so, we seem to have two opposing aspects to Cavendish's thought: on the one hand, a commitment to the contingency of all opinion and the power of the individual imagination and on the other hand, a commitment to peace that may trump this philosophical belief in the inevitability of diverse opinions. So we have not quite resolved this problem and neither has the Empress. Let me turn briefly to some recent ways of thinking about some of these issues in order to set up a reading of the text's efforts to address this problem.

Violence, Protection, Worlds

The question of the politics of the concept of "the world" has a long philosophical tradition, one that sees critics split on whether worlds are inherently violent or peaceful and tolerationist (or better). Martin Heidegger's conception of a world rests on its relation to protection and to how a world's inhabitants imagine themselves in relation to God: "[I]n a world's worlding," Heidegger writes, "is gathered that spaciousness out of which the protective grace of the god is granted or withheld."[39] So once one imagines a world, protection is imperative and is imagined as proceeding from a power outside the world, from a god whom the world's inhabitants must share if they are to be considered as inhabiting the same world. The etymology of toleration is derived from toll, which is a tax to be paid at the polity's boundary, and is also related to telos, a tax for the gods and also a limit of the polity.[40] For Heidegger, the telos must be established in order for a world to world – that is, to protect. This is why governments, religions, and worlds are coterminous, why worlds need gods, and why acts of imagination or worlding necessarily invoke the instinct to protect. Emmanuel Levinas' critique of Heidegger's philosophy of the world rests on the fact that this need to protect permits the universalizing tyranny of the state.[41] But this critique of Heidegger leads also to a sense that in the conception of the "world," in the ways that "world" necessitates encounters with others and other worlds, lies the possibility of encounters that are hospitable rather than violent – that is, encounters between others that go even beyond mere peace and tolerance. In Derrida's reading of Levinas, the protectionism and violence fundamental to worlds is centered on the decisionism that founds both politics and religion. When a community recognizes that it must make a decision (e.g., to protect itself), it recognizes the prior decision that founded their community, a decision inevitably authorizing violence and ascribed to an entity that transcends the world. For Derrida, this means that "the world" is that in which the "absence-presence of God *plays*" – a play that allows us to "think the essence *of God*."[42] If God plays at the borders of worlds, this explains why religious difference is a fundamental issue for worlds: At the borders of worlds, the encounter with the essence of God (or with other religions) may either authorize violence or may soften the world's boundaries. Gilles Deleuze and Felix Guattari are sanguine about the positive (tolerationist, at a minimum) possibilities of encounters between worlds, arguing that in the encounter with the other lies the possibility of peace via the dissolution of the boundaries of the self

Figuring: Margaret Cavendish's Critique of Imagining 119

and world. The other appears, in their account, as "neither subject nor object but as something that is very different, a 'possible *world*' (emphasis mine)"; an encounter with such an other/world can redistribute "subject and object [...] figure and ground, margins and center."[43] For Deleuze and Guattari, the encounter with the possibility of another world is both frightening and hopeful, ultimately salutary if one opens up to the experience – it can be a way of destabilizing the self and the world, or making the "world go by" (Deleuze and Guattari, 18). Philosophers thus differ on the centrality of violence to worlds but they pose the central question – will an encounter with others and other worlds be violent or peaceful? – that *The Blazing World* ends by asking. Its answer is less hopeful than Deleuze and Guattari's.

The importance of this philosophical debate to literature has been taken up by a number of literary critics.[44] Eric Hayot argues for literature as a place where such conflicts between "the world" and other worlds (or the universe) are mediated at the level of form. For Hayot, there exists an inherent affinity between literature and the world, because literature involves always toggling between parts and wholes and because the idea of "the world" is bounded and embedded in an idea of the universe. "The world" necessitates the development of a concept of wholeness in relation to greater wholeness. For Hayot, modernity is defined by the arrival of "the universal" as a history-making event and the literary as a process whereby that conception is formalized in literary worlds. So when Descartes says "the matter of the heavens and the earth is one and the same, and there cannot be a plurality of worlds" and Spinoza concurs with "life is always the same and everywhere one," we, according to Hayot, "recognize the seemingly paradoxical combination of universalism and multiplicity as central to the entire modern world view."[45] In modernity, we assume that everyone lives in the same world and therefore must see themselves as part of the same thing, enough at least to tolerate each other. For Hayot, this means that the world is "whatever one has a good theory of," and literature is a means of formalizing such a worldview. Pheng Cheah comes at these questions differently from Hayot, arguing that literature can "world" because of its receptivity and because of its temporality, factors that allow it to contest the hegemony of one world – global capitalism – and through this contestation to bring about new worlds.[46] For Cheah, because literature's temporality underlies its world-remaking power, its possibilities go beyond the mediation of conflict (in the real world) that Hayot describes, to imagining a future utopia. Cavendish might be up to something similar to what both Hayot and Cheah claim as literature's special role, insofar as she uses the literary imagination to address questions of worlding. Cavendish, however, sides with form and figuration against theory, and thereby is more materialist and formalist than Hayot. She also seems much more resolutely committed to the material and the formal connections between imagined and real worlds than Cheah is, a commitment that limits the political imaginary of such form and figuration.[47] Cavendish's philosophical positions on the nature of the literary imagination (contra Hayot and Cheah) help to explain why the Blazing World, which can seem rather utopian (or at least peaceful) when it is, on the diegetic level, the only world, turns quite violent when worlds encounter each other.

After the Empress and Margaret Cavendish's world-creating exercise, in which they experience the figuring power of the mind as productive of peace and harmony, they endeavor to influence other worlds, ones that seem at once more real and more difficult to govern. The central conflict in the "real" Margaret Cavendish's life was the loss of her husband's lands and fortune during the interregnum. Cavendish devoted a great deal of effort to right what she considered this political wrong. In *The Blazing World*, this real aspect of Cavendish's life has an analogue: the fictional Cavendish and the Empress travel "as lightly as two thoughts" to Cavendish's home in order to try to resolve a similar conflict that Cavendish's husband is having (*BW*, 190). The problem is figured via personification: Prudence and Honesty are aligned with the Cavendish's cause, while Fortune is the Cavendish's antagonist, with Folly and Rashness on its side. The Empress and Margaret Cavendish convene a trial to mediate the conflict, but the judge, Truth, proves ineffectual at resolving the conflict between these personifications. This experience – of reflecting upon the nature of conflict and the impossibility of changing opinions that are fundamentally connected to identity and/or to other worlds (and personification is the trope for this, an antagonist to simile) – offers a counterpoint to the elation of the world-imaginings of these two characters. This is because the liberating potential of the imagination is also the threat to the security and protection of worlds. If Margaret Cavendish can enter the Blazing World and if the two of them can travel "as lightly as two thoughts" from one world to another, the security of each individual world is at stake (*BW*, 190). The glorious power of the literary imagination gives each individual the power to construct a world and, thus, to threaten others' worlds. If every individual – or even every sovereign nation – can construct a world, each world in fact becomes part of a larger whole.[48] The text asks this question directly: Is "man a little world?" it wonders (*BW*, 169). We more commonly hear its cousin, also relevant given the topography of the

Blazing World: whether every man is (or no man is) an island. In this collapsing of the individual and the world, the text's central conflict can be seen, whereby the freedom inherent in matter – and that is central to emergent liberal political theory – comes into conflict with the protection that secular worlds demand – and thus with the postsecular conservative worldview that follows, in Cavendish's case, from this.

The Blazing World, like all worlds, is made up of "parts." On a textual level, this partitioning relates not only to the philosophical and literary texts but also to the two highly unequal parts of the literary text. The first part, by far the longest (making up about eighty percent of the whole), fulfills the promise of the title by being mainly description; the governing actions, such as they are, of the Empress are revoked by the end and the imaginary worlds easily dissolved, leaving the Blazing World – as well as the worlds of Margaret Cavendish (fictional and real) – more or less as it was when the protagonist arrived. The much shorter second part, by contrast, is a fast-paced tale of massive military innovation and destruction. Elaborate planning allows the Empress to travel to her original world, where the nation of her nativity is besieged by enemies. The problem in this world is precisely that it is partitioned into "several sovereign governments" (*BW*, 189). The Empress solves this problem by exploiting the physical realities and the knowledge of her Blazing World: The firestone that allows water to burn (in the Blazing World) proves militarily as well as spectacularly useful when transported to this other world, and the telescopes of the bear men that were divisive in the singular Blazing World prove useful in military affairs in this divisive world. In a relentless series of sieges, which rely on equal parts science, spectacle, and the Empress' command of her diverse troops, the Empress routes out all the enemies – actual and potential – of her native land, bringing all other inhabitants of that world into submission, that is, into one world, which is monitored and symbolized by the tribute they must all pay to the sovereign.

Thus, the text's celebrated exploration of literary world-creation offers a view of the literary imagination as producing the experience of the world not as parts but as a whole and at the same time as producing a recognition of the limits of the human imagination: As self-moving rational matter itself, the literary imagination can only produce vitalistic worlds that resemble our own – worlds that are close to it and that, therefore, threaten it. This is how Cavendish refutes political solutions, such as those of Hobbes, that rely on *ex nihilo* creation of a body politic, because they violate the laws of nature that are discoverable in the literary imagination. This is perhaps why Cavendish's Blazing World is not separate from the real world but rather connected to the globe of earth, discovered accidently by a woman fleeing violence and entered accidently because of the natural law of magnetic poles. The literary imagination can experience the unity and the thoroughgoing materiality of the world that we experience as diverse, and thus it can manage – via figuration – the "opinions" that are produced by these natural laws but that create religio-political strife. But in the end, Cavendish's text produces a very ambivalent attitude toward toleration and early liberalism: The literary imagination both understands the inevitability of diversity of opinion (thus of worlds) and fails to imagine a solution other than state violence.[49]

Actual, Possible, and Fictional Worlds

In order to contextualize Cavendish's resolution to the relationships among worlds, violence, and the literary imagination, it might help to compare her with Gottfried Wilhelm Leibniz's later and more famous meditation on these relationships. In his *Theodicy* (1710) Leibniz's resolution to the question of evil hinges on a theory of possible worlds: Evil can be accounted for (and God's benevolence redeemed) by recognizing that, despite evil, this is the best of all possible worlds.[50] Leibniz's culminating example involves a fable about the founding of Rome and the evil that Sextus Tarquin committed by raping Lucretia. Leibniz's story compares the possible world in which Sextus lives a happy life – Lucretia's life, happiness, and suffering are shockingly uninteresting to Leibniz – with the actual world. In the actual world, the good produced by Sextus' "wicked" "crime" is evident both in the beauty of the pyramid that represents all possible worlds (with the actual one its culmination) and by the generalization that Roman civilization was crucial to making our world the best possible world: "[T]he crime of Sextus serves for great things: it renders Rome free; thence will arise a great empire, which will show noble examples to mankind."[51] For Leibniz, possible worlds exist in the real world only through fiction: A "skilled writer of fiction" can delve into situations "not impossible" (93), but these possible worlds will necessarily be inferior to the actual world. This is why in order to explain his theory of possible worlds, Leibniz must resort to, and apologize for doing so, fables that imagine different worlds for Sextus (and others).[52] "Fiction for fiction" is Leibniz's method, as well an apology for engaging in fictionalizing.[53] Leibniz's political argument is proto-conservative in several respects. Sextus' possible worlds prove that the choice is not between worlds but between the world and the individual – individual happiness

Figuring: Margaret Cavendish's Critique of Imagining

(and perhaps especially female happiness) is sacrificed for the world. This is the central insight of Leibniz's theodicy, which posits God as an architect of a political system that favors the greater good, and it is Leibniz's case for refuting secular thinkers who extoll human ethical, epistemological, and political accomplishments. Whereas Hobbes and Spinoza, according to Leibniz, argue that "wisdom, goodness, justice are only fictions in relation to God," and this constitutes, presumably, their case for human secular political culture, Leibniz puts individual happiness and agency on the side of fiction.[54] For Leibniz, fiction is merely the exploration of possible worlds that are individualistic and thus inherently inferior to the real world. As such, the violence necessary in the real world is justified by the greater good in that world compared with any other possible world. This might provide some context not only for Cavendish's difference from Leibniz but also for Leibniz's response to 1688–89 – in which he argued that the legal right to require obedience derives from a sovereign's ability to provide protection.[55]

The seventeenth-century fascination with the concept of the world, which always entails grappling with other worlds – whether real, possible, or imagined – registers something about how political groups, both within and among sovereign states, can be potentially managed. Cavendish situates her meditation on this question within scientific debates about parts and wholes and uses it to explore the function and the limits of the literary imagination. She is exploring the kinds of questions – about nation-state relations in an increasingly global economy, about balancing individual freedoms and sovereign power, and about the relationship between literature and politics – that will become flash points after the Restoration. Jürgen Habermas, one of the central architects of the secularization thesis – and also someone who has partially recanted it – argues that the concept of "the public" replaces the idea of the world beginning in mid-seventeenth-century England.[56] Michael Warner expands this thesis by pointing out a curious thing about the concept of public: It is infinitely pluralizable, and yet it masks this capacity by always appearing in the singular. As Warner puts it, "a public, in practice, appears as the public."[57] This capacity of the concept of public is why it is central to democracy, to managing the diversity inherent to the liberal world with a sleight of hand, similar to but less concrete than Hobbes' Leviathan (as discussed in Chapter 1), that makes plurality into singularity. The concept of the world, at least as far as Cavendish (and Leibniz too) deploys it, works in the opposite way: it appears as something pluralizable (other worlds) but in fact resolves into the normativity of one world. For Leibniz, the thought experiment of possible worlds reassures the thinker that our world is not only the real world but also, despite its violence, the best of all possible worlds. For Cavendish, something more complicated happens: she imagines – or figures – a world that is at once more singular and more peaceful than her real world. The possibility of doubling expressed in the text's title and its paired publication (with the *Observations*) resolves into the reality that the two worlds are inextricable: The natural world and the political world are not just connected but mutually informing, and so too the world of reality and the imagination. The possible worlds of the imagination may be more peaceful than the real world(s), and worlds may appear whole and singular, but worlds are inevitably tethered to other worlds, and thus one cannot escape the natural laws of the globe or of the mind.

Cavendish, however much she insists on the connection between real worlds and imaginary ones, nonetheless puts so much more narrative and imaginative energy into her fictional world that one might conjecture that the fictional world exists merely to shed light on just how un-ideal the real world is. The eighty percent of the text devoted to the Blazing World and produced by the imagination of a very singular woman (who imagines women both more powerful and more content in the Blazing World than in the actual world) is not superseded, if the record of critical readings of the *Blazing World* can be taken as evidence, in readers' minds by the second part, in which the conflict between worlds – and the discrepancy between the literary imagination and the real world – is rectified (and erased) by state violence. The analysis in this chapter contradicts critics who have read a feminist utopian possibility in Cavendish's literary imagination of worlds and rather posits figuration as the way that the imagination – following vitalistic and monistic laws of nature – works to underscore the limits of human political agency and the inevitability of violence. This is the case for the conservative Cavendish. But perhaps it is possible to reconcile these readings with mine: The literary world (in this case the Blazing one) is not, as in Leibniz, inferior to the actual world – in fact it is superior. Cavendish's possible Blazing World, figured as it is and as it only can be, as a simile for the real world, is nonetheless more peaceful. This is Cavendish's justification for state violence (in the real world) and intolerance (in the imaginary one) but also perhaps for the function of the literary imagination. Given that Cavendish's imagined world is more peaceful than her actual world, the literary imagination may serve a purpose, both for the individual and the collective, in the real world. Cavendish, that is, unlike Leibniz, allows for the possibility – in fact she imagines it in vivid detail – that imaginary worlds could impact the actual world for the better, or at least could offer a temporary alternative in the fantasy of human imaginative agency. But this possible reading of Cavendish is ultimately no more convincing or real than her Blazing World. I turn in Chapter 4 from imagined worlds to imagined readers and thus to the imagination of literary history, a different way of thinking about how the literary field grapples with questions of forming communities. Like Cavendish, Dryden used exile from the center of political power to experiment in literary form in order to explore the limits of human knowledge and power and to imagine how human communities can, given those limits, be imagined by literature, and reading in particular.

Notes

1 Following current scholarly convention, I will use her married name, Cavendish, throughout.
2 On the importance of "worldviews" to both liberalism and conservatism, see George Lakoff, *Moral Politics: How Liberals and Conservatives Think*, 2nd ed. (Chicago: University of Chicago Press, 2010), 24–40.
3 Margaret Cavendish, *The Blazing World and Other Writings*, ed. Kate Lilley (London: Penguin, 1992). Hereafter abbreviated to *BW*. All further references will be to this edition, unless otherwise stated.
4 On the seventeenth-century conception of worlds and universes, and its impact on the literary imagination, see Mary Baine Campbell, *Wonder and Science: Imagining Worlds in Early Modern Europe* (Ithaca, NY: Cornell University Press, 2004). She situates Cavendish within the early modern "impulse to bring a world into imagined being" and the literary tradition that this impulse spurred (Campbell, *Wonder*, 185). There were many manifestations of this tradition, with different emphases. For example, compared with Robert Hooke's *Micrographia*, whose microscope figures the internal, domestic world, Cavendish is exploring the larger political dimensions of this literary tradition. *Micrographia, or, Some Physiological Descriptions of Minute Bodies Made by Magnifying Glasses: With Observations and Inquiries Thereupon* (London: Printed by J. Martyn and J. Allestry, 1665). On the tradition of possible worlds as a species of counterfactual thinking that typically supports theodicy, see Catherine Gallagher, *Telling It Like It Wasn't: The Counterfactual Imagination in History and Fiction* (Chicago: University of Chicago Press, 2018), 16–47.
5 Margaret Cavendish, *Observations upon Experimental Philosophy*. Cambridge Texts in the History of Philosophy (Cambridge: Cambridge University Press, 2001). Hereafter abbreviated *OEP* for the purposes of citation. On the significance of description to eighteenth-century epistemology, see Joanna Stalnaker, "Description and the Nonhuman View of Nature," *Representations* 135, no. 1 (2016): 72–88; and Cynthia Wall, *The Prose of*

Things (Chicago: University of Chicago Press, 2014). Stalnaker's analysis of Georges Cuvier gets at my point about Cavendish, for whom "Description" in the title suggests "broad sweeping view" of the world, which does not privilege human perspective ("Description and the Nonhuman View of Nature," 75).

6 From the dedication "To All Worthy and Noble Ladies" in the 1668 edition of *The Blazing World*, when *The Blazing World* was published separately (Boston: Northeastern University Women Writers Project, 2002).

7 Eric Hayot, *On Literary Worlds* (Oxford: Oxford University Press, 2012); Martin Heidegger, "The Origin of the Work of Art," in *Poetry, Language, Thought*, trans. Albert Hofstader (New York: Harper & Row, 1971), 15–73.

8 For feminist readings of Cavendish that celebrate these world-creating gestures, see Sylvia Bowerbank, "The Spider's Delight: Margaret Cavendish and the 'Female' Imagination," *English Literary Renaissance* 14, no. 3 (1984): 392–408; Catherine Gallagher, "Embracing the Absolute: The Politics of the Female Subject in Seventeenth-Century England," *Genders* 1 (March 1988): 24–29; Elaine Hobby, *Virtue of Necessity: English Women's Writing, 1646–1688* (Ann Arbor: University of Michigan Press, 1989); Rosemary Kegl, "The World I Have Made: Margaret Cavendish, Feminism, and the *Blazing World*," *Feminist Readings of Early Modern Culture: Emerging Subjects*, eds. Valerie Traub et al. (Cambridge: Cambridge University Press, 1996), 119–41; Lisa Sarasohn, *The Natural Philosophy of Margaret Cavendish: Reason and Fancy during the Scientific Revolution* (Baltimore: Johns Hopkins University Press, 2010); and Rachel Trubowitz, "The Reenchantment of Utopia and the Female Monarchical Self," *Tulsa Studies in Women's Literature* 11, no. 2 (1992): 229–45. I am reading against this tendency in Cavendish studies to read her as proto-feminist – not because I question the validity of her early feminist tendencies, but because I think such approaches obscure the more conservative aspects of her writing.

9 As I mentioned in the Introduction, "conservative" is anachronistic – there would be no full-blown ideology of conservatism until the nineteenth century. I use this term here colloquially to indicate what it is that critics, typically liberal, find distasteful about Cavendish's politics: monarchism, Catholicism, and, in the case of the *Blazing World*, intolerance. But Mannheim's larger points about conservative thought are consonant with my argument about Cavendish. For Mannheim, conservative thought is marked by "intuitive, qualitative, concrete forms of thought," which oppose the kind of rationalizations and generalizations that mark liberal thinking and that are generally consistent with the idea of a "world" view. Karl Mannheim, "Conservative Thought," *From Karl Mannheim*, ed. Kurt H. Wolff (New York: Oxford University Press, 1971), 273.

10 Charles, England and Wales, Sovereign. *His Majesties Gracious Letter and Declaration Sent to the House of Peers: By Sir John Greenvill, Kt. from Breda, and Read in the House the First of May, 1660* (London: Printed by John Macock and Francis Tyton, 1660), 9–10. Its discussion of the elimination of "discord, separation and difference of parties" promotes political unity, not

the toleration of political and social diversity that we have come to know as toleration, but it was an important step in defining the state's key stake in what we now call toleration and also secularization: Difference of opinion in religion was to be separated from politics (ibid., 12).
11 Charles, *His Majesties Gracious Letter*, 12. Similar language, but with an important difference in which freedom of religion is just example and not exception, appears in the *Declaration of the Rights of Man and the Citizen* adopted by French assembly during the French revolution: "No-one shall be interfered with for his opinions, even religious ones, provided that their practice does not disturb public order as established by the law" (*Declaration of the Right of Man and the Citizen*, France, August 26, 1789).
12 Charles issued the *Royal Declaration of Indulgence* in 1672 but was forced to withdraw it in 1673. James II's move in 1687 to issue an even more capacious indulgence precipitated his downfall in 1688 and also William's *The Act of Toleration in 1689 (King William's Toleration: Being an Explanation of that Liberty of Religion, Which May Be Expected from His Majesty's Declaration. With a Bill for Comprehension & Indulgence, Drawn Up in Order to an Act of Parliament*. London: Printed for Robert Hayhurst, at the sign of the Axe, in Little Britain, 1689). Parallel events were happening with the Huguenots in France. Charles' motives for promoting religious tolerance have always been suspect. I speak here more to his rhetoric than his motives. For more on this topic, see Chapter 2.
13 I am grateful to Alison Conway for helping to understand this problem and this history in these terms.
14 See Scott Sowerby, *Making Toleration: The Repealers and the Glorious Revolution* (Cambridge, MA: Harvard University Press, 2013), 59. Sowerby observes that granting freedom of conscience was perhaps even a way that the Stuarts endeavored to strengthen monarchy.
15 Elena Russo, "How to Handle the Intolerant: The Education of Pierre Bayle," in *Imagining Religious Toleration: A Literary History of an Idea, 1600–1830*, eds. Alison Conway and David Alvarez (Toronto: University of Toronto Press, 2019), 119–35.
16 For a sense of the long history of this problem in philosophy, see the essays in Ann Ward, ed., *Matter and Form: From Natural Science to Political Philosophy* (Lanham, MD: Rowman & Littlefield, 2009).
17 The obverse of this movement, and synergistic with it, is the imagining of nature as matter that, once its rules are understood, could be managed and manipulated. Francis Bacon is credited with the strong articulation of this idea, which has been the subject of much scholarly critique. Cavendish, and my argument about her take on worlds, can also be seen as in conversation with Baruch Spinoza and Leibniz. As Garth Kemerling puts it, "Spinoza saw the world as a single comprehensive substance like Descartes's extended matter, while, Leibniz supposed that the world is composed of many discrete particles, each of which is simple, active, and independent of every other, like Descartes's minds or souls" (https://brewminate.com/early-modern-philoso

phy-spinoza-and-leibniz/). My argument about Cavendish positions her between these two views, though the philosophical and political nuances of this possible connection are beyond the scope of this essay.

18 This assumption persists in the twenty-first century, as exemplified by trends in new materialism and object-oriented ontology. See, for example, Jane Bennett, *Vibrant Matter: A Political Ecology of Things* (Durham, NC: Duke University Press, 2009); Karen Barad, *Meeting the Universe Halfway: Quantum Physics and the Entanglement of Matter and Meaning* (Durham, NC: Duke University Press, 2007); Graham Harmon, "The Well-Wrought Broken Hammer: Object-Oriented Literary Criticism," *New Literary History* 43, no. 2 (2012): 183–203; and the essays in Diana Coole and Samantha Frost, *New Materialisms: Ontology, Agency, and Politics* (Durham, NC: Duke University Press, 2010). We might ask why and when thinkers take this approach and what its limitations are (a question Colin Jager posed to me when I presented this paper). Answering it is beyond the scope of this essay, but I do think my argument here counters such critical trends that assume natural science and politics can be solved together, by showing the dead end of Cavendish's approach to this problem.

19 Samuel Pepys, *The Diary of Samuel Pepys*, vol. 9, *1668–1669*, eds. Robert Latham and William Mathews (London: G. Bell & Sons, 1970), 123. For context on this event, see Samuel I. Mintz, "The Duchess of Newcastle's Visit to the Royal Society," *Journal of English and Germanic Philology* 51, no. 2 (April 1952): 168–76.

20 On Cavendish's self-representation as a solitary genius, see James Fitzmaurice, "Fancy and the Family: Self-Characterizations of Margaret Cavendish," *The Huntington Library Quarterly* 53, no. 3 (1990): 199–209.

21 Gallagher accounts for Cavendish's commitment to absolutism as a means of imagining autonomous subjectivity for a woman, in Gallagher, "Embracing the Absolute." Trubowitz builds on this argument by arguing that the "competing demands of radical feminism and social conservatism" account for Cavendish's generic innovations, in "The Reenchantment of Utopia and the Female Monarchical Self: Margaret *Cavendish's Blazing World*," *Tulsa Studies in Women's Literature* 11, no. 2 (1992): 229.

22 For a post-humanist reading of *The Blazing World*, see Aaron R. Hanlon, "Margaret Cavendish's Anthropocene Worlds," *New Literary History* 47, no. 1 (2016): 49–66. For Cavendish's critique of subject/object relations, see Eve Keller, "Producing Petty Gods: Margaret Cavendish's Critique of Experimental Science," *ELH* 64, no. 2 (1997): 447–71. For her general critique of the Royal Society, see Anna Battigelli, *Margaret Cavendish and the Exiles of the Mind* (Lexington: University Press of Kentucky, 2015). On her vitalism see John Rogers, *The Matter of Revolution: Science, Poetry, and Politics in the Age of Milton* (Ithaca, NY: Cornell University Press, 1998).

23 Alexandra Bennett, "Margaret Cavendish and the Theatre of War," in *Margaret Cavendish*, ed. Sara Heller Mendelson (Farnham: Ashgate, 2009), 103.

24 Cavendish reflects on the implications of England being an island nation in "An Oration concerning Shipping," in *Margaret Cavendish: Political Writings*, ed. Susan James (Cambridge: Cambridge University Press, 2003), 137–38.
25 Deborah Boyle, "Margaret Cavendish on Perception, Self-Knowledge, and Probable Opinion," *Philosophy Compass* 10, no. 7 (2015): 438–50. In Boyle's account, Cavendish's philosophy does not equate all opinions (some are more probable than others), but I think Cavendish, especially in The Blazing World is engaged in thinking about the political problem, not just the epistemological one, of difference of opinion.
26 Peter Dear, "A Philosophical Duchess: Understanding Margaret Cavendish and the Royal Society," in *Science, Literature and Rhetoric in Early Modern England*, eds. Juliet Cummins and David Burchell (Aldershot: Ashgate, 2007), 130.
27 For a helpful introduction to the problem of vitalist politics with respect to new materialism (and hence also seventeenth-century materialism) see the introduction to *The New Politics of Materialism: History, Philosophy, Science*, eds. Sarah Ellenzweig and John H. Zammito (Oxfordshire: Routledge, 2017).
28 For examples of the way that critics locate a feminist politics in her vitalist science, see Lisa Sarasohn, who takes Cavendish as describing "the freedom that inheres in matter" (*The Natural Philosophy of Margaret Cavendish*, 91–92); John Rogers, who argues that seventeenth-century vitalism "necessitated feminism" (*The Matter of Revolution*, 15); and Gabrielle Starr, who links Cavendish's vitalism to her anti-Platonic aesthetics, grounding both in her situation as a woman ("Cavendish, Aesthetics, and the Anti-Platonic Line," *Eighteenth-Century Studies* 39, no. 3 [Spring 2006]: 295–30). The potential of vitalism for liberation is once again, in the twenty-first century, something of a critical darling – see, for example, Jane Bennett (*Vibrant Matter*). Speculating about this longer tradition is beyond the scope of this essay, but I can suggest that then and now, vitalism offers a means to measure the success or failure of liberal politics, including toleration, or to leverage its yet unrealized possibilities. But more to my point, vitalism has been a way to redeem the more unseemly aspects of Cavendish's politics: her monarchism or even absolutism.
29 Benjamin Kaplan, *Divided by Faith: Religious Conflict and the Practice of Toleration in Early Modern Europe* (Cambridge, MA: Harvard University Press, 2007), 8. Kaplan's approach to toleration comes close to how I am reading Cavendish here: toleration is typically seen as philosophical (enlightenment theory) or political (government action) but he takes it up as a practice – a habit of peaceful coexistence (ibid., 8).
30 Battigelli, *Margaret Cavendish and Exiles of the Mind*, 61–65.
31 Alan Ryan, "Hobbes, Toleration, and the Inner Life," in *The Nature of Political Theory*, eds. David Miller and Larry Siendentop (Oxford; New York: Clarendon Press, 1983), 215–17. Ryan argues that while Hobbes does not seem to have much to say about the "inner life," he nonetheless offers an argument for toleration – one based on epistemological not moral reasons: The sovereign is bound by expediency and it is impossible to get people to

agree on everything – to completely control what they think. Therefore, there is no point in trying ("Hobbes," 217). Though Hobbes argues for "real Unitie" there is "no submergence of individual substances in some superior whole."

32 If we take John Locke as exemplary of the tradition of British empiricism, he defines what we know as analysis thusly: "[A]ll our complex Ideas are ultimately resolvable into simple Ideas, of which they are compounded, and originally made, though perhaps their immediate Ingredients, as I may so say, are also complex Ideas." John Locke, *An Essay Concerning Human Understanding*, 4th ed., ed. P.H. Nidditch (Oxford: Oxford University Press, 1975), xxii, 9). So analysis is the reverse of amalgamation – but both are processes that in Locke's terms involve "combining" or "composing" (or their reverse). Gottfried Leibniz is also interesting here. In trying to explain how a subject/predicate can be reduced to an "identity," he explains the "great value" of algebra (i.e., the "art of symbols") consists in the way it "unburdens the imagination." Gottfried Wilhelm Leibniz, *New Essays on Human Understanding*, trans. and ed. Peter Remnant and Jonathan Bennett (Cambridge: Cambridge University Press, 1981), IV.xvii. 487–88. Immanuel Kant defines synthesis as unification of a concept with another not contained in it – he distinguishes analysis from synthesis on the basis that synthesis produces new knowledge. Immanuel Kant, *Critique of Pure Reason*, 1st ed., 1781, 2nd ed., 1787, trans. Paul Guyer and Allen W. Wood (Cambridge: Cambridge University Press, 1997). While these enlightenment definitions are revealing, a full consideration of their relevance to Cavendish is beyond the scope of this essay. Here I am taking synthesis as much less philosophically specific, as a general concept of knowledge that exceeds analysis or amalgamation, that includes the more specific concept of figuration, and that also in Cavendish's case, contra Leibniz, involves the imagination.

33 See Chapter 2 for analysis of the distinction between indulgence and toleration.

34 These other worlds, those that are not the Blazing World, are called "E" and "ESFI." Both are imagined doubles of England – The Duchess calls her world the "Blinking world of Wit" (*BW*, 220).

35 Anne Thell argues in a related line that for Cavendish the imagination "is a potent generative force that supersedes sense perception yet also remains material," in "'[A]s Lightly as Two Thoughts': Motion, Materialism, and Cavendish's *Blazing World*," *Configurations* 23, no. 1 (2015): 17.

36 For Oddvar Holmesland, Cavendish's idea of unity is based in nature (not in worlds). For him the phrase "nature tends to Unity" means that the imagination is capable of communing with nature, being composed of natural motions. Oddvar Holmesland, *Utopian Negotiation: Aphra Behn and Margaret Cavendish* (Syracuse, NY: Syracuse University Press, 2013), 97.

37 For an incisive reading of Cavendish's narrative strategies and their relation to diversity of opinion, see Battigelli, *Margaret Cavendish and Exiles of the Mind*, 73–80.

38 "Orations of Divers Sorts, Accommodated to Divers Places," in *Margaret Cavendish, Political Writings*, ed. Susan James (Cambridge: Cambridge University Press, 2003), 168.
39 Heidegger, "The Origin of the Work of Art," 144. I recognize that the theories of Heidegger – along with Cavendish – are problematic to a liberal perspective. Heidegger's politics – and their relation to the world-domination aspirations of Nazi Germany – have been the subject of no small amount of criticism, so I will not rehearse that argument here, except to say that insofar as my reading of "worlds" in Cavendish relates to Heidegger, then I side with those who cannot separate his aesthetic, philosophical, and political theories and activities, just as I cannot separate Cavendish's conservatism and her literary innovation.
40 For these multiple denotations, see the *OED*. For a discussion of the critical tradition, see Wade Sikorski, "Toleration and Shamanism," *New Political Science* 13, no. 1 (1993): 3–20.
41 Emmanuel Levinas, *Totality and Infinity: An Essay on Exteriority*, trans. Alphonso Lingis (Dordrecht: Kluwer, 1991), see especially 130–35. In comparing Levinas and Heidegger on the question of totality, Graham Harmon invokes the idea, relevant for my point about the geography of the Blazing World, of islands as spaces where the totalizing force of worlds can be escaped. For Levinas (unlike Heidegger), Harmon claims, "the tool-system is riddled with gaps and tropical islands where individual things take shape for our enjoyment" ("Levinas and the Triple Critique of Heidegger," *Philosophy Today* 53, no. 4 [2009]: 409).
42 Jacques Derrida, "Violence and Metaphysics," in *Writing and Difference*, trans. Alan Bass (London: Routledge, 1978), 133.
43 Gilles Deleuze and Félix Guattari, *What Is Philosophy?* (New York: Columbia University Press, 2014), 17.
44 The larger scholarly conversations about "world literature" and the critiques of universal cosmopolitanism (as, in Kant's words, the means to perpetual peace) would be avenues to take these questions further, though it is beyond the scope of this essay. On world literature see Emily Apter, *Against World Literature: On the Politics of Untranslatability* (London: Verso Books, 2014); Amir Mufti, *Forget English!: Orientalisms and World Literature* (Cambridge, MA: Harvard University Press, 2016); and Gayatri Spivak, "Rethinking-Comparativism," *New Literary History*, 40, no. 3 (2009): 609–26. On cosmopolitanism, see Kwame Anthony Appiah, *Cosmopolitanism: Ethics in a World of Strangers (Issues of Our Time)* (New York: W. W. Norton & Company, 2010); Seyla Benhabib, *Another Cosmopolitanism* (Oxford: Oxford University Press, 2008); Jacques Derrida, *On Cosmopolitanism and Forgiveness*, trans. Mark Dooley and Michael Hughes (London: Routledge, 2001); Eddy Kent and Terri Tomsky, *Negative Cosmopolitanism* (Montreal: McGill-Queen's University Press, 2017); and Mufti, *Forget English!*
45 Hayot, *On Literary Worlds*, 108.

46 Pheng Cheah, *What Is a World?: On Postcolonial Literature as World Literature* (Durham, NC: Duke University Press, 2016).
47 I am not taking a position on the feasibility of any of these positions. I will say that my concern about Hayot's argument is that it relies on a limited notion of the literary "worlds" (with its centrality of the concepts of Realism, Romanticism, and Modernism) in ways that seem unlikely to be able to address the problems of diversity of opinion and worlds in either the seventeenth or the twenty-first century. Cheah's argument, with its championing of postcolonial literature as the site of reimagining the "world" of "global" capitalism offers a more politically appealing locus of literary world reimagining, but I, like Cavendish, tend to be more skeptical about claiming such wholescale powers for the literary imagination.
48 Susan Mendus identifies the roots of toleration as respect for the other person, as it is supported by the Kantian imperative, in the Introduction to *Justifying Toleration: Conceptual and Historical Perspectives* (Cambridge: Cambridge University Press, 1988). Kobi Assoulin glosses this imperative as the demand for subjects to "[r]ecogniz[e] the other as an autonomous entity, who is entitled to shape her *private world*," in "Beyond 'Good': Richard Rorty's Private Sphere and Toleration," *Iyyun: The Jerusalem Philosophical Quarterly* 60 (January 2011): 63, emphasis mine. So this world-creating faculty that *The Blazing World* celebrates is also the fundamental problem of toleration.
49 Geraldine Wagner, *"Romancing Multiplicity*: Female Subjectivity and the Body Divisible in Margaret *Cavendish's Blazing World*," *Early Modern Literary Studies* 9, no. 1 (2003): 1–59; B. R. Siegfried, "The City of Chance, or, Margaret Cavendish's Theory of Radical Symmetry," *Early Modern Literary Studies*, Special Issue 14 (2004): n.p. Critical solutions to the violence at the end of the text have been, to my mind, unsatisfactory and based on a desire to preserve Cavendish as an avatar of female modernity. Geraldine Wagner, for example, argues "although Margaret and her characters have trouble escaping this oppressive dialectic of domination and submission (they repeatedly assume the roles of conquerors and rulers), the text shows a way out by constructing the self as multiple" (Wagner, "*Romancing Multiplicity*," 59). According to John Rogers, Cavendish engages "the science of animist materialism with the unembarrassed intention of exploring the revolutionary potential of its antipatriarchal logic" (*The Matter of Revolution*, 181). For B. R. Siegfried, "Singularity makes good on the promise of liberty and Cavendish's seeming autocracy is precisely because people have agency" (Siegfried, "The City of Chance," para. 29).
50 Gottfried Wilhelm Leibniz, *Theodicy: Essays on the Goodness of God, the Freedom of Man and the Origin of Evil*, ed. Austin Farrer, and trans. E. M. Huggard (New Haven, CT: Yale University Press, 1952).
51 Ibid., 372–73.
52 Ibid., 93.
53 Ibid., preface, 72.

54 Gottfried Wilhelm Leibniz, "Reflexions on the Work that Mr. Hobbes Published in English on 'Freedom, Necessity and Chance,'" in *Theodicy: Essays on the Goodness of God, the Freedom of Man and the Origin of Evil*, eds. Austin Farrer, and trans. E. M. Huggard (New Haven, CT: Yale University Press, 1952), 393–404, 399.

55 On this issue, see Nicholas Jolley, "Leibniz on Hobbes, Locke's Two Treatises and Sherlock's Case of Allegiance," *The Historical Journal* 18, no. 1 (1975): 21–35. Jolly states that for Leibniz, "The creation of political society must be understood in terms of divine intervention: it cannot be given a purely secular interpretation" (32).

56 Jürgen Habermas, *The Structural Transformation of the Public Sphere: An Inquiry into a Category of Bourgeois Society* (Cambridge, MA: MIT Press, 1989), 26. Recently, Habermas' writing has taken a decidedly postsecular turn, in asking "what is missing" from civil society. See Jürgen Habermas, *An Awareness of What Is Missing: Faith and Reason in a Post-Secular Age* (Cambridge: Polity, 2010).

57 Michael Warner, "Publics and Counterpublics," *Public Culture* 14, no. 1 (2002): 51. Warner ends up connecting publics and worlds, arguing that the "embodied creativity" of publics is linked to its "world-making" power (54) and that "writing to a public helps to make a world" (64).

CHAPTER 4

Reading
John Dryden's Postsecular Apostolic and the Time of Literary History

John Dryden (1631–1700) was the Restoration's poet laureate and most prolific playwright, England's first modern literary critic, and one of English Catholicism's most famous converts. His was a remarkably varied literary career, at once shaped by and creatively responsive to the political events of the Restoration. Dryden's trajectory was politically and religiously conservative if not downright perversely anachronistic; according to his detractors he wound up on the wrong side of history by converting from Puritanism to Anglicanism to Catholicism.[1] With these conversions, Dryden moved in a historically retrograde manner along the spectrum of available seventeenth-century politico-religious models, beginning with the most modern and winding up, by the end of the Restoration, with the most medieval, or the most conservative. Such movement was not only historically retrograde but retrograde about history itself, for while his era moved inexorably toward a whiggish, progressivist, and secular worldview, Dryden retreated, at least as far as his Catholicism goes, to a worldview that preceded modern conceptions of history. Thus, it is somewhat ironic that Dryden was, as Samuel Johnson pronounced, the father of modern literary criticism and that one of his most enduring contributions to literary criticism was the very idea of literary history.[2] Dryden began to conceive of nature as historical, and, according to Earl Miner, he developed modes of comparison that are key to critical techniques employed in our own age of secularization; according to Miner, the idea of an "age" is Dryden's own, and thus Dryden is the exemplar not only of the "Age of Dryden" but also of the modern secular notion of historical "ages," an idea that was literary before it was historical.[3] Both Poet Laureate and Historiographer Royale, Dryden was at the forefront of thinking about how literature and history would come to relate in modernity and how reading might mediate this.

Historical events transformed Dryden's own political and religious views, most notoriously in his conversion to Catholicism, in tandem with

James II's ascension in 1685, and his literary career followed suit. The Exclusion Crisis of 1678–81 and the dynastic disruption of 1688–89 were watershed moments that put Dryden permanently outside the ruling party and state religion, necessitating changes in his profession and practice of literature. Dryden's later-life translations and fables are his most famous post-conversion productions, but I focus here on Dryden's mid-career writings of the 1680s, with a particular emphasis on Dryden's deployment of allegory and the modes of interpretation it makes possible. The confessional debates in which Dryden embroils himself hinge on questions of how to read and interpret scripture. In a variety of ways, Dryden tries to secularize these sacred literary practices, but I read this ostensibly secularizing process as postsecular, translating Catholic practices of reading into a postsecular practice. His mid-career literary experiments employ allegorical forms congruent with older religious models of time, causation, and agency. Political typology, beast fable, and heroic tragicomedy all fall loosely under the category of allegory, but Dryden experiments with these allegorical literary forms in ways that inaugurate a new literary age and new models of reading and interpretation. While allegory was a medieval form based on a view of time as cyclical, Dryden's experiments remake allegory as a means for defining how one historical age relates to or communes with another, as well as how individual readers might use the literary past to interpret and even to live their lives.[4] He adapts a form that had always presumed a reading method based on uncovering increasingly important levels of meaning and adapts it for a secular world. In short, over the course of the 1680s, Dryden was working out the transformation from sacred to secular reading practices. To explore this hypothesis, we will turn first to two poems *Absalom and Achitophel* (1681) and *The Hind and the Panther* (1687), which take an innovative approach to allegory and allegoresis. We will then look at his heroic tragicomedy *Don Sebastian* (1689), with which Dryden begins to articulate a theory of a modern postsecular reading practice.

During the 1680s, as he sought to develop alternatives to both emergent secular political narratives and residual cosmological views, Dryden experimented with the genres and modes of allegory and tragicomedy. In these writings, the past is not fossilized, disavowed, or sentimentalized, and the present does not reliably repeat the past in a natural cycle or in a typological fashion that can be interpreted via biblical hermeneutics. Dryden's practices of literature and literary criticism make sense of time in nonchronological ways and of causation in a non-linear fashion. This view of temporality (which we might call *literary time*) is committed to the complexity of a material, archeological, embodied, and coded past requiring living interpreters. It demands a reading practice committed to materiality, complexity, mystery, and participation rather than to transcendent meaning or causation. I will call Dryden's vision of literary time and meaning "postsecular apostolic," to indicate a literary aesthetic and a hermeneutic practice that are social, historical, and embodied. Dryden's proposed practice of reading is postsecular in that it resembles the sacred theories it displaces but without recourse to a transcendent beginning or ending. It is apostolic because it depends upon a historical community of interpreters that is embodied and temporal in ways that differ from the religious models being supplanted as well as from the Whig interpretation of history and politics with which his views are coterminous.

How "Latter Ages on Former Wait": Allegory and Literary History in *Absalom and Achitophel* and *The Hind and the Panther*

Absalom and Achitophel (1681) employs the story of the rebellion of Absalom against King David as told in the Old Testament Second Book of Samuel to forge a representation of the Exclusion Crisis, which was an attempt to exclude the Stuart heir James II from the throne. Biblical history forms the vehicle for a tightly constructed representation of current events by which the poem explores allegory's relevance to contemporary history; the poem is also a political act designed to affect the Exclusion Crisis. The tension between allegory and political action gives the poem its unique energy. According to Steven Zwicker, Dryden's political typology attempts to show "how the present day embodies the past and, through that association, comes itself to participate in an eternal repetition of the events that the Bible records."[5] But the typological repetition in *Absalom and Achitophel* is decidedly not sacred – it renders the anti-Stuart revolutionaries simultaneously unoriginal and on the wrong side of biblical history. And as political allegory it is somewhat oxymoronic: Dryden's attempts to make the poem didactic or rhetorical for purposes of political impact are to some extent stymied by its typological structure. The intense energy in the famous opening lines reflects this tension:

> In pious times, ere priestcraft did begin,
> Before polygamy was made a sin;
> When man on many multiplied his kind,
> Ere one to one was cursedly confined;
> When nature prompted, and no law denied,
> Promiscuous use of concubine and bride;
> (1–6)

This opening signals both historical difference (the "pious Times" are differentiated from the time of "sin and law") and, via its exuberant alliteration, an unchanging cycle in which events repeat. But the repetition is based in human rather than divine nature: Like David and Absalom, King Charles is promiscuous and his illegitimate son Monmouth is a rebel. The poem opens with language that insists on historical difference – different "times" – but this is a secular view that posits even biblical time as historically contingent. The poem treats biblical narrative as history, a key way that the bible was secularized under the reformation.[6] As a "time," the biblical story participates in the idea of "times" itself; its corollary, which the poem satirizes, is the revolutionary fantasy that human political culture can create fundamental change. The emphasis is not on God's transcendence but on the impotence of human political culture: with or without laws made by humans, human activities, including both promiscuity and rebellion, continually repeat because the human sexual and political desires that we might call sin and the political impulses that create laws do not change.[7] While the particulars of sin and law may change in relation to one another, human sinful impulses are so reliable that wildly different historical events can be paralleled in one of the most tightly constructed political allegories in English.[8] The secularity of the poem's political typology – its focus on the eternal truths of humanity's promiscuity and propensity to rebellion rather than transcendent religious truth – makes Dryden's allegory a conservative response to emergent ideas of political progress and the fantasy of the significance of revolution that are central to Whig history and that I take up more thoroughly in Chapter 6.

The Hind and the Panther is like a mirror image of *Absalom and Achitophel*. Both poems were written as attempts to influence volatile political situations, and both experiment with allegory by using religious sources to illuminate contemporary politics – but in quite opposite ways. *Absalom and Achitophel* is a poem animated by the revolutionary energy it satirizes and was written in a historical moment in which revolution was forestalled. *The Hind and the Panther*, on the other hand, was written on the eve of a revolution in order to influence a political conflict that was moot by the time the poem was published. Thus, there is a sense of historical belatedness about it.[9] *The Hind and the Panther* is both Dryden's longest poem and also perhaps the least action-packed long poem ever written. In this complicated beast fable, the Hind represents the permanence and infallibility of the true religion of the Catholic Church. Over the course of the poem, the Hind takes no action except to engage in conversation and tell her own beast fable, as she patiently waits out a historical period in which her truths are neglected by the rebellious religious sects who are her illegitimate offspring. The opening, like that of *Absalom and Achitophel*, clearly establishes that two temporal systems, and two theories of action and meaning, are in conflict:

> A milk-white Hind, immortal and unchanged,
> Fed on the lawns, and in the forest ranged;
> Without unspotted, innocent within,
> She fear'd no danger, for she knew no sin.
> Yet had she oft been chased with horns and hounds,
> And Scythian shafts; and many winged wounds
> Aim'd at her heart; was often forced to fly,
> And doom'd to death, though fated not to die.
> (I. 1–8)

The very body of the Hind integrates her experience of the violence and capriciousness of the temporal animal world with the mystery and permanence of the true church: Although she has experienced "many winged wounds," the Hind is "unspotted" (I.7, 8). The trope of the Hind as both embodied experience and eternal truth is the central oddity of the poem. Samuel Johnson complained "what can be more absurd than that one beast should counsel another to rest her faith upon a pope and council?", and C. S. Lewis famously suggested that a design blending beast fable and theological controversy suggests a mind "bordering on aesthetic insanity."[10] Such "absurd[ity]" and "insanity" obtain in how closely the poem brings together the contingent animal and the transcendent spiritual worlds in the body of the Hind, even as it insists on their radical difference: human activity "*doom[s]*" the hind "*to death*" while spiritually she is "*fated not to die*" (I.8). If in *Absalom and Achitophel* Dryden utilized a religious form to represent the radically secular world of politics, in *The Hind and the Panther* he makes quite an opposite move, by using a literary form designed for simplifying human morals to represent mysterious religious truths.[11]

In both poems, the relationship between literal and allegorical meaning is clear. *Absalom and Achitophel* may be complex due to the topical references and the knottiness of the political situation, but getting from the literal to the allegorical (i.e., from a historical figure to a contemporary one) does not reveal more meaning, and the higher levels of allegoresis (moral, spiritual, etc.) are seemingly absent. In *The Hind and the Panther*, the references are obvious (the Hind is the Catholic Church and the Panther is Anglican), as are all the other levels of allegoresis (the idea that the Catholic Church is the true church basically suffices for every level of interpretation), but this is likewise not the point of the poem. Dryden is writing allegories that are not amenable to allegoresis, or the slow revealing of layers of meaning, and hence the form and the hermeneutic of reading are dissonant. While *Absalom and Achitophel* at least offers a dense landscape of topical referentiality and political complexity that might engage readers' intellectual faculties or desire for political gossip, *The Hind and the Panther* satisfies neither sacred nor secular demands for complexity or transcendent meaning. Its dense materiality is not especially gratifying in terms of literal meaning or readerly interpretive pleasure: the beasts, the fables, and the "church" are all richly material and yet un-literal (or un-referential) in a profoundly unsettling way. Unlike *Absalom and Achitophel*, this poem does not offer any difficult human problem in need of solution – the Hind's equanimity, infallibility, and immortality pervade it. As a result, it has been a much more difficult poem for readers. In this poem, Dryden's integration of secular and sacred models does not produce the attractive simplicity of a revolutionary beginning or an aphoristic moral, nor does it reward literary analysis by allowing for competing or nuanced interpretations of meaning. The aesthetic and material complexity of *The Hind and the Panther* has confounded readers for over 300 years, less in terms of meaning than because of its bizarre materiality and its presumed and actual effect on audiences.

Critics who seem most comfortable working with *The Hind and the Panther* tend to be archivists, bibliographers, and philologists. Much good work has been done on the history and the materiality of the poem; for example, the *Works of John Dryden* includes 110 pages of footnotes to the poem.[12] And yet the poem's "meaning," has been either elusive or too obvious, or perhaps simply too Catholic to inspire much critical notice or debate. The liveliest work done on it has theorized it in terms of its method and effect, treating it as a mystical or emotional experience rather than representing reality or interpreting it rationally. J. M. Armistead is exemplary here: "The cosmic vision in which the allegory participates is, of course Roman Catholic, so that an unwary reader who invests himself in the play of figures and ideas is likely to espouse the Catholic cause without fully realizing it."[13] In a related vein, William Myers says: "Its meanings lie in the risks it takes and the insecurities they create."[14] For these critics, the poem is an experience that resists secular critique, which privileges synthesis and depth of rational meaning. The poem instead provokes an emotional experience. One of the poem's earliest readers, Thomas Brown, for example, writes:

However if *Mr. Bayes* [Dryden] would be pleased to abate a little of the exuberancy of his Fancy and Wit; to dispense with his Ornaments and Superfluencies of *Invention and Satyr*, a Man might consider, whether he should submit to his argument; but take away the *Railing*, and *No Argument remains*; so that one may beat the Bush a whole day, and after so much labour, only spring a *Butterfly*, or start an *Hedge-hog*.[15]

Brown here suggests that reading this bizarre beast fable – which Brown sees as a kind of "labour" to read – should produce something important, more important than another animal, whether a butterfly or a hedge-hog. But the poem offers no transcendence from its animality and materiality into the world of ideas, and this fact incites Brown and countless other readers, then and now, to dismiss it. Brown's comments also point to another unsettling issue at stake in Dryden's method: the need for a clear and logical argument to which the reader has a choice of whether or not to "submit." But the political problem of submission is of course something completely different from logical assent to argument.

Dryden opens his dedication to the reader of *The Hind and the Panther* by averring that the world is in "too high a ferment" for his poem to get a fair reading. Nonetheless, his poem, like its protagonist the Hind, goes out into the world, in which chaotic emotions, self-interested modes of interpretation, and physical violence are constant. In the poem, the "Milk white *Hind*" takes no action besides discoursing with the Panther and inviting her to share her humble retreat (1); she merely exists and speaks (in the languages of both theology and fables). Her emotional equanimity and sincerity are in contrast to the emotionality and deceptivity of the beasts: the boars who "Bristle" and the bears who "groan" are beasts of prey who are "Wild in effect, though in appearance tame" (I.43, I.36, I.157). The beasts fear and admire the Hind, which creates in them an aesthetic and emotional hypocrisy: they "grin'd as They pass'd, and with a glaring eye/ Gave gloomy signs of secret enmity" (I.29–30). Their emotions are both hidden – the grin is false – and available, perhaps unconsciously, via "signs." In this sense, the beasts are rather modern. They instrumentalize and code their emotions, and they prioritize private happiness over truth or peace. So too the Reformers, "All" of whom, "would be happy at the cheapest rate," and they accomplish this by replacing the "drudging works of grace" with "marriage pleasures." (I.375, I.371, I.367) "The jolly *Luther*," for example, endeavors to "make the paths of Paradise more sweet" and marries because "'twas uneasy travailing alone" (I.380–5). If, as Jonathan Kramnick has argued, Locke will account for human desire as being motivated by "unease," Dryden takes a related path: The desire for ease, seen as the avoidance of unpleasant, threatening, or publicized emotions, is the motivator of secular politics and happiness.[16] And rather than being a revolutionary assertion of autonomy from authority or even a mode of maximizing self-interest, marriage is instead portrayed as a lazy response to fear and complexity. The Hind herself is no exemplar of chaste and secular companionate marriage. In fact, she appears to be a bit wanton, fruitful as she is with her riotous brood of half-breed animal sects. Her children are full of "zeal," but, unlike their mother, are neither fruitful nor immortal. Their effects are "fiery tracks of dearth" and a "teemless earth" (I.227–8). In this poem, what we now call secularization is promoted as a path of ease, a negation of the difficulty of human (or animal) existence: Fear and unease are banished, so that "happiness," as well as a sense that human action matters, can reign supreme in the human experience. But of course that promise is an *ignis fatuous*: the emotional beasts and the reformers in search of ease and meaningful action transform the world into a barren and violent place.

The Hind and the Panther is centrally concerned with the problem of sacred hermeneutics. The Hind and the Panther devote most of their conversation in parts I and II to a consideration of the Catholic priesthood's role as interpreter of the Bible. The Hind argues that the true faith is apostolic, passed from one live interpreter to the next. Her argument emphasizes not only tradition but also the complexity, ambiguity, and deceptiveness of language, against the Reformer's position that everyone can read the Bible because its meaning as well as its language are both clear and derived from God. For Reformers, the apostles' experience of revelation belongs to a period of history radically different from the secular world of seventeenth-century England, in which revelation is foreclosed, forcing the faithful to rely upon scripture – this is a position that Dryden explored most directly in *Religio Laici*.[17] For the Hind and in this poem, however, scripture (especially the New Testament) is not revelation: Jesus' words were oral, and the mediation of the apostles in having written them down means that they are subject to the rules that govern all language and especially all reading. The main concern about language in confessional debates about scripture versus apostolic transmission is whether human's self-interest motivates them to willfully misinterpret language. The Hind emphasizes the fallibility both of language and of humanity and thus the fallibility of the apostles who did the original writing. As such, scripture demands a complex reading practice.

Besides scripture, the central object of dispute in the poem is the Eucharist. Dryden's treatment of it reveals what is at stake in these debates about apostolic transmission and, for Dryden, allegory. With respect to the Eucharistic debates, the Hind claims that the Reformer's position has effectively changed the meaning of the Eucharist, and "what may change may fall" (II.35). A number of critics have argued that with respect to his royalism Dryden manages to find pragmatic arguments to support a conservative position when the transcendental ones no longer suffice.[18] Here, that logic applies to the most divisive object of interpretation between Catholics and Reformers. At stake here is not only the Catholic Church, but also the possibility of any political stability if there is no epistemological stability, and the Hind's position is that because language is inherently unstable and humans inherently self-interested, such stability comes (besides via innate authority) only over the course of many historical ages and via personal, apostolic transmission. As described by the Hind, the Reformer's position is that everyone can read the apostles' writing because their "sense so obvious, and their words so plain," in response to which the Hind paints a picture of the violence that results from the Reformers' efforts to stabilize meaning: "Luther, Zuinglius, Calvin, holy chiefs,/ Have made a battle of royal beliefs;/Or, like wild horses, several ways have whirl'd/ The tortured text about the Christian world" (II.116–119). The effort to make the sociable transmission of ideas through writing and reading unnecessary leads to aggression and hostility. Sharon Achinstein has eloquently described how violent this seemingly inactive poem is; she links the "violent predation" of the dissenting animals to the "willful interpretation" of Anglicans, creating a pervasive sense of the links between political and literary menace.[19] In this poem, textual complexity and the inherent complexity of language support the Hind's case for acknowledging the difficulty of texts and thus the need for "Latter ages" to "on former wait" (I.110) as the way to political security. Moreover, the Hind hinges its argument for the mystery of the Eucharist on the idea that "one single place two bodies did contain" (I.101), which is a mystery beyond human understanding. Dryden's allegories, which after all are a way of making "one single place" contain "two bodies," are a formal experiment in this sacred mystery as well as a formal means of making sure that "latter ages on former wait" (I.110).

The Hind makes a case for the sacred apostolic transmission of the Catholic faith, but her argument also applies to both conservative political theory and literary history: "Latter ages must on former wait" (I.110) because the "weight of ancient witness" is an "unerring guide" (I.62, I.65) to matters of faith.[20] But such ancient witness is "unerring" precisely because humanity and language inevitably err (I.65). Only by removal from the current moment, in which self-interest clouds writing and interpretation, can error be revealed and truth confirmed, and thus only those ideas that survive into subsequent ages can possibly be free of error. This argument about scriptural interpretation is thus the corollary of early theories of political conservatism, which emphasized the Ancient constitution and common law.[21] In the confessional debates in *The Hind and the Panther*, this historical scaffolding traces back to a transcendent and sacred "innate authority" (I.453), but when the logic of the Hind's arguments is translated into the secular realm of literary history, the reasoning holds. "As long as words a different sense will bear/ Our airy faith will no foundation find" might well be the founding problem not only of scriptural interpretation and of political judgment but also of literary critique, one often solved by consulting the OED or engaging in other historicist critical methods (I.463–5).

It is a commonplace that literary methods derive from religious hermeneutics, but Dryden is doing something quite specific in linking sacred and literary transmission and reading.[22] The narrator of *The Hind and the Panther* makes a number of direct comparisons between the poem and sacred scriptures, including the fact that both are occasional ("all those letters were not writ to all;/Nor first intended but occasional" (II.339) as well as "mysterious[ly] writ" (III.2). By depicting the scriptures as occasional writings, the narrator links them to a key practice of a poet laureate and implies that such occasions offer a chance for a writer to process highly contemporary events while using the material of the past.[23] The occasion is an opportunity for mediation of the present by the past rather than an occasion for willful intention or interpretation. Occasionality is thus part of what makes both scripture and poetry "mysteriously writ."[24] The poem lingers lovingly on the body ("milk white" and "unspotted") of the Hind, and this reinforces the apostolic transmission. Although she "represents" ideas, which is what gives many critics pause (a talking beast offends the spirituality of humans), the Hind's animality and physicality are central to Dryden's purpose: Ideas must be passed through physical bodies (I.1–3). Thus, the Hind represents the Catholic Church's positions on the scriptures and the Eucharist in her speech, while her body also symbolizes them by embodying and animating the need for apostolic transmission, via occasions in the present.

While the simplicity of meaning of *The Hind and The Panther* tends to leave critics unsettled, the ending of *Absalom and Achitophel* offers some relief from its political and satiric complexity:

> Henceforth a series of new time began,
> The mighty years in long procession ran:
> Once more the god-like David was restored,
> And willing nations knew their lawful lord.
>
> (1028–31)

Like its beginning, the ending of *Absalom and Achitophel* strikes a careful balance between sacred and secular ideas about temporality. As an agent of God (or *deus ex-machina*), David must decide the conflict and end the poem via recourse to the transcendent authority of divine absolute law, a process that involves inaugurating a new age. This ending is made welcome by the unrelenting stalemate that the poem depicts as the result of human struggles for power. But the ending, with its "new time," does not supersede for most readers the lively portraits of humanity's complexity (including David as a sexual human being and a loving father) upon which the poem's appeal depends. *Absalom and Achitophel* stages a problem in the present that is paralleled by a problem in the past, but the solution must necessarily differ: in Restoration England, no *deus ex machina* can inaugurate a "new time" (1028). In *The Hind and the Panther*, the central issue at stake is not explicitly political authority or sexual desire but rather scriptural/historical interpretation, and the poem offers no such promise of a new time or a divine intervention to resolve the political situation. Instead, after each telling a beast fable with obvious relevance to their respective religio-political views, the Hind and the Panther drift off to sleep.[25] While it seems that nothing is resolved between them, this ability to sleep in peace as a result of a literary experience seems crucial to the poem's purpose or at least to its occasion: a political event that offers the opportunity to meditate on history and literary hermeneutics and that offers apostolic transmission as a substitute for – or at least the salve for – political factionalism and violence.

Taking up Where History Left Off: Apostolic Literary Interpretation in *Don Sebastian*

Don Sebastian (performed 1689, published 1690) is based on the Portuguese king who disappeared at the battle of the Alcazar in 1578 under circumstances equal parts romantic and foolhardy.[26] His body was never found, although pretenders to his birthright made frequent enough appearances, and he lived on as a romance figure in the hearts and minds of his Portuguese subjects. His story circulated in published form before

Dryden's treatment, but Dryden takes a unique approach by avoiding the known facts of Sebastian's life and imagining a sequel.[27] Dryden says his version is "purely fiction" because he takes up the story of Sebastian "where the History has laid it down," and he means that quite specifically: at the moment where there is no historical record because Sebastian disappears (67). Dryden bases his *Don Sebastian* on the possibility that the king survived the battle and yet did not return to rule. What, the play asks us to consider, might be the possible justification for and ramifications of such an abdication of power and responsibility? Dryden invents elaborate reasons – slavery, incest, and remorse – for the king's disappearance: having met and unwittingly married his sibling while battling against and enslaved in a Muslim empire, Sebastian mistrusts his ability to balance his passionate and political selves (his love and honour), and he comes to the conclusion that secretive monastical sequestration is the only practical political action and also the only way to save his soul. Despite his version of Don Sebastian's story having little historical or literary precedent, Dryden wrote a very long play. In its first production, the play was, by Dryden's own account, too long to be enjoyed in the theater, and while he cut 1,200 lines for the staged version, he published the full text, along with a lengthy dedication and preface, for reading. He also, in both the play and the paratext, theorizes a method of reading that responds to the political events his imagined readers need to interpret.

Don Sebastian is Dryden's most direct response to the events of 1688–89 and has been called by Steven Zwicker the only real piece of "literature" that resulted from those events.[28] Indeed, it is replete with literary technique including classical allusions, a mix of blank verse and prose, and a complex form. The tragicomic structure of Dryden's *Don Sebastian* is based on multiple kinds of doublings and parallels: sixteenth-century Portugal and seventeenth-century England, high and low plots, and Christian and Muslim cultures.[29] The main plot follows the exploits of Sebastian and his loyal followers (Antonio and Alvarez) as they are imprisoned by the tyrannical emperor Moley Moluch. The virtuous Sebastian and the villainous Moley Moluch vie for the love of the beautiful Almeyda, the illegitimate child of Sebastian's father. Sebastian incites fierce devotion in his subjects, while Moley Moluch is the subject of an attempted usurpation, which is the central feature of the low plot. The play allegorizes this complex plot to events in England, making a parallel between the sixteenth-century Portuguese king, who went missing on the field of battle but lived on for years in the memory and the desires of his subjects, and the recently exiled, abdicated, or deposed (depending on your perspective) King James II and the events in England more broadly. In contrast to both *Absalom and Achitophel* and *The Hind and the Panther*, which compare contemporary events with biblical history or eternal truth, *Don Sebastian* parallels two decidedly human events relatively closely connected in time. Dryden also chooses an event with a historical mystery and a vibrant literary tradition to parallel an event that will have, though Dryden could not have known it, an opposite dynamic: historical significance and literary obscurity. Finally, as with many of the representations of 1688–89 studied here, Dryden allegorizes revolution, moving revolutionary activity out of England, further in the past, and onto a group that is religiously and racially other.

This formal structure allows the play to present a complicated view of human reason, causation, and agency. Literary devices (rather than causal logic or consistent politics or values) connect the high with the low plot and the political events with the romantic: for instance, both politics and romance are figured as usurpation. Rather than being purposeful agents, the play's characters are mired in interpretive errors and quandaries, stymied by the weight of the past, and subject to the vicissitudes of illogical literary effects, as words, feelings, and error transmute like an infection across the various plots without clear causal or temporal explanation. Ruth Mack has argued that the problem of causation animates the way that later eighteenth-century literature – as a direct result of the events of 1688–89 – will solve the problem of how literature can represent history (as experience).[30] Here, on the cusp of that transition, the problem is posed more as a problem of the present: Where history "leaves off" we find a chaotic scene where causation is impossible to understand. Metaphor, etymology, parodic imitation, and the "magical causation" (in Angus Fletcher's term) of allegory – what Steven Zwicker characterizes as an "unsteady system of analogies and parallels, proximities and disparities" – control the events in this play."[31] Both material and literary effects transfer across the tragicomic form in ways that cannot be predicted or controlled and that must be mediated retroactively by a literary hermeneutic. The denouement comes when the aging courtier Alvarez reveals the incest of Don Sebastian and Almeyda by showing how their rings interlock, proving their shared paternity. This moment, requiring human interpretation of the material evidence of the past, secularizes the apostolic role and provides a metaphor for literary history and the need for embodied knowledge. Alvarez is thus another example of the apostolic vision I attribute to Dryden, a postsecular and mortal version of the Hind. Alvarez's aging body contrasts with the Hind's purity and immortality, but this is quite to the point. While

Alvarez can unlock the meaning needed for the lovers in the play, his mortality means the play itself will depend upon readers to carry on this apostolic practice. The elaborate (even for Dryden) paratextual writing included in the printed version offers a vision of the kind of reading and interpretation that Dryden envisioned might be needed in postsecular England.

In order to connect *Don Sebastian* with a history of modern literary critique and modern secularization, I start with the simplest and most historically literal connection between secularization and literature: Monasteries were the incubators of religious-based academic training and often became literally the physical locations of secular academies. And here is a place to start also with *Don Sebastian*, which begins, in Dryden's preface, with an account of its literary production and reception and ends with a king resolved to spend the remainder of his days as an anchorite in religious sequestration. I am suggesting that the ending, in which a king enters a religious sanctuary and thereby dismantles the religio-political structure, mandates the beginning, a new postsecularized theory of reading. The play thus predicts that abdication will lead to a new way of reading. This is the case for *Don Sebastian's* status as the most "literary" production resulting from the events of 1688–89: instead of being merely a literary allegory of the events, it posits literary experience itself as a response to the events, and thus perhaps as an alternative to revolution.

Both the play and its paratext repeatedly reference and evaluate practices of reading and their propensity to fail. It is not incest that drives the central conflicts of the play; the incest is itself a consequence of poor reading and interpretation. Although Nostradamus decreed that he was fated to marry incestuously, Sebastian denies the applicability to his situation, saying: Ere this unhappy war my mother died,/ And sisters I had none; – vain augury!" (II.i.581). Sebastian of course does not know that his father and Almeyda's mother had an adulterous affair. But he ignores the information that he does have. Reminded that his father explicitly told him not to marry Almeyda, Sebastian analyzes what he assumes to be his father's logic and obviates the command: He decides that his father's injunction must have been because of Almeyda's Muslim religion, and he reasons that since she has converted to Christianity he may safely marry her. He remembers his father's admonition to defend Almeyda's crown and sees this as evidence of disinterested nobility on his father's part; he cannot imagine that it might be due to guilt about or love for an illegitimate daughter. Sebastian, as a king and a lover who is "Brave, Pious, generous, great and *liberal*" [emphasis mine], is caught between the desire to maintain the legitimacy of his birthright and the rebellious desire to make his own romantic choices (I.i.103). He is motivated to protect his memory of his father's perfections yet does not want to pay a "blind obedience" to his father's will; he argues that "justify[ing]" his father is more important than obeying him (V.i.238, 242). Don Sebastian thus makes two opposite kinds of errors: in the first case he uses new circumstances (Almeyda's conversion) to rewrite a past sovereign decree, and in the second he uses old information (his father's admonition to defend Almeyda) to support his desire. While one is rebellious and indeed secularizing (liberal) and the other upholds tradition and the mystical value of the monarch (traditionalist), both of course serve his desires in the present and thus are problematic modes of interpretation and reasoning.

If Sebastian's crime is to misinterpret prophecy and command in order that he may follow his desires and protect his romantic ideas, and if he does so by failing to integrate past ideas with present circumstances or present ideas with past circumstances, the villains of the play make similar, if slightly more egregious yet less catastrophic, errors. Moley Moluch, the Barbary emperor and a stand-in to some extent for Anglican secularization (and specifically for Henry VIII), also wants to marry Almeyda. He commands his religious advisor to reinterpret the Koran so that he may marry a Christian. His injunction "Make it, I charge thee, make my pleasure lawful" encapsulates his theory of language and governance – he declares that the mufti must make the Koran "speak my sense" or he is no "prophet" (III.i.87, 65–66). The emperor's tyrannical and arbitrary rule, which needs no reasoning beyond desire, is based on the completely arbitrary relationship between words and meaning, which he believes he controls. His religious advisor must choose between "literal" interpretation of scripture and the more creative interpretations that the emperor demands; the literal meaning is aligned with "the Vulgar" while the elite are aligned with the power of individual interpretation (I.i.180–1). Tyranny thus functions via an arbitrary theory of language that makes it pliable to new meanings as a tool of power, leading to tragic results. It is also the basis for comedy via the assumptions of the same ideas and behaviors by the characters in the low plot: The faithful yet flexible Antonio survives his transposition from high to low plot by gamely playing a horse, an enslaved person, a lover and a hero, as the situation demands. And "the Rabble" seems to pick up this ethic of arbitrary signification by osmosis: Their revolutionary rallying cry becomes, both comically and tragically enough, "Another Religion, a new Religion, another religion" (IV.iii.161). The villainy, unintentional evils, and the comedy in the play all result from improper interpretive practices, which are motivated by rebellious or selfish political and romantic desire. Throughout the play – in high and low plots, in politics and romance – human nature, especially our propensity to misinterpret and misunderstand historical facts and processes based on our own desires, creates cascading revolutions and interpretative impossibilities. Revolution in *Don Sebastian* is not the time-erasing beginning of a new regime of meaning. Rather it is one means – allegory is another – whereby people change places (from high to low, from king to enslaved) and experience the limits of their power and understanding. An allegory of revolution then is doubly suited to Dryden's purposes here.

How then, to read the turn to the monastery at the end? Sebastian's retreat could perhaps be read as a recognition of the ceremonial and public role of the king: in seclusion and secrecy, he is maintained as an idea in the minds of his people, an idea of sovereignty that holds the system in place but that is better as a pure abstraction (fiction or romance) or transcendental ideal than an actual person. But I want to take seriously the idea that Dryden is meditating on the possibility of living in a world in which the king has abdicated – a world in which subjects cannot rely on either abstract ideals or transcendent meaning. Sebastian retreats at once from kingship and this world, saying, "The world was once too narrow for my mind,/But one poor little nook will serve me now" (V.i.547). He renounces both royal sovereignty and romance in favor of friendship and reflection. In the throes of horror over his incest and with the realization that his intentions, desires, and interpretations do not prepare him to continue acting in the world in a manner either efficacious or ethical, Sebastian considers suicide, so that he may "think no more" (V.i.450). Dorax, Sebastian's oldest and recently reconciled friend, induces Don Sebastian to change his mind by forcing him to see his situation from a different perspective. At first, Sebastian can only think about his role as king, which is incompatible with the crime of incest, until Dorax reminds him that he has a private spiritual destiny, which suicide will destroy. Dorax says that he knows if he could just give Sebastian "leisure" enough to "think" – time to reinterpret the events of his life and of his "history" – then he could be dissuaded from suicide. Sebastian renounces his crown and his love to join the monastery (V.i.533).

The imagery of streams, fruits, and blood permeates the text, creating metaphorical and symbolic clues to the chain of causation that leads to the tragedy and to the connections between high and low plots. The monastical retreat – the "poor little nook" – to which Sebastian retires is described as a place of "purling streams," "savage fruits," and "unbloudy feasts" (V.i.674). These symbolic patterns are exemplary of the way the play functions as a study in literary experience. For example, "fruit" recurs repeatedly as the unwarranted or undesired outcome of an action and stands in for human error or futility with respect to reproduction, political rule, or labor.[32] The metaphor of "fruit" serves many meanings in the play, but they converge around consequences and temporality, and collectively they offer a check on human agency: Cultured fruits raise questions about human ability to control the relationship between means and ends. Moreover, the metaphor of fruits connects the different plots, occurring repeatedly in ways that suggest the distinctions that humans make – between Christian and Moor, high and low – do not obtain when it comes to consequences of actions. Almeyda's royal blood is called a "purer stream," and she desires the "fruitful head of *Hydra*" that could "bourgeon" more heads as needed, as a means of producing enemies for Moley Moluch. The botanical metaphors are not limited to fruit: weak princes are like "tender plants" while strong governments as are "old Oak"; Sebastian must be killed because "the vine will cling while the tall poplar stands"; and Dorax counsels Moley Moluch that by allowing preachers to make meaning he allowed a "limb to be lopt" from his Prerogative." And in a minor but perhaps telling moment, Dorax claims that "Slaves are the growth of *Africk*, not of *Europe*," criticizing slavery but blaming Africa for the enslavement of its people. Moraya makes the plays' more direct critique of imperialism and slavery, when she says of the jewels she steals form her father "the Spoils of Orphans are in these Jewels, and the Tears of Widows in these Pearls." And yet as the Africans here stand for English people (and as it is the Europeans, including Sebastian, who are enslaved), the causation and blame for slavery is almost impossibly complicated. "Fire" is another pattern of literal/metaphorical meaning that permeates the play, possibly as a counterpoint to fruits. The Emperor for example suggests that he and Sebastian share affinities and that perhaps their souls had split "one spark to *Africk* flew and one to Portugal." And the motivations of characters are often referred to as "flame" or "flashing lightening," but these fire-based metaphors do not suggest any more effective human agency than "fruits." Almeyda brings these two patterns of metaphor (fruits and fire) together – she thinks her Christian religion will lead to more positive "fruits" but she also believes, wrongly and despite, like Sebastian, being warned against marriage, that her love is a "flame, so holy and so clear, that the white taper leaves no soot behind." The pattern of fire is connected to that of poison (poison should work "like a slow fire that works against the wind"). Thus while the various plots may have no obvious causal connections and while the characters insist on differentiation, the metaphorical patterns suggest clues to their shared meaning, or at least their shared experience. There are many other examples of such metaphorical patterns.[33] "Nook" too was first metaphorical: long before Sebastian retreats to his monastical nook, Dorax calls Sebastian's drawing of the black ball that should randomly assign him to death a "nook of fate" (I.i.324). And, "Sacred retreat," which at the end is literally a monastery, is first offered as a simile for the "thoughts of Kings" (II.i.3). So it is not just that the actions have doubles and metaphors, but the metaphors themselves are parallels for human action, a way that human agency and action are further complicated via literary devices. I am suggesting then that metaphors have agency and are alternatively fighting each other or collaborating. Like personification in Chapter 1 and simile in Chapter 3, a literary device is used here to explore human agency.

All of these patterns of the metaphorical traveling between registers of plot, of the metaphorical becoming literal (thoughts becoming reality) or the critical becoming literary (thoughts becoming plots) contribute to Dryden's aesthetic and political vision, one where meaning travels across registers of society and representation, where actions have unpredictable consequences, and thus one in which reading and interpretation are needed. Thus the monastical retreat, where "savage fruit," presumably grow without intent, may seem to be a refuge from the human world of error, metaphor, typology, and literary interpretation (V.i.674). But "fruit," "Sacred retreat," and "nook" have all been introduced before the monastical retreat, thus suggesting that it will not be a space wholly separate from the world (V.i.674, II.i.3, I.i.324). Rather it might be a way to interpret, or to live in, the world.

In *Don Sebastian*, as in so much writing of the long eighteenth century, political authority and marriage are tropologically connected: The freedom to marry according to one's own choice is a corollary of – and a figure for – political freedom. It is a means by which both conservative and liberal writers figure the possibilities of human agency. Thus the abdication at once of political power and romance by a king at the end of the play, and his decision to enter a monastery, would signal a reaction against both royal privilege and liberal narratives of human freedom. In this respect, *Don Sebastian* builds upon (but also signals a departure from) not only the two poems discussed earlier but also the representation of marriage in Dryden's earlier plays, such as *Marriage a la Mode* and *All for Love*. Those plays often display a view of marriage that fits with mainstream Restoration libertinism and royal privilege; in them, Dryden demonstrates an awareness of the emergent episteme in which monogamous heterosexuality is the center of affective life and an analogy for political change, and the plays offer checks on or counterpoints to that ideology, with honour or political duty typically triumphing over (whether tragically or comically) passion.[34] During the 1680s, Dryden takes this critique of revolutionary/liberalizing romance further. Both *The Hind and the Panther* and *Don Sebastian* feature endings in which the protagonists wind up neither married nor tragically dead from passion but in seclusion: The Hind ends the poem alone in her hermitage after failing to convince even her closest descendent, the Anglican panther, to share her worldview. The royal lovers of *Don Sebastian*, united by genuine affection and married in good faith, must separate, and abdicate, when it turns out that, by dint of misinterpretation of familial injunctions, signs, prophesies, and material inheritances, they discover that they have married incestuously. In other words, in the choice between love (or freedom) and honor (or sovereignty), this play rejects both.

In place of the lonely sovereignty of a powerful king or the political and affective stability of marriage, Dryden offers friendship and reading. The denouement of *Don Sebastian* hinges on forgiveness and friendship as catalysts for overcoming the play's affective, political, and interpretive dilemmas. The very basis of the king's prerogative is destroyed: The royal "kindness" of Sebastian's father for Almeyda's mother turns out to have been motivated by his adulterous love, and Sebastian's own love for Almeyda is revealed to have been a sociopathic attraction of likes. No one, least of all the royals, is so "passionately fond of noble Acts" as to avoid misreading their affections in ways that are politically dangerous (V.i.297). Once the king's incest and the former king's adultery are revealed, all relations of love and conventional loyalty are dissolved in a pageant of friendship, which is based on emulation of the king's mercy but which winds up dissolving class, gender, religious, and national distinctions. Sebastian responds to Dorax's compassionate catechism of him, "I am no more thy King/But still thy friend" (V.i.564–5). The "Holy name" of friend is also invoked with respect to Sebastian's former enemy Muley-Zeyden and by Almeyda, who wishes that she and Sebastian had been the same sex because, "we had been friends, and friendship is not incest" (V.i.565, 607). And finally of course it is Alvarez's friendship with Don Sebastian's father that makes the resolution possible. Hence, both royal privilege and romantic exclusivity are subordinate to friendship. The practice of friendship is the basis for an ethic and a hermeneutic of reading that values the importance of materiality, tradition, generational knowledge, and emotion. It eschews abstraction, the tyrannical imposition of meaning, the emotional exclusivity of marriage and private happiness, and the lure of revolutionary beginnings.[35]

Still, it is unclear how readers might apply the play to their own lives, in particular the retreat to the monastery of "savage fruits" (V.i.674).[36] While the play offers many parallels with the secular world of Restoration England, and perhaps with the affective entanglements of individual readers, monastic retreat is not an option anymore in seventeenth-century England. Nor are most of the readers or audience members royalty, for whom such retreat signifies quite differently. And the audience of the play (in the seventeenth century or now) does not live in a Dryden play, insofar as real life is not conducted via poetry and neoclassical allusion. On this problem, Joseph Addison's response is telling: He found the play ridiculous; it would be impossible, he insists, for a Barbary Emperor to be well enough versed in Ovid to talk as if he were Dryden.[37] But Dryden is not interested in such realism and would not be defensive about the bleeding boundaries between literary and literal activities. This imbrication of historical reality and the literary is the point of the play and why it requires the paratextual material and to be read as well as performed.

The dedication of *Don Sebastian* meditates on the nature of historical "ages" and thereby on whether human activity differs over time. The preface addresses the problem of the length of the play, positing it as a consequence of the relationship between action and literary effects. "The most poetical parts," Dryden says, "which are Descriptions, Images, Similitudes, and Moral Sentences" were pared away because "the body was swoln into too large a bulk for the representation of the Stage" (66). In the performed, excised version, some events had to be, he says "precipitated"; that is, the causal relations among acts are obfuscated, if they exist at all. One assumes, then, that meanings existed in those "Poetical parts" that have been excised (66). Dryden here again is referencing questions about the difference between literal and figurative meanings in the Bible, a point which earlier in his career had him siding with, at least according to Colin Jager, the literal, but in the *Hind and the Panther* has him suggesting the impossibility of literality and thus need for an immortal and infallible guide.[38] But in this preface, Dryden explains, "there is a vast difference betwixt a publick entertainment in the Theatre, and a private reading in the Closet" (66). Dryden signals that a particular reading practice will produce a very different, and indeed preferable, response to the text. The reader who takes time to peruse the text in their "closet" can find out those "beauties of propriety" that "escap'd him in the tumult and hurry of representing" and will, according to the preface, be rewarded with a second moral to the story, "couched" within the more obvious one (66, 71).[39] When Dryden says that the play offers a "moral," he is gesturing to the practice of allegoresis, specifically to the third (tropological) level in which morals provide a basis for actions. Moral truths are intended to influence personal/political actions and in turn affect spiritual belief and destiny.[40] In the dedication, Dryden argues for a practical and flexible philosophy, because "stiffness of Opinion is the effect of Pride, not philosophy" (62). As such, simple morals will not suffice; some meaning or moral may be "couched" within the play, but in ways that demand time-intensive and private reading practices to uncover (71). Instead of simple morals or clear causation, Dryden offers complex literary form and literary contemplation: The reader's closet stands in for the hero's nook, replacing a religious space of contemplation with postsecular space of reading. The retreat to the monastery represents not just a rejection of romance and sovereignty but also the rejection of the larger possibility (of which sovereignty and romance are examples) of simple meaning and therefore simple paths of action.

The composition of *Don Sebastian*, as described by Dryden in the preface, consisted of contracting action, ignoring history, and eschewing temporal and logical causation in order to make room for literary activity: both the paratextual material and the experience the play offers to its audience, especially to its readers. He explains the reasons he "take[s] [the story] up where the history leaves off" thus (66):

> where the event of a great action is left doubtful, there the poet is left master. ... declaring it (the incest) to be fiction, I desire my audience to think it no longer true, than while they are seeing it represented; for that once ended, he may be a saint, for aught I know, and we have reason to presume he is. (68)

Pondering the ethical implications of fabricating the incest, he justifies it by asking the reader to imagine it only "while they are seeing it represented" (68). The time of seeing or reading, like the composition of the play itself, is temporally and causally dissonant from the events being depicted, and the reader must be willing to toggle between fiction and history – to presume that Sebastian may be a "Saint" in real life but also to ponder the meaning of his abdication and retreat as fictional constructs (68). Temporal discontinuity is crucial to Dryden's method. If one meaning of secular was out in the world (and hence the movement of *Don Sebastian* is from secular to religious) another definition of secular grounds it in temporality: secular time moves linearly forward rather than repeating allegorically, and thus one age is discontinuous with another age and also discontinuous with sacred or messianic time. In his preface, Dryden says that in the theater "we are confined to time," but by contrast the "reader is judge of his own convenience; he can take up the book and lay it down at his pleasure" (66). All reading is thus a kind of occasion, a corollary of occasional poetry in which the present offers an opportunity to reimagine or recycle the past in order to understand or moralize – and thereby take action in – the present. The preface also addresses the issues of literary precedent. *Don Sebastian* draws on literary predecessors ranging from Greek tragedy to French romance. Dryden states in the preface that such literary deployment of the past and past literature are not "plagiaries" but rather the manner by which poets use the common "*Materia Poetica*" to make their own "property" (69). Similarly, the reader in their private closet searching for a couched moral will experience the materials of the play as temporally discontinuous and thus available for reappropriation (71). Dryden asks his reader to imagine this fictional (and literary) story of incest and abdication anachronistically and to experience it as a literary event. He creates a fictional and temporary space for experiencing moral uncertainty, causational irrationality, and temporal discontinuity.

Dryden says he had to write *Don Sebastian* "against his will" (65). What he means by this, perhaps, is that if he had a tyrannical and arbitrary will, then the king (James II) would still be on the throne and there would therefore be no such worry about a tyrannical and arbitrary will. Dryden's polemical and allegorical projects such as *Absalom and Achitophel*, and *The Hind and the Panther* – which we might take as efforts to exert political will – have not had Dryden's desired effect on the political outcome of 1680s, and thus he has turned to a different kind of project, a literary project that turns away from a direct connection to politics. This chapter has been analyzing how Dryden modernizes allegory and allegoresis and thereby models a practice of literary writing and reading that demands a view of temporality, agency, and causation that differs from allegorical and historical theories of action and meaning. Ruth Mack argues that "what modernity requires is not only a new model of causation but also new ideas about the reader and writer to the text of history."[41] Dryden offers a unique solution to this problem, one that is at once literary and postsecular. In *Don Sebastian*, present events do not reenact past events. Past events do not provide a heuristic for present events, but rather the past and the future haunt the present in ways that are not logical but rather material and literary. *Don Sebastian* constructs an idea of a literary memory, practice, and ethic that are ritualistic and must be embodied, not only in plays that may be preserved for future readers but also in human bodies: in the aging bodies of Alvarez and Dorax, who remember Sebastian's past for him; in Sebastian's live body that takes up a sacramental role; and finally in the reader's body, in their private closet, searching for "couched" morals that rather than existing can only be contingently produced in the present (71).[42] Dryden's proleptic response to critics of the play and to charges that the characters are inconsistent is: "let them read the Play, and think again" (70), thereby drawing a link between readers and the hero of play. Dryden's literary gambit here is to create an interpretive problem for readers, a set of mysterious material representations that must be lived out and worked out, hermeneutically and ethically. The fruits of such activity are unknown because the occasion of reading in the present is necessarily unknown. If this argument thus seems to position Dryden as usurping the role of God (in ignoring history, he claims to be "Master"), in fact Dryden as author situates himself much closer to the position of the reader or of Sebastian than to a god (68). Confronted with historical circumstances that are irretrievably and yet obscurely factual, armed with morals that are obvious in the abstract but never exactly convenient to the situation, the reader or writer must, at some point, take action. Like the characters in a play, real people live in a world of precipitation, and yet they must interpret and take action. Dryden's preface suggests that interpretation is contingent and cannot be separated from action: The reading of the play in the present of the reader's life means that its meaning depends on that occasion. Writing and reading are thus occasions for participation in a postsecularized apostolic literary historical experience. We might connect this account of Dryden to the argument about indulgence in Chapter 2, with Dryden's vision of the scene of reading a kind of readerly indulgence: a formal submission to the mysterious realities of the text that can only take place when disjunctions among text, reader, and meaning are assumed. Rose Zimbardo calls *Don Sebastian* a novelized play, and we might productively put Dryden's paratexual arguments in conversation with the arguments about Behn's narrators that I am developing (in Chapters 2 and 5): The paratext tells the reader how to read but not what to make of the text (the "couched" moral is a red herring). As such, the form of this play enacts some of the same ambivalence about the relationship between action and ethical judgment, and thus the same antirevolutionary ethos, that Behn's proto-novels do.[43]

Karl Mannheim's influential account of conservatism provides a lens for understanding the conservatism of *Don Sebastian*. For Mannheim, conservatism (as opposed to traditionalism) only takes hold when all individual events connect to society as a whole.[44] While its aristocratic main characters may argue against such a reading (and for their exceptionality as sovereigns), I find that *Don Sebastian* fulfills this spirit at the literary, if not the representational, level in several ways. The tragicomic form and allegorical modes intimate that all human action reverberates into other realms, although in ways that are literary rather than causal: People and objects are haunted by connections that are resolutely material but obscurely causal. Mannheim's idea of conservatism as a style builds on Justus Möser's argument about property, which defines feudalism as an amalgamation of person and thing, a mode of perception in which property is bound up in a vital relation with its owner and is both a source of rights and inalienable.[45] *Don Sebastian*'s treatment of the relation of person and thing (and meanings) registers a distinction between feudalism and conservatism. In Mannheim's account, the progressive uses the future to interpret things, while the conservative uses the past, and of course this describes what Dryden is up to in *Don Sebastian*.[46] Dryden's conservative turn to the past, though, is not a desire to return to a feudal political, religious, or representational system. Rather, he makes a case for a literary approach to the past, both in literary history and in literary interpretation. In later work – his fables and translations – Dryden further develops his theory of how the literary realm engages with the past and with other cultures, how literature from a different age can be made relevant to the present. The allegories of the 1680s show literary experience emerging as a counterpoint to political, historical, and religious ways of thinking about human action and interpretation. This is why literary history – that is, literature posited as ages in which both difference and similarity partake and in which interpretation is complex and meaningful but never abstract – and literary experience – reading and thinking for oneself in one's nook or closet – were Dryden's answers to two possible political positions available to him in the 1680s: to maintaining a traditional idea of sacred kingship or to embracing modern, secular ideas of agency and revolution. Dryden's response is to head to a nook to read and "think again."

The Postsecular Dryden

This chapter has endeavored to argue that Dryden's mid-career experiments in literary form offered a new way to think about the relationship of reading to an emergent secular age and to see Dryden's literary techniques – and the modes of reading and critique they produce – as responses to emergent secular ideas about temporality, causation, and human capacity and agency: those things, in short, that make both revolution and progressivist history not only possible but desirable. It seeks to posit Dryden not as conservative in the sense of moving backwards in time, but rather as a postsecular conservative in the sense of one who is committed to the vitality and the importance of the past with respect to the present and the future as well as one who sees the need for an alternative voice – a literary voice in Dryden's case – to an emergent episteme of temporality and agency. The literary forms – beast fable, allegory, tragicomedy, and translation – that Dryden would pursue during the 1680s and after his conversion to Catholicism reveal something about the emergent relationships among literature, politics, and history in a secular age: if politics, Dryden seems to be suggesting, wants to begin anew and structure time linearly, then the literary realm must take a more three dimensional approach to time, one that is both historical and discontinuous.[47] And with a literary and conservative approach to time comes a particular reading method, one that Dryden based on his adopted Catholic religion and that is grounded not in human reason but in mystery, complexity, and participation, a postsecular apostolic. In one sense, Dryden is a straightforward secularizer in the way Carl Schmitt describes, whereby religious institutions, forms, and practices (in this case scriptural interpretation and apostolic transmission) are transferred into secular ones (literary studies).[48] But Dryden's conversion complicates his case as a model of secularity, and it is possible to read his turn to Catholicism and its particular vision of postsecular apostolic transmission as a response to and a critique of secularized practices of history and reading – as postsecular rather than secular. I am not suggesting that conversion to Catholicism is the proper response to reading Dryden but rather that Dryden may have leveraged Catholicism as a template for a modern reading practice.

   Dryden's career, especially the relationship between his political orientation(s), his conversion, and his literary trajectory, has been the subject of critical speculation and has meant that his reputation has depended on trends in criticism. Given the breadth and variety of his writing, critics have often made distinctions between his pre- and post-conversion (or pre- and post-1688) writings and between his politico-religious orientations and his writing. Dryden has been particularly problematic for criticism with ideological ambitions, as his conservatism – especially his conversion to Catholicism – was so prominent in his career trajectory. For critics focused on ideological critique and a hermeneutics of suspicion, where the purpose of form is often to reveal an ideology at odds with content, Dryden could only be interesting if his obviously conservative politics and/or religion were undermined by his literary technique.[49] Laura Brown's "divided" Dryden reveals something about the way the relationship between Dryden's writing and authentic self (or as Zwicker puts it between "real and ideal") has been approached in this vein of critique (395).[50] In order to resolve the ideological contradictions she sees in Dryden, Brown splits the man and the writing. She credits Dryden, as a man of his time, with a "blind advocacy of a conservative and static ideal" and yet credits his "poetry" with representing, perhaps even being committed to, "the realities of a progressive and dynamic historical process" (405). She argues that Dryden's poetry by "persistently subverting its own assertions ... knows more than it can say" (405). The hero of Brown's story, and it is an argument designed to appeal to literary critics, is literary criticism itself. The more we condemn Dryden's politics, the more we can credit the scholarly realm with overcoming them.

Such ideological approaches to reading Dryden, and to reading literature more broadly, position the critic as having more insight than the author, and this tendency has been prevalent in literary criticism since the 1970s at least. This trend has not been kind to Dryden's conservatism or his Catholicism, both of which have often been posited as at odds with his literary contributions. Dryden has been treated more sympathetically by critics working in a deconstructive mode, because in this vein "paradox and contradiction," as Zwicker puts it, constitute an auto-critique of writing.[51] But this vein of critique tends to ignore both Dryden's Catholicism and his political ambitions, and it assumes that literature can be ideological but not political and that religion is of interest only at the level of form. Even when critics have tried to take his conversion seriously in terms of his literary accomplishment, the critical grammar has often demanded that every engagement about Dryden's conservatism or Catholicism be hedged.[52] Colin Jager, for example, distinguishes Dryden's pre-conversion commitment to "literal" interpretation, which separates form and content, from his post conversion sacramental poetics, yet Jager measures the value of this poetics in terms of whether it promotes liberal multiculturalism.[53] There has been a twenty-first century trend to take seriously the relation between Dryden's Catholicism and his literary career. Some critics seem to want to recover both Dryden and Catholicism at once – we might characterize these as partaking of a "religious" turn in critical studies, rather than a postsecular one, and thus one that is historicist rather than allowing for a living literary history.[54] More relevant to my argument has been renewed critical interest in The *Hind and the Panther*, perhaps influenced by Margaret Doody's effusive claim that it is "the great, the undeniable, sui generis poem of the Restoration era."[55] Matthew Augustine convincingly demonstrates that interest in this poem exemplifies the larger critical problem of trying to see Dryden as "whole," a desire that often rests on seeing *The Hind and the Panther* as a means of proving the poet's spiritual integrity and ultimately the integrity of his character.[56] Augustine's intervention in this problem is to propose "Transversion" as a model for taking seriously the influence of Catholicism on Dryden's writing.[57] Steven Zwicker's argument that Dryden's poetry works to displace meaning – and thus participates in Catholic mysticism – is an influence on my approach, but for Zwicker the replacement for "meaning" is ambiguity and irony, whereas I am trying to explore the poem not as meaning but as experience. Molly Murray's account of the poem – in which the contingency of experience makes religious conversion "a redefinition of a believing self" – offers a way of thinking about how to explore what the poem's curious combination of simplicity (of meaning) and complexity of both form and content have to do with secularization.[58] Along with Augustine, closest to my own thinking is Melissa Pino's argument that Dryden's theory and practice of translation offer a "communion between the translator and the original author" (56) and that "Dryden's evolving ideas of translation theory were intimately bound to his changing religious beliefs" (62).[59] My account of Dryden hinges on communities of readers, and thus I do not criticize or supersede these account of the poem; rather I build upon them (and reconfigure them) in order to conceptualize how a new mode of readings came out of Dryden's representational strategies of the 1680s. This chapter offers a prehistory of Dryden's turn to translation and fleshes out the connections between Dryden's literary practice and theory and his conversion, in order to discover what it means to take seriously, and in tandem, Dryden's Catholicism, his interest in political abdication (his own and the Stuarts), and his theorization of the reading experience.

Like other writers studied in this book, Dryden's prescience about the literary is related to his conservatism with respect to the religio-political. However, while Dryden was once – and for a long time – the most celebrated poet and exemplar of his age (the age of Dryden, after all), he is rather less of interest to readers in the twenty-first century than many of the authors I study here. Aphra Behn, for example, is the subject of both cult-like acclaim and wide-ranging interest. Margaret Cavendish's critique of science and her singularity are according her a twenty-first century scholarly renaissance. Meanwhile Dryden, it seems, is read by only a few monkish devotees, secreted in their own closets. This chapter might explain why this is an appropriate legacy for Dryden, one he even predicted in the preface to *Don Sebastian*. Still, I would like to make the case that Dryden may be more widely relevant to twenty-first century readers, an argument that hinges on accepting a particular view of the literary sphere as conservative and on what we might take to be Dryden's relevance to postsecular critique.

A number of critics have recently called for post-hermeneutic or post-critical reading practices, some of which bear similarities to Dryden's modes of reading. Calls for a new philology by critics such as Jerome McGann and Frances Ferguson historicize the practice of literary criticism, tracing the current crisis in literary studies to the demise of philology in favor of philosophy.[60] For McGann, a key date is the publication of Francois Lyotard's *Postmodern Condition* in 1975.[61] As I argued with respect to the *Hind and the Panther*, philology was well suited to Dryden's aesthetic of the 1680s. For McGann, the shift from philology to philosophy set up the current "crisis in the humanities," but it can be traced all the way back to the Enlightenment project's commitment to "new norms for understanding."[62] Dryden's literary reputation tracks more or less in tandem with McGann's historicization of the Enlightenment project of critique. According to McGann's account, Dryden's relevance would be eclipsed when self-referential and philosophical forms of critique peak. Calls for post-hermeneutic methods of reading might thus make Dryden's work interesting once again.

The postsecular turn also makes it possible to reexperience Dryden's mid-career writing differently, thanks to critics who are analyzing the affect and the reading methods of secularity in order to propose alternatives to hegemonic literary hermeneutics. Talal Asad for instance shows how the Christian secular critique of Muslims hinges on a disdain for their reading practices: from this secular perspective, the Quoran "forces" Muslims to be guided by it; hence the text is determinate, magical, or infectious and readers passive. By contrast, Christians are free to "interpret" the bible as they please: the text is passive and readers are active.[63] In a related postsecular vein, Saba Mahmood argues that under secularization, feelings shift from being adverbial – a manner of doing something and thus one aspect of an action – to agential – a cause or a motivator of action.[64] This makes it impossible for secular feeling and embodied experience to be personally transformative. For Mahmood, secular notions of feeling – and the ethics on which they are based – are static. By contrast, the religious practices of the Muslim women she studies are based on exemplarity, on repeating the prophet's speech and actions. Such piety is a form of critique – a reading practice that produces an engagement with the world that is open to transformation, both of the subject and the world. While early modern Catholicism emphasized ritual and liturgy, most dramatically in the affective engagement with the passion of Christ and in agape, Reformation spirituality de-emphasized embodied, repetitious, and emotionally mimetic actions, creating, in Charles Taylor's account, a spiritual impoverishment, and in Mahmood's account foreclosing a mode of being that offers a dynamic alternative to the static secular emphasis on individual privatized feeling and action.[65]

Such lines of post-hermeneutic and postsecular critique, which I take to be related, allow us to recover the ways that Dryden's literary practices may have been responding to an emergent liberal hegemony. Blair Hoxby's argument about neoclassical tragedy is relevant here: He argues that such tragedy has been misunderstood by critics because it focuses on representing and producing passions, not on tragic action. My point is to suggest that a critical emphasis on both action and interpretation has obscured Dryden's goals in his writings of the 1680s and that his conversion to Catholicism may have functioned to leverage a theory of reading that constitutes early postsecular critique of emergent liberalism, one that combines a kind of submission to the mysterious materialities of a text with acknowledgment of its transformative potential. If one thing characterizes the literature of the 1680s, as Michael McKeon has argued, it is the wild genre experimentation that inaugurates a transition in the concept of genre itself.[66] The 1680s represents a moment of transition between the traditional genre system, which was idealist, and the emergence of literary history, which is largely nationalist and secular and which allows for narratives of historical and aesthetic development, methods of historical contextualization, and ideological interpretations of texts. Dryden neither creates nor foresees all of these developments. However, his experimentation with the various possibilities that allegory affords for telling secular stories opened up new perspectives of how one story relates to another story, one life relates to another life, one age relates to another age, and how one reader relates to another reader. The resulting reading practice and hermeneutic are not progressively historical, geographically limited, or causal but rather are based on mysterious communion of stories across time and space. Dryden's allegories of the 1680s are historically specific efforts to resist emergent models of secular history in favor of a ritualized, affective, transformative, and postsecular reading practice, one based on his adopted religion. Dryden endeavored – in the wake of the liberalizing turn of 1688–89 – to imagine that he could be relevant to the occasions of future readers via a vision of literary experience that we might see as a postsecular response to 1688–89 and that might, once again, be relevant to a twenty-first century turn away from critical practices derived from such liberalism.

Notes

1 Dryden's career has often been approached in relation to these personal and national experiences. Dryden's contemporaries set the tone of being cynical about his conversion that would persist for centuries. Matthew Prior and Charles Montagu, as early as 1687, satirized Dryden's propensity "to change sides meerly to keep his hand in ure," in *The Hind and the Panther, Transvers'd to the Story of the Country Mouse and the City-Mouse* (London, 1687), A6. On the influence of Samuel Johnson, Dryden was through the nineteenth century typically criticized as an opportunist. Alexandre Beljame, for example, argues that Dryden's changes of mind/party/religion were due to "worldly motives" and "personal advantage" (*Men of Letters and the English Public in the 18th Century: 1600–1744, Dryden, Addison, Pope* [London; New York: Routledge, 2013], 206). Thomas Babington Macaulay tellingly levels a critique at Dryden that is also a critique of his age and the idea of ages: "For, in fact, it is the age that forms the man, not the man that forms the age" ("Art. I – The Poetical Works of John Dryden," *The Edinburgh Review* 93 [January 1828]: 2). Subsequent critics have tried to nuance this critique, by various methods and emphases. Louis Bredvold argues that skepticism about human reason was key to Dryden both before and after his conversion (with the key distinction begin that his conversion marked a desire for an extra-human explanatory framework), in *The Intellectual Milieu of John Dryden: Studies in Some Aspects of 17th-Century Thought* (Ann Arbor: University of Michigan Press, 1956). As Maximillian Novak points out, subsequent critics challenged this view, claiming that Dryden was not antirationalist, though this made it difficult, as Novak explains, to explain his conversion. For his part, Novak treats Dryden as a product of his time, as "eminently politically incorrect" and finds his politics consistent, insofar as Dryden advocated for strong sovereignty against a fear of the "rabble" ("John Dryden's Politics: The Rabble and Sovereignty," in *John Dryden (1631–1700): His Politics, His Play, and His Poets* (Newark: University of Delaware, 2004), 88. Later I use Laura Brown as an example of this hermeneutics of suspicion ("The Ideology of Restoration Poetic Form: John Dryden," *PMLA* 97, no. 3 [1982]: 395–407). This essay, as with other recent work on Dryden, tries to take his Catholicism more seriously. See for example Geremy Carnes, *The Papist Represented: Literature and the English Catholic Community, 1688–1791* (Newark: University of Delaware Press, 2017); and Melissa Pino, "Translating toward

Eternity: Dryden's Final Aspiration," *Philological Quarterly* 84, no. 1 (Winter 2005): 49–75.

2 Samuel Johnson, *The Lives of the Poets a Selection* (Oxford: Oxford University Press, 2009), 121–217. Johnson calls Dryden the "father" of English criticism, a telling metaphor, but one that my reading of apostolic transmission might call into question or at least nuance (166). Johnson's case rests on the idea that Dryden developed "principles" to use in determining the "merit of the composition" (166). We might thus see Johnson's account of Dryden's significance as a secularization of literary – part and parcel of a shift from allegory and moralizing to aesthetic critique, but my reading of literary experience as practice complicates this idea. Johnson is closer to my argument when he says: "with Dryden we are wandering in quest of truth, whom we find, if we find her at all, drest in the graces of elegance; and if we miss her, the labour of the pursuit rewards itself; we are led only through fragrance and flowers" and an "author proves his right of judgement by his power of performance (167–68).

3 Earl Miner argues that Dryden theorizes progress and ages differently from his contemporaries. By combining translation and progress, stasis and motion, art and nature, Dryden invents a literary criticism that involves drawing upon both transcendent standards and notions of human progress – in a sense, this is Miner's case for a conservative Dryden ("Dryden and the Issue of Human Progress," *Philological Quarterly* 11, no. 1 [January 1961]: 120–29). In a later piece, Miner proposes that this argument might not apply after 1688, when Dryden's idea of an age become less "optimistically progressive" ("Introduction: Borrowed Plumage, Varied Umbrage," in *Literary Transmission and Authority: Dryden and Other Writers*, eds. Jennifer Brady and Earl Roy Miner [Cambridge: Cambridge University Press, 1993], 23n3). For Miner, as for me, 1688 and Dryden's conversion to Catholicism are key to a shift in how Dryden thinks about literary activity. Later in the essay, I build on Miner's idea that Dryden's later (post-conversion and post 1688) work formulates a theory of literary morality as grounded in affect and action; see "Ovid Reformed: Fable, Morals and the Second Epic?" in *Literary Transmission and Authority: Dryden and Other Writers*, eds. Jennifer Brady and Earl Roy Miner (Cambridge: Cambridge University Press, 1993), 79–120. This chapter fleshes out some of these ideas of Miner's, by looking closely at the 1680s as transitional in terms of developing these ideas. In the end, I disagree with Miner only one small point – Miner emphasizes Dryden's commitment to an idea of a hierarchy of readers where I will insist (a position suggested by my use of the gender-neutral pronoun "they") that Dryden's theory of readership might be even more diverse than Miner suspected.

4 Here I build upon Ruth Mack's understanding of "literary historicity" (*Literary Historicity: Literature and Historical Experience in Eighteenth-Century Britain* [Stanford, CA: Stanford University Press, 2009]). While Mack focuses on how literature makes possible an experiential understanding of the past, my reading of Dryden will focus more on the ways that literature

allows one to use creatively transcend the past to make sense of the present as well as to write in the present with future readers in mind.
5 Steven N. Zwicker, *Dryden's Political Poetry: The Typology of King and Nation* (Providence, RI: University Press of New England, 1972), 101.
6 For an overview of this historical and scholarly project, see Hans W. Frei, *The Eclipse of Biblical Narrative: A Study in Eighteenth and Nineteenth Century Hermeneutics*, rev. ed. (New Haven, CT: Yale University Press, 1980); Scott Hahn and Benjamin Wiker, *Politicizing the Bible: The Roots of Historical Criticism and the Secularization of Scripture*, 1300–1700 (Chicago: Crossroad, 2017); and Jon Douglas Levenson, *The Hebrew Bible, the Old Testament, and Historical Criticism: Jews and Christians in Biblical Studies* (Louisville, KY: Westminster/John Knox Press, 1993).
7 I am reading against critics who want to find either a transcendent ideal or the possibility of equivalence in the poem. Bernard Schilling, for example, reads the poem as effecting a loyalty "beyond contamination by its object, by whatever happened to embody it in passing" and argues that the poem functions like other moral allegories by presuming "its superiority to immediate historical reference" (*Dryden and the Conservative Myth: A Reading of Absalom and Achitophel* [New Haven, CT: Yale University Press, 1961], 14). Wasserman exemplifies the trend to find a synthetic relation between the tenor and vehicle of Dryden's literary tropes, in *The Subtler Language: Critical Readings of Neoclassic and Romantic Poems* (Baltimore: Johns Hopkins University Press, 1968). Michael McKeon is typical of the trend that sees Dryden's verse as exhibiting conflict between traditionalist (royalist) and progressive (capitalist) ideologies, in *Politics and Poetry in Restoration England: The Case of Dryden's Annus Mirabilis* (Cambridge, MA: Harvard University Press, 1975). I also read against critics like Laura Brown who want to read absolute difference in these parallels. For Brown, Dryden's aesthetic move is to insist on the "failure of functional equivalence" ("Ideology," 398).
8 Michael McKeon, for example, reads the poem as opening up distinctions between the sacred and secular figures, with the thrust of meaning invested in the contemporary story, in "Historicizing Absalom and Achitophel," in *The New Eighteenth Century: Theory, Politics, English Literature*, eds. Felicity Nussbaum and Laura Brown (New York: Methuen, 1987).
9 The poem was written in the midst of debates about the Test Act, which enforced the view that only communicants of the Anglican Church were eligible for public office. Before it was published, James issued the Declaration of Indulgence. According to William Myers, this accounts for the poem's mixed tones – it satirizes James' political ineptitude, which among other things "castrated" the poem's original intentions ("Politics in *The Hind and the Panther*," *Essays in Criticism* 19, no. 1 [January 1969]: 33).
10 Samuel Johnson, "Dryden," in *Lives of the Poets* (Oxford: Oxford University Press, 2006), 140; C. S. Lewis, "Shelly, Dryden, and Mr. Eliot," in *Selected Literary Essays* (Cambridge: Cambridge University Press, 2013), 187–208, 191.

11 While other critics (Earl Miner and Jennifer Brady, eds., *Literary Transmission and Authority: Dryden and Other Writers* [Cambridge: Cambridge University Press, 1993]; and Schilling, *Dryden and the Conservative Myth*, for example) see such structures as evidence that Dryden is balancing progress and transcendence, I am reading these poems as transitional, toward a more limited view of transcendence.

12 John Dryden, *The Works of John Dryden*, eds. Earl Miner and Vinton Dearing, vol. 3, *Poems, 1685–1692* (Berkeley: University of California, 1969).

13 J. M. Armistead, "The Mythic Dimensions of Dryden's *The Hind and the Panther*," *SEL* 16, no. 3 (1976): 380.

14 William Meyers, *Dryden* (London: Hutchinson, 1973), 117.

15 Thomas Brown, *Notes upon Mr. Dryden's Poems in Four Letters / by M. Clifford . . .; to Which Are Annexed Some Reflections upon the Hind and Panther, by Another Hand* (London, 1687), 19–20.

16 Jonathan Brody Kramnick, "Locke's Desire," *The Yale Journal of Criticism* 12, no. 2 (October 1, 1999): 189–208. Kramnick identifies, in Locke's revision to the *Essay*, "a restlessness that founds modern society" (204). Vivasvan Soni offers a compelling argument about the de-politicization of happiness in this period, in *Mourning Happiness* (Ithaca, NY: Cornell University Press, 2010).

17 For a discussion of this poem, and its relation to toleration, see Colin Jager, "Common Quiet: Tolerance around 1688," *ELH* 79, no. 3 (2012): 569–96. For a discussion of *The Hind and the Panther* and its stance on revelation, see Anne Cotterill, "'Rebekah's Heir': Dryden's Late Mystery of Genealogy," *Huntington Library Quarterly* 63, no. 1/2 (2000): 201–26.

18 This argument often hinges on critics making a case for Dryden's literary style as an effect of this pragmatism. Leo Braudy for example argues, "Dryden, in attempting to re-establish the legitimacy of the royalist view of history to accompany the pragmatic restoration of the monarchy, succeeds paradoxically in established instead the primacy of a certain sort of heightened language we call literary" ("Dryden, Marvell, and the Design of Political Poetry," in *Enchanted Ground: Reimagining John Dryden*, eds. Jayne Lewis and Maximillian E. Novak [Toronto: University of Toronto Press, 2004], 52–69, 58). In a similar vein, A. E. Wallace Maurer has argued that in *Absalom and Achitophel*, the complexity of the political situation is transformed into an intellectual and aesthetic complexity that supports a conservative politics ("The Form of Dryden's *Absalom and Achitophel*, Once More," *Papers on Language and Literature* 27, no. 3 [1991]: 320). For his part, David Bywaters characterizes it thus: "The rhetorical authority that Dryden had habitually drawn from his claim to represent a unified or unifiable nation is replaced by a different kind of authority drawn from the poet's professed mastery of and participation in a venerable and transcendent literary tradition" (*Dryden in Revolutionary England* [Berkeley: University of California, 1991], 10–11).

19 Sharon Achinstein, "Dryden and Dissent," in *Enchanted Ground: Reimagining John Dryden*, eds. Jayne Lewis and Maximillian E. Novak (Toronto: University of Toronto Press, 2004).

20 That *The Hind and the Panther* leverages religious debates to make a point about literary interpretation is nothing new, as the poem's first readers argued about the appropriateness of this project. Thomas Brown for example said "For all this, is it not great pity to see a Man in the flower of his *Romantick* Conceptions, in the full vigour of his Studies on *Love and Honour*, to fall into such a distraction, as to walk through the *Thorns and Briars* of Controversie, unless his *Confessor* hath commanded it, as a *Penance* for some past sins: that a Man, who hath read *Don Quixot* for the greatest part of his Life, should pretend to interpret the *Bible*, or trace the Footsteps of *Tradition*, even in the darkest Ages?" (*Notes*, 19–20). George Etherege said the poem "has a noble ambition to restore poetry to its ancient dignity in wrapping up the mysteries of religion in verse" (*The Letterbook of Sir George Etherege [1928]*, ed. Sybil Rosenfeld [Oxford: Oxford University Press, 1928], quoted in James Kinsley and Helen Kinsley, eds., *Dryden: The Critical Heritage* [London: Routledge, 1971], 174).

21 Burke's interest in the Ancient Constitution is articulated most famously in *Reflections on the Revolution in France*, ed. Paul Langford (Oxford: Clarendon, 1996). The career of J. G. A. Pocock has brilliantly excavated this concept in writers before Burke. See, for example, *The Ancient Constitution and the Feudal Law: A Study of English Historical Thought in the Seventeenth Century*, 2nd rev. ed. (Cambridge, NY: Cambridge University Press, 1987); and *The Machiavellian Moment: Florentine Political Thought and the Atlantic Republican Tradition*, rev. ed. (Princeton, NJ: Princeton University Press, 2016). For a helpful overview of Pocock's career on these issues, see Glenn Burgess, "From the Common Law Mind to 'The Discovery of Islands': J.G.A. Pocock's Journey," *History of Political Thought* 29, no. 3 (2008): 543–61.

22 For an overview of religious and literature hermeneutics, see David Jasper and Daniel Anlezark, "Biblical Hermeneutics and Literary Theory," in *The Blackwell Companion to the Bible in English Literature*, eds. Rebecca Lemon, Emma Mason, Jonathan Roberts, and Christopher Rowland (Hoboken, NJ: Wiley Online Books, 2010), https://doi.org/10.1002/9781444324174.ch3.

23 On Dryden's use of the occasion for political purposes while Poet Laureate, as a way of molding public opinion in a new era of party politics, see Phillip Harth, *Pen for a Party: Dryden's Tory Propaganda in Its Contexts* (Princeton, NJ: Princeton University Press, 2015).

24 Johnson has this to say about the character of Dryden's occasional poetry: "His criticism may be considered as general or occasional. In his general precepts, which depend upon the nature of things and the structure of the human mind, he may doubtless be safely recommended to the confidence of the reader; but his occasional and particular positions were sometimes interested, sometimes negligent, and sometimes capricious" (*Lives*, 168). I want to argue something quite different: that Dryden responds, on the occasion of his demotion from Poet Laureate and freedom from all duties calling for occasional poetry, with an account, in the paratext of *Don Sebastian*, of why all literature is occasional.

25 Anne Coterill has commented helpfully on this ending and its ironic lack of precept, arguing that the poem "acknowledges fable's ambiguity of pretended reticence and evasion coupled with aggression, and it holds the reader suspended in that tension indefinitely" ("'Rebekah's Heir,'" 202). In other words it is the fact of transmission, not any particular knowledge or moral, that the poem exemplifies.

26 John Dryden, *Don Sebastian*, in *The Works of John Dryden*, eds. Earl Miner and George R. Guffey, vol. 15, *Plays: Albion and Albanius, Don Sebastian, Amphitryon* (Berkeley: University of California, 1976). All references are to this version, with Act, scene and line number for references to the play and page numbers for references to paratextual material.

27 There was one previous novelization: *Don Sebastian, King of Portugal an Historical Novel in Four Parts* (London: Printed for R. Bentley and S. Magnes, 1683). An earlier treatment (a short – fourteen pages – translation from the Spanish) was also published in England in 1602 (José Teixeira, *The True Historie of the Late and Lamentable Aduentures of Don Sebastian King of Portugall after His Imprisonment in Naples, Vntill This Present Day, Being Now in Spaine at Saint Lucar de Barrameda* [London, 1602]).

28 Steven N. Zwicker, *Lines of Authority: Politics and English Literary Culture, 1649–1689* (Ithaca, NY: Cornell University Press, 1993), 173–74.

29 One way of reading such doublings is that the porousness of play's boundaries between such elements reveals, in Derek Hughes' words, a "spiritual kinship" between the disparate classes, geopolitical situations, and time periods ("Dryden's *Don Sebastian* and the Literature of Heroism," *Yearbook of English Studies*, 12 [1982]: 84). Dryden's use of the tragicomic form is distinct; typical Restoration tragicomedy, on Laura Brown's account "is based upon a strong aristocratic and neoclassical assumption that forbids the interaction of high and low characters on the stage," in "The Divided Plot: Tragicomic Form in the Restoration," *ELH* 47, no. 1 (1980): 68.

30 For Mack, the literary historicity that will characterize post-Restoration literature involves situating history as a "field of independent yet related causes" in "individual experience as the primary means of constructing temporality" (*Literary Historicity*, 8, 3). Dryden anticipates some of these developments, but my argument here is that Dryden emphasizes reading and interpretation – apostolic transmission – as central to understanding the causation that seems chaotic when experienced. Where Mack is concerned with how literature allows readers to experience history, Dryden is concerned with literary experience as coming after history and thus preparing readers for living in the present (and the future).

31 Angus Fletcher, *Allegory, the Theory of a Symbolic Mode* (Princeton, NJ: Princeton University Press, 2012), 181–220. For Zwicker, these formal characteristics, including the invention of incest (which has no historical parallel), work to make *Don Sebastian* seem less political (*Lines of Authority*, 186).

32 I take this to be a response to two biblical phrases. First "Wherefore by their fruits ye shall know them" (Matthew 7:20)," which turns up repeatedly in Restoration texts and in this play as "judge them not by their doctrine but by their fruits." And second, to the admonition to "be fruitful, and multiply" (Genesis 1:28). In the first case, people are to be judged not by their stated or real beliefs but rather by impacts in the world: the "fruit" of their beliefs and actions. This is by far the most common suggested meaning of "fruits" in the play. When the second, procreative, meaning of fruits is suggested, the implication is that the sins of the parents will redound upon their progeny (or lack thereof). As Dorax puts the moral to the play, "The unrepented Crimes of Parents dead,/Are justly punish'd on their Children's head." In the play, the metaphorical pattern of "fruits" has a complex array of meanings that build upon these two biblical references. Muley Moloch is called by Benducar a "wild and fruitless plant" but Benducar also thinks that he himself deserves the fruit of his own toil, even if it is "guilt and damnation." Almeyda takes a more positive, because Christian, stance on fruits when she expects that her conversion to Christianity will eventually result in forgiveness and charity; "though [such] Fruits come late, and are of slow increase" she says, as an explanation for her continued anger against Moley Moluch. "Fruits" is also used in reference to sexual intercourse and love: Benducar advises Moley Moluch that though rape is legal is it better to let "fruit" ripen than to "pluck the green distastful fruit." Mustapha makes the argument that those who are "preaching up rebellion" should "have the first fruits of it." And Antonio claims that, as a way of controlling Moryama, he may "take his revenge and turn Gardener again" – suggesting that producing children is a way to limit the female freedom that life in Christendom will afford her. Morayma, who is the central wit of the play, retorts that Antonio needs to be concerned that "some young Antonio" may turn up in his own family – that is, that Antonio's falseness and not his biology will be what is reproduced.

33 There is a pattern of keys and locks alongside a related pattern of insides and outsides ("You have the key, he opens inward to you"; "the gloomy outside, like a rusted chest"). And the "poison" which promises, though fruitlessly, to be an agent of rebellion, also moves from the preface to the play and then from a metaphoric register to a literal one: In the play Dorax, upon recognizing Sebastian, proclaims "he's poyson to me," and he wishes to avoid embracing Benducar so he can "keep Infection distant." Later, both Benducar and the Mufti try to poison Dorax, but the two different poisons, one hot and one cold, cancel each other out. In the preface, Dryden uses "poison" metaphorically, for the author's choice to kill ("butcher") a character "when the poet wants the brains to save him," a reference to Dryden's imagination of a continued life for Sebastian but one that also suggests why the poisoning of Dorax will fail – neither poets nor revolutionaries can rely upon death to resolve conflicts.

34 So, for example, the libertine lovers in *Marriage à la Mode* make a rational calculation that monogamy makes sense for them. The higher plot of that

comedy, in which the royal characters have a committed affective attachment to each other, only ends happily in marriage because, after toying with the possibility of a series of mismatched identities, it so happens that history, class status, and political expediency collude with the lovers' desires. *All for Love* refracts these issues slightly differently: Mistaken identity and misaligned politics plague the libertine-inclined lovers of the low plot, but events conspire to make marriage the most practical resolution for them. Anthony and Cleopatra's passionate attachment, by contrast, causes all manner of tragic effect, personal, political, and material, suggesting that uncontrolled passions are inimical to politics. To the extent that feelings figure, they are the "passions" of the seventeenth century, seen mostly, as Susan James has argued, in a quasi-Aristotelean schema that views passions, in their passivity and their irrationality, as opposed to both rational calculations of interest and what we will later think of as emotional intimacy (*Passion and Action: The Emotions in Seventeenth-Century Philosophy* [Oxford: Oxford University Press, 1997]). The passions are a mode of being imposed upon that can be creative but that must be regulated, and they are not easily made amenable to a sociable, ethical, or spiritual project.

35 James Horowitz makes a compelling case for a "queer" Dryden, but this is based not on sexual politics but on Dryden's binary approach to partisan politics in "Partisan Bodies: John Dryden, Jacobite Camp, and the Queering of 1688," *Restoration: Studies in English Literary Culture, 1660–1700* 39, no. 1 (November 10, 2015): 17–60.

36 As a post-exemplarity form of representing history, it fits with Ruth Mack's understanding of the trajectory of literary history (*Literary Historicity*, 9–10).

37 Joseph Addison, "Number 110: The Guardian," in *The Works of Joseph Addison*, vol. 4. (London, G. Bell & Sons, 1889), 208.

38 Jager, "Common Quiet," 584–85.

39 Morals, of course, are never the things that make a text long or obscure (as fables, including Dryden's, well exemplify). As Dryden will later write in the preface to his *Fables:* morals that "leap ... into sight without the Reader's trouble of looking after them" are "tedious" (IV: 1447). I concur with Richard Kroll that no such clear second moral emerges, but other critics have taken up the challenge to find a couched moral ("The Double Logic of Don Sebastian," in *John Dryden: A Tercentenary Miscellany*, ed. Steven N. Zwicker [San Marino, CA: Huntington Library, 2001], 47–69). David Bywaters for example finds the moral to be clear, that by "overthrowing the settled power that ensures the stability of the state and their own safety, the Protestants had in the Revolution entailed on their own posterity the war and anarchy passed on to them by the rebels of the 1640s" (*Dryden in Revolutionary England*, 42). Elaine McGirr argues that the play is "antimoral," in *Heroic Mode and Political Crisis 1660–1745* (Plainsboro Township, NJ: Associated University Press, 2009), 124. I would also point out that the mere need of a preface suggests that no precept can clearly be drawn from the examples. I would also recall the critical response from Matthew Prior and Charles Montagu to the *Hind and*

the Panther, which took issue with "this is his new way of telling a story and confounding the moral and the fable together," in *The Hind and the Panther Transversed to the Story of the Country Mouse and the City Mouse* (London, 1687) A2. Looking ahead to Dryden's fables, this question of morals becomes yet more complex: according to Jayne Lewis the morals there are "cynical and pragmatic" (*The English Fable: Aesop and Literary Culture, 1651–1740* [Cambridge: Cambridge University Press, 2006], 20).

40 Here is how I take the hidden "moral" of *Don Sebastian* in terms of Dryden's critical method: it is anti-allegoresis in the sense that it could be literally there – it is not an unsubstantial idea. It is also anti-allegoresis because the idea that the moral is (planted) physically in the story suggests that there is no moral that transcends the particulars of the story.

41 Mack, *Literary Historicity*, 9–10.

42 Johnson's account of Dryden's own reading is telling here: Dryden "had a more pleasant, perhaps a nearer, way to knowledge than by the silent progress of solitary reading. I do not suppose that he despised books or intentionally neglected them ... but that his studies were rather desultory and fortuitous than constant and systematical" (Johnson, *Lives*, 170). I concur with Johnson that Dryden is not advocating for systematic reading, because the idea of a canon read in order would violate the argument I am making here about temporality and reading.

43 Rose Zimbardo, "The Late Seventeenth-Century Dilemma in Discourse: Dryden's *Don Sebastian* and Behn's *Oroonoko*," in *Rhetorics of Order/ Ordering Rhetorics in English Neoclassical Literature*, ed. Clifford Earl Ramsey (Newark: University of Delaware Press, 1989), 46–67. My argument also differs in that I am emphasizing the ways that allegory persists in *Don Sebastian*.

44 Karl Mannheim, "Conservative Thought," in *From Karl Mannheim*, ed. Kurt H. Wolff (New York: Oxford University Press, 1971).

45 Ibid., 162.

46 Ibid., 169.

47 On Dryden's view of time, see Michael McKeon, who analyzes how Dryden combines cyclical and progressivist models of time, in "The *Politics of Pastoral Retreat: Dryden's Poem to His Cousin*," in *Enchanted Ground: Reimagining John Dryden*, eds. Jayne Lewis and Maximillian Novak (Toronto: University of Toronto Press, 2004), 91–110. Cedric Reverend shows how Dryden's view of literary history can be progressivist, in "Dryden and the Canon: Absorbing and Rejecting the Burden of the Past," in *Enchanted Ground: Reimagining John Dryden*, eds. Jayne Lewis and Maximillian Novak (Toronto: University of Toronto Press, 2004), 203–25. Michael Worth Gelber describes Dryden's literary-historical method by arguing that Dryden had been trying to arrange things chronologically, but then saw unusual connections, and thus the path of literature is "wayward and confused," in "Dryden's Theory of Comedy," *Eighteenth-Century Studies* 26, no. 2 (1992), 261–83. Steven N. Zwicker sees

Dryden as poised precisely between ancient and modern, in *The Cambridge Companion to John Dryden* (Cambridge: Cambridge 2004) 280–85.
48 Carl Schmitt and George Schwab, *Political Theology: Four Chapters on the Concept of Sovereignty* (Chicago: University of Chicago Press, 1985).
49 Even positive readings in this vein work by assuming a split between form and content, or the literary text and the author. Bywaters, for example, argues that Dryden hides political and polemical argument in the fabular form of Aesop (*Dryden in Revolutionary England*).
50 Brown, "Ideology"; Zwicker, *Dryden's Political Poetry*, 119.
51 Similar cases for a deconstructive Dryden can be found in Matthew Augustine, "Dryden's 'Mysterious Writ' and the Empire of Signs," *Huntington Library Quarterly: Studies in English and American History and Literature* 74, no. 1 (March 2011): 1–22; and Horowitz, "Partisan Bodies." Jayne Lewis accords more single-minded purpose to Dryden but posits an open-endedness about interpretive mediation. While Dryden "hotly pursues a single, highly interested perspective" his writing nonetheless "invites appropriation by competing interests" (Lewis, *English Fable*, 3).
52 Anne Cotterill, for example, argues that the turn to Catholicism is responsible for both the interiority of Dryden's late works (which is presumably on the right side of history) and their "burying" of female characters ("'Rebekah's Heir,'" 204).
53 In this reading, "Religio Laici" is anti-intellectual and anti-literary and "pursues a conservative, Counter-Reformation end through a most radical means" (Jager, "Common Quiet," 580). For Jager, the purpose of Form in Dryden (or at least "Religio Laici") is to hollow out meaning.
54 For a comparison of the religious turn versus postsecularism, see Alison Conway and Corrinne Harol, "Toward a Postsecular Eighteenth Century," *Literature Compass* 12, no. 11 (November 2015): 565–74. Geremy Carnes, whose works exemplifies a religious turn, argues that critics should take *Don Sebastian*'s "engagement with religious subjects as seriously as its engagement with political subjects," an important point and one that produces a fascinating (if to me unconvincing) way of reading marriage and Catholicism in the play, but, in its instance on the play's relevance to "contemporary concerns specific to the English Catholic community" of 1688, the reading reduces the literariness of the play to a kind of political shell game ("Catholic Conversion and Incest in Dryden's Don Sebastian," *Restoration: Studies in English Literary Culture, 1660–170*, 38, no. 2 [2014]: 5, 6). Ann Barbeau Gardiner goes much further, imagining the *Hind and the Panther* as a spotless monument to Dryden's conversion. Her argument about Dryden's "Ulyssean eloquence" indexes the authenticity of his religious conversion rather than anything about his literary project ("Division in Communication: Symbols of Transubstantiation in Donne, Milton, and Dryden," in *Religion in the Age of Reason: A Transatlantic Study of the Long Eighteenth Century*, ed. Kathryn Duncan [New York: AMS, 2009], 1–17).

55 Margaret Anne Doody, *The Daring Muse: Augustan Poetry Reconsidered* (Cambridge: Cambridge University Press, 1985), 85.
56 Matthew C. Augustine, *Aesthetics of Contingency: Writing, Politics, and Culture in England, 1639–89* (Manchester: Manchester University Press, 2018), 205.
57 Ibid., 199.
58 Molly Murray, *The Poetics of Conversion in Early Modern English Literature: Verse and Change from Donne to Dryden* (Cambridge: Cambridge University Press, 2009), 172.
59 Pino, "Translating," 56, 62.
60 Frances Ferguson, "Philology, Literature, Style," *ELH* 80, no. 2 (2013): 323–41; Jerome McGann, "Philology in a New Key," *Critical Inquiry*, 39, no. 2 (2013): 327–46.
61 McGann, "Philology," 330.
62 Ibid., 332.
63 Talal Asad, *Formations of the Secular* (Redwood City, CA: Stanford University Press, 2003).
64 Saba Mahmood, *Pious Formations: The Islamic Revival and the Subject of Feminism* (Princeton, NJ: Princeton University Press, 2004).
65 Charles Taylor, *A Secular Age* (Cambridge, MA: Harvard University Press, 2007).
66 For an overview of the modern "decay" and "disenchantment" of the genre system, see Michael McKeon, "Genre Theory," in *Theory of the Novel: A Historical Approach*, ed. Michael McKeon (Baltimore: Johns Hopkins University Press, 2000), 1–4, 3.

PART III

Political Agents and Novel Forms

CHAPTER 5

Passivity
The Passion of *Oroonoko* and the Ethics of Narration

Chapters 3 and 4 explored how Cavendish and Dryden leveraged their conservative commitments and their literary endeavors to explore questions of how literary experience can shape communities: Margaret Cavendish's investigation of possible worlds and Dryden's imagination of future readers register the desire and the difficulty of imaging different political and social worlds from the emergent secular liberal ideal. Chapters 5 and 6 introduce a related theme of human agency: the ways that individual political agency is figured in novels. Focusing on two concepts – passivity and revolution – that might seem to be opposite, I explore in these last chapters the ways that the novel form facilitated an exploration of the limits of human agency via counterrevolutionary figures of failed agency: the royal slave and the Jacobite. The intention is not to claim that accounts of the novel that emphasize individual agency or that focus on capital accumulation or the marriage plot – that is, that tie the novel form to a secular liberal worldview – are wrong, but rather to explore the connections between certain literary forms (limited narration and historical fiction) and conservative (here meaning antirevolutionary) political positions. This chapter, which builds on my analysis of Aphra Behn in Chapter 1, explores the way that *Oroonoko*'s narrative strategies represent the possibility of ethical human action – and ethical human narration – in a colonial setting, linking passive obedience with novelistic narration. Both practices stake a claim to ethics but are impotent in the immanent world of eighteenth-century (colonial and slave-holding) England.

When the "royal slave" protagonist of Aphra Behn's *Oroonoko* (1689) encounters the Surinam war captains and hears that their right to military leadership is established via self-mutilation, he deems this "passive valour" to be "too brutal to be applauded."[1] Nonetheless, Oroonoko expresses his "esteem" of the war captains, who prove their bravery in a "debate" that involves "contemptibly" cutting off ears, noses, and lips, among other things (56). This fast-paced text's sole mention of "passive" occurs here.

But this belies the text's reliance on passivity as a thematic and a plot device. The grandfather's impotence, the numb eel's ability to paralyze its victims, Oroonoko's inability to execute his plan for revenge: these are just a few examples of the way that passivity dominates the plot of *Oroonoko*. *Oroonoko* is a text fundamentally concerned with political obedience, written at precisely the moment in British history when that question was more or less being resolved in favor, according to the Whig interpretation of history, of the subject's right to refuse obedience to political authority, indeed even, according to John Locke and others, in favor of the obligation that the subject rebel against a tyrannical authority.[2] Behn, as is well known but not so comfortably assimilated, was a political conservative who was loyal to the king and probably Catholic, culturally and politically if not spiritually.[3] In her poem, "To His Sacred Majesty, King James the Second," she celebrates the Catholic monarch's "patience, suffering, and humility."[4] What, then, are we to make, and indeed why has so little been made, of a text in which the hero, very much celebrated by the female pen who narrates his story, spends such a noticeable amount of the text passive, almost supernaturally so, and in which the main actions are an impotently executed revolt and a Christ-like execution? In general, a modern, Whiggish perspective derogates passivity and obedience and valorizes the congruence of belief and action. Oroonoko's passivity, the narrator's celebration of him, and, most of all, the narrator's own inaction, are thus key critical problems in the text. According to Victoria Kahn, in the seventeenth century "passion and action" replace "virtue and vice" as explanations for human motivation – and thus for human ethics and politics.[5] *Oroonoko*, written during a crucial overlap between these two systems of value and in the thick of the events of 1688–89 and its renewed debates about passive obedience, offers a unique theorization of the virtues of passivity. It makes a pragmatic, if not a religious, case for passive obedience negatively, by repeatedly showing the consequences of active disobedience as well as the immorality of most action. It makes that case universally, by having its exemplar be both royal and enslaved, British and African. And it makes its case through its aesthetic, locating ideal human behavior in the values that will dominate realist novels (emotional passion, passive witnessing, and political detachment) over the values of politics (activity and power) and theater (heroic romance and "applau[se]," 56). *Oroonoko*'s case for passivity rests not on divine right, contract, or historical precedent. Rather, in response to the opposition claim that passive obedience is "contrary to the Law of Nature," *Oroonoko* demonstrates passivity to be a law of nature, linked to procreation and to death and not susceptible to human will, contract, or politics.[6] This articulation of a universal law of passivity takes place in the context of a white woman who narrates the abuse of a black man, and the passivity of these figures is inherently connected. The argument in this chapter can support a reading of *Oroonoko* as a critique of the exclusion of women and black people from models of liberal agency, but it can also be read – with the same evidence – as apologizing for it and offering, in novelistic narration, an alibi for liberalism's exclusion of women and black people and for pitting their needs against one another.

The Politics of Passivity

The loyalist doctrine of passive obedience, associated in a political sense with the Stuarts at this critical moment of their demise, is frequently conflated with nonresistance. But nonresistance is only the negative value in a theory of political obligation that has three parts: active obedience, passive obedience, and nonresistence.[7] In his 1689 tract on passive obedience, the Anglican clergyman Abednego Seller (1646/7–1705) offers a typical definition of political obligation: "the duty of every Christian, in things lawful, actively to obey his superior; in things unlawful, to suffer rather than obey, and in any case, or upon any pretense whatsoever not to resist, because whoever does so shall receive to themselves Damnation."[8] Thus, passivity relates not to obedience (which is active), nor to resistance (which is prohibited), but rather to the acceptance of punishment in cases of non-obedience. When a sovereign demands something unlawful, the subject may choose to "suffer rather than obey." The injunction against resistance is thus not absolute in terms of what it demands of its adherent, who must decide when it is appropriate to "obey" and when to "suffer," and it allows for a discrepancy between conscience and action. Seller, quoting "Dr. Jackson," describes passive obedience as "subjection of the outward man."[9] This "subjection" depends upon the prioritizing, morally if not politically, of inward conscience; thus, the outward, less important, part is subjugated, but the conscience remains pure.[10] As John Kettlewell (1653–95) says, "religion, is an internal thing" and "any outward force upon us, must stop at the outside of us: or, if it pierce further, it will force away our Lives, before it reach our Hearts."[11] Richard L. Greaves locates the genesis of this emphasis on conscience and interiority as a basis for political subjectivity in Elizabethan Protestant, including Puritan, dogma: "Conscience was the key in determining the proper object of obedience, for it was never justifiable to violate one's conscience in order to comply with a magistrate's decree. In fact, conscience bound one not to fulfill such commands."[12] The doctrine of passive obedience, thus, was not so much a call to complete submission but rather an explanation of how to respond to disagreements with a political ruler and thus a primer on non-obedience (and according to J. C. D. Clark, a precursor to modern forms of civil disobedience) rather than a mandate to obey.[13]

When passive obedience is discussed, both by its critics in the seventeenth and eighteenth centuries and in later analyses, it is often described as fundamentally proscriptive and absolute, in that it prohibits rebellion in all circumstances. John Toland (1670–1722), for example, glosses it as "PASSIVE, or unlimited OBEDIENCE," that inculcates obedience to commands "tho' never so strange, illegal, unjust, or prejudicial."[14] But passive obedience's roots in theories of conscience – which developed in the seventeenth century into the emphasis on law over government – allowed seventeenth-century writers to use the concept as a way of articulating the crucial role of subjects in evaluating their rulers. As James Ellesby (b. 1644 or 1645) put it, "Let our Governours be never so Bad, Actual Obedience is due to all their Lawful Commands, and Submission to those that are Otherwise."[15] Writers on passive obedience are thus theorizing different options available to subjects, who must make decisions based on their own evaluation of the legitimacy of the ruler's commands; passive obedience thus offers ways for the subject to act no matter how ungodly the king. This subtlety in theories of obedience, in which conscience has to be weighed against the good of political stability, goes back at least as far as Thomas Aquinas (1225–74), and it positions the politico-religious subject in a complex and thoughtful relationship to the ruler.[16] "We must," one writer explains, "be patients or Agents; Agents, when he is good and godly; patients, when he is tyrannous and wicked."[17] Thus while the Whig interpretation of history would suggest that in 1688–89 there were two camps – those for complete subjection and those for liberty – in fact, the landscape was much more nuanced. Up until 1688–89, and for some time afterwards, nearly all political theory was based in some form of obedience.[18] Moreover, absolute positions on obedience were hard to come by. For example, the notoriously conservative Robert Filmer (d. 1653) argues that the rules of obedience "cannot be learnt without a relative Knowledge of those Points wherein a Sovereign may Command," and he thus makes a case for the importance of education and individual reason in determining obedience.[19] And from the other side, Samuel Johnson (1649–1703), passive obedience's most ardent critic, celebrates forms of resistance practiced by early Christians – prayers, words, and noncompliance with orders – that are in fact congruent with, indeed are even the exemplars of, passive obedience.[20]

The doctrine of passive obedience is often conflated with divine right, but in fact these two concepts are quite distinct, as the example of Christ proves.[21] Passive obedience has no necessary relation to the king's divinity; to the contrary, it theorizes the mandate for obedience under the conditions of an illegal and tyrannical rule. The traditional exemplar of this mode of passive obedience was Jesus's suffering under unjust Roman rule. From him, Englishmen should learn to, "take vp the Cross" instead of rebelling.[22] Christ's active obedience consists in following the will of God, and his passive obedience consists in suffering the punishments that such (dis)obedience entails. Seventeenth-century sermons about the "active and passive obedience" of Christ stress that the two are inseparable: Christ followed both God's will and the law whenever possible, but when his religious conscience made following secular law impossible, he continued to follow God's will and suffered whatever the secular authorities demanded. Thus, Christ's Passion stood as the ultimate example of passive obedience, in that he suffered in submission to God's law. It also provided a way to theorize split allegiances: between sacred and secular authority and between body and soul. The major distinction between active and passive obedience thus involves not God's will, nor the subject's will or obedience, but rather the experience of the subject's body. As one Civil War tract put it, obedience consists in allowing the ruler's will to work "either of us, or on us; of us, when they command for Truth; on us, not by us, when they command against the Truth."[23] Thomas Bainbrigg (1636–1703) puts the case thusly: passive obedience, he complains, "sets Body and Soul at variance."[24] The passivity of Christ's body thus offered a complex heuristic for thinking about the nature of passivity – and of the body/soul relationship – in the political arena.

While Christ, as one writer put it, "never exercised any act of Civil Government," and thus a case could be made for a quietist version of Christic political subjectivity, the nature of Anglicanism as a national religion required some accommodation between religious and political modes of subjectivity.[25] During the Civil Wars, loyalist writers staked their claim to the moral and political high ground by representing Jesus' Passion as the ultimate expression of passive obedience and Catholic loyalty to the pope as its opposite. But after the Restoration of the Stuarts in 1660, Christ posed problems for a loyalist position, insofar as his suffering at the hands of a manifestly unjust ruler did not offer a model for Stuart loyalism. Christ as an exemplar of passive obedience also posed problems for an emergent Whig politics of sincerity as well as for writers interested in asserting a more nuanced, casuist, or radical position on political subjectivity.[26] Thus, while Christ figures importantly in this longer history of passive obedience, during 1688–89, writers – Behn excluded – more frequently turned to the Old Testament and to the primitive Christians, whose resistance to tyrannical rulers like Constantius and Julian could be more easily marshaled to support their position.[27]

Discussions of passive obedience – for, against, and descriptive – rightly point out that it frequently finds its moral justification in the afterlife. The biblical source on which theories of passive obedience rest is Romans 13, which argues, as is echoed in the quotation above by Seller, "they that resist, shall receive to themselves damnation."[28] Nonetheless, passive obedience is not an apolitical doctrine. It makes possible modes of political agency that are expressive rather than active, and thus it legitimizes particular methods – we might call them literary – of political activity. Bainbrigg, for example, argues that options for subjects who disagree with their ruler include: "make their Defenses and plead their Causes," "pray to God," and "accept of deliverance"; he argues that passive obedience does not mean that one should "court Suffering" because there is always the option, of which the French Huguenots are the most relevant example, of exile: "[O]ur Savior has given us leave," he says, "when they persecute us in one City to flee into another."[29] Many writers refer to the "Prayers and Tears" that the performance of passive obedience can produce in political and military terms; one writer, for example, calls these forms of expression a "thundering Legion of Prayers and Tears," thus implying their capacity for political or moral effects.[30] On the opposing side, writers argued that Romans 13 is not applicable to the current situation of James II's tyrannical rule for, as Johnson writes, "no Tyrant can put in so much as his Nose at the 13th of the Romans," and thus James is an "outcast" of Romans.[31] Supporters and critics of passive obedience in 1688–89 agree that Romans 13 explains the limits of political obedience: For loyalists, this limit space is where passive obedience becomes potentially efficacious as oppositional discourse in "Prayers and Tears," while for Whigs, this space is where political obedience is suspended and genuine autonomous political action can happen.[32]

The historical trajectory and political alignments of passive obedience reveal some surprising plot twists. The English Protestant embrace of what came to be known as passive obedience had deep roots in the politics of English anti-Catholicism. In anti-Catholic propaganda, as Greaves and

John Neville Figgis have argued, Catholics are portrayed as clearly and treasonously prioritizing their allegiance to the pope over any secular authority.[33] Passive obedience was thus originally a Protestant, even Puritan, articulation of difference from Catholicism. After the Restoration, it came to be "the defining symbol of the Anglican middle ground" according to Clark. And then, during 1688–89, it came to be thoroughly identified with the Catholic James II and his most ardent supporters.[34] Derided by radical Whigs and their later historians, it could nonetheless be made congruous with 1688–89; for example, according to George Hickes, "the majority of Subjects" at that time "were merely passive, and surprized into deliverance."[35] Passive obedience also allowed loyalists to align their Whig opposition with Catholics. The Whig opponents of passive obedience criticize Catholics but have, according to one author, "carried along with them one of their most pestiferous Opinions," insofar as both legitimate rebellion against kings: Catholics via their allegiance to the pope and Whigs via vesting authority in the people.[36] In another irony of the history of passive obedience, its most famous critic, Johnson, while being whipped for his writings against passive obedience, invoked Christ's sufferings to buoy his supporters.[37] In sum, no writers on passive obedience during this time considered it to be apolitical or irrelevant, and as a concept it had a certain plasticity that made it politically volatile.[38]

Writings on passive obedience repeatedly invoke the New Testament parable in which Jesus' response to the question of paying taxes to an unjust ruler is to "Render ... vnto Cesar the things which be Cesars."[39] The phrase "render vnto Cesar" means render unto to the king that, and only that, which the king deserves, since the following phrase instructs followers to render "vnto God the things which be Gods." That which is Caesar's includes taxes, specifically the coins that already bear the image of Caesar, and, in most loyalist interpretations, the lack of active resistance. But, in the hands of writers both for and against passive obedience, this passage is ultimately more about what cannot be "render[ed] to Cesar," not only conscience but in fact everything outside of tax money.[40] In *Oroonoko*, this mandate to "render vnto Cesar the things which be Caesars" is deeply ironic, as Oroonoko's enslaved name is Caesar. The choice to call him Caesar reflects his amphibious nature as royal slave, and it perhaps prefigures his grotesque cutting/cesarean at the end, a plot development that, I will argue, reflects a complicated politics of passivity. As a violent history of a largely passive royal slave who chooses exile over revolt, *Oroonoko* investigates the possibility of meaningful political action in a body whose ultimate destiny is desacralized passivity.[41]

Oroonoko has proved incredibly fertile ground for scholars working in a diversity of critical methods and fields, as Srinivas Aravamudan pointed out when he characterized the phenomenon as "oroonokoism."[42] Feminist scholars working on the history of women writers, postcolonial scholars working on slavery/colonialism, and those researching the prehistory and roots of the novel have all found things to love – or to hate – about *Oroonoko*. On its path to canonization, two camps of *Oroonoko* critics have emerged: those doing ideological readings about gender (Ros Ballaster, Margaret Ferguson, Moira Ferguson, Charlotte Sussman) or about race and colonialism (Laura Brown, Laura Doyle, Albert Rivero), and those who argue that such readings are anachronistic (George Guffy, Derek Hughes, Richard Kroll, Adam Sills).[43] In simple terms, these camps differ in whether they approach *Oroonoko* retrospectively, as an avatar of the novel and of the ideological issues that concern modern critics, or whether they see the text as a product of the seventeenth-century aesthetic values and the specific political issues that provide its context. These camps reflect the amphibious nature of the text: like its royal enslaved protagonist, *Oroonoko* straddles two worlds. It reveals its roots in seventeenth-century politics and aesthetics via its baroque investments in the physical body, in allegory, and in its fantasy attachment to the possibility of virtuous transcendence. It reveals its commitments to modernity in its realism and in its commitments to the notion that the particulars – of race, class, and gender but more importantly of the contingent ethical choices one can make in this realistic world – matter. In terms of politics, it shows how and perhaps why literature leaves behind the kinds of specific political concerns of those in power, including God – and the allegorical mode that reflected and represented those concerns – to focus, in novels, on more abstract ideological issues, while simultaneously investing in the specific details of individual lives. Hence the use of the term "baroque realism," my own contribution to oroonokoism, is an effort to explain this hybrid quality of *Oroonoko* and its eponymous protagonist, the passive royal slave. While most scholars have followed the Whig interpretation of history, which finds passive obedience to be absurd both politically and intellectually, I read *Oroonoko* as a specific product of 1688–89, as a hybrid text on many levels, and as part of the complex loyalist counter-theorization to emergent Whig orthodoxy about political subjectivity.

Passivity, Plot, and Genre

Oroonoko is a curious text in which none of the significant actions of the hero – except for his initial disobedience – actually relate to the plot developments.[44] Oroonoko slays tigers, narrowly escapes a numb eel, and he even fights real battles in Africa, but none of this bears upon the events that structure the course of Oroonoko's life and narrative, all of which are motivated by linguistic, symbolic, representational, or external forces. His two great acts – leading the exodus of other slaved people and killing Imoinda – are not so much actions as withdrawals from the theater of action. His lack of labor, that fact which makes him a "slave" "only [in] name," also marks something important about his political position: because he is not asked to do anything for the ruling authority, he has little occasion to withhold his obedience (46). Oroonoko, as a royal slave, is supposed to be the exception to all rules, for example to the rule that all women belong to his grandfather and to the rule that enslaved people must labor. But *Oroonoko* repeatedly demonstrates that exceptionality – and autonomous activity – can only be sustained fictionally, in romance.

While enslaved, Oroonoko engages in a series of heavily symbolic heroic activities, in which his power to command rather than perform obedience is fictionalized in a romance mode. When he goes tiger hunting, Oroonoko's physical command over the natural world both provides the entertainment for the colonialists and keeps the peace in their society. Even here, where his activity is largely romantic symbolism and undertaken for amusement ("applau[se]" 56) and indeed as a form of keeping him politically passive, Oroonoko is not so very active. In slaying the first tiger, Oroonoko calmly gets his friends to "obey" him by leaving the tiger to him, he fixes his "aweful stern Eyes" on the tiger, puts himself "into a ... posture of defense" and runs his sword through the tiger in a manner that suggests static posing and aesthetic restraint – as in classical sculpture – rather than impassioned activity and representational excess – as in baroque art (49). In pursuit of "trophies and garlands" Oroonoko then proceeds to stalk a tiger who has unfathomably withstood several bullets to the heart, and, again, it is Oroonoko's patience and technique with a bow and arrow, "so good a will, and so sure a hand," not any extreme physical feat, that allow him to slay the tiger (50–51). In killing both of these tigers, Oroonoko and his colonizer friends fictionalize him as a romantic hero, able to perform feats that others find to be impossible. But Oroonoko is also acting politically: Both tigers have infringed upon private property, the second tiger stealing sheep and oxen that "were for the support of those to whom they belonged" (49). This casual mention of private property within this ostensible diversion reveals these tiger episodes to be deeply implicated in the colonial economy, so deeply that the beneficiaries of these actions ("those to whom they belonged") never enter the narrative. Within

Oroonoko's narrative, these actions are performative or fictionalized heroic activities. Their real effect is Oroonoko's political passivity: his own refrain from taking any private property, including his own enslaved body, away.

These heavily romanticized and fictionalized episodes are followed by one that is seemingly anomalous. In their continued pursuit of mutually favorable goals – Oroonoko's real passivity and romantic entertainment for all – Oroonoko, in one of the greatest ironies in this highly ironic text, next pursues a numb eel, a creature whose sole power is that of making its victim passive. This episode teaches Oroonoko that he is indeed like others, that his special statuses – as a royal and as an enslaved person who does not labor – do not exempt him from the numb eel's powerful mandate to passivity. The Surinam natives who save Oroonoko from his plight are nameless, peripheral to the main narrative; their rescue of Oroonoko exists only as a sideline to their own lives and merely postpones Oroonoko's ultimate passivity within his own narrative. The eel episode meditates on the impotence of physical force and the inevitability of passivity, even in a prince without a people and an enslaved person who does not labor. In all three of these encounters between the royal slave and power of nature, the denouements rehearse the vulnerability of the natural body: the first episode ends with the tiger whelp being thrown at the narrator's feet; the second with the supernatural tiger, whose heart has absorbed seven bullets, being anatomized; and the third with the eel, who had a seemingly supernatural power to make Oroonoko passive, being eaten by the colonizers and Oroonoko in a civilized meal. All of these episodes are not about the human power over nature, but rather the natural law of passivity: both Oroonoko's and the animals'. These fictionalized stagings of what we might anachronistically call Oroonoko's agency – but which prove nothing so much as his lack of agency – take place within a larger plot structure in which Oroonoko's activities are structurally irrelevant.[45] In the main events of the narrative, Oroonoko is even less active and less politically relevant than he is during these staged heroics. This representation shares features seen in Chapter 3 with Cavendish's *Blazing World* in that limitations on human knowledge and action are grounded in natural laws, although here it is the human body specifically, not the larger laws of nature, that we might see as the foundation of Behn's conservatism.

In Africa, during the chronological beginning of the story, we see a traditional monarchy functioning, albeit imperfectly, under the mandate of political obligation, including passive obedience. Oroonoko and Imoinda submit, for the most part, to the grandfather's rule, despite his impotence and the illegality of his actions. The charming young protagonists must mask their true feelings, which are revealed by nonverbal communication and by the narration. As long as they do not act on their true feelings, calm reigns in Coramantien, with both Oroonoko and the grandfather prohibited from sexual activity. In this first part of the novel, a conservative doctrine of political obligation is explicitly invoked: Imoinda and Oroonoko base their actions on the maxim that "They pay a most absolute resignation to the monarch," an "obedience" that is "not at all inferior to what they paid their Gods" (14–15).[46] The first and only significant action that Oroonoko takes in the story is to defy his obligation to his grandfather and sovereign by having sex with Imoinda. In this romantic betrayal of political obligation, which is presented as background to the main narrative, the original dilemma in Coramantien reveals an ambivalence about political obligation that permeates the rest of the text, in so far as the story reinforces passivity and obedience, but it would not have occurred without this initial disobedience and the love story that motivated it. The prioritizing of passion over obedience that sets the action of *Oroonoko* on its tragic course is simultaneously romantic and antiromantic. It is romantic because romance eschews the limits of both nature and politics. Victoria Kahn has argued that in romance, "the ongoing consent and affections" are more important than obligation and thus there is no such thing as an "irrevocable act of consent."[47] Still, romance usually defers consummation; typically, the refrain from sexual activity marks the virtuous control of the passions that authorizes other forms of activity, often seemingly supernatural ones (like slaying tigers). The grandfather points out that according to their code of political obligation, not only should Oroonoko not have consummated his love for Imoinda, but also the grandfather should have put her to death rather than exiling her. Thus, according to both political and generic laws current in 1688–89, the rest of *Oroonoko* should never have happened. Oroonoko himself only lives because of the sacrifice of Imoinda's father, who becomes a "hero" when he passively "bow[s] his head" to "receive" the arrow "in his own body" that would have killed Oroonoko (10–12). The main events of the text thus operate outside the boundaries of stable social and political spheres – as well as the codes of romance – which are made possible by acts of obedience and passivity. The initial action of Oroonoko – to prioritize his affections and passions over parental approval and obedience – will be the plot that animates many eighteenth- and nineteenth-century novels. But here, in 1688–89, we are in relatively uncharted territory.

Thus, one way to gloss the tale of *Oroonoko* could go like this: an erstwhile perfect prince disobeys his grandfather's orders and subsequently suffers pain, misfortune, and a gruesome death (punctuated by a short period of sexual and domestic happiness). In this accounting, at the level of plot, Behn's gambit is to show that political obedience applies to all, as Oroonoko's disobedience takes him from a prince to enslaved. Imoinda, by contrast, is the perfectly obedient subject and a completely static character. When Oroonoko kills her, he only completes what the grandfather should have done in the first place. This is perhaps why Imoinda is "brave," "beautiful," and "constant," as well as why she gets the last word of the text (73). In order to make this reading work, the suffering that Oroonoko endures in Surinam must somehow be a result of the disobedience in Coramantien. But the two parts of the story – its two plots, two aesthetics, and two politics of obedience – do not have any causal relationship. For *Oroonoko* is also the tale of a prince whose claim to the "honour" adjudged by the narrator is not for heroic battles but rather for passivity and suffering.[48] Bainbrigg defends passive obedience by arguing that suffering for a good cause is what "men of worth" do in every age. "In the exercise of Vertue," Bainbrigg argues, "Man must have nothing of the Slave in him." A man who would "flinch from his duty" on account of suffering is "slavish."[49] Neither Oroonoko's initial disobedience nor his behavior in Surinam has anything to do with flinching from suffering. Hence, the suffering that Oroonoko endures – that which he endures because he is enslaved – is, paradoxically, that which keeps him from being "slavish." His disobedience takes him from royal to enslaved, and it is not his heroic deeds but rather his resulting suffering that constitutes his heroism.

Throughout its narrative, *Oroonoko* remains a text in which every action, no matter how benign (such as reproducing with the one you love and are married to) brings danger. Passivity, by contrast, has political and moral value. When asked, for example, why he has not acted on his desire for Imoinda, Trefry reports that her "modesty and weeping so tender and so moving" effectively "overcame" and "disarm[ed]" him and caused him, gratefully, to "retire" (42). Imoinda's expressive and moral passivity reproduce themselves in Trefry's avoidance of sexual assault upon her, just as, to some extent, they had that effect on the grandfather when she, "all in tears," tells him he is committing a sin and a crime to be with her (16). These repeated references to the moral and social effect of tears quite closely reflect the discourse about passive obedience, and they make a case for the moral superiority of passivity and expressivity over activity and agency. *Oroonoko* thus, via its meditation on passive obedience, offers some insight to the historical divorce of morality and ethical political action. The "prayers and tears" of political subordinates may not change either the political structure or the mandate to passivity, though that does not mean that they are unimportant, for they are the heart of the text's ethical project, as they will be for the novel of the eighteenth century.[50] In all the systems of value in the text – heroic, Christic, African, European – the passivity of the human subject is the foundation of virtue. This is why the generic and geopolitical vertigo of *Oroonoko* is important.

Lying and Lying Down

For Whigs writing during 1688–89 and its aftermath, passive obedience represented not only an abrogation of political rights but also a dangerous form of hypocrisy. The Whig critique of passive obedience was part of a larger critique of what they considered to be their opponents' hypocritical tendencies to divorce material, verbal, and visual forms of expression – including political action – from subjective truths and beliefs. Passive obedience, in which a subject's beliefs are not acted upon, along with other forms of hypocrisy, provided grounds of negation upon which Whigs theorized the legitimacy, the authenticity, and the morality of the modern individual, who makes ideas and actions coincide.

This is why it matters that rather than actions, the main plot motivators and thematic obsessions of *Oroonoko* have to do (as others have noted) with truth and oaths.[51] *Oroonoko* has typically been read as a conflict between honor (romance and monarchism) and contract (truth, realism, and so forth). Both of these systems rely on harmony between representation and action. In a world based on contracts, meaning what you say and doing what you say you will do are the foundation of social stability. Thomas Hobbes' natural law, for example, includes the provision that *"men perform their covenants made."*[52] The romance's commitment to honor is based on a similar commitment to the congruence of belief and action/agency. The key difference between honor and contract is that moral obligation underpins honor while contract establishes legal obligation.[53] But the dividing lines between these concepts, like the geographical boundaries in the text, are difficult to establish.

Behn's decision to begin *Oroonoko* with a description of the natives of Surinam before narrating the Coramantien passages that some critics have found so romantic violates chronology (not to mention confusing readers, perhaps deliberately, about which culture is being described). But it allows

Behn to posit an "absolute idea of the first state of innocence" before narrating the "history" of her hero (8). Her claim that the natives are prelapsarian rests substantially on their lack of a word for "a man who promised a thing he did not do," and the Englishmen provide the word "liar," as well as many occasions in which they demonstrate its meaning by unscrupulously lying (8). The critical consensus about this thematic in the text is redacted in the footnote to the Oxford edition: "Oroonoko is easily duped because his notion of honour is no match for those who lie" (270n8). That is, the English colonialists' blatant willingness to lie contrasts unfavorably with Oroonoko's romantic and prelapsarian "honour," even as it defeats it. From our postcolonial and Whiggish perspectives, the colonialists' repeated lying is not only an unfair way to enslave Oroonoko but it is also a failure of ethical liberal subjectivity more generally.[54]

However, it is not only the unethical but efficacious colonialists who lie. The lying, or the "Promis[ing] a thing [one does] not do" begins with the grandfather who banishes Imoinda to slavery because he believes "he had made a great conquest over himself, when he had once resolved, and had performed what he resolved" (28), but who then proceeds to lie to Oroonoko about what he has done (as well as to admit that he really should have killed her). If liar is the word for a "man who promised a thing he did not do," that definition applies not only to the English colonialists, who lie in the sense of deliberate deception, but also to the impotent Coramantien king, to the narrator, who lies about her ability to predict the governor's manumission of Oroonoko, and finally to Oroonoko himself, who lies repeatedly despite his commitment to a code of honor. As such, *Oroonoko*'s meditation on lying and passive obedience exceeds the demand for congruence between language and action that underlies both honor and contract.[55] It also responds to Behn's concerns (described in Chapter 1) about faith and belief in the absence of a figure of transcendent authority.

The prevalence of lying across geographical and cultural boundaries helps to account for the text's complex spatial and temporal organization. At the level of story (as opposed to plot), the geographical flow of the text moves from England across the Atlantic to Surinam and from Africa across the Atlantic to Surinam. With Surinam as the cosmopolitan meeting point and as the locus of all the action witnessed by the narrator, its status as a prelapsarian state of nature does not quite work. Rather – following Walter Benjamin, who argues that the baroque transposes original temporal data into spatial simultaneity, Chi-ming Yang, who has remarked that *Oroonoko*'s romance set in the New World make time and place "notably elusive," and Sills, who argues against a modern cartographic view of geography in the text – I want to take seriously the anti-mimetic representation of chronology and geography in the plot of *Oronoko*.[56] According to the narrative of lying and obedience that this chapter been developing, Oroonoko's story begins in history – with honor and contract as two competing but ultimately similar foundations for political action – and moves toward nature, where the body is inherently unable to comply with promise or desire. The action catalyzed by the definition of "liar" moves from history to nature in that it moves from lying about what has happened, to breaking promises about the future, to lying, and here the meaning begins to disaggregate, about what you are capable of doing. That is, the plot moves from lying as a mental act (whether representational or contractual) to lying as a physical act, or more properly a lack of physical action. For ultimately in *Oroonoko* lying – that is, lying down – is the one action that can be reliably performed. One can promise to take action or one can lie about one's intention to lie passively obedient, but inevitably, these all turn out to be lies.

Thus, while Oroonoko, the narrator, and the scholars who have written about the text focus more frequently on the broken promises of the colonialists and slave traders, for the purposes of this chapter, Oroonoko's own vows to "never lift a weapon, or draw a bow, but abandon the small remains of his life to sighs and tears" (29), to "make no resistance" (37), and to "lift [no] hand" (46) are the key to the text's engagement with passive obedience. Oroonoko promises to "act nothing upon the white people": he would prefer to "forfeit his eternal liberty, and life itself, than lift his hand against his greatest enemy," a promise he will fail to keep, except for the part about forfeiting his life (46). In this, he is not so different from the English colonialists who promise his freedom and repeatedly renege. I have already shown how Oroonoko's inaction dominates most of the plot. According to proto-conservative seventeenth-century theories of political obedience, active resistance to authority is never an option. In extreme cases of abuse or intolerable discrepancy between conscience and political demand, the final option, according to writers on passive obedience, is exile, as exemplified in Moses's exodus as well as the French Huguenots' exile in England.[57] This is why it is important that Oroonoko does not rebel but rather leads an exodus: he does not try to change the political system, such as it is, in Surinam, but rather to leave it. He convinces the other enslaved people to leave their politico-social situation, based on the religious (rather than political) rhetoric that their treatment as more like "senseless brutes than human souls" had robbed them of their "divine quality" and would continue for "eternity" (57–58). Their path to potential freedom is through what seems to be an uninhabited swath of land, that is, a land without a sovereign who must be obeyed.[58] Thus, in a way, Oroonoko does comply with his promise not to rebel. In order to carry out this plan, he must essentially leave the world of politics, in which questions of activity and passivity are framed and given meaning. Oroonoko's great action is thus a withdrawal from the theater of political action. It is motivated by modern notions of passion (his initial passion for Imoinda and his concern for their unborn child) and not politics, and it also falters at least partially due to passion: his fellow enslaved men's commitment to their own families. The exodus also has affinities with classical notions of honor: Oroonoko repeatedly claims that they are better off losing their lives than living "in perpetual slavery" (59). The mixed rhetoric – of Christian ideas about the soul and heroic ideals of military honor – in Oroonoko's speech reveals something about the text's attitude toward passivity. Despite the conflict between Christian and classical notions of interiority – with Christianity privileging the interior realm of conscience and heroic romance insisting that interiority and activity coincide – that seems to be at the heart of the text's moral dilemmas, Oroonoko's speech and *Oroonoko* more generally suggest that in both cases, passivity of the body is the ultimate moral position and the ultimate narrative outcome.

Baroque Realism: A Mangled King, Smoking

In the dedication of *Oroonoko*, to Richard Maitland, Behn describes her innovative prose fiction as a mixture of allegorical and novelistic modes, and of baroque and neoclassical aesthetics. She opens by suggesting that her art contrasts with painting, which is ideally mimetic and classical in nature, in so far as the "original alone gives it its perfection" and a "good hand cannot augment its beauty" (3). Writing, at least her kind of writing, instead draws "the nobler part, the soul and mind" (3). Given that *Oroonoko* will be written in a heavily plotted and (especially in the second half) richly detailed style, this claim to draw the soul (assuming it applies beyond the dedication) suggests a baroque technique of spiritual animation via immersion in the sensual. Indeed, such lives as Oroonoko's and Maitland's, Behn's dedication suggests, would "lie neglected" (a phrase I hope that this chapter has animated) without her written effort to resurrect them to "immortal fame" (3–4). She pairs this baroque claim with a neoclassical one: she hopes the "lazy nobility" will be elevated via the examples of the resurrected Maitland and Oroonoko (4). Thus, the baroque technique of resurrection and the neoclassical technique of imitation in the service of didacticism, both described here as forms of animation, promise to work together to fulfill Behn's political and aesthetic vision. But this double animation proves mostly to produce negation, insofar as it represents and exalts passivity. Indeed the dedication itself supports this: via her comparison of her writing to painting, whether neoclassical or baroque, Behn evinces a politics of virtue that can be representational and affective but that is not primarily active or narrative.

While *Oroonoko* is often considered an early novel, it draws heavily on the residual mode of baroque allegory and the worldview that it represented. As argued in the last section, the theme of lying (and lying down) in the text does not pit cynical modernity against innocent nativism, but rather it suggests that lying and passivity inhere in the ahistorical human experience. Similarly, Oroonoko's baroque commitments – as contrasted with romance, where the body is no obstacle, and also realism, where it is there to be overcome and is vastly overshadowed in importance by interiority – locate shared humanity in the body that lacks both agency and grace. Beginning with the grandfather's impotence, the vulnerability, incapacity, and intractability of the body is everywhere in evidence. Imoinda's pregnancy, Oroonoko's easy inebriation, the enslaved men's attention to the difficulties of rebelling with women and children: it is ultimately the body's incapacity that collapses historical, racial, and national distinctions. This theme is best exemplified in the final image of a mangled king smoking. According to Oroonoko's heroic design he will "first ... kill [Imoinda], and then his enemies, and next himself" (67). He manages the first part of the triple promise (the part that was already mandated by his initial disobedience), but this action is followed by Oroonoko's most debilitating moment of paralysis. After killing Imoinda (which is described in a highly stylized way, almost a neoclassical tableau), Oroonoko lies prone, immobilized as his promise of revenge turns into a lie, while Imoinda's body rots under the leaves. Laura J. Rosenthal's claim that Oroonoko really "goes native" here is quite apt.[59] For he is about to replicate the natives' most puzzling ritual: the war captains' self-mutilation, which Oroonoko initially finds "too brutal to be applauded" (56). The seemingly blithe way that the Surinam war captains conduct a "debate" that entails hacking off body parts in order to prove what they "dare do" collapses the distinction between promise and action. In lieu of any "reply" to the challenge to demonstrate their courage, that is in lieu of any promise (about what they are willing, able, or dare to do), the war captains "prove their activity" by what the narrator calls a "passive valour" (56). The narrator takes the war captains to be "hobgoblins or fiends," and indeed the parallel is apt, because their "debate" challenges the relationship between representation and reality and the distinction between conscience and action by insisting, ironically enough, on the total passivity of the body (55–56). Via the brutalization of their passive bodies, the war captains earn the right to be "obeyed with great resignation" (8).

The brutality of the war captains' self-mutilation, by a process of mysterious causation typical of allegory (as I discussed in Chapter 4) leads to Oroonoko's own self-mutilation (his auto-caesarian if you will) and then to the colonialists' mutilation of him, all described in brutally realistic terms. Here, at the very end of the text, the parallels among England, Surinam, and Africa coalesce most uncannily in the image – so extreme even for the baroque that its seems almost a satirical baroque – of Oroonoko's ghastly pipe-smoking as his mutilated and dying body takes on the resonance of a "mangled king" (73). This final image of Oroonoko, smoking a pipe as he "gave up the ghost," might be seen as suggesting some agency – the evidence of conscience or of faith that audiences to the execution of martyrs were trained to look for (72).[60] But Oroonoko's interiority and his agency disappear over the course of the text, and this grotesque image of his demise does not bear witness to any individual or religious transcendence. While at the beginning of the narrative, his expressive eyes revealed the discontinuity between his passion and his political situation, in the end the only evidence of Oroonoko's interiority, or of a transcendent truth beyond his body, is his tobacco smoking. But tobacco would have been the crop that enslaved people were laboring to produce, and it would have also been associated, particularly by the method of pipe smoking, with Native Americans.[61] In yet another of the text's deep ironies, many of which revolve around our hero's name, "Orinoco" designates not only a river in South America, not only an African prince, but also, according to the *OED* – and as Stephanie Athey and Daniel Cooper Alarcón have noticed – tobacco itself; not only that, but an inferior form of tobacco to boot.[62] Rather than demonstrating "resilience of character," this image of Oroonoko smoking orinoco is thus profoundly ironic, almost a parody of both religious ideas about conscience and emergent Whiggish ideas about agency.[63] And the tableau around this figure, with Oroonoko surrounded by his ruthless executioners and impotent admirers, parodies the Passion of Christ.[64] Oroonoko's execution parallels Jesus's in many ways. While the *King James Bible* translates several deaths as a process of giving up "the ghost," Oroonoko's death is most comparable to Jesus' death, translated as "And Jesus cried with a loude voice, and gave vp the ghost."[65] Oroonoko cries out, in his penultimate bout of suffering, the rather heterodox promise that the colonialists will "no more find a faith in me" (70). The ghost (which is etymologically and doctrinally related to "breath") that he breathes out when he "[gives] up the ghost" would have been mingled with the tobacco that he has "learnt" to smoke (72). His "learnt" habit of smoking tobacco, I'm arguing, offers no evidence of spiritual transcendence, individual agency, or Christic sacramentalism. Rather, it proffers a claim about the shared humanity of enslaved people, natives, and royals. This final image thus leaves us with a baroque aesthetic, but one that questions rather than affirms spirituality and interiority. It aestheticizes the passive suffering body as a natural and universal truth.

The arguments in 1688–89 about passive obedience – as well as about succession, rights, the rule of law, and so on – were frequently, from both sides, grounded in history, and in the specifics of England's "ancient Laws."[66] By setting *Oroonoko*, allegorically and/or globally, outside of England, by setting it repeatedly and increasingly in settings with no legitimate ruler, and by making her protagonist both royal and enslaved, Behn's representation of the fundamental passivity of the human body levels a critique, from a perspective with both spiritual and materialist elements, of political and nationalist ways of thinking about individuality and political agency.[67] This global context of *Oroonoko* pits the exceptionalism expected in realism against the capacity for similitude provided by allegory. And it pits the self's capacity to objectify the world (exemplified in the logic of modern slavery) against the baroque allegorical commitments, in Gordon Teskey's words, to "mythopoetic and visionary" participation, between local and cosmic forces and between signs and referents.[68] It pits neoclassical modes of accommodation and didacticism against the baroque obsession with the inevitability of death, decay, and sorrow. And finally, and most relevantly, it pits both romance and realistic modes of thinking about agency against what Benjamin has described as the baroque's genius for depicting "man's subjection to nature."[69] Loyalist theories of passive obedience were founded on the notion that "political duties had a religious basis"; Behn's baroque realism grounds passivity in nature, not politics or religion.[70]

The Passively Obedient Novel

The novel, at least the realist and sentimental novels of the eighteenth century, is an anti-allegorical form. Novels happen when we begin to think, in Lorna Clymer's terms, that "not repeating oneself – or anyone else" is a "sign of mastery."[71] This chapter has been arguing that this is the sign that Oroonoko is unable to perform. In his lying, in his ultimate impotence, and in the narrator's repetition not only of the colonialists' lies but also of the lying of Oroonoko, we find a text unable to stop repeating and also unable to sustain a fiction of exceptionality: royals, enslaved people, and protagonists of novels are destined to embody the universal law of passivity. Teskey has argued that allegory is a form of ritual interpretation that produces a depoliticized form of hope that we belong to one spiritual project. Politics, he says, "puts the body at risk," while allegory "cares without risk."[72] Teskey's critique of allegory might lead to a reading of *Oroonoko* as a deeply traditionalist response to the emergence of modern politics: Behn's allegory represents all efforts at political activity as impractical and as violations of our shared humanity. This chapter's analysis of passivity in the text could support this reading. But this is not the only possible interpretation of the baroque body politic in *Oroonoko*. *Oroonoko*'s emphasis on the sexual, suffering, impotent body about which no promises can be made, the ground of Behn's baroque aesthetic and her conservative critique of modernity, is the same ground upon which rests the recent critique of the liberal emphasis on human rights – Giorgio Agamben's theorization, for example, of the implications of how "bare life" (or "life exposed to death") emerges from natural life.[73] According to Agamben, following Carl Schmitt's theory of sovereignty, late liberal capitalism, in a logic both foundational and unjust, works by a proliferation of the state of exception. As a conservative, Behn was uniquely positioned to predict the dangers of this increasingly secular world that was emerging as she was writing *Oroonoko*. Her interrogation of Oroonoko's double and oxymoronic exceptionality – that is, her depiction of a world with no monarch, justice, or true exceptionality – shows how the denial of the law of passivity leads not to active agency or freedom but rather to a proliferation of injustice and suffering.[74] As discussed in Chapter 2, the political crisis that brought down the Stuarts and that thus provides the immediate context for *Oroonoko* involved James II's 1689 Declaration of Indulgence, which rested on the notion that king's exceptionality allows him the prerogative to grant liberty, or exception, to his subjects.[75] Behn's gambit in *Oroonoko* is to make a royal, the one person who is an exception to the rule of law at least under royalist theory, into a slave, the one category of person excluded from liberal rights theory, and to show that even in these bodies, indeed even as the exception to these exceptions, the human body lacks the possibility of either transcendence into spirituality or abstraction into rights.[76] The end game of the logic of the exception in *Oroonoko* is that all bodies are subject to unjust practices, to violence and decay, and they cannot be made congruent with human languages of desire, agency, or command. While we may, and the narrator does, dream that a just ruler (James II or Oroonoko himself) might be different, or at least not quite as bad, that Surinam, or Coramantien, or England itself might prove the exception to the rule, the novel ultimately provides a vision of continual passivity in human affairs, one in which questions of justice and the reality of the vulnerable human body are all too easily divorced from legal, political, and discursive modes of social interaction.

Oroonoko documents Oroonoko's inability to provide an alternative to the lying, deceiving, brutal world of colonialism and slavery, because his capacity for expression and his exceptionalities, his two possible modes of political action, have been eroded throughout the narrative. It is thus important, in terms of the relationship between the history of passive obedience and the development of the novel form, that Oroonoko's story is mediated by a surrogate, a narrator whose own position within the story is just as physically implicated and even less agential than his own but who nonetheless acts as a witness to and a judge of his story: as an "eye-witness" (6) she deems him to have been "a great man" (73) who is "worthy of a better fate" (73). The narrator, as Athey and Alarcón have argued, retains a position of "reflection and moral judgment," even as all she can do is to admonish Oroonoko, for reasons that are extremely compromised, to "rest yet a little longer with patience" and then to describe the brutal reality of her hero's passive and suffering body when that strategy fails (46).[77] Scholars have often noticed, and criticized, the narrator's inaction in the story, her ghostlike presence that never acts on Oroonoko's behalf even as she exalts him.[78] Her inaction is a modern form of passive obedience and is integral to her politically and ethically complicated role as witness and narrator. It is important to notice that she is not fully detached from the action. Her body is exposed and vulnerable: to the natives when they examine her dress; to the violent potential revolt and, by implication, to the sexual or political violence of male colonizers; and finally to "fits of dangerous illness upon any extraordinary melancholy," the occasion of her ultimate passivity, because she is absent, during the scene of Oroonoko's death (72). Her implicated and passive body, like Oroonoko's, is not a vehicle for individual agency or spirituality. She bears witness, via various modes of removal, to Oroonoko's suffering, but this limited witnessing comes "from the ground," not from any place of participation or transcendence.[79] The tragedy of Oroonoko perhaps inheres precisely in this fact that she can neither participate in his life politically nor transcend his death spiritually. Sacrifice, as Graham Ward has argued, depends upon communion among community.[80] Oroonoko can, in Agamben's terms be "killed but not sacrificed" precisely because of this lack of communion between the narrator and her hero, a lack that marks the text's distance from baroque participation. This aspect of the text also marks a distinction between this chapter's analysis of the narration and Catherine's Gallagher's summation of a line of thinking in which the distance between character and narrator contributes to the consolidation of the reader's ego.[81] If Oroonoko's attitude toward the war captains was that he could "esteem" but not "applaud" them, then Behn's narrator makes both applause and esteem seem impossible. Applause is, by definition, a visible display of approval, while esteem refers to the interior judgment of approval, often directed toward a deity, rather than to the representation of approval.[82] The setting of the story – in a place without a monarch or shared ideals – and the techniques of narration – a tragedy narrated by an eyewitness/participant – make both esteem and applause unavailable. Esteem and applause – those effects of heroic, religious, and theatrical modes – are replaced here with the practices and the complicated agency of passive obedience. The narrator is expressive; she pleads a case, assumes a discrepancy between justice and reality, and accommodates a discrepancy between belief and action. Moreover, as an early prose fiction, *Oroonoko* not only participates in a modern form of lying, but it can, to push its connection with passive obedience a bit and in contrast with predecessor forms like theater and baroque religious art, be experienced by readers while lying down.

In short, *Oroonoko* uses the occasion of debates over passive obedience to instantiate the modern narrator: passive and thus politically compromised because partially detached from the situation and partially implicated, a narrator whose liberty of conscience, whose right to a different moral standard from the one depicted – indeed even from the one in which she participates as an actor – depends upon passivity and expressivity even as it precludes active agency.[83] The text's ambivalence about its own generic regulations, and their political implications, is perhaps why the narrator wishes a "more sublime wit" than her own could do justice to Oroonoko's story (73). With the narrator in *Oroonoko*, Behn suggests that in the emergent political landscape only a certain kind of inaction – the compromised and contingent witnessing available in the passively obedient novel form – is consonant with a discursive practice devoted to justice.

Oroonoko, then, predicts both the novel and the modes of agency with which modernity would grapple, insofar as it works by a logic of surrogacy and representation, and insofar as it is ideological but not political. It is a modernized mode of passive obedience for a world in which there is no sovereign to which one can appeal, no exception who can make exceptions, and in which enslaved people may have sympathy but no political recourse. In terms of its place within the history of the novel, *Oroonoko* presents the typical novelistic plot, in which virtuous and passionate young people rebel against a tyrannical parental figure. That Behn's young lovers find realism rather than romance and passivity rather than rebellious transcendence does not preclude a novelistic sensibility that valorizes individuality, but it predicts a great deal of compromise for the future citizens of democracy. From this perspective, *Oroonoko* is not advocating for passive obedience. Instead, it is a formal thought experiment that uses passive obedience to dismantle a liberal account of political subjectivity, laying bare a system in which slavery is both necessary and disavowed. This is the ground of Behn's political conservatism, her critique of liberalism and revolution, and her literary innovation.

This chapter has been treating passivity, in a baroque and Christian sense, as both a law of nature and as a form of moral resistance that applies equally to princes, enslaved persons, the son of God, and narrators. This chapter has also treated *Oroonoko* formally, as a hybrid between allegory and realism, or we might say between royalty and slavery. Insofar as *Oroonoko* is allegory or romance, Oroonoko's race is incidental: in an allegorical and monarchist worldview, an African Prince may be paralleled with a British king, and indeed Oroonoko has been read as allegorical of both Charles I and James II, English Kings whose subjects rebelled against them. But *Oroonoko* is not just an experiment in human nature and politico-religious obligation; nor is it pure romance. It is also a text in which gender and race figure importantly and one often credited as an early realist novel form. The interactions of race and gender have been a critical problem in the text, articulated most prominently by Margaret Ferguson.[84] Because Oroonoko is not just a royal but also a black African, his race, and the text's realism in its representation of new world slavery, are central to an understanding of its perspective on liberal ideas about agency and freedom. And because the narrator is a woman, one (fictionally at least) whose connection to colonial powers is complicated, as is her position as both character and narrator, her gender matters as well as her race and nationality. It is not, I am suggesting, a coincidence or irrelevant that the form of passive witnessing that this chapter elucidates occurs between a white English woman and a black African man: the female narrator who cannot or does not act and the black enslaved person whose failed rebellion and torture she narrates. The narrator's passivity (as character) contributes to both the enslavement and the death of Oroonoko. Her empathy (as narrator) with him and her judgment against the colonizers who abuse him do nothing to interrupt the system of chattel slavery that is present in the text not only in "in name" but also in brutality against Africans. The narrator's empathic moral witnessing ameliorates or provides an alibi for liberalism's dependence on slavery, and the logic of racism that it in turn depends, but it has, at best, only ethical or ideological – not political – force. Scholars in black studies have made a convincing case that the liberal order depends upon racialized slavery, and even that it relies upon transcendentalizing or enchanting that system, making it impervious to human agency.[85] In *Oroonoko*, the passivity of both the white woman and the enslaved black person keeps the system of racial slavery functioning and also mystified. *Oroonoko*, then, offers insight into the special relationship between gender and race – and in particular between white women and black men – under liberalism. In Chapter 1, I recounted the narration of *Love Letters*, arguing that the narrator there could not participate in the transcendent religious experience she narrates. Something parallel but more revealing and sinister happens her. Here it is racialized slavery, not God, that constitutes the realm of the unparticipatable but that nonetheless creates and authorizes – and whose absence would threaten – the narrator's world. The white woman and the black man are (as Chapter 2 discussed) left out of a liberal logic of agency and rights, left to depend upon indulgence and passive forms of both resistance and moral logic, and their relationship is, as the argument about *Oroonoko* demonstrates, morally and formally complex. Their passivity operates as both physical law (realism) and as a mystical ceremony (allegory). If liberalism aspires, in its ambition to abstractions such as freedom and rights, to become a secular crypto-theology, the passive and vulnerable bodies of the white woman and the black man resist that abstraction. As such, *Oroonoko* lays bare liberalism's dependence on racism and slavery and upon the figure of the white woman to perpetuate it. This happens not despite but because of her witnessing, in which she stands passive, ceremonially, before the transcendent logic of liberal racialized slavery. The double logic of the narrator/character as passive allows *Oroonoko* to be read as a postsecular critique of this system or, alternately, as a secularization of the logic of witnessing Christ's passion, transformed here into passivity before the brutal reality of slavery. This is, ultimately, *Oroonoko's* triumph of hybridity, a literary model of how liberalism will have it both ways when it comes to gender and racial (in)justice. This chapter has been recounting a failed or impotent slave rebellion. Chapter 6 will take up the ways that the literary/liberal collaboration works to forestall revolution, and revolution by enslaved and oppressed people is of course the prime example of the kind of revolution that liberalism must preclude.[86] On this account, it is significant that *Oroonoko* was written and published during the events of 1688–89, and that it allegorizes those political events via the logic of slave rebellion, linking England's ambivalent bourgeoise revolution with its concern about slave rebellion. Together, these chapters show how the forms of prose fiction contribute to the logic of revolution under England's nascent liberalism.

Notes

1. Aphra Behn, *Oroonoko, and Other Writings*, ed. Paul Salzman (Oxford: Oxford World's Classics, 1998), 56. Hereafter cited parenthetically by page number.
2. See John Locke, *Two Treatises of Government and a Letter Concerning Toleration*, ed. Ian Shapiro (New Haven, CT: Yale University Press, 2003).
3. Little is known about Behn's religious background and leanings. See Sara Heller Mendelson, *The Mental World of Stuart Women: Three Studies* (Amherst: University of Massachusetts Press, 1987); Mary Ann O'Donnell, "Private Jottings, Public Utterances: Aphra Behn's Published Writings and Her Commonplace Book," in *Aphra Behn Studies*, ed. Janet Todd (Cambridge: Cambridge University Press, 1996), 285–309; and Alison Shell, "Popish Plots: The Feign'd Curtizans in Context," in *Aphra Behn Studies*, ed. Janet Todd (Cambridge: Cambridge University Press, 1996), 31–49. Elsewhere Mary Ann O'Donnell notes a variant in *Oroonoko*'s dedication that focuses on Maitland's Catholicism; see *Aphra Behn: An Annotated Bibliography of Primary and Secondary Sources* (New York: Garland, 1986), esp. 122–23, 129–30.
4. Aphra Behn, "To His Sacred Majesty, King James the Second," in *Oroonoko, and Other Writings*, ed. Paul Salzman (Oxford: Oxford World's Classics, 1998), 255–56. These adjectives are all terms that appear repeatedly as analogues of passive obedience.
5. Victoria Ann Kahn, *Wayward Contracts: The Crisis of Political Obligation in England, 1640–1674* (Princeton, NJ: Princeton University Press, 2004), 13.
6. *Passive Obedience in Actual Resistance* (London, 1691), 1.
7. For overviews of history of political obedience in early modern England, see John Neville Figgis, *The Divine Right of Kings*, 2nd ed. (Cambridge: Cambridge University Press, 1914); and Richard L. Greaves, "Concepts of Political Obedience in Late Tudor England," *Journal of British Studies* 22,

no. 1 (1982): 23–34. In 1709–10, the case of Henry Sacheverell revisited these debates, linking passive obedience clearly with the lost Stuart cause.
8 Abednego Seller, *The History of Self-Defense* (London: printed for Theodore Johnson 1689), A3.
9 Abednego Seller, *A Defence of Dr. Sacheverell. Or, Passive-Obedience Prov'd to Be the Doctrine of the Church of England* (London, 1710), 51. He presumably refers to the divine Thomas Jackson (1579–1640).
10 Hence, passive obedience is not the kind of annihilation of the self discussed in Scott Paul Gordon, *The Power of the Passive Self in English Literature, 1640–1770* (Cambridge: Cambridge University Press, 2002). Passive obedience does not, especially as it becomes secularized, make a claim to complete oneness with God. What is at stake in passive obedience is not the power of God but the power of the conscience, and the need to balance secular and sacred beliefs.
11 John Kettlewell, *Christianity, a Doctrine of the Cross: Or, Passive Obedience* (London, 1695), 4–5.
12 Greaves, "Concepts of Political Obedience," 29. J. C. Davis argues that the claim to liberty of conscience "had virtually nothing to do with a claim to direct or manage ourselves"; rather it is a claim to "be free to submit to the governance of God [over] any other authority," in "Religion and the Struggle for Freedom in the English Revolution," *Historical Journal* 35, no. 3 (1992): 515.
13 See J. C. D. Clark, *English Society, 1660–1832: Religion, Ideology, and Politics during the Ancien Regime* (Cambridge: Cambridge University Press, 2000).
14 John Toland, *Mr. Toland's Reflections on Dr. Sacheverells Sermon* (London, 1710), 11. George Berkeley is one of the few major thinkers after 1688–89 who supports passive obedience; see Berkeley, *Passive Obedience* (London, 1713). Berkeley bases his support – for nonresistance and acceptance of punishment – on human reason and the practicalities of governance. By contrast, David Hume says "in all our notions of morals we never entertain such an absurdity as that of passive obedience" (*A Treatise of Human Nature*, 3 vols. [London, 1739–40], 3:163–64). William Blackstone later calls passive obedience a "slavish and exploded doctrine" (*Commentaries on the Laws of England*, 4 vols. [Oxford: Clarendon Press, 1765–69], 1:326).
15 James Ellesby, *The Doctrine of Passive Obedience* (London, 1685), 15.
16 In *De Regimine Principum*, Thomas Aquinas argues that monarchy is the best form of government and counsels that violent resistance to a tyrannical government is unwise, but he distinguishes tyrants from monarchs and allows for the possibility of communal resistance to tyranny (Thomas Aquinas, *De Regimine Principum Ad Regem Cypri: Et De Regimine Judaeorum Ad Ducissam Brabantiae*, 2nd ed., ed. Joseph Mathis [Taurini: Marietti, 1986]).
17 W. J. Welwiller, To peace and truth, *Obedience Active and Passive Due to the Supream Povver* (London, 1643), 9.
18 Howell A. Lloyd argues that political obedience was a central tenet of all European political theory and that its demise was much less rapid and

profound than a Whig interpretation might suggest, in the Conclusion to *European Political Thought 1450–1700: Religion, Law and Philosophy*, eds. Howell A. Lloyd, Glenn Burgess, and Simon Hodson (New Haven, CT: Yale University Press, 2007), 498–509. On the importance of obedience to all sides in 1688–89, see also Mark Goldie, "The Revolution of 1689 and the Structure of Political Argument," *Bulletin of Research in the Humanities* 83 (1980): 473–564; and J. P. Kenyon, *Revolution Principles: The Politics of Party, 1689–1720* (Cambridge: Cambridge University Press, 1977). Most writers assumed the importance of political obedience, but of course there were radical Whigs who argued that political power resides within the people, who can revoke their rulers' power by acts of rebellion.
19 Robert Filmer, *Patriarcha: Or, the Natural Power of Kings* (London, 1680), 5–6.
20 See Samuel Johnson, *Julian the Apostate* (London, 1682). Johnson, who was the chaplain to William Russell (a major proponent of exclusion and the right of subjects to resist), argues that early Christians legitimately resisted the rule of the pagan Julian. For a history of this text, see Dorothy Auchter, *Dictionary of Literary and Dramatic Censorship in Tudor and Stuart England* (Westport, CT: Greenwood Press, 2001), 174–78. The most famous interlocutor for Johnson is George Hickes (1642–1715), the English divine who would become a nonjuror, in *Jovian, or, an Answer to Julian the Apostate by a Minister of London* (London, 1683). The radical argument that Johnson and other Whigs make is that it is the law, and not the king, that one is obliged to obey, and thus that active rebellion is justified if the king subverts the law. Johnson was tried and imprisoned for seditious libel. But his most famous example in fact complies with passive obedience. For an overview of Johnson's career, see Melinda Zook, "Early Whig Ideology, Ancient Constitutionalism, and the Reverend Samuel Johnson," *Journal of British Studies* 32, no. 2 (1993): 139–65.
21 This is a complex problem, but divine right and passive obedience are often erroneously conflated. Writers who argued strongly for passive obedience frequently did so on the basis of either "Hereditary or Elective" right. See, for example, John Walker, *The Antidote: Or, a Seasonable Discourse on Rom. 13.1* (London, 1684), 36.
22 Mark 10:21 (*King James Version*, 1611). According to Ellesby, Christ was "so far from offering at Resistance ... that he did not ... make shew of the least Murmuring or Discontent," and his apostles "rejoyc'd in Affliction, and gloried in Tribulations" (Ellesby, *Doctrine*, 6–7).
23 Welwiller, *Obedience*, 9.
24 Thomas Bainbrigg, *Seasonable Reflections on a Late Pamphlet Entitled a History of Passive Obedience since the Reformation* (London, 1689–90), 15. Bainbrigg argues that all obedience is active.
25 John Norton, *A Discussion of that Great Point in Divinity, the Sufferings of Christ; and the Questions about His Righteousnesse Active, Passive* (London, 1653), A2.

26 See J. S. McGee, "Conversion and the Imitation of Christ in Anglican and Puritan Writing," *Journal of British Studies* 15, no. 2 (1976): 21–39. As George Hickes puts it, the Church of England "thinks her self obliged to suffer, as her *Saviour*, like a Lamb brought to the slaughter; and dares pretend to take up no Arms but those of the Primitive Christians (Whose true Copy she is) Tears, Arguments and Prayers" (*The Judgment of an Anonymous Writer* [London, 1684], 2). Jeremy Taylor (1613–67) notes that Christ "esteemed it his *Meat and drink to do the will of his Father*, and for his obedience alone obtain'd the greatest glory: and no man ever came to perfection but by obedience" (*The Rule and Exercises of Holy Living* [London, 1650], 191).

27 There were loyalist accounts featuring Christ. See, for example, Thomas Pierce, *A Prophylactick from Disloyalty in These Perilous Times* (London, 1688).

28 Rom. 13:2 (*King James Version*, 1611).

29 Bainbrigg, *Seasonable Reflections*, 28–32.

30 Francis Turner, *Sermon Preached before the King on the 30/1 of January 1680/1* (London, 1681), 24. For a similar example, see Welwiller, *Obedience*, 16–17. See also this exact phrase in *Oroonoko*, 30.

31 Samuel Johnson, *An Answer to the History of Passive Obedience* (London, 1709/10), 5. *Passive Obedience in Actual Resistance* satirizes such "prayers and tears" as a mechanism of "Thraldom and Bondage" based on specious interpretation of scripture (2).

32 This political notion is often deeply imbricated in religious ideas. In one text, passive obedience is wrong because it makes God "Unmerciful, Cruel, Barbarous, and Tyrannical" (*Vox Populi, Vox Dei* [London, 1709], 38). There are also, of course, writers who deny the political import of such affective displays. Robert Filmer, for example, says there is "no Remedy in the Text against Tyrants, but in Crying and praying unto God in that Day" (*Patriarcha*, 80–81).

33 Greaves cites a gloss of the Great Bible of 1539, which says that Christians must "obeye Ungodly rulers" ("Concepts of Political Obedience," 24) because "the actions of both [kinds of rules] can be controlled by God for his ends" (31). See also Figgis, *Divine Right*. Obviously this is not a completely new idea. Rather, my point is that after a period of insistence, under the Stuarts, on the divine right of kings in England, writers in 1688–89 began to theorize the meaning and practice of obeying an unjust king in new ways. Joseph Priestley will later (ironically in a critique of passive obedience) describe passive obedience as a necessary counter to the "king-killing principles" of Catholics (*An Essay on the First Principles of Government* [Dublin, 1768], 29).

34 Clark's influential argument recovers the "shared ideological inheritance" (*English Society*, 88) of Whigs and Tories throughout the long eighteenth century, and passive obedience is a centerpiece of this "middle ground" (58). Besides the fact that ideological change comes slowly, and that England's history was one of compromise, no government, as Clark points out, has incentive to support the right to resistance.

35 George Hickes, *A Sermon Preach'd before the Honourable House of Commons* (London, 1692), 22–23. Thomas Long (1621–1707) makes a similar case: "[B]eing no Men at Arms" the clergy had fulfilled its duty by standing still and waiting *"for the salvation of God"* to relieve them from their terror and oppression (*The Historian Unmask'd* [London, 1689], 6). For a discussion of the history of passive obedience and the complex ways it interacted with the revolution, see George F. Sensabaugh, "Milton and the Doctrine of Passive Obedience," *Huntington Library Quarterly* 13, no. 1 (1939): 19–54.

36 *The Doctrine of Passive Obedience and Nonresistance, as Established in the Church of England* (London, 1710), 26. In another example, Henry Sacheverell links Republicans, who think people can remake government, with "Papists" who think Rome can overrule Britain (*Perils of False Brethren* [London, 1709], 86).

37 See Zook, "Early Whig Ideology," 147.

38 See Clark, *English Society*, 58, who argues that the emergent democratic society of England was deeply rooted in the values of passive obedience.

39 Luke 20:25; see also Matt. 22:21 and Mark 12:17 (KJV).

40 In an example of an argument against passive obedience invoking this language, one writer, Welwiller, *Obedience*, argues that what is received from the sovereign must be returned in kind, "because they keep our Tillage safe, they must have Tribute out of our Lands" (*Obedience*, 8). Charles Taylor will, much later, argue quite oppositely that conscience is defined by participation in social institutions. Traditional despotism, Taylor argues, could require only that people "remain passive and obey the laws," while a democracy asks that citizens be "motivated" to contribute not only "treasure" but also "blood" and participation in governance ("Nationalism and Modernity," in *Theorizing Nationalism*, ed. Ronald Beiner [Albany: State University of New York Press, 1999], 228).

41 It also investigates what difference it makes for an enslaved person or group (versus a religious minority) to choose exile. I am grateful to Michael O'Driscoll for this observation, which bears more analysis than I can give it here.

42 Srinivas Aravamudan, *Tropicopolitans: Colonialism and Agency, 1688–1804* (Durham, NC: Duke University Press, 1999), 29–70.

43 For examples of gender criticism see the following: Ros Ballaster, "New Hystericism: Aphra Behn's *Oroonoko*: The Body, the Text and the Feminist Critic," in *New Feminist Discourses: Critical Essays on Theories and Texts*, ed. Isobel Armstrong (London: Routledge, 1992), 283–95; Margaret W. Ferguson, "Juggling the Categories of Race, Class, and Gender," *Women's Studies* 19, no. 2 (1991): 159–81; Moira Ferguson, "*Oroonoko*: Birth of a Paradigm," *New Literary History* 23, no. 2 (1992): 339–59; Charlotte Sussman, "The Other Problem with Women: Reproduction and Slave Culture in Aphra Behn's *Oroonoko*," in *Rereading Aphra Behn: History, Theory, Criticism*, ed. Heidi Hutner (Charlottesville: University Press of Virginia, 1993), 212–33. For race and colonial studies, see Laura Brown,

"The Romance of Empire: *Oroonoko* and the Trade in Slaves," in *The New Eighteenth Century*, eds. Laura Brown and Felicity Nussbaum (New York: Methuen, 1987), 41–61; Laura Doyle, *Freedom's Empire: Race and the Rise of the Novel in Atlantic Modernity, 1640–1940* (Durham, NC: Duke University Press, 2008); and Albert J. Rivero, "Aphra Behn's *Oroonoko* and the 'Blank Spaces' of Colonial Fictions," *SEL Studies in English Literature, 1500–1900* 39, no. 3 (1999): 443–62. For examples of critics who see such readings as anachronistic, see the following: George Guffey, "Aphra Behn's *Oroonoko*: Occasion and Accomplishment," in *Two English Novelists: Aphra Behn and Anthony Trollope* (Los Angeles: William Andrews Clark Memorial Library, UCLA, 1975), 1–41; Derek Hughes, "Race, Gender, and Scholarly Practice: Aphra Behn's Oroonoko," *Essays in Criticism* 52, no. 1 (January 2002): 1–22; Richard Kroll, "'Tales of Love and Gallantry': The Politics of *Oroonoko*," *Huntington Library Quarterly* 67, no. 4 (2004): 573–605; and Adam Sills, "Surveying 'The Map of Slavery' in Aphra Behn's *Oroonoko*," *Journal of Narrative Theory* 36, no. 3 (2006): 314–40. The dichotomy I mention oversimplifies the critical field; see for example, Joanna Lipking, "'Others', Slaves, and Colonists in Oroonoko," in *The Cambridge Companion to Aphra Behn*, eds. Derek Hughes and Janet Todd (Cambridge: Cambridge University Press, 2004), 166–87. *Oroonoko*'s critical fame, the reason for oroonokoism, has largely rested on its innovations in the novel form and the kind of ideological questions about the individual's place in society that concern the novel and its critics. But *Oroonoko* should also be treated as belated rather than new, or as allegory rather than novel. Scholars have recently, and rightly so I think, been thinking about *Oroonoko*'s affinities with theater; see Sills, "Surveying"; and Marta Figlerowicz, "'Frightful Spectacles of a Mangled King': Aphra Behn's *Oroonoko* and Narration through Theater," *New Literary History* 39, 2 (2008): 321–34.

44 As Hughes points out, this dynamic has not been taken up enough by critics ("Race," 9).

45 Laura M. Ahearn's definition of agency as "the socioculturally mediated capacity to act," and thus quite opposite of both free will and resistance, is apt here ("Language and Agency," *Annual Review of Anthropology* 30 [2001]: 112).

46 This quotation suggests, unlike the situation in 1688–89, a culture that does not distinguish sacred and secular forms of power. One has to take these references to absolute political obedience in *Oroonoko* with some degree of irony, as they are always referenced exactly when they are being violated.

47 Kahn, *Wayward Contracts*, 173.

48 "Honour" is referenced at least thirty times in the text.

49 Bainbrigg, *Seasonable Reflections*, 15–16.

50 See note 31.

51 Vernon Guy Dickson notes, correctly I think, that Oroonoko's obsession with truth is related not to factual truth but rather to moral truth; see "Truth, Wonder, and Exemplarity in Aphra Behn's Oroonoko," *SEL: Studies in English Literature, 1500–1900* 47, no. 3 (2007): 573–94.

52 Thomas Hobbes, *Leviathan*, ed. J. C. A. Gaskin (Oxford: Oxford University Press, 1996), 95.
53 For a discussion of this difference, see Kahn, *Wayward Contracts*, 47.
54 Kahn, in explaining how John Milton prefigures Friedrich Nietzsche, defines the "conscientious and 'calculable' ethical subject" as one who can keep ones promises and that thus presupposes a kind of internal contract (*Wayward Contracts*, 133).
55 This fundamental truth about humans, that they "lie," also suggests something about why and how a royal can also become enslaved, since the two routes to slavery are physical passivity and being duped – both forms of lying.
56 Chi-ming Yang, "Asia out of Place: The Aesthetics of Incorruptibility in Behn's Oroonoko," *Eighteenth-Century Studies* 42, no. 2 (2009): 235. See also Walter Benjamin, *The Origin of German Tragic Drama*, trans. John Osborne (London: Verso, 1998/1977), esp. 81; and Sills, "Surveying."
57 For example, in *Obedience*, W. J. writes: "Moses ... had not ... any power committed to him to incite the people to take up armes against *Pharaoh* their King" but "only to intreat *Pharaoh* to let them goe" (11–12).
58 This is perhaps why the New-World setting is important – it is the only way to imagine an exodus away from political situations. But of course, this is not really so: The exodus has a leader/prince, and the enslaved all have family obligations that they bring with them.
59 Laura J. Rosenthal, "*Oroonoko*: Reception, Ideology, and Narrative Strategy," in *The Cambridge Companion to Aphra Behn*, eds. Derek Hughes and Janet Todd (Cambridge: Cambridge University Press), 162.
60 See Elizabeth Hanson, "Torture and Truth in Renaissance England," *Representations* 34 (Spring 1991): 53–84. Hanson argues that torture in Renaissance England, as part of the "developing practice of criminal investigation," was congruent with the emergent scientific epistemology of discovery, in that it assumes the "victim [is] in possession of a hidden truth ... and ... the interrogator's task was 'discovery'" (54–55). By contrast, the ideal Catholic victim maintained secrecy, defining truth as discontinuous from "utterance and representation" (75). Between these two competing positions emerged the idea that the conscience was fully and intensely private, unconnected to the flesh, a zone of "secrecy and discovery" (72). Methods of discovery thus "revealed that impenetrable sanctum it had created" (77). My point, though, is that *Oroonoko* satirizes all these ways of reading martyrdom.
61 On history of tobacco, see E. R. Billings, *Tobacco; Its History, Varieties, Culture, Manufacture and Commerce* (Middlesex: Wildhern Press, 1875); Todd Butler, "Power in Smoke: The Language of Tobacco and Authority in Caroline England," *Studies in Philology* 106, no. 1 (Winter 2009): 100–18; and Jason Hughes, *Learning to Smoke: Tobacco Use in the West* (Chicago: University of Chicago Press, 2003).
62 *Oxford English Dictionary Online*, s. v. "Orinoco, n.," December 2011, www-oed-com.login.ezproxy.library.ualberta.ca/view/Entry/132715. See Stephanie Athey and Daniel Cooper Alarcón, "*Oroonoko*'s Gendered Economies of

Honor/Horror: Reframing Colonial Discourse Studies in the Americas," *American Literature* 65, no. 3 (1993): 425.
63 Yang, "Asia out of Place," 244. While I'm arguing against Yang's reading of agency in this scene, a similar point to mine is made by George Boulukos, who reads the smoking as a parody of Foxean Protestant martyrdom (*The Grateful Slave: The Emergence of Race in Eighteenth-Century British and American Culture* [Cambridge: Cambridge University Press, 2008], 70). In *The Rover* Part 2, Behn represents tobacco quite negatively, when, in a discussion of sex and marriage as "lying," Beaumont threatens Aria with the image of an old lover: "the compound of nasty Smells about him, stinking Breath, Mustachoes stuff with villainous snush, Tobacco, and hollow Teeth" (*The Second Part of the Rover* [London, 1681], act 2 scene 2, 31).
64 Kroll has noticed the parallels between Oroonoko's death and Christ's Passion, including the witnessing by women ("'Tales of Love and Gallantry,'" 576).
65 Mark 15:37 (KJV).
66 *Vox Populi, Vox Dei*, 18.
67 In this "natural law" approach, though not in its conclusions, she is modern for 1688–89, following (or leading) such figures as Locke, whose "highly rationalized, ahistorical idiom" contrasted with the more common law/history approach of other Whigs and Tories. Melinda S. Zook, *Radical Whigs and Conspiratorial Politics in Late Stuart England* (University Park: Pennsylvania State University Press, 1999), 140.
68 Gordon Teskey, *Allegory and Violence* (Ithaca, NY: Cornell University Press, 1996), 101.
69 Benjamin, *Origin*, 166.
70 Clark, *English Society*, 135.
71 Lorna Clymer, *Ritual, Routine and Regime: Repetition in Early Modern British and European Culture*, (Toronto: University of Toronto Press, 2006), 4.
72 Teskey, *Allegory and Violence*, 132.
73 Giorgio Agamben, *Homo Sacer: Sovereign Power and Bare Life*, trans. Daniel Heller-Roazen (Stanford, CA: Stanford University Press, 1998), 88.
74 I undertake this argument with trepidation, as I think it is always a risk to revive conservative views of the past to critique the present. In a way, this is just the flip side of the Whiggish habit, as Blair Worden phrases it, of congratulating "the past on becoming more like the present" ("Toleration and the Cromwellian Protectorate," in *Persecution and Toleration*, ed. W. J. Sheils [Oxford: Blackwell, 1984], 199).
75 James II, King of England (1633–1701), *A Declaration of His Most Sacred Majesty, King James II to All His Loving subjects in the Kingdom of England* (London, 1689).
76 I use the term "slave" here (as opposed to "enslaved person") and throughout only when it is relevant to understanding what Behn is doing with the phrase "royal slave": that is, suggesting that such seeming identities are merely circumstances that may change.

77 Athey and Alarcón, "*Oroonoko's* Gendered Economies," 423. They argue, following Nancy Armstrong's argument about the rise of the novel, that this is the source of both Behn's modernity and her moral authority – her "metaphysical subjectivity" (431). See Armstrong, *Desire and Domestic Fiction: A Political History of the Novel* (New York: Oxford University Press, 1987).

78 See Ferguson, "Juggling," esp. 165–66; see also William C. Spengemann, "The Earliest American Novel: Aphra Behn's *Oroonoko*," *Nineteenth-Century Fiction* 38, no. 4 (1984): 384–414. Spengemann attributes the narrator's inactivity to genre, while Ferguson's reading is more about the strictures of gender/power relations.

79 This language is from Graham Ward's reading of the death scene in *Romeo + Juliet*, which he says is shot so there is "an inability to gain moral high ground, and perspective that can change the situation" (*True Religion* [Malden, MA: Blackwell, 2003], 29). As in that film, there is "no sense of resurrection" in *Oroonoko* – except perhaps in the unexpected revival of the name "Imoinda" at the very end. Or perhaps in the promise (or the consolation) that only literature – or perhaps literary scholarship – can resurrect the righteous or transcend the unethical world. For an interesting account of how witnesses became separated from judicial functions, see Matthew Wickman, *The Ruins of Experience: Scotland's "Romantic" Highlands and the Birth of the Modern Witness* (Philadelphia: University of Pennsylvania Press, 2007).

80 See Ward, *True Religion*, 14–17.

81 Agamben, *Homo Sacer*, 90. On Gallagher's account, the discrepancy between narrator and reader provides "subjective blanks" that will be "overcome" by the reader's "idealized ego," and it also results in the reader recognizing her material "reality" as "ontologically plentiful" (Catherine Gallagher, "The Rise of Fictionality," in *The Novel: Volume 1: History, Geography, and Culture*, ed. Franco Moretti [Princeton, NJ: Princeton University Press, 2006], 360–61). Against this reading of the reader's psychological subjectivity and material reality being at stake in novels, this reading posits the third person narration as a kind of ethical alibi (and/or accusation). As such, it follows Frances Ferguson's argument discussed in Chapter 6; Frances Ferguson, "Romantic Memory," *Studies in Romanticism* 35, no. 4 (1996): 509–33.

82 In the tracts on passive obedience, "esteem" is due to "higher powers"; see for example Walker, *The Antidote*, 60–62.

83 For Laura Doyle, the narrator's position, writing from exile, allows her to "re-anchor ... displaced persons and events" (*Freedom's Empire*, 102).

84 Margaret Ferguson's argument – which posits both affinities and conflict between the white woman and the black man – has been especially influential ("Juggling"). Critics of this argument include Derek Hughes, who argues that Ferguson imposes a relationship between the white woman and the black man (imagining rape most egregiously) that is not there ("Juggling").

85 Charles Mills' influential and controversial arguments are just one of many. Mills connects racism and liberalism but imagines that liberalism can be

purged of this racialization of freedom and slavery (*Black Rights/White Wrongs: The Critique of Racial Liberalism* [Oxford: Oxford University Press, 2017]). Other scholars disagree. Partha Chatterjee for example argues that the theories and institutions of liberal democracy developed precisely in response to the needs of colonization, including slavery (*Lineages of Political Society – Studies in Postcolonial Democracy* [New York: Columbia University Press, 2011]). Nathan Hensley argues that the logic of liberalism's ambition to universality is founded in "the most basic form of human interchangeability: slavery" ("*Armadale* and the Logic of Liberalism," *Victorian Studies* 51, no. 4 [2009]: 607). See also his *Forms of Empire: The Poetics of Victorian Sovereignty* (Oxford: Oxford University Press, 2016). For a discussion of how liberal theories of freedom connect to slavery, including how they differ from those in slave narratives and republicanism, see Barnor Hesse, "Escaping Liberty: Western Hegemony, Black Fugitivity," *Political Theory* 42, no. 3 (2014): 288–313.
86 This line of thinking is indebted to Jared Hickman, *Black Prometheus: Race and Radicalism in the Age of Atlantic Slavery* (Oxford: Oxford University Press, 2016).

CHAPTER 6

Revolution and Nostalgia
Walter Scott and the Forms of Jacobite Nostalgia

> We have before us a Work, that seems to our selves a Dream, and that will appear to Posterity a Fiction.
> Gilbert Burnet, 1689

> We have never dreamt that parliaments had any right ... to force a currency of their own fiction in the place of that which is real.
> Edmund Burke, 1790

> What is a merit in the writer may well be a vice in the statesman, and the very qualities which go to make great literature can lead to catastrophic revolutions.
> Alexis de Tocqueville, 1856

The first Whig historian Gilbert Burnet, writing on the first anniversary of the events of 1688–89 in the epigraph above, offers a distinctly modern observation about the relation of fiction and politics.[1] In projecting the effects of the events of 1688–89 toward posterity, Burnet reveals an understanding of politics as an imaginative force that can bring about historical changes. Politics in the moment of its labor ("work") and desire ("Dream") will appear later as the fictional imagination striving for a future so distinctly different from the present as to be almost unimaginable – it will be, one way of putting it might be, revolutionary but not violent. For Burnet, the events of 1688–89 offer a fantasy of transformation that is based in the salutary effects of fiction: Whereas politics must be intentional, active, and perhaps violent, fiction can effect positive political change almost magically. 1688–89 is the exemplar of a fictional revolution in the eyes of Burnet and other early Whig historians because they deemed it nonviolent and perhaps even non-intentional, "bloodless" in common parlance or in Burnet's terms here a "Dream." In this version of events, William was responding to an invitation, and James II was peacefully, almost unconsciously, abdicating. Edmund Burke, writing just after the hundredth anniversary of the 1668–89 "revolution" and one year after its more famous French cousin, takes an equally positive view of the events of 1688–89 but a more wary stance towards the relation of fiction and politics.[2] Not surprisingly, the more conservative Burke is aligned with a more retrograde view about fiction's positive political intentions: In the seventeenth century, fiction was often represented as the usurper of the real, and its implication in politics almost inevitably problematic. For Burke, the violence of political revolution is related to a fictional "force" that restructures reality based on theoretical or imaginative grounds, and this magical "force" of fiction is precisely its threat – the kind of liberal dream that causes Burnet's reverie but that Burke depicts as a nightmare. Burke's disparagement of the French revolution held up the events of 1688–89 as an antirevolutionary exemplar – neither fictional nor revolutionary but rather incremental and resolutely attached to material and historical reality. For Burke, the fictional imagination is linked to revolution and this connection accounts for his different opinion of the two events: where 1688–89 was based on customs and practices instituted slowly over time – and thus it was neither a revolution nor a fiction – the French revolution endeavored to remake the society wholesale, based on a fiction. Alexis de Tocqueville splits the difference between Burnet and Burke, arguing that literature can sustain the fantasy of fictional rebellion and wholesale social remaking, but the real world cannot.[3] We might take Tocqueville as expressing approval for the full disciplinary distinction between fiction and politics as well as for providing the motto for this chapter: revolutions belong in fiction.

Together, these writers suggest that the poverty of fictional representations of 1688–89 has a certain logic, as the event was justified because it was grounded in the habits and practices of English law and custom, because it eschewed the force of fiction, and because it has been ambivalent about its status as a revolution. Kathleen Wilson has argued that 1688–89 took on the status of myth; this may be another way of explaining why it could not withstand representation.[4] We might take these arguments collectively as suggesting that 1688–89 proposed a tenuous orthodoxy about fiction's relation to politics, which was threatened by the revolutions in the later eighteenth century and which would lead to the disciplinary ghettoization (thus interdependence) of literature and politics. Anthony Jarrells supports and nuances this argument – and shows the synergy between the political and the literary fields – by arguing that in wake of the French revolution, the literary sphere functioned like the "bloodless" revolution of 1688: to forestall revolution in favor of reform.[5] On Jarrell's account, this is why 1688–89 – in the Whig's account of it as bloodless – was the Romantic solution to the problem of revolution, which was a local, global, and most of all a colonial threat in the early nineteenth century. Jared Hickman has shown how the romantic interest in the Prometheus myth reveals the deep racial logic of liberalism, which depends upon the revolutionary myth of a white Prometheus while shadowed by the disavowed possibility of revolution by enslaved black people.[6] This chapter too will offer an account of how revolution comes to be forestalled – and perhaps how racism comes to be disavowed – by being fictionalized and formed in literature, with 1688–89 as the central object facilitating this process. This book has been nuancing the story of the Restoration and 1688–89 by exploring the ways that conservative writers – those who were against the revolution, who did not see it as bloodless or salutary – experimented with literary forms and techniques in order to explore the implications of the events in arenas not typically (with the exception of Hobbes and Cavendish) seen as political. Even where the literature could be seen as representational of 1688–89 or directly political, I have focused not on representation but on the kinds of commitments – to faith, to indulgence, to apostolic transmission, to passive obedience – that these writers were concerned with and to the kinds of literary engagement and innovation – in narration, allegory, imagination, and literary history – that they deployed. The last chapter began to address the racial and colonial implications that these conservative writers have been both addressing and avoiding in their fictional experiments. In the two chapters that deal most directly with the events of 1688–89, the mode of allegory has moved those events off the English island. Significantly, in both Dryden's *Don Sebastian* and Behn's *Oroonoko* (as well as, in a different way, *Cavendish's Blazing New World*) revolutionary activity is removed and located in other times and places: the Portuguese/Muslim dispute in *Don Sebastian*, the complex slave economy of Surinam, and the diverse fictional world of Cavendish. All of these allegorical others layer religious and racial difference. This is a complex representational strategy, in which revolution in England, and particularly the events of 1688–89, are allegorized in order, perhaps, to manage concern with rebellion in England's colonies.

In this chapter, I look more directly at 1688–89 and to the Jacobite cause that was its most obvious descendent. Yet even in so doing, 1688–89 remains a vanishing point: an event that exits to give perspective rather than something to be represented. This dynamic has something to do with the way that it has always raised questions – perhaps ones we do not like the answers to – about how human agency is fictionalized and forestalled and thus about how politics and fiction relate. For example, when I presented the first piece of writing that would become the germ of this book, on the warming pan scandal that may or may not have precipitated the dynastic change, a historian asked me why, if the scandal was both untrue and not a provable cause of revolutionary political change, that is if it had no agency or historical effect, why would I bother to write about it?[7] The warming pan scandal and the events of 1688–89 more broadly were, I tried to answer then and this book endeavors to answer more completely now, a literary event, because they were about the "dream" and the "force" of fiction that allowed writers the occasion for meditating on the nature of literary fictionality, literary historicity, and the political imagination. In this chapter, I take on the most direct and controversial question about 1688–89: was it a revolution at all? In so doing, I argue that this problematic, the ambivalent status of 1688–89 as revolution, accounts for its centrality to the British political imaginary; I explain why it is not 1688–89 but rather later Jacobite uprisings that have been more commonly represented in the literary field and how this may be a way to manage colonial rebellion, at least fictionally; in so doing, I account for why 1688–89 has been a catalyst for literary experimentation, not representation.

For historians, the significance of 1688–89 has inhered mostly in the ways it has allowed them to debate the nature of history and the significance of revolutions to history. The period 1688–89 is described by its Marxist critics as a bourgeois or conservative revolution, not really a revolution at all because it was "bloodless," incremental, and engineered by a ruling class. But for those interpreters who deem it a "glorious" revolution, its significance abides not only in its bloodlessness but also because it inaugurated what has become known as the Whig interpretation of history, which is one of the key models of modern historiography, a way of viewing history as progressive change in which the reactionary forces of absolutism are slowly but inevitably defeated by the human desire for liberty, along with which comes scientific progress and economic prosperity. This human desire for liberty is the fundamental ideological premise of modern revolution, and in the Whig interpretation of history, liberty itself is an always already preexisting condition of human nature. Revolutions are thus at least as much about returning to a fundamental nature – freedom and the rights of man – as they are about the forward thrust of history: the world-remaking power of individuals or of fiction. The etymology of the word revolution reveals the fundamental ambivalence at the heart of modern notions of revolutions and revolutionary temporality: "[R]evolution" is based on the astronomical notion of cyclical revolving and thus grounded in cosmological ideas of return and repetition.[8] But modern revolutions also stake a claim for origins. One of the characteristics of revolutions is that they reconfigure time, often setting the year to zero in order to mark the beginning of not only a new political regime but also a new concept of time itself. For revolutions not only begin things anew but they also, as Hannah Arendt has argued, are fundamentally defined by their commitment to the notion of beginning.[9] Revolution is grounded in the belief that human actions have meaning, that humans can begin something new and lasting, even, or perhaps especially, when that change is incremental or obscure and thus when an historian is needed to recount its trajectory.

Steve Pincus argues that 1688–89 was the first "modern" revolution.[10] Taking issue with characterizing the conflict, ideologically and materially, as being between traditionalists, who wanted to maintain politico-economic status quo, and liberals, who pushed for progress, Pincus argues instead that what was at stake were two competing visions of modernity. He maintains that 1688 was not bloodless nor consensual but rather violent and ongoing and that it was motivated not by attachments to archaic forms of political subjectivity but rather by competing visions of modernity. In his account, James II is not an inept, unimaginative, retrograde king protecting a dying tradition but rather a canny political operator whose vision for large-scale, state-controlled capitalism, based on the model of Louis XIV in France, was defeated by the Dutch vision of a competitive free market liberalism.[11] While I cannot weigh in on the historical plausibility of this argument and while I find its tone a bit uncritically whiggish, I do want to take up Pincus' suggestion that 1688–89 was the first modern revolution, and as such that it exemplifies something about revolution and indeed political subjectivity in modernity – in particular about conservative political ideology as modern. Conal Condren's argument about this period would seem to be the very reverse of Pincus'. Condren argues that there was "no radical/conservative dichotomy," as we understand it, in the seventeenth century. Instead, there were "rival claimants to the language of conservatism – to tradition, integrity, and obedience. If radical was used at all – and it hardly was – it meant simply to cut back to the roots, to remove all unwelcome accretions and innovations."[12] The perspective in this book reconciles these two views by seeing the conservative/liberal dynamic not as conflict but synergy. Conservatism is not so much a commitment to the past and a resistance to change but rather part and parcel of the modern political imaginary, more often seen to be liberal. This project does not offer a new version of the historical events or a new definition of conservative but rather explores conservative writers' contributions to the literary field.

This chapter develops this line of inquiry by linking nostalgia to revolution and to historical fiction. While nostalgia would seem to be emblematic of the conservative worldview and revolution of the progressive or liberal, they share a history and are related, specifically insofar as together they provide the formal energy of historical fiction. Taking seriously the idea that there is something foundationally "revolution"-like about the events of 1688–89 and building on what appears to be mere historical anecdote – that the term "nostalgia" was coined in 1688 – this chapter endeavors to explain a central irony in the literary/political imaginary: that the exemplary nostalgic subject is the Jacobite counterrevolutionary, the follower of the deposed Stuarts monarchs who staged two major rebellions in the eighteenth century, hoping to restore the Stuarts to the throne. *Waverley*, Walter Scott's paradigmatic representation of nostalgic Jacobitism and exemplary case of the historical novel, forms the central literary example.[13] If 1688–89 is the first modern revolution, then it shares a birthday with both Jacobitism and nostalgia. Revolution, nostalgia, and Jacobitism are thus triplets with a long and complicated relationship – one that begins in 1688, that is central to the fields of literature and politics, and that is exemplified in *Waverley*.[14]

1688–1689, the Ambivalence of Revolution and the Emergence of Nostalgia

Revolution is central to secular theories of human action and to the theories of temporality, causation, emotion, and meaning that are entwined with it. A great part of the political ideology and affective appeal of secular liberal modernity derives from the fact that secular temporality ascribes historical importance to human action. John Locke argues that liberty consists "in a power to act, or to forbear acting, and in that only."[15] In Stefan Collini's account of the "rhetoric of sincerity" that emerged in the eighteenth century, the modern subject becomes and remains true to itself by deriving action from feeling.[16] Enlightenment literacy, as Matthew Wickman argues, is not merely an empirical approach to the world but also an understanding of time as a chronological movement within which human actions have meaning.[17] Revolution is a powerful modern fantasy of human agency derived from what is assumed to be the most basic of human feelings – the desire for liberty. But revolution's complex approach to temporality and causation reveals a good deal of ambivalence about this enlightenment view of agency. Hannah Arendt sees revolution, and modernity's love affair with revolution, both as a watered-down version of a past ideal – classical politics – and as a seminal practice of secularity, based on a model of political action as grounded in the human capacity to begin something new. For Arendt, revolution has both a past and a future orientation, and beginnings derived from human action must not be instrumental – something is true political action when we begin something without knowing what its consequences will be.[18] This is partially at least because we may not live to see the effects of our actions, but also fundamentally because political action cannot be seen as fulfilling the particular interests of an individual. We celebrate revolutionary moments of human action as beginning something significant, but we necessarily cannot predict their fruition nor understand their full meaning. With a characteristic commitment to open-endedness, revolutions in this sense only exist in a world committed to progress in a secular sense; for Arendt, revolution is the only possible successor to religion.[19] It is ironic, of course, that Arendt finds this revolutionary model of beginnings and succession in the past and that an ideal of individual agency leads to a theory of unforeseen consequences. But these ironies are at the heart of the modern notion of political action and progress that this chapter will be exploring, via both the ironic figure of the Jacobite and the ironic form of historical fiction.

For Charles Taylor, as for Arendt, revolution is an inherently secular ideal, and for Taylor the Reformation (not 1688–89) was the first modern revolution, the beginning of the age of both secularity and revolutions.[20] The word secularity originally related to time: It meant that which pertains to this present world, to temporal as distinguished from spiritual or eternal interests. Secular time as exemplified by revolution can be seen as fossilizing the past; it is chronological and causative, rather than cyclical and prophetic. The idea of an age, on which modern views of history so depend is more or less synonymous with secularity. (Thus, the title of Taylor's *A Secular Age* is redundant.) Secularization opposes messianic models of eternal, unchanging or cyclical time, in which truth and meaning are permanent and human actions, by contrast, are neither original nor generators of meaning; rather, human actions in messianic time are modes of participation in meaning: mediums and sites of change but not intentional instigators of it. In Taylor's argument, revolutions are something like secular "kairotic knots" – those momentous religious experiences of eternity in which reversal and rededication occur.[21] But revolutions define that kairotic experience in a very different way. Secular revolutions do not partake of the "higher time" of god, experienced momentarily in the secular world; instead they celebrate the human potential to make the world our own. Revolutions are a fantasy that the kairotic may be made permanent via human political action; they are thus central to the cryptotheology of liberalism. What I am getting at, then, via Taylor and Arendt, is that revolution, as an ideal of secular modernity, tries to transcend time, even as it valorizes the possibility of human action in time. Revolutions are the sites of tension between the vestiges of sacred time in the modern world and the secular fantasy that the time of human action has open-ended (i.e., progressive in a whiggish sense) meaning for the future. In this sense, we might say that revolutions are postsecular.

The Whig interpretation of 1688–89 insists that British political subjectivity is founded in liberty and ancient laws and that it mandated not only the right but in fact the obligation to rebel against unjust authority.[22] But the mainstream Whig account of the "revolution" of 1688 also deemed it to be bloodless and its subsequent counterrevolutionary Jacobite uprisings to be impotent and inept as well as politically anachronistic. In other words, the increasing secular liberal commitment to a theory of revolution as fundamental to political liberty and individual agency were balanced, in accounts of 1688–89, by the denial that English subjects had engaged in such revolution and by the transferal of the revolutionary character to their historical – and stuck in the past – Jacobite antagonists. The notion of considering 1688–89 a revolution was not always a foregone conclusion: For decades afterward, the events were more often described as an abdication than a revolution, a strange way of putting the agency, albeit the agency to surrender sovereignty, on James II rather than seeing the members of Parliament as revolutionary agents – or rather than seeing 1688–89 as a continuation of the Puritan Revolution of the 1640s, an event that was much more radical in its ideology, aims, and methods.[23] In the dominant seventeenth-century version of 1688–89, Whigs merely issue an "Invitation" – a civilized and polite gesture rather than a revolutionary one – to William and Mary. And despite the massive military force that joined William, much effort was made to perpetuate this view. *The English Current* for December 1688–89, for example, describes William as "entertain[ing] in discourse" and with "cheerful countenance" the Lords who invited him.[24] Toni Bowers shows how David Hume's influential account of the event, in which an "abdicated family" is at the center, further complicates any idea of revolutionary agency. The passive construction of (the already agentially strange) "abdicated" and its coupling with a collective "family" rather than an individual, places the deposed royal family in a strange position to 1688–89 as well as to the Jacobite counterrevolutionary cause that would be its legacy.[25] Hence it is ironic, an irony grounded in an ambivalence about revolution that gets managed by nostalgia, that 1688–89 has come to be seen as revolutionary. When referred to as a revolution, the events of 1688–89 always take an adjective – glorious, Protestant, or bourgeois – but one nonetheless credited with the kind of historical agency that revolution requires. Because of this ambivalence about its revolutionary quality, 1688–89 has become a touchstone for thinking about the nature of history in general and the course of British history in particular: Did the events instantiate a break or turning point in the linear teleology of progress or was it a regenerative incident in a cyclical history?[26] In either case, the legacy of 1688–89 is to depict Jacobites, at least on the surface, as wholly left behind by modern political subjectivity: committed to obedience, non-resistance, and an aberrant chapter in British history that allowed the Catholic and, absolutist Stuarts to very nearly enslave English subjects. At the same time, the Jacobite becomes a figure of revolutionary energy, or nostalgia for revolution.

Nostalgia would seem to be the opposite of revolution, a return to the past instead of a new beginning. "Nostalgia" was coined in 1688 by physician Johannes Hofer to describe the experience of Swiss soldiers returning from war.[27] The word combines the Greek words *nostos* (return home) and *algia* (pain). According to Hofer, nostalgia works by "arousing especially the uncommon and ever-present idea of the recalled native land in the mind."[28] Over the course of the eighteenth century, the meaning of nostalgia shifted from medical pathology to aesthetic ideal and from place to time.[29] Immanuel Kant plays a central role in this historical redefinition of nostalgia. Kant notes that nostalgics who do return home are usually disappointed, because, in fact, they did not want to return to a *place*, but to a *time*, a time of youth.[22] Nostalgia thus refuses the enlightenment project of growing up.[30] Nicholas Dames reconciles the two aspects of nostalgia, arguing that nostalgia integrates the temporal and the spatial, that nostalgic narratives are chronotropic. According to Dames, narratives of nostalgia operate as sites of "temporal processes that reflect, and manage dislocation."[31] This perspective on nostalgia allows us to see why and how Jacobites, with their location in Scotland and their futile commitment to a doomed historical position, were central to the English political imaginary in the eighteenth century.[32]

For many critics – especially those like Frederic Jameson and others working from the Frankfurt School tradition – nostalgia is dangerously apolitical and anti-critical: By drawing people to the past and/or out of their political context, nostalgia – whether seen as disease or aesthetic experience – siphons away the possibility of political action.[33] Unable or unwilling to understand the reality of their temporal or spatial context, nostalgic political subjects, when they act at all, almost inevitably appear incompetent, inadequately prepared, and easily confused, and they produce unanticipated effects. The nostalgic political subject is a failed modern subject on at least two counts: because the nostalgic is out of place, they cannot gather the empirical evidence that makes effective action possible. The nostalgic, moreover, does not have the understanding of time that makes political activity meaningful. The failure to historicize and thus to enable (in Linda Charnes' account) time to have a political dimension is what makes nostalgic political action oxymoronic, at least in some accounts.[34] This is why for Kevis Goodman, nostalgia is a "disturbing disease of historicity" and why Charnes posits in nostalgia "a compulsion, perhaps, to abandon the ship of the present."[35]

Working against the Frankfurt School critique of nostalgia, some critics see in nostalgia an important role for radical, progressive, anti-modernist political subjectivity, or at least its imaginative potential.[36] Bradley Bryan, following Nietzsche, for example, argues that political commitment begins in the desire for revenge, which is an important symptom of nostalgia.[37] For John Su, fictionalized nostalgia can provide a space for ethical visions that may not find outlets for action in the present.[38] For some critics, nostalgia's seductive lure is in the collective roots of the past, which suggest a possible political subjectivity from which to act, but this turns out most often to be a false promise, because an attachment to a fantasy past rooted in community draws one out of one's own political context.[39] This can be convenient to a colonial power, because colonial subjects are displaced from community, from place. According to these two camps of nostalgia critics – those who see it as politically impotent and those who want to see it as potentially generative – the political potential of nostalgia inheres in its capacity or its incapacity to create communal attachment and thus communal forms of action. While novels and enlightenment philosophy celebrate individual action, revolutions demands action on behalf of a communal or collective identity; nostalgia for revolution is one way to manage these disparate ideals. Thus, while we might typically align revolutionary action with liberal or progressive ideas and mature resigned conservatism with what we see as conservative politics' commitment to the continuity of community, an aversion to revolution because it breaks the continuity of time and thus the continuity of a community, the dynamic between revolution and nostalgia suggests that these two ideological commitments are related. The possibility to take political action is founded on an attachment to a community in time and place and at the same time an individual desire – in revolutionary action – to transform that time and place. The function of nostalgia is to manage this disjunction between attachment and political transformation. In the particular case of revolution in the English context, this alliance of nostalgia and revolution means that revolution can only be undertaken as a patriotic act, to defend one's own country. As such, it delegitimizes other kinds of revolution, especially those of colonialized or enslaved people.

This tendency of nostalgia to promote communal attachment and political commitment while positing individual political action as being out of time is what makes the Jacobite a political figure, even an exemplary one, who reconciles conservative and liberal ideas of political action. Jacobite nostalgia as a literary phenomenon unites the secular liberal philosophical commitment to rebellious political subjectivity with a political aversion to rebellion in the present time and place and thereby reveals a fundamental ambivalence at the heart of modernity's ideas about political agency and in particular at the heart of British imperial subjectivity. As such, it responds both to the Frankfurt School critique of nostalgia and to those more recent scholars working on nostalgia who have been arguing for a rehabilitation of nostalgia's political function. The Jacobite reveals something about the ambivalence of the modern idea of political action: one based equally in collective action and consequential agency, one that acknowledges the effects of the past and the attachments to community and yet one that maintains the possibility of individual agency. Revolution itself, in this reading, cannot escape nostalgic ambivalence, and this is the way that revolution is forestalled.

Jacobite Nostalgia

The Jacobite is crucial to the history of nostalgia in England because Jacobites were among the first sufferers from the medical disease of nostalgia and because Jacobites were also among the first identified with the patriotic strain of nostalgia that evolved from the medical diagnosis. The anachronistic but loyal and independent figure of the Jacobite offered Great Britain both a justification for progress and a noble past from which that justification gained legitimacy. Eighteenth-century British literature is heavily ornamented with politically inept Jacobites, though it will take a century for the Jacobite to become fully nostalgic and an object for British nostalgia.

The literary Jacobite first appears in late seventeenth-century political ballads, where we find him drinking and singing ye olde ballads about passive obedience and nonresistance – a phenomenon I have discussed elsewhere as a collaboration between Whigs and Jacobites, an early indication of their fundamental entanglement and thus the entanglement of liberalism, conservatism, and literature.[40] Later representations shift this caricature of the Jacobite toward both nostalgia and revolution. Colley Cibber's *The Nonjuror* (1718), for example, recounts the seduction of Woodvil, a country gentleman, by an insinuating Jacobite, who is tellingly named Dr. Wolf, in an homage to the violent and wild aspects of Scotland that would be both feared and celebrated by British subjects in their nostalgia for Jacobites. In mainstream and decidedly Whig novels of the midcentury, such as *Tom Jones* and *Tristram Shandy*, the Jacobite appears as a menacing but ultimately inept member of the aging, about-to-be eclipsed, generation. *Tristram Shandy*'s whole plot can be seen as an attempt to generationally transcend not only the blow to the nose that Dr. Slop, the inept Jacobite midwife, gives Tristram but also Uncle Toby's obsessive (and child-like) recreation of the siege of Namer. It is telling that Toby reenacts a battle not of 1688–89 or 1714, that is not of a decisive Whig victory but rather one that is part of the ongoingness and ambivalence of the Jacobite cause. Toby is the nostalgic in the novel, as well as an impotent Whig, while the forward-looking Jacobite is the agent of psychic menace, and these ironies are part of what give the novel its comic energy. In *Tom Jones*, the comedy revolves around the fact that Jacobite revolutionary is bested by the rebellious female protagonist: Sophie Western refuses her father's choice of husband and thereby distracts him from participating in the battle of Culloden. Later in the century, such comic deflations of the menace of Jacobitism diminish, and the Jacobite appears in gothic fiction in more sinister disguises: as a ghost, a devil, or a monk.[41] The appearance of the Jacobite as a Scottish Highlander on a craggy rock is the invention of romantics such as Robert Burns, James MacPherson, and Walter Scott, an invention that inaugurates the English nostalgia for the Scottish nostalgic revolutionary, which persists into the twenty-first century, for example in the books and television series *Outlander*. What these various literary representations share is that the Jacobite is typically displaced spatially or temporally, and often both. The Jacobite who appears in gothic fiction as a ghost or a devil is thus a hyperbolic representation, but nonetheless one still connected to the earlier and later representations of the Jacobite whose potential political menace appears to be rendered impotent because of his or her temporal (generational) or spatial (Scottish) discontinuity.[42]

The Scottish Highlander constitutes the apogee of the Jacobite's literary history and its most influential instantiation. Stuck in the past and in a remote location, they were, and remain, the object of romantic and nostalgic literary attention but social and political derision. In a typical nineteenth-century account, John Stuart Mill, the great theorist of liberalism, argued that it is better for the Scottish highlander to be a British citizen "than to sulk on his own rocks, the half-savage relic of past times, revolving in his own little mental orbit."[43] The use of "relic" is interesting here, for it positions the Highlander as a scholarly object of study, one with religious implications. The Highlander in their own "mental orbit" contrasts with the imperialist, whose idea of citizenship is inclusive (the Highlander can become a British citizen) and with the secular academic, Mills himself, who can reach beyond his own mental orbit to imagine this half-savage relic, mired in a superstitious religion, as a future British citizen. The use of "savage" both distances the Highlander from rebellion (which takes enlightened reason) and hints at a racial disparity, linking (as scholars have noted as a larger trend in such representations) the Highlander with Indigenous and African peoples, whose propensity to rebellion must be managed.[44] This problem of the savagery and the potential rebelliousness of colonized peoples helps to explain how and why the Jacobite became Scottish and the symbol of rebellion. Obviously, the two major eighteenth-century Jacobite uprisings were in Scotland, but this erases both the religious (Catholic) and nationalist (France, Italy) associations with earlier Jacobitism. Focusing on 1714–15 and 1745 as Scottish and as paradigmatic Jacobitism makes the history of Jacobitism a threat from within Great Britain, one rooted in a British past, but only if one squints at history a bit, ignoring not only 1688–89 itself but also the temporal, spatial, and politico-religious differences between England and Scotland that make the Union, ostensibly settled in 1707, precarious. Hofer's prescient definition of nostalgia as a mechanism whereby the "native land" is at once both "present" and "recalled" explains why it becomes possible that when a nineteenth-century Englishman depicts eighteenth-century Jacobitism as (misplaced) nostalgic he is at once embracing Scotland as British (because it has been so for so long according to the strange temporal logic of nostalgia) and diminishing the revolutionary potential of Scotland – as well as England's colonies.

The nostalgia of and for Jacobitism – including its location in the Scottish Highlands and its secularization into a nationalist or tribal instead of a religious, ethnic, or political project – was a fiction, one that depended on a great deal of irony and one that was central to Great Britain's developing sense of itself – and its political actions – as a modern political nation.[45] A view of Jacobitism as indigenous English threat relies on understanding the imperialist destiny of Great Britain and on holding an ironic and/or fictionalized historical perspective toward it. Hugh Trevor-Roper, Murray Pittock, and Gerald Porter, among others, have argued that the myth of a backward yet nostalgically appealing Highland tradition was invented, and also that it was connected to England's imaginative management of Jacobitism.[46] The Highlander as British Patriot, who balances according to Pittock the "two-edged quality" of conservative nostalgia and radical subversion, was "formally adopted by the British state" by the early nineteenth century.[47] In order for this to happen, the Highlander had to become English, shedding the associations with the "savages" who still troubled the imperial project. For Geoffrey Plank, this transformation of Highlanders into "useful settlers and champions of the imperial cause" was central to English colonialism.[48] In short, the Highland atavistic attachment to clan, land, and to the ancient Stuart monarchy was produced by and for a British nationalism now based on international trade and future-oriented capitalism, Protestant Christianity, and the racialization and oppression of colonial subjects.[49]

The Jacobite's rebellious nostalgia for a different place and time is connected to the non-Jacobite English nostalgia for the Jacobite. This dynamic, which indexes the fundamental paradox at the heart of modern British political subjectivity, animates historical fiction. The Jacobite's willingness to rebel, which put him on the wrong side of history during the eighteenth century but on the right side of philosophy and political theory, makes the Jacobite a key figure to reconcile the tensions in mainstream political subjectivity in eighteenth- and nineteenth-century England. As such, there is usually an element of irony in depictions of Jacobites: "Prodigious indeed!" says the man on the hill in *Tom Jones*, "A Protestant rebellion in favor of a popish prince!"[50] We might continue this perspective on the ironies of Jacobitism by exclaiming "prodigious indeed that the loyalist turns revolutionary!" or "prodigious indeed that the purpose of the revolutionary is to foreclose revolution!" In short, the Jacobite's unwavering loyalism, their unmediated access to the justification for action (because it never changes), their connection to clan and to the homeland, and their willingness to rebel unsuccessfully made the Jacobite become, over the course of the eighteenth century, a figure for authentic and patriotic political action, even as Jacobite politics were inevitably represented as anachronistic. But of course it is precisely this combination – lauding the independent and rebellious personality while descrying their politics – that can support revolution in theory but prevent revolution in practice. For this was the mainstream position of English citizens by the end of the eighteenth century, Whigs and Tories included. Its mechanism was nostalgia while its form was historical fiction. Thus, it should not surprise us that for most of the eighteenth century the main figure for rebellion was the Jacobite and that the Jacobite would become not only nostalgic but an object of British nostalgia and the protagonist of historical fiction.

Along with proving to be an important watershed moment for revolution, nostalgia, and Jacobitism, 1688–89 also proved to be a seminal moment in the history of the novel. For example, Aphra Behn's important short fictions, including *Oroonoko*, were all published in 1688–89, and perhaps written and published as novels precisely because political events would have made getting plays produced, for Behn, impossible.[51] Something similar happens, as I discussed in Chapter 4, with John Dryden, whose *Don Sebastian* is a kind of novelized play and foundational manifesto for literary history, in which reading is imagined as taking place in the future. Both texts, significantly, are concerned with rebellions by racialized others, even as they allegorize English political events. But more generally, I am giving the novel a birthday of 1688–89, because of the way that its generic features and ideological orientation are often seen to be connected to the political transformations credited to 1688–89: the rise of individualism, empiricism, middle-class values, and above all a secular notion of progress, which is tied to the idea of revolution.[52] A larger consideration of the novel's connection to 1688–89, revolution, and nostalgia would have to connect the Jacobite to another ambivalent and novelistic revolutionary: the virtuous protagonist of the domestic novel who rebels against patriarchal authority. This path might more fully evaluate Sophie Western's relationship to her father, and it would complicate the discussion of *Clarissa* as clinging to indulgence in Chapter 2 as well as the discussion of Behn's interest in the narrative inaction of the female narrator in Chapter 5. But in order to track the history of nostalgia, revolution, and Jacobitism, I turn to a later and more masculinist novel, Walter Scott's *Waverley*. A defining event in the legitimization of the novel and the historical novel in particular, *Waverley* is the exemplar of the culmination of eighteenth-century linkage of nostalgia, revolution, and Jacobitism.[53] This chapter thus takes up *Waverley* under the premise that it

Waverley, Historical Fiction, and Nostalgia

is a watershed in the history of the novel and that its status as a historical novel about Jacobitism has something to do with this.

The plot of *Waverley* accounts for how the politically ambivalent protagonist, Edward Waverley, finds himself – inadvertently, by miscellaneous accidents and via a romantic attraction to a beautiful woman – seduced into rebellion by a clan of Highland Jacobites. The protagonist's political ambivalence and personal immaturities have been the subject of no small amount of critical attention; the character of Waverley is often credited with transforming the ideal of heroism beyond recognition. György Lukács refers to Scott's "mediocre heroes" and Alexander Welch to his "passive heroes," while George Levine credits Scott (and *Waverley*) with "the death of the hero."[54] Caught between the incredibly efficient modern Hanoverian state and the seductive forces of the fiercely clannish Jacobite rebels, Waverley finds autonomous political thinking or activity – should they interest him, which they do not – impossible. His political passivity results in all kinds of mayhem, mainly for himself but also for his friends, who suffer and die as a result of his naiveté, passivity, and mediocrity.[55] Waverley's individuality consists mainly in his mediocrity: He is "Edward" Waverley to the extent he distances himself from the Waverleys and their historical connection to Jacobitism. Thus, the title indicates in advance the impossibility of such detachment – Edward's dalliance with the Highland rebels is signaled as inconsequential (historically at least) by the title, as the familial Waverley's attachment to Jacobitism (on his uncle's side) has already been decided (in favor of the Hanoverian/Whigs on his father's side) by the time of the novel's publication. The title *Waverley* does not quite conform to the conventions of titling novels, which rely on the given names of characters. Female names are often singular – *Pamela, Clarissa, Emma*, and so on – while male names more commonly include both given and surname – *Robinson Crusoe, Tom Jones, Tristram Shandy*, etc. – but both conventions work to establish, in Ian Watt's influential account, the character's characteristic individualization.[56] Scott's introduction stakes a claim for the "uncontaminated" nature of the name Waverley, and perhaps we might take him at his word and accept that Scott was trying to avoid the "preconceived notions" (based in typology) that well-known names bring about (33). We might take this as Scott's liberal side, as staking a claim to a blank slate for his protagonist, except of course the Waverley family name is a harbinger of Edward's destiny. "Uncontaminated" also suggests an ethnic purity and perhaps even whiteness, something that may distance Waverley from the Highland rebels he will romanticize. But Scott's conservatism (and thus his tendency to take as David Devlin puts it a "middle way" in terms of his approach to history) is also indicated by his choice to title the novel only with a last name, howsoever uncontaminated, and thus to make Edward Waverley more Waverley than Edward, more connected to his family and to England's destiny – both of which will situate Jacobitism in the past – than to his individual agency and his Highland adventure.[57]

The subtitle of *Waverley* is "'tis sixty years since." *Waverley* was published in 1814 but written, according to Scott, in 1805. In fact, Scott claims the date of composition (at least of the introductory chapter) to be November 1, 1805, exactly sixty years after the Jacobite insurrection of 1745, which the novel fictionalizes via the perspective and story of its mediocre protagonist (34). Sixty years before that, in 1685, James II ascended the throne, setting the stage for the revolution of 1688–89 and subsequent Jacobitism. Scott is not alone in finding 1745 a more interesting subject of representation than 1688.[58] In fact, his horizon of "sixty years" is a kind of sleight of hand that alludes to 1688–89 but puts it well into the past, beyond the possibility of what Scott considers to be the proper horizon of historical fiction. In the introductory chapter to *Waverley*, Scott claims that the setting, "sixty years since" means that his tale will not be romantic. He rejected the more ambiguous subtitles "A tale of other days" as too gothic and "a tale of the times" as creating a readerly expectation of "anecdotes" and "dashing sketch[es] of the fashionable world" (34). Situated between "a romance of chivalry" and a "tale of modern manners," *Waverley's* popularization of historical fiction, then, and its legitimation of the novel genre, rests on a span of sixty years at a time, just barely within the memory of a lifetime, or two generations removed at the most, and yet still a lifetime away, in the sense that a progressive reading of history means that sixty years is enough time to partially eclipse or to confound time and space – and thus to commingle revolution and nostalgia. A "generation" is generally agreed to be about thirty years. For Karl Mannheim, the idea of a generation is rooted in biology and means that the parents will always stand for conservatism, thus providing an alibi for youthful rebellion and a sense of history as liberal progress.[59] This might give a clue as to why Scott uses sixty years: The double generation gap opens up the possibility for the younger generation (Edward) to act conservatively and rebelliously at once. This time span and the question of generations haunts many of the texts taken up in this study: The absence of fathers in *Oroonoko* and *Don Sebastian* creates the kind of generation gap that means authority and knowledge are interrupted and also that the young have no conservative generation against which to rebel. But in *Waverley* this time span – sixty years or two generations – constitutes the wager of nostalgia. The nostalgic moment or object is just within generational memory, and we are living its consequences but absolved from individual responsibility for its larger motives and effects. It is thus interesting amount of time for thinking about the consequences of political action. If Arendt is right about the nature of revolutionary beginnings, then perhaps sixty years is the proper temporal perspective from which revolutionary actions can be viewed and historical fiction is the proper genre for representing such action. If this is the case, then it is interesting that *Waverley* doubles down on the nostalgic perspective, positioning 1688–89 as two nostalgic eras away, too far away, in Scott's gambit, to be suitable for historical fiction. In fact, 1688–89, as political event in which Waverley's family might be still involved, is erased in the novel. The Jacobite, starting in the eighteenth century and continuing until now, is always fighting an already lost cause. They may be valiantly fighting – and kitted out in their dashing plaids – in 1745. But we rarely see them fighting in 1688–89; at that time they are singing ballads while William is entertained by the Lords who invited him to be king, leaving the counterrevolutionary spotlight to their descendants. Revolution as a punctual event makes little sense with respect to literary representations of 1688–89 and the history of Jacobitism: The period 1688–89 is almost never the subject of representation of Jacobitism, even though it haunts the nostalgic investment in 1745. Part of the point of this book has been to explore the lack of representations of 1688–89; this chapter shows how and why it is 1745, rather than 1688–89, that becomes the object of nostalgic investment in general and Scott's historical fiction in particular.

   The political choices of two generations of Waverley's family and of England more generally have created the context whereby Waverley is seduced by Jacobite nostalgia but also whereby both he and the Highland Jacobites are incompetent politically. In fact, they are, in comparison with the ruling Hanoverians, not political at all but rather almost wholly domesticated, living in an isolated geographic and metal orbit that leaves them quite afield from the kinds of political questions that were pressing at the time of *Waverley*'s publication, when England was at war with its former colonies.[60] The most consequential outcome at stake in the novel is not the political destiny of England, as that is easily enough settled and has been for sixty years or even sixty more, but rather the personal consequences – to his friends, family, and associates, and to himself – that Waverley's inadvertent rebellion causes. Waverley can be seen as being seduced into revolution because he is interested in people and not politics. The novel *Waverley* follows this logic out by not holding Waverley responsible for his actions: The denouement of the novel sees the historically, empirically, and militarily superior British political machine absolving Waverley, and even most of the more active revolutionaries, from paying legal consequences for their crimes. The clergyman who first makes the case for Waverley's innocence reasons thus: "Justice, when she selects her victims . . . must regard the moral motive. He who [rebels due to] ambition, or hope of personal advantage . . . let him fall a victim to the laws; but surely youth, ... mislead . . . may plead for pardon" (252). Critics have read this absolution of Waverley as indicative of the novel's commitment to motive over consequences: Waverley is not guilty because he did not mean to do wrong and because in fact he did not mean to do anything. He is an accidental, reluctant, or naive revolutionary – that is, the only kind of modern British revolutionary possible. By personalizing the question of Waverley's guilt, the novel depoliticizes human rebellion as youthful naiveté, provincialism, and narcissism. In short, it makes revolution a counterpoint of nostalgia and thus allows one to be nostalgic for revolution because it is a symptom of youth and thus of the past.

This dynamic allows us to think about ethical questions regarding responsibility for actions and how they are embedded in form. In her essay on "Romantic Memory," Frances Ferguson describes the modern episteme of memory as reliant on the ongoing possibility of revising the morality of past actions by reevaluating them in light of later consequences.[61] One can imagine going back in time with the benefit of understanding the consequences – and thus the morality and the narrative arc – of events. Romantic memory depends upon knowing how the story ends, and this knowledge withdraws moral choice from the realm of action in the present, situating it in the past. Moral choice is never really a choice because romantic memory provides moral certainty. In the episteme of romantic memory, children cannot legally act. They are not legally responsible for the things they do because they could not have been aware of the consequences. The legal attitude toward children demonstrates how society suspends its judgment of actions when it deems that actors could not have been aware of the consequences of their actions. Nostalgia, by contrast, is childish because it does not concern itself with consequences. In fact, the present, as a potentially undesirable consequence of the past, is denied in the nostalgic imagination, and this is part of its lure. In the Scottish Enlightenment stadial theory of history as the progress of civilization, the past is filled with children, and thus returning to the past in historical fiction is also returning to a state of naive childhood.[62] According to Kant's famous view, enlightenment derives from a conscious move away from "self-incurred immaturity."[63] For Kant, nostalgia mourns the loss of childhood or an earlier stage of development, and thus historical fiction positions its readers as nostalgic for their childhood. For Linda Charnes, this dynamic of nostalgia is what allows it to posit a "glorious, and misrecognized, past" as the justification for imperialism.[64] From this perspective, it is interesting that the *Waverley* novels become children's novels as Great Britain's imperial power increases. Likewise, it is interesting to note how historical fiction itself has become, in large part, a children's genre.

Nostalgia acts as a mirror image of romantic memory. Romantic memory revisits the past so that one can imagine acting differently: more politically active and more ethically correct. That is, romantic memory returns to the immoral past to imagine that one could redeem it with one's own political action. Nostalgic memory, by contrast, returns to the past and to its scenes of individual guilt to absolve the past itself of political violations. We return to the past to imagine that its politics have not affected us adversely or that the past was a necessary, if childish, stage. But what is being mourned or celebrated in this formulation? In *Waverley*, 1745 is not the right time for revolution and the Jacobite cause is not the right cause, but its rebellious Jacobites are the moral center of the novel and the objects of nostalgic investment in the possibility of rebellion. Because the nation has not been influenced adversely, British readers can, in 1814 – when the British were at war with its former (revolutionary) colonies – be nostalgic for the Jacobite. This keeps open the possibility that revolution might have an appropriate time and place; nostalgia for the inept revolution is the mechanism whereby revolution can be maintained as an ideal: the ethical but impractical choice. Sandra MacPherson's argument that eighteenth-century novels can be read as investigations of harm rather than rights is relevant here: Waverley has the right to rebel should a sovereign actually be unjust, but that is not the case in his temporal and spatial (his geopolitical) situation.[65] This is why the harm caused by his action redounds not on the nation but on his personal relations and also why it can be explored in literature. In MacPherson's account, literature offers persons "consolations of form" in place of "exigencies of embodiment."[66] In *Waverley*, historical fiction provides form to political action while evading responsibility and, largely, consequences – at least to the Waverleys and to England more generally. Scott's historical novel is the formal instantiation of a nostalgic, rather than a romantic, memory.[67]

Waverley ends with a mourning of highland culture that is at once nostalgic of Jacobite culture and dismissive of Jacobite politics:

> [Jacobitism] has now almost entirely vanished from the land, and with it, doubtless, much absurd political prejudice; but, also, many living examples of singular and disinterested attachment to the principles of loyalty which they received from their fathers, and of old Scottish faith, hospitality, worth, and -honour. (363)

The dismissive prepositional phrase "with it much absurd political prejudice" makes the nineteenth-century political aversion to Jacobite politics a commonplace, while the main clause syntactically links "vanish[ing]" to idealized cultural values, making both the fact (the fact of vanishing) and the norm (the ideals of faith, hospitality, etc.) equally important.

What this attitude toward the highland Jacobites of 1745 allows us to say about the Walter Scott's politics is something the critics cannot agree upon. William Hazlitt's famous condemnation of Scott as a "bigoted admirer of the good old world" rests on the claim that for Scott "the moral world stands still."[68] Hazlitt's denunciation has been a source of critical anxiety for Scott scholars – we might assume that this is because those of us working on Scott find something appealing in *Waverley*, and yet we demur to consider conservatism and bigotry to be the source. Yet the nature of Scott's political orientation remains a dynamic question. The critical commonplace that Scott is conservative has given way, in critics such as Judith Wilt and Jerome Christianson, to seeing him as a skeptic or as politically ambivalent.[69] Scott as a reluctant liberal is probably the one he would most recognize, the Scott closest to Edward Waverley. The question of Scott's political orientation is intimately linked to the questions of form, and critics have predictably divided on the politics of historical fiction and on Scott's formal methods in particular. The link between temporality and agency is the center of such disagreements. For Richard Slotkin, historical fiction provides a way to recover past time, to "explore ... alternative possibilities for belief, action, and political change," but as novels, they must see it "from within, from the limited and contingent perspective of those who are caught up in the action."[70] Slotkin argues that historical fiction embeds a theory of "heroic" individual agency and action and thus that that historical fiction is undergirded by a theory that "human agency, consciousness and action really make a difference in historical outcome."[71] The category of historical fiction might sometimes develop in the direction of such political faith as Slotkin describes. Popular historical fiction often operates this way (this is why it is often a children's genre or romance), and Scott's career may represent a microcosm of this trend.[72] But *Waverley*, that is the first Waverley novel, does not see human agency as salutary nor efficacious; it does not ascribe to the "political faith" of revolution.[73]

György Lukács offers what is perhaps still the most influential account of the relation of Scott's politics to his chosen literary form, and one with a more nuanced idea of how temporality and agency relate. In this account, conservatism means siding with the worldview of those members of society "precipitated into ruin" by economic and political modernization.[74] For Lukács, revolutions are "great" – and interesting for historical fiction – because through them latent human capacities for greatness are liberated. But such greatness of action, for Lukács, springs from the fact that its mediocre protagonists chart (because they are embedded in) a "middle course" between the extremes of important historical conflicts. In the framing of action as historical necessity – precipitated by the "here and now" (*hic et nunc*) of an historical past – and in treating the past as the "prehistory of the present," Scott's conservatism, according to Lukács' historical materialist perspective, inheres in the fact that Scott's historical novels account for human action as historical necessity.[75] But this is less true of *Waverley* than it might be of Scott's other fictions, because Edward Waverley is already nostalgic, already acting on behalf of two generations of previous Waverleys, for whom he happens to find a corollary in the Highland rebels. The temporal/spatial discontinuity (against Lukács *hinc et nunc*) of *Waverley* makes it more nostalgic than Lukács' account. Conservative in this sense takes an historical approach to human agency, one that countenances a youthfully naïve belief in agency and revolution or even nostalgically invests in them but (or perhaps precisely because of this belief in progress) necessarily sees at least some action – revolutionary action – as a denial of progress. This is strange dynamic of the nostalgic revolutionary. George Levine thinks Scott's conservatism paved the way for more subversive uses of history and that this potential is encapsulated by the difference between Edward Waverley and *Waverley* "what Edward Waverley must dismiss, *Waverley* preserves."[76] But this chapter's account of nostalgia instead supports Juliet Shields' argument that the purpose of *Waverley* and its foundational techniques of historical fiction are to put revolution in the past.[77] *Waverley*, with its perspective of (only) sixty years, finds a fantasy of faith in revolution (or more generally any kind of postsecular faith) at once dangerous and outmoded. Katey Castellano describes what she calls "romantic conservatism" as an "imaginative attachment to past and future generations."[78] Not just past and future generations but also past and future political positions: nostalgia for the wrong political party paradoxically functions to make *Waverley* ironic – in the sense that it posits a liberal idea of progress and Whig governance as the tradition that must be accepted and as the community to which one owes an admission of political and moral sensibility. Thus, Scott produces a representation of the dynamic between liberalism and conservatism that is fundamentally ironic: The Jacobite is on the wrong side of the Restoration and 1688–89, and thus in their counterrevolutionary instantiation later in the century, they can be the exemplar at once of both revolution and the conservative commitment to tradition. This allows the fictions of enlightened progress and British sovereignty to coexist, and this is why Scott, the ambivalent progressive, perpetuates a conservative worldview. And it is also why he chose historical fiction, which forecloses the revolutionary possibilities of beginnings in favor of historical perspective, and why in particular he chose a historical fiction about the Jacobite – mediocre, ineffectual, and attractive all at once – to reconcile his ambivalence. On one level, historical fiction is conservative simply because it is historical – all historicization is conservative according to Mannheim – and also because it is fiction: a way of imaginatively living through the past, not abstracting it. Fiction can be seen as a subset of conservatism, insofar as it is, in Mannheim's words, an "intuitive, qualitative, concrete form of thought."[79] Scott's historical fiction, covering the space of sixty years, allows for such an imaginative attachment, even across the political borders of Scotland and England, Whig and Jacobite. But not, we might add, outside the patriotic border of Britain: Revolution by colonized or enslaved peoples is not justified by the nostalgic logic of *Waverley*. This is why, at least in 1814, *Waverley* is a novel for adults not for children, a novel of nostalgic memory not romantic memory.

Compared with other writers in this study, Scott does not really qualify as a postsecular conservative. But I have been tracing the ways that the conservatism of these writers took them in unexpected directions. In some cases, the connection from their conservative opinions to their literary contributions is fairly straightforward: Dryden's conservatism and his withdrawal from the domain of party politics can be seen as leading to his theories of literary history as future literary experience using the occasions of the present and the material of the past – political theology secularized as literary history, which may or may not itself be conservative.

But in other cases, conservative opinions or conservative forms led to surprising literary outcomes: Faith becomes a model for narrative relations in Aphra Behn and indulgence persists in theories of mental and imaginative freedom in David Hume. I have been tracing, in other words, effects of conservatism on the literary field, which turn out to be multifarious and not always themselves conservative. Scott may by this standard be more conservative than other writers – insofar as his calibration of the relationship between nostalgia and revolution in historical fiction proves exemplary of how seemingly liberal (revolution) and conservative (nostalgia) commitments are entangled and how they together work toward the stability of Britain, and past and future. *Waverley* is the end of this study because with it, the form (historical novel) and the content (antirevolutionary) of representing a conservative position on the Restoration are reconciled. I conclude by suggesting that this is, perhaps, why nostalgia for Jacobitism, as evidenced by a minor explosion in critical work on Jacobitism in history and literary studies, seems to be peaking once again. *The Outlander* novels and television series, which center on a kind of double nostalgia – a twentieth-century woman, who might have nostalgic appeal for twenty-first century audiences, goes back to the always-already nostalgic time of Jacobitism – provide only the most relevant examples. We are, still, or once again in the early twenty-first century – post Arab Spring, *en media res* of the postsecular phenomena of ISIS, Brexit, and Donald Trump – an age ambivalent about revolution and mediating that ambivalence via cultural forms.

Notes

1. Gilbert Burnet, *A Sermon Preached in the Chapel of St. James's, before His Highness the Prince of Orange, 23rd of December, 1688* (Edinburgh, 1689), 1.
2. Edmund Burke, *Reflections on the Revolution in France*, ed. Frank M. Turner (New Haven, CT: Yale University Press, 2003).
3. Alexis de Tocqueville, *The Old Regime and the French Revolution*, trans. Stuart Gilbert (Garden City, NJ: Doubleday Anchor, 1955), 147.
4. Kathleen Wilson, "Inventing Revolution: 1688 and Eighteenth-Century Popular Politic," *Journal of British Studies*, 28, no. 4 (1989): 362.
5. Anthony S. Jarrells, *Britain's Bloodless Revolutions: 1688 and the Romantic Reform of Literature* (New York: Palgrave Macmillan, 2005), 1–2.
6. Jared Hickman, *Black Prometheus: Race and Radicalism in the Age of Atlantic Slavery* (Oxford: Oxford University Press, 2016).
7. Corrinne Harol, "Misconceiving the Heir: Mind and Matter in the Warming Pan Propaganda," in *Vital Matters*, eds. Helen Deutsch and Mary Terrell

(Toronto: University of Toronto Press, 2012), 130–46. As I explained in the Introduction, while a couple of early publications related to this project explored Whig writing about the revolution, as the book progressed, I focused more on the conservative writers.
8 As Reinhardt Koselleck has argued, this idea of a natural cycle of revolution has its corollary the historical meaning of political revolution, in which the constitutional movement from monarchy to democracy cyclically repeats (*Futures Past: On the Semantics of Historical Time*, trans. Keith Tribe [Cambridge, MA: MIT Press, 1990], 41–43).
9 Hannah Arendt, *On Revolution* (London: Penguin, 1977), 1–58.
10 Steve Pincus, *1688: The First Modern Revolution* (New Haven, CT: Yale University, 2009).
11 Ibid., 6–7.
12 Conal Condren, *The Language of Politics in Seventeenth-Century England* (Basingstoke: Macmillan, 1994), 155–58, 10.
13 Walter Scott, *Waverley: Or, 'Tis Sixty Years Since* (London: Penguin, 1985). All references will be to this edition.
14 A similar argument can be found in Amanda Louise Johnson "Thomas Jefferson's Ossianic Romance," *Studies in Eighteenth-Century Culture* 45 (2016): 19–35. Johnson explores Thomas Jefferson's interest in *Ossian* and its romanticizing of the lost Scottish Highlands as a foundation for ideas about America.
15 John Locke, *An Essay Concerning Human Understanding* (Oxford: Oxford University Press, 2008), chap. 21, para. 24.
16 Stefan Collini, *Public Moralists: Political Thought and Intellectual Life in Britain, 1850–1930* (Oxford: Oxford University Press, 1993), 276.
17 Matthew Wickman, *The Ruins of Experience: Scotland's "Romantick" Highlands and the Birth of the Modern Witness* (Philadelphia: University of Pennsylvania Press, 2007).
18 Arendt, *On Revolution*.
19 Arendt says, "it is as though the beginner had abolished the sequence of temporality itself," Ibid., 206. Regarding religion and revolution, Arendt says, "Indeed, it may ultimately turn out that what we call revolution is precisely that transitory phase which brings about the birth of a new, secular realm. But if this is true, then it is secularization itself, and not the contents of Christian teachings, which constitutes the origin of revolution," Ibid., 26.
20 Charles Taylor, *A Secular Age* (Cambridge, MA: Harvard University Press, 2007), 61. Taylor's argument about modern revolutions would make 1688–89 just one subset of the larger Protestant Reformation. Pincus' emphasis on economic issues and his de-emphasis on religion make him see 1688 as having more importance. In some ways their disagreement, with Taylor aligned with a Catholic postsecularity and Pincus with a mainstream liberalism, demonstrates how the conflict of 1688–89 is still shaping the way we frame political debate, though things have come back around, in a postsecular time, to the extent that Taylor's argument seems the more radical.

21 Taylor, *A Secular Age*, 53–54.
22 This argument is generally credited to John Locke's *Second Treatise on Government* (London, 1689/90), chap. 19.
23 This is a point about which historians disagree: both in terms of how prominent "abdicate" was (versus "revolution") and what each term meant. For an overview of these positions, as well as an account of the meaning of "abdicate," see Thomas P. Slaughter, "'Abdicate' and 'Contract' in the Glorious Revolution," *The Historical Journal* 24, no. 2 (June 1981): 323–37.
24 *English Currant: From Friday Dec. 21 to Wednesday Dec. 26, 1688*, no. 5 (London, England, 1688), *17th–18th Century Burney Collection Newspapers*.
25 Toni Bowers, "'The Abdicated Family': Hume's Partisan Grammar in 'Of the Protestant Succession,'" *Restoration* 39, no. 1/2 (2015): 61–81.
26 Juliet Shields discusses how these ideas were worked out in Scott's writing, in *Sentimental Literature and Anglo-Scottish Identity, 1745–1820* (Cambridge: Cambridge University Press, 2010).
27 Johannes Hofer, "Medical Dissertation on Nostalgia," trans. C. K. Anspach, *Bulletin of the History of Medicine* 2, no. 6 (1934): 376–91.
28 Ibid., 381.
29 A number of critics follow this history of nostalgia, including Svetlana Boym, *The Future of Nostalgia* (New York: Basic Books, 2008); Kevis Goodman, "'Uncertain Disease': Nostalgia, Pathologies of Motion, Practices of Reading," *Studies in Romanticism* 49, no. 2 (2010): 197–227; David Lowenthal, *The Past Is a Foreign Country* (Cambridge: Cambridge University Press, 1985); Michael S. Roth, "The Time of Nostalgia: Medicine, History and Normality in 19th-century France," *Time & Society* 1, no. 2 (1992): 271–86; Jean Starobinski and William S. Kemp, "The Idea of Nostalgia," *Diogenes* 14, no. 54 (June 1966): 81–103; Susan Stewart, *On Longing: Narratives of the Miniature, the Gigantic, the Souvenir, the Collection* (Baltimore: Johns Hopkins University Press, 1984).
30 A refusal, in Kant's terms, to emerge from "self-incurred immaturity." Immanuel Kant, *An Answer to the Question: "What Is Enlightenment?"* (London: Penguin UK, 2013).
31 Nicholas Dames, *Amnesiac Selves: Nostalgia, Forgetting, and British Fiction, 1810–1870* (New York: Oxford University Press, 2001), 12.
32 This relationship between time and place may be reversed. David Daiches argues something like this when he says "place survives, however altered, where time dissolves … to look at the present site of historic actions … is to invite the imagination both to reconstruct the past and to dwell on its relation to the present," in *Sir Walter Scott and His World* (London: Thames & Hudson Ltd., 1971), 9.
33 Fredric Jameson argues that nostalgia diminishes "our lived possibility of experiencing history in some active way," in *Postmodernism, or, the Cultural Logic of Late Capitalism* (Durham, NC: Duke University Press, 1991), 21.
34 Linda Charnes, "Anticipating Nostalgia," *Textual Cultures: Text, Contexts, Interpretation* 4, no. 1 (2009): 74.

35 Kevis Goodman, "Romantic Poetry and the Science of Nostalgia," in *The Cambridge Companion to British Romantic Poetry*, eds. James Chandler and Maureen N. McLane (Cambridge: Cambridge University Press, 2008), 197; Charnes, "Anticipating Nostalgia," 81.
36 For this trend, see Alastair Bonnett, *Left in the Past: Radicalism and the Politics of Nostalgia* (New York: Continuum, 2010); Kimberly K. Smith, "Mere Nostalgia: Notes on a Progressive Paratheory," *Rhetoric & Public Affairs* 3, no. 4 (2000): 505–27; William Stafford, *Socialism, Radicalism, and Nostalgia: Social Criticism in Britain, 1775–1830* (Cambridge: Cambridge University Press, 1987).
37 Bradley Bryan, "Revenge and Nostalgia," *Conference Papers – Western Political Science Association* (2009): 1–22.
38 John J. Su, *Ethics and Nostalgia in the Contemporary Novel* (Cambridge: Cambridge University Press, 2005).
39 See, for example, Fabil B. Dasilva and Jim Faught, "Nostalgia: A Sphere and Process of Contemporary Ideology," *Qualitative Sociology* 5, no. 1 (1982): 47–63. Nicholas Dames divides these camps of nostalgia critics into those that produce symptomatic readings of disease and those interested in the kinds of functions that nostalgia may perform in specific circumstances (an approach that Dames prefers), in "Nostalgia and Its Disciplines: A Response," *Memory Studies* 3, no. 3 (2010): 269–75.
40 Corrinne Harol, "Whig Ballads and the Past Passive Jacobite," *Journal for Eighteenth-Century Studies* 35, no. 4 (2012): 581–95.
41 For a discussion of this see Diane Long Hoeveler, "Anti-Catholicism and the Gothic Imaginary: The Historical and Literary Contexts," *Religion in the Age of Enlightenment* 3 (2012): 4. An extensive discussion of the pope's association with the devil during the Guy Fawkes festivities can be found in Colin Haydon, *Anti-Catholicism in Eighteenth-Century England, c. 1714–80: A Political and Social Study* (Manchester, NY: Manchester University Press, 1993), chap. 1. The devil's literal appearance in any number of gothic novels (in particular, those by Matthew Lewis and Charles Maturin) suggests that the gothic imaginary worked by transforming historically distant but lingering political and historical fears such as the gunpowder plot, the Spanish Armada, the Irish massacre, and the Jacobite rebellions, and presenting them in slightly disguised forms (the pope and devil now represented by a "possessed" monk or his amorous seductress).
42 This sketch of the literary Jacobite in eighteenth-century England is of course very limited. Fuller accounts have been provided by other critics and would include: Boswell's use of highland culture to reflect, according to Leith Davis, the heterogeneity of Britain (*Acts of Union: Scotland and the Literary Negotiation of the British Nation 1707–1830* [Stanford, CA: Stanford University Press, 1998]); Defoe's Jacobites who inhabit, as Evan Gottlieb puts it, the "refuge of the disaffected," in *Feeling British: Sympathy and National Identity in Scottish and English Writing, 1707–1832* (Lewisburg, PA: Bucknell University Press, 2007), 39; Jery Melford in Tobias Smollet's

Humphrey Clinker; Sir Pertinax Macsychophant in Charles Machlin's *Man of the World*; Macartney in Frances Burney's *Evelina*; Mary Douglas in Susan Ferrier's *Marriage*, among many others.

43 John Stuart Mill, *On Liberty and Other Essays*, eds. Mark Philp and Frederick Rosen (Oxford: Oxford University Press, 2015), 375. Mill is referring to both Scottish and Welch people.

44 Comparisons between highlanders and African (as well as Indigenous New World peoples) were common. Geoffrey Plank makes this case, and also makes the distinction between "rebel" and "savage" (*Rebellion and Savagery: The Jacobite Rising of 1745 and the British Empire* [Philadelphia: University of Pennsylvania Press, 2005], 12, 22). See also Colin Kidd, "Race, Empire, and the Limits of Nineteenth-Century Scottish Nationhood," *The Historical Journal* 46, no. 4 (2003): 873–92; Silvia Sebastiani who argues that such language was first applied to Celtic people (*The Scottish Enlightenment: Race, Gender, and the Limits of Progress*, trans. Jeremy Carden [New York: Palgrave Macmillan, 2013], 165); and Silke Stroh, *Gaelic Scotland in the Colonial Imagination: Anglophone Writing from 1600 to 1900* (Chicago: Northwestern University Press, 2017), 185–212.

45 For a sense of the anomalousness of the Scottish situation vis-à-vis Great Britain and its effect on the Scottish literary tradition generally, see Robert Crawford, *The Scottish Invention of English Literature* (Cambridge: Cambridge University Press, 1998); David Daiches, *The Paradox of Scottish Culture: The Eighteenth Century Experience* (Oxford: Oxford University Press, 1964); Davis, *Acts of Union*; Kenneth Simpson, *The Protean Scot: The Crisis of Identity in Eighteenth Century Scottish Literature* (Aberdeen: Aberdeen University Press, 1988); and Katie Trumpener, *Bardic Nationalism: The Romantic Novel and the British Empire* (Princeton, NJ: Princeton University Press, 1997).

46 Hugh Trevor-Roper, *The Invention of Tradition* (Cambridge: Cambridge University Press, 2015); Murray Pittock, *The Invention of Scotland: The Stuart Myth and the Scottish Identity, 1638 to the Present* (London: Routledge, 2014); Gerald Porter, "'Who Talks of My Nation?' The Role of Wales, Scotland, and Ireland in Constructing "Englishness," in *Imagined States: Nationalism, Utopia, and Longing in Oral Cultures*, eds. Luisa Del Guidice and Gerald Porter (Logan: Utah State University Press, 2001), 101–35.

47 Murray G. H. Pittock, *Poetry and Jacobite Politics in Eighteenth-Century Britain and Ireland* (Cambridge: Cambridge University Press, 2006), 213. In this sense, English nostalgia for Scottish Jacobitism is a function of imperialism. Renato Rosaldo argues that this is typical of imperialist nostalgia, "where people mourn the passing of what they themselves have transformed," in *Culture & Truth: The Remaking of Social Analysis: With a New Introduction* (Boston: Beacon Press, 1993), 69. Sari Makdesi sees in *Waverley* a "virtual reinvention of the colonized territory as a space that can be put to use in various ways" ("Colonial Space and the Colonization of Time in Scott's

Waverley," *Studies in Romanticism* 34, no. 2 [1995]: 156). My point is that English nostalgia for Jacobitism is also (1) based on the Jacobite's own nostalgia and (2) at the same time a nostalgia for revolution itself. For more on how Scott's novels respond to the Union, see also James Chandler, *England in 1819: The Politics of Literary Culture and the Case of Romantic Historicism* (Chicago: University of Chicago Press, 1999).
48 Plank, *Rebellion and Savagery*, 26.
49 For a revisionist account of this, including the role that women writers (and Irish women writers) played in making nationalism central to the historical novel, see Fiona Price, "The Uses of History: The Historical Novel in the Post-French Revolution Debate and Ellis Cornelia Knight's *Marcus Flaminius* (1792)," in *Reading Historical Fiction: The Revenant and Remembered Past*," eds. Kate Mitchell and Nicola Parsons (New York: Palgrave MacMillan, 2013), 187–203 and Trumpener, *Bardic Nationalism*.
50 Henry Fielding, *The History of Tom Jones, a Foundling* (London, 1749), book 8, chap. 14. (Note: This part of the narrative was included in the first edition but was later excised.) The irony that "a Popish Prince may be the defender the Protestant Church" was somewhat of a commonplace; *The Jacobite's Journal* 1748 January 2, cited in Raymond D. Tumbleson, *Catholicism in the English Protestant Imagination: Nationalism, Religion, and Literature, 1660–1745* (Cambridge: Cambridge University Press, 1998), 39. I do not treat these representations at length because I feel they are satires – that is, true Whig critiques of Jacobitism – whereas I am positing that with Scott we get a more fully formed (and therefore ambivalent) nostalgia for Jacobitism.
51 Joanna Lipking describes *Oroonoko* as the first realistic novel, in *Oroonoko: A Norton Critical Edition*, by Aphra Behn (New York: Norton, 1997), xi.
52 For a similar argument, see Jarrells, *Britain's Bloodless Revolutions*, 15–16.
53 The claim for Waverley's significance to the history of the novel is a critical commonplace. Hayden White credits Scott with the "invention" of the historical novel ("Introduction: Historical Fiction, Fictional History, and Historical Reality," *Rethinking History* 9, no. 2–3 [June 1, 2005]: 147–57). Frederick Jameson calls Scott's fiction "an emergent new form," (Introduction to *The Historical Novel*, by György Lukács, trans. Hannah Mitchell and Stanley Mitchell [Lincoln: University of Nebraska Press, 1983], 1). For George Levine, Scott "transformed the history of narrative in Western Europe, even though (or precisely because) Scott downplayed the seriousness of his fiction (*The Realistic Imagination: English Fiction from Frankenstein to Lady Chatterley* [Chicago: University of Chicago Press, 1981], 81–82). The legitimization of the novel is also its de-feminization and its transformation into historical fiction. Ina Ferris finds evidence that this happened rights away: Reviewers of the Waverley novels perceived them as rescuing the novel from its feminization by historicizing romance, as that is a "manly intervention into an overblown and enervated form" (*The Achievement of Literary Authority: Gender, History, and the Waverley Novels* [Ithaca, NY: Cornell University Press, 1991], 1–8, 1). For other perspectives on Scott's legitimation of the

novel, see Homer Obed Brown, *Institutions of the English Novel from Defoe to Scott* (Philadelphia: University of Pennsylvania Press, 1998); Ian Duncan, *Modern Romance and Transformations of the Novel* (Cambridge: Cambridge University Press, 1992); Jarrells, *Britain's Bloodless Revolutions*; Jane Millgate, *Walter Scott: The Making of the Novelist* (Toronto: University of Toronto Press, 1984); Fiona Robertson, *Legitimate Histories: Scott, Gothic, and the Authorities of Fiction* (Oxford: Clarendon, 1994); and Trumpener, *Bardic Nationalism*. I would like to thank Max Novak for making me think along these lines. As a graduate student in a course on the eighteenth century, I asked him when the novel lost its scandalous feminine character, and he said, "in 1814, with *Waverley*." It has taken me decades to come back to this question to try to understand his answer.

54 György Lukács, *The Historical Novel*, trans. Hannah Mitchell and Stanley Mitchell (Lincoln: University of Nebraska Press, 1983), 33. George Levine credits Scott with the "death of the hero" *The Realistic Imagination*, 85. Michael Gamer calls Scott's reformation of the hero as an "evacuation of agency" that "alienate[s] conduct from character" ("Waverley and the Object of [Literary] History," *Modern Language Quarterly* 70, no. 4 [December 1, 2009]: 520). Katie Trumpener notes that the name Waverley and this mediocrity of character were already established in other historical novels: for example, in Jane West's *Loyalists: An Historical Novel* (1812) or in Charlotte Smith's *Desmond* (1792) (*Bardic Nationalism*). Wolfgang Iser calls them passive or neutral heroes, in "Fiction – The Filter of History," in *New Perspectives in German Literary Criticism*, eds. Richard E. Amacher and Victor Lange (Princeton, NJ: Princeton University Press, 2015), 86–104.

55 For Andrew Lincoln, this is the foundation of Scott's politics, which suggest that in personal relations loyalty and principle are good but in politics they produce fanatics (*Walter Scott and Modernity* [Edinburgh: Edinburgh University Press, 2007], 8). Overall, Lincoln disagrees (with me and other critics) that Scott's use of the past is nostalgic.

56 Ian Watt, *The Rise of The Novel* (Berkeley: University of California Press, 1697), 18–21.

57 David Douglas Devlin, *The Author of Waverley: A Critical Study of Walter Scott* (London: Palgrave Macmillan, 1971), 41.

58 Leith Davis argues that the novels of Smollett and Fielding were centrally concerned with using the occasion of the 1745 uprising to reshape readers as British subjects (*Acts of Union*, 46–73).

59 Karl Mannheim, "The Problem of Generations," in *Karl Mannheim Essays*, ed. Paul Kecskemeti (London: Routledge, 1972), 276–322.

60 The point is not that the political issues raised by Jacobitism are actually far afield of issues in the war of 1812 – including England's relationship with Canada and the USA and the ongoing questions about revolution that these raised – but rather that they could seem remote and that the techniques of historical fiction accomplish this.

61 Frances Ferguson, "Romantic Memory," *Studies in Romanticism* 35, no. 4 (1996): 509–33.
62 On Scott's response to stadial theory, which begins with William Hazlitt's attack, see George Levine (*Realistic Imagination*, 86) and Sari Makdesi ("Colonial Space").
63 Immanuel Kant, "An Answer to the Question: What Is Enlightenment?" in *What Is Enlightenment?: Eighteenth-Century Answers and Twentieth-Century Questions*, trans. and ed. James Schmidt (Berkeley: University of California Press, 1996), 58.
64 Charnes, "Anticipating Nostalgia," 72.
65 Sandra Macpherson, *Harm's Way: Tragic Responsibility and the Novel Form* (Baltimore: Johns Hopkins University Press, 2010), 4.
66 Ibid., 174. I am arguing that in *Waverley*, the material consequences are always threatened, but in the end the form of the historical novel encapsulates both action and responsibility while evading consequences.
67 Hamish Dalley, "Temporal Systems in Representations of the Past: Distance, Freedom and Irony in Historical Fiction," in *Reading Historical Fiction: The Revenant and Remembered Past*, eds. Kate Mitchell and Nicola Parsons (New York: Palgrave Macmillan, 2013), 33–49. Dalley reviews the way that critics have approached the mixture of history and fiction (or distance and agency): In short, Waverley balances the demands of history and the novel by segregating them and Dalley concludes that "this temporal system lends itself to conservatism, as we are invited to look ironically on the strivings of individuals, and accept that the past could only have turned out as it did" (37–38).
68 William Carew Hazlitt, *The Spirit of the Age; or, Contemporary Portraits* (London: G. Bell & Sons, 1886) 110.
69 Judith Wilt, *Secret Leaves: The Novels of Walter Scott* (Chicago: University of Chicago Press, 1985), 17; Jerome Christensen, *Romanticism at the End of History* (Baltimore: Johns Hopkins University Press, 2000), 175. For a discussion of this critical trend, see Lincoln, *Walter Scott and Modernity*, vii–viii.
70 Richard Slotkin, "Fiction for the Purposes of History," *Rethinking History* 9, no. 2–3 (June 1, 2005): 225.
71 Ibid., 231.
72 It is beyond the scope of this project to discuss Scott's larger career. I focus on *Waverly* because of its primacy, its significance to 1688–99 and its centrality to literary history. For a discussion of this question of *Waverley*'s priority in literary history, see Gamer, "Waverley."
73 Slotkin, "Fiction for the Purposes of History," 231.
74 Lukács, *The Historical Novel*, 32.
75 Ibid., 60, 53.
76 Levine, *The Realistic Imagination*, 82.
77 Shields, *Sentimental Literature*, 12. For Juliet Shields, the genre of historical fiction puts revolution in the past. I am building on her argument by showing how this movement also allows us to be nostalgic for revolution. Critics of Walter Scott often reference nostalgia, but few treat it substantially, and it has

not been linked to revolution. I am not claiming that my approach – linking revolution and nostalgia – leads to an original reading of *Waverley* (and certainly not of Scott's oeuvre more generally); rather, *Waverley* is the example of the larger theory I am working out in terms of how a liberal/conservative dynamic is mediated via revolution/nostalgia in historical fiction.

78 Katey Kuhns Castellano, "Romantic Conservatism in Burke, Wordsworth, and Wendell Berry," *SubStance: A Review of Theory and Literary Criticism* 40, no. 2 (2011): 73–91.

79 Karl Mannheim, "Conservative Thought," in *From Karl Mannheim*, ed. Kurt H. Wolff (New York: Oxford University Press, 1971): 273.

Coda
On Literary Conservatism as a Formal Category

The book has argued – via keywords and close readings – that certain forms of literary representation derive from their author's concerns about what we now call secularization. It posits that cultural concepts (faith, worlds, nostalgia), forms of mentation (indulgence, figuring), literary forms (novelistic narration, historical fiction), and even fiction and modes of reading themselves result from the conservative orientation of their authors. In so doing, it argues for treating the secular and the postsecular as relevant not just to politics or religion but also to literary forms and innovation, theories of mind, and conceptualizations of temporality and mentation more generally. In fact, a central insight of the book is that the postsecular is motivated not necessarily by political or religious opposition – or even by a renegotiation of the relationship between the religious and the secular – but rather by changes wrought by secularization across the spheres of cultural and social life, and it argues that the literary sphere provided both the site and the methods for that process. This study has also demonstrated that secularization and liberalism are not separate from postsecularization and conservatism – rather, they are interdependent, as this study's keywords suggest: Faith and indulgence, transformed for a secular system, make possible belief and toleration; imagining worlds and reading literary history are embedded in secular spatiality and temporality, even as they reveal the offenses and limitations wrought by these secular categories; passivity and the revolution/nostalgia dynamic both keep alive and keep in check the liberal fiction of human agency. The conservative and the postsecular are thus constantly in tension with the liberal and secular. This is why it is no coincidence that the concerns of people not well served by liberalism – not just royals but also women and enslaved people – occur repeatedly in this study. This is also why the two characteristics that most distinguish these conservative writers – their opposition to revolution and their innovative literary formations – are connected.

Hence literary conservatism constitutes a formal, not a political, category. On a basic level, my interest in the formation of literary conservatism indexes the efforts to account for the literary aspects – rather than the political orientation – of these writers. This is reflected in the fact that the central contributions of this book consist not in any overarching theory but in the arguments of each chapter, treating the writers and texts in their historical and formal specificity. This may be seen as formally conservative, committed to the local and material rather than the general and the abstract, and as such, conservatism is not just the content but also the form of this book. In most of the chapters, I am not interested in theorizing form – which would contravene the concepts of conservatism taken up here – but rather in taking up particular forms as ways that authors shaped their conservative/literary responses to political issues. The arguments about Margaret Cavendish and David Hume are exceptions, places where I take up form as a theory of making literature, and in these cases my theory of form is conservative. In tracing how "figuring" tracks between Cavendish's literary and philosophical projects, I argue that Cavendish's conservatism inheres in her theory and practice of figuration. This argument reconciles a seeming contradiction in Cavendish (and in strains of conservatism more generally) between a discourse or a defence of freedom and a recognition of the organic limitations of such freedom, and I theorize an inherent conservatism in the notion of figuring and thus of literary form and fictionality. In the account of David Hume, I explore how indulgence as a mental process is related to the monarchical function in a mixed government, allowing a freedom from both opinion and law that, if properly checked, allows for the slow development of society that characterizes Hume's conservatism. This formal (as opposed to historical or ideological) definition of conservatism emphasizes its antitheoretical character, its emergence as a critique of the theoretical fundamentalism of nascent liberalism. In this sense, the interrogations of form in Cavendish and Hume are inherently connected to the dynamic between conservatism (as form) and liberalism (as theory) and thus between literature and politics.

This account of form explores the extent to which these writers grappled with the relationship between the material world and their own capacity as both authors and political subjects. One such relevant account of this dynamic is Victoria Kahn's treatment of how poesis in the early modern period links literary and political acts.[1] But Kahn's account of poesis is grounded in liberal theories and values: Poesis is the making new or making original, emphasizing human potency and agency, whereas form, on my account, explores the connection between human agency, which is limited, and the matters at hand. In arguing for the *ex nihilo* origin of politics, Hobbes proposes that you can only know what you have made.[2] Literary formation by contrast, constitutes a way of knowing and a way of making, but it need not – contrary to Kahn's account of Hobbes and the maker's knowledge – claim to have created the matter nor the knowledge one shapes.[3] Form is, as Henry Turner has defined it, an action, a verb, a response to the material reality of one's world and an effort to engage with it, to shape it, not as a means of invention *ex nihilo* but as process that can be epistemological, aesthetic, and political but that is always connected to an understanding of matter's own forces.[4] Such a position rejects a form/content divide because literature (in individual cases but also in general categories of genre as well as literary history) necessarily combines form and content. Whereas poesis and the concept of the maker's knowledge align with a liberal view of agency and politics, this study's account of form suits a conservative ethos in which human actors cannot impose meaning on the material world but may be able to shape it. These form and forming functions of literature provide a counterpoint to what postsecular scholars have revealed about how liberalism aspires to a transcendence that might replace theology; literary form offers a place to critique the theories of liberalism and its aspirations to abstraction and universality. This is one argument for why conservative writers, in favor of restoration and against revolution, would be aligned with formal innovation, for why, that is, conservative writers have been so influential in literary history during the long Restoration.

One goal of the book has been that treating these writers as postsecular can bring this period of literary history in conversation with postsecular scholarship and with other periods while also pointing to new directions in scholarship on this period. Its intention is to expand our idea of the secular and the postsecular: to include both early periods and aspects of life beyond religion and politics. By attending to how the postsecular emerges in the long Restoration, and in realms beyond religion and politics, this book makes the case that secular and postsecular must be thought together and must be considered in every aspect of culture. This may be controversial, because neither secularization nor postsecularization are historically accurate to this period. Jordan Alexander Stein describes secularization as a "misrecognition...the history of a story we told, not of a thing that happened."[5] That is, secularization functions more as a lens or an ideology – one with inherent blind spots – than a historical fact. As such, a case could be made for discarding the term as overly simplistic or misleading.

But this study has revealed that what we now call secularization was a locus of concern for conservative writers, and it has shown how the secular orientation of scholars has limited our ability to see these concerns. Hence my case for bringing a postsecular lens to these early critics of what we now call secularization, in order to nuance the stories we tell about both secularization and literary history. While I have insisted that this study is literary rather than political, it does offer some insights into the ways that the liberal state "lives on premises that it is not able to guarantee by itself."[6] As such, it suggests that models of governance including liberal capitalism that are disciplinary or atomizing or that abstract the full range of human experience out of politics will continue to experience postsecular resistance. This is not to argue for a conservative position, but rather to offer insight into what liberalism cannot provide or reconcile.

Finally, I do not claim that conservatism explains these writers or formal experiments fully. Literature—individually, generically, and as a larger field—can be many things at different (or even the same) times. I can read these texts as literary conservatism, but this does not mean they cannot offer other insights, ones that even oppose my interpretations here. This is why I have purposefully resisted proposing a new monolithic account of this period, its literature, secularity, or postsecularity. I follow Lori Branch and Mark Kinght in calling for the postsecular as a method that must refuse the "rituals of ... re-secularization" that turn new critical practices into "certain secular knowledge."[7] This call to remain in uncertainty is, in this study, a call also to attend to the specificity of the close readings and formal concerns of the chapters rather than any larger theories of the concepts treated here. My intention, beyond the arguments in the chapters, is not to inspire other scholars to agree with my view of conservatism, literature, or postsecularity but rather to attend to the concepts and the formal innovation in the literature they study, in order to explore the historical and formal specificity of texts beyond the monolithic – and often invisible – secularism of the methods and interests we have pursued for so long.

Notes

1 For Kahn's accounts of the fictive and poetic nature of both law and literature, see *Wayward Contracts: The Crisis of Political Obligation in England, 1640–1674* (Princeton, NJ: Princeton University Press, 2009), *The Future of Illusion: Political Theology and Early Modern Texts* (Chicago: University of Chicago Press, 2014), and *The Trouble with Literature* (Oxford: Oxford University Press, 2020). *Wayward Contracts* focuses on the linguistic turn to

contract as constitutive of the ways that modern politics and literature collaborate to bring new political entities into being. *The Future of Illusion* develops the idea of poesis, as an early modern account of (and an accounting of the value of) human secular agency. *The Trouble with Literature* explores the idea of the maker's knowledge in Hobbes.
2 Hobbes is building on a tradition of empiricism to make a case for *sciencia* in politics. He puts it this way, "Geometry therefore is demonstrable, for the lines and figures from which we reason are drawn and described by ourselves; and civil philosophy is demonstrable, because we make the commonwealth ourselves." William Molesworth, *The English Works of Thomas Hobbes Volume VII* (London: Longman, Brown, Green, and Longmans, 1845), vol. 7, 184. For a discussion of this tradition of the "maker's knowledge," see also Antonio Pérez-Ramos, *Francis Bacon's Idea of Science and the Maker's Knowledge Tradition* (Oxford: Oxford University Press, 1988).
3 In Kahn's account, one of the consequences of this difference is that liberalism winds up committed to ideas of "form" over content: formal equality over substantive value, for example (*The Future of Illusion*, 13). But on my account, form rejects this distinction.
4 Henry S. Turner, "Lessons from Literature for the Historian of Science (and Vice Versa)," *ISIS: Journal of the History of Science in Society* 101, no. 3 (September 2010): 578–89.
5 Stein, Jordan Alexander Stein. "Angels in (Mexican) America." *American Literature: A Journal of Literary History, Criticism, and Bibliography* 86.4 (2014): 683–711, 684.
6 Ernst-Wolfgang Böckenförde, *Staat, Gesellschaft* (Berlin: Suhrkamp, 1976) [English translation: *State, Society and Liberty: Studies in Political Theory and Constitutional Law* (Oxford: Berg, 1991], 60.
7 Lori Branch and Mark Knight, "Why the Postsecular Matters," *Christianity and Literature* 67, no. 3 (2018): 493–510, 504.

Bibliography

Achinstein, Sharon. "Dryden and Dissent." In *Enchanted Ground: Reimagining John Dryden*, edited by Jayne Lewis and Maximillian E. Novak, 70–90. Toronto: University of Toronto Press, 2004.
Addison, Joseph. "Number 110: The Guardian." In *The Works of Joseph Addison*, vol. 4, 207–10. G. Bell & Sons, 1889.
Agamben, Giorgio. *Homo Sacer: Sovereign Power and Bare Life*. Translated by Daniel Heller-Roazen. Stanford, CA: Stanford University Press, 1998.
Ahearn, Laura M. "Language and Agency." *Annual Review of Anthropology* 30 (2001): 109–37.
Althusser, Louis, and Étienne Balibar. *Reading Capital*. Translated by Ben Brewster. London: New Left Books, 1970.
Alvarez, David. "Reading Locke after Shaftesbury: Feeling Our Way towards a Postsecular Genealogy of Religious Tolerance." In *Mind, Body, Motion, Matter: Eighteenth-Century British and French Literary Perspectives*, edited by Mary Helen McMurran and Alison Conway, 72–109. Toronto: University of Toronto Press, 2016.
Alzate, Elissa B. *Religious Liberty in a Lockean Society*. New York: Palgrave, 2017.
Anidjar, Gil. "Secularism." *New German Critique* 33, no. 1 (2006): 52–77.
Appiah, Kwame Anthony. *Cosmopolitanism: Ethics in a World of Strangers (Issues of Our Time)*. New York: W. W. Norton & Company, 2010.
Apter, Emily. *Against World Literature: On the Politics of Untranslatability*. London: Verso, 2014.
Aquinas, Thomas. *De Regimine Principum Ad Regum Cypri: Et De Regimine Judgeorum Ad Ducissam Brabantiae*, 2nd ed. Edited by Joseph Mathis. Taurini: Marietti, 1986.
Aravamudan, Srinivas. *Tropicopolitans: Colonialism and Agency, 1688–1804*. Durham, NC: Duke University Press, 1999.
Arendt, Hannah. *On Revolution*. London: Penguin, 1977.
Armistead, J. M. "The Mythic Dimensions of Dryden's The Hind and the Panther." *SEL* 16, no. 3 (1976): 377–86.
Armstrong, Karen. "Let's Revive the Golden Rule." Filmed July 2009. TED video, 9:38. www.ted.com/talks/karen_armstrong_let_s_revive_the_golden_rule.

Armstrong, Nancy. *Desire and Domestic Fiction: A Political History of the Novel.* Oxford: Oxford University Press, 1987.
Asad, Talal. *Formations of the Secular.* Stanford, CA: Stanford University Press, 2003.
Ashcraft, Richard. *Revolutionary Politics & Locke's Two Treatises of Government.* Princeton, NJ: Princeton University Press, 1986.
Assoulin, Kobi. "Beyond 'Good': Richard Rorty's Private Sphere and Toleration." *Iyyun: The Jerusalem Philosophical Quarterly* 60 (January 2011): 53–71.
Athey, Stephanie, and Daniel Cooper Alarcón. "Oroonoko's Gendered Economies of Honor/Horror: Reframing Colonial Discourse Studies in the Americas." *American Literature* 65, no. 3 (1993): 415–43.
Auchter, Dorothy. *Dictionary of Literary and Dramatic Censorship in Tudor and Stuart England.* Westport, CT: Greenwood Press, 2001.
Augustine, Matthew C. *Aesthetics of Contingency: Writing, Politics, and Culture in England, 1639–89.* Manchester: Manchester University Press, 2018.
  "Dryden's 'Mysterious Writ' and the Empire of Signs." *Huntington Library Quarterly: Studies in English and American History and Literature* 74, no. 1 (March 2011): 1–22.
Avis, Paul. *The Church in the Theology of the Reformers.* London: Marshall, Morgan and Scott, 1982.
Bainbrigg, Thomas. *Seasonable Reflections on a Late Pamphlet Entitled a History of Passive Obedience Since the Reformation.* London, 1689–90.
Baker, J. Wayne. "Sola Fide, Sola Gratia: The Battle for Luther in Seventeenth-Century England." *The Sixteenth Century Journal* 13, no. 1 (Spring 1985): 115–33.
Ballaster, Ros. "New Hystericism: Aphra Behn's Oroonoko: The Body, the Text, and the Feminist Critic." In *New Feminist Discourses: Critical Essays on Theories and Texts*, edited by Isobel Armstrong, 283–95. London: Routledge, 1992.
  Seductive Forms: Women's Amatory Fiction from 1684–1740. Oxford: Oxford University Press, 1998.
  "'The Story of the Heart': Love-Letters between a Noble-Man and His Sister." In *The Cambridge Companion to Aphra Behn*, edited by Derik Hughes and Janet Todd, 135–50. Cambridge Companions to Literature. Cambridge: Cambridge University Press, 2004.
Barad, Karen. *Meeting the Universe Halfway: Quantum Physics and the Entanglement of Matter and Meaning.* Durham, NC: Duke University Press, 2007.
Barthes, Roland. *Mythologies.* Translated by Annette Lavers. New York: The Noonday Press, 1957/1972.
Battigelli, Anna. *Margaret Cavendish and the Exiles of the Mind.* Lexington: University Press of Kentucky, 2015.
Baucom, Ian. *Specters of the Atlantic: Finance Capital, Slavery, and the Philosophy of History.* Durham, NC: Duke University Press, 2005.

Behn, Aphra. *A Congratulatory Poem to Her Sacred Majesty, Queen Mary upon Her Arrival in England by Mrs. A. Behn*. London: Printed by R.E. for R. Bentley ... and W. Canning ..., 1689.

"To His Sacred Majesty, King James the Second." In *Oroonoko, and Other Writings*, edited by Paul Salzman, 255–56. Oxford: Oxford World's Classics, 1998.

Oroonoko, and Other Writings. Edited by Paul Salzman. Oxford: Oxford World's Classics, 1998.

Oroonoko and Other Writings. Oxford: Oxford University Press, 2009.

The Project Gutenberg eBook of the Works of Aphra Behn. Edited by Montague Summers. London: William Heinemann [1960] 2009.

The Second Part of the Rover. London, 1681.

The Works of Aphra Behn. Vol. 2, Love-Letters between a Nobleman and His Sister (1684–7). Edited by Janet Todd. Charlottesville, VA: InteLex, 2004 and London: Pickering & Chatto, 2000–1.

Bejan, Teresa. *Mere Civility: Disagreement and the Limits of Toleration*. Cambridge, MA: Harvard University Press, 2017.

Beljame, Alexandre. *Men of Letters and the English Public in the 18th Century: 1600–1700, Dryden, Addison, Pope*. London; New York: Routledge, 2013.

Benbaji, Hagit, and David Heyd. "The Charitable Perspective: Forgiveness and Toleration as Supererogatory." *Canadian Journal of Philosophy* 31, no. 4 (2001): 567–86.

Benhabib, Seyla. *Another Cosmopolitanism*. Edited by Robert Post. Oxford: Oxford University Press, 2008.

Benjamin, Walter. *The Origin of German Tragic Drama*. Translated by John Osborne. Reprint. London; New York: Verso, 1998/1977.

Bennett, Alexandra. "Margaret Cavendish and the Theatre of War." In *Margaret Cavendish*, edited by Sara Heller Mendelson, 103–13. Farnham: Ashgate, 2009.

Bennett, Jane. *Vibrant Matter: A Political Ecology of Things*. Durham, NC: Duke University Press, 2009.

Berger, Peter. "Protestantism and the Quest for Certainty." Religion Online. Accessed June 20, 2017. www.religion-online.org/showarticle.asp?title=239&gt.

Berkeley, George. *Passive Obedience*. London, 1713.

Bernstein, Richard J. "The Secular-Religious Divide: Kant's Legacy." *Social Research* 76, no 4 (Winter 2009): 1035–48.

Billings, E. R. *Tobacco: Its History, Varieties, Culture, Manufacture and Commerce*. Middlesex: Wildhern Press, 1875.

Binhammer, Katherine. *The Seduction Narrative in Britain, 1747–1800*. Cambridge: Cambridge University Press, 2009.

Blackstone, William. *Commentaries on the Laws of England*. 4 vols. Oxford: Clarendon Press, 1765–69.

Böckenförde, Ernst-Wolfgang. *Staat, Gesellschaft* (Berlin: Suhrkamp, 1976) [English translation: *State, Society and Liberty: Studies in Political Theory*

and Constitutional Law. Translated by James Amery Underwood. Oxford: Berg, 1991].
Bonnett, Alastair. *Left in the Past: Radicalism and the Politics of Nostalgia*. New York: Continuum, 2010.
Boulukos, George. *The Grateful Slave: The Emergence of Race in Eighteenth-Century British and American Culture*. Cambridge: Cambridge University Press, 2008.
Bowerbank, Sylvia. "The Spider's Delight: Margaret Cavendish and the 'Female' Imagination." *English Literary Renaissance* 14, no. 3 (1984): 392–408.
Bowers, Toni. "'The Abdicated Family': Hume's Partisan Grammar in 'Of the Protestant Succession.'" *Restoration* 39, no. 1/2 (2015): 61–81.
Boyd, Diane E., and Marta Kvande. *Everyday Revolutions: Eighteenth-Century Women Transforming Public and Private*. Newark: University of Delaware Press, 2008.
Boyle, Deborah. "Margaret Cavendish on Perception, Self-Knowledge, and Probable Opinion." *Philosophy Compass* 10, no. 7 (2015): 438–50.
Boym, Svetlana. *The Future of Nostalgia*. New York: Basic Books, 2008.
Branch, Lori, and Mark Knight. "Why the Postsecular Matters." *Christianity and Literature* 67, no. 3 (2018): 493–510.
Braudy, Leo. "Dryden, Marvell, and the Design of Political Poetry." In *Enchanted Ground: Reimagining John Dryden*, edited by Jayne Lewis and Maximillian E. Novak, 52–69. Toronto: University of Toronto Press, 2004.
Bredvold, Louis. *The Intellectual Milieu of John Dryden: Studies in Some Aspects of 17th-Century Thought*. Ann Arbor: University of Michigan Press, 1956.
Brewer, David A. "The Even Longer Restoration." *Restoration: Studies in English Literary Culture, 1660–1700* 40, no. 2 (2016): 96–104.
Brown, Gillian. *The Consent of the Governed*. Cambridge, MA: Harvard University Press, 2001.
Brown, Homer Obed. *Institutions of the English Novel from Defoe to Scott*. Philadelphia: University of Pennsylvania Press, 1998.
Brown, Laura. "The Divided Plot: Tragicomic Form in the Restoration." *ELH* 47, no. 1 (1980): 67–79.
  "The Ideology of Restoration Poetic Form: John Dryden." *PMLA* 97, no. 3 (1982): 395–407.
  "The Romance of Empire: Oroonoko and the Trade in Slaves." In *The New Eighteenth Century*, edited by Laura Brown and Felicity Nussbaum, 41–61. New York: Methuen, 1987.
Brown, Thomas. *Notes upon Mr. Dryden's Poems in Four Letters / by M. Clifford ... ; to Which Are Annexed Some Reflections upon the Hind and Panther, by Another Hand*. London, 1687.
Brown, Wendy. *Regulating Aversion: Tolerance in the Age of Identity and Empire*. Princeton, NJ: Princeton University Press, 2009.
Bryan, Bradley. "Revenge and Nostalgia: Reconciling Nietzsche and Heidegger on the question of coming to terms with the past." *Philosophy & Social Criticism* 38, no. 1 (2012): 25–38.

Burgess, Glenn. "From the Common Law Mind to 'The Discovery of Islands': J. G. A. Pocock's Journey." *History of Political Thought* 29, no. 3 (2008): 543–61.
Burke, Edmund. *An Account of the European Settlements in America: In Six Parts: Each Part Contains an Accurate Description of the Settlements*, vol. 1. London, 1757.
  "A Letter to a Peer of England on the Penal Laws against Irish Catholics." In *The Works and Correspondence of . . . Edmund Burke*. F. & J. Rivington, 1852.
  "Letters to the Sheriffs of Bristol." In *The Writings and Speeches of Edmund Burke. Vol. 3, Party, Parliament, and the American War*, edited by Paul Langford, 289–99. Oxford: Clarendon, 1996.
  "A Letter to William Elliot, Esq., Occasioned by the Account Given in a Newspaper of the Speech Made in the House of Lords by the **** of ******* in the Debate Concerning Lord Fitzwilliam," 1795.
  A Philosophical Enquiry into the Origin of Our Ideas of the Sublime and the Beautiful. In *The Writings and Speeches of Edmund Burke. Vol. 1, The Early Writings*, edited by Paul Langford, 185–320. Oxford: Clarendon, 1997 [1757].
  Reflections on the Revolution in France. Edited by Frank M. Turner. New Haven, CT: Yale University Press, 2003.
  "Speech on American Taxation. April 19, 1774." In *The Writings and Speeches of Edmund Burke. Vol. 2, Party, Parliament, and the American Crisis*, edited by Paul Langford, 406–62. Oxford: Clarendon, 1981.
  "Speech in General Reply, June 7, 1794. . ." In *The Works of the Right Honorable Edmund Burke*. Little, Brown, 1881.
  "Speech on Moving His Resolutions for Conciliation with the Colonies. March 22, 1775."
  "Speech on the Sixth Article of Charge. May 5, 1789."
  The Writings and Speeches of Edmund Burke. Edited by P. J. Marshall. Oxford: Clarendon Press, 1981.
Burnet, Gilbert. *Bishop Burnet's History of His Own Time*. London: Printed for Thomas Ward, 1724.
  A Sermon Preached in the Chapel of St. James's, before His Highness the Prince of Orange, 23rd of December, 1688. Edinburgh, 1689.
Burns, F. D. A. "Holyday, Barten (1593–1661)." In *Oxford Dictionary of National Biography*. Oxford University Press, September 23, 2004. https://doi.org/10.1093/ref:odnb/13625.
Burtt, Shelley G. *Virtue Transformed: Political Argument in England, 1688–1740*. Cambridge; New York: Cambridge University Press, 1992.
Butler, Todd. "Power in Smoke: The Language of Tobacco and Authority in Caroline England." *Studies in Philology* 106, no. 1 (Winter 2009): 100–18.
Butterfield, Herbert. *The Whig Interpretation of History*. New York; London: W. W. Norton, 1931.

Bywaters, David. *Dryden in Revolutionary England*. Berkeley: University of California Press, 1991.
Campbell, Mary Baine. *Wonder and Science: Imagining Worlds in Early Modern Europe*. Ithaca, NY: Cornell University Press, 2004.
Capaldi, Nicholas, and Donald W. Livingston, eds. *Liberty in Hume's History of England*. Dordrecht: Springer Netherlands, 1990.
Carnell, Rachel. *Partisan Politics, Narrative Realism, and the Rise of the British Novel*. New York: Palgrave Macmillan, 2006.
Carnes, Geremy. "Catholic Conversion and Incest in Dryden's Don Sebastian." *Restoration: Studies in English Literary Culture, 1660–1700* 38, no. 2 (Fall 2014): 3–19.
The Papist Represented: Literature and the English Catholic Community, 1688–1791. Newark: University of Delaware Press, 2017.
Casanova, José. *Public Religions in the Modern World*. Chicago: University of Chicago, 1994.
Castellano, Katey Kuhns. "Romantic Conservatism in Burke, Wordsworth, and Wendell Berry." *SubStance: A Review of Theory and Literary Criticism* 40, no. 2 (2011): 73–91.
Cavendish, Margaret. "To All Worthy and Noble Ladies." In *The Blazing World [1668]*. Boston, MA: Northeastern University Women Writers Project, 2002.
The Blazing World and Other Writings. Edited by Kate Lilley. London: Penguin, 1992.
Observations upon Experimental Philosophy. Cambridge Texts in the History of Philosophy. Cambridge: Cambridge University Press, 2001.
"An Oration Concerning Shipping." In *Margaret Cavendish: Political Writings*, edited by Susan James, 137–38. Cambridge: Cambridge University Press, 2003.
"Orations of Divers Sorts, Accommodated to Divers Places." In *Political Writings*, edited by Susan James, 111–293. Cambridge: Cambridge University Press, 2003.
Chadwick, Owen. *The Secularization of the European Mind in the Nineteenth Century*. Cambridge: Cambridge University Press, 1990.
Chandler, James. *England in 1819: The Politics of Literary Culture and the Case of Romantic Historicism*. Chicago: University of Chicago Press, 1999.
Charles, England and Wales, Sovereign. *His Majesties Gracious Letter and Declaration Sent to the House of Peers: By Sir John Greenvill, Kt. from Breda, and Read in the House the First of May, 1660*. London: Printed by John Macock and Francis Tyton, 1660.
Charles II, King of England. *His Majesty's Declaration to All His Loving Subjects, 26 December 1662*. Quoted in J. P. Kenyon, *The Stuart Constitution*. Cambridge: Cambridge University Press, 1986.
Charles II, King of England. *His Majesty's Declaration to All His Loving Subjects, March 15, 1672*. Quoted in J. P. Kenyon, *The Stuart Constitution*. Cambridge: Cambridge University Press, 1986.

King Charles II, His Declaration to All His Loving Subjects of the Kingdom of England. Dated from His Court at Breda in Holland, the 4/14 of April 1660 ("Declaration of Breda").

Charnes, Linda. "Anticipating Nostalgia." *Textual Cultures: Text, Contexts, Interpretation* 4, no. 1 (2009): 72–83.

Chatterjee, Partha. *Lineages of Political Society – Studies in Postcolonial Democracy*. New York: Columbia University Press, 2011.

Cheah, Peng. *What Is a World?: On Postcolonial Literature as World Literature*. Durham, NC: Duke University Press, 2016.

Christensen, Jerome. *Romanticism at the End of History*. Baltimore: Johns Hopkins University Press, 2000.

Clark, J. C. D. *English Society, 1660–1832: Religion, Ideology, and Politics during the Ancien Regime*. Cambridge: Cambridge University Press, 2000.

——— *English Society 1688–1832: Ideology, Social Structure and Political Practice during the Ancien Regime*. Cambridge: Cambridge University Press, 1985.

Clymer, Lorna. *Ritual, Routine and Regime: Repetition in Early Modern British and European Culture*. Toronto: University of Toronto Press, 2006.

Collini, Stefan. *Public Moralists: Political Thought and Intellectual Life in Britain, 1850–1930*. Oxford: Oxford University Press, 1993.

Condren, Conal. *The Language of Politics in Seventeenth-Century England*. Basingstoke: Macmillan, 1994.

Conway, Alison, and Corrinne Harol. "Toward a Postsecular Eighteenth Century." *Literature Compass* 12, no. 11 (November 2015): 565–74.

Cook, Elizabeth. *Epistolary Bodies: Gender and Genre in the Eighteenth-Century Republic of Letters*. Stanford, CA: Stanford University Press, 1996.

Coole, Diana, and Samantha Frost, eds. *New Materialisms: Ontology, Agency, and Politics*. Durham, NC: Duke University Press, 2010.

Cotterill, Anne. "'Rebekah's Heir': Dryden's Late Mystery of Genealogy." *Huntington Library Quarterly* 63, no. 1/2 (2000): 201–26.

Crawford, Robert. *The Scottish Invention of English Literature*. Cambridge: Cambridge University Press, 1998.

Daiches, David. *The Paradox of Scottish Culture: The Eighteenth Century Experience*. Oxford: Oxford University Press, 1964.

——— *Sir Walter Scott and His World*. London: Thames & Hudson, 1971.

Dalley, Hamish. "Temporal Systems in Representations of the Past: Distance, Freedom and Irony in Historical Fiction." In *Reading Historical Fiction: The Revenant and Remembered Past*, edited by Kate Mitchell and Nicola Parsons, 33–49. New York: Palgrave Macmillan, 2013.

Dames, Nicholas. *Amnesiac Selves: Nostalgia, Forgetting, and British Fiction, 1810–1870*. New York: Oxford University Press, 2001.

——— "Nostalgia and Its Disciplines: A Response." *Memory Studies* 3, no. 3 (2010): 269–75.

Dasilva, Fabil B., and Jim Faught. "Nostalgia: A Sphere and Process of Contemporary Ideology." *Qualitative Sociology* 5, no. 1 (1982): 47–63.

Davis, J. C. "Religion and the Struggle for Freedom in the English Revolution." *Historical Journal* 35, no. 3 (1992): 507–30.
Davis, Leith. *Acts of Union: Scotland and the Literary Negotiation of the British Nation 1707–1830*. Stanford, CA: Stanford University Press, 1998.
Dear, Peter. "A Philosophical Duchess: Understanding Margaret Cavendish and the Royal Society." In *Science, Literature and Rhetoric in Early Modern England*, edited by Juliet Cummins and David Burchell, 124–42. Aldershot: Ashgate, 2007.
Declaration of the Rights of Man and the Citizen. France, August 26, 1789.
Deleuze, Gilles, and Félix Guattari. *A Thousand Plateaus: Capitalism and Schizophrenia*. London: Bloomsbury, 1988.
 What Is Philosophy? New York: Columbia University Press, 2014.
Derrida, Jacques. *The Beast and the Sovereign*. Translated by Geoffrey Bennington. 2 vols. Chicago: University of Chicago Press, 2009.
 On Cosmopolitanism and Forgiveness. Translated by Mark Dooley and Michael Hughes. London: Routledge, 2001.
 "Violence and Metaphysics." In *Writing and Difference*, trans. Alan Bass. London: Routledge, 1978: 79–153.
Devlin, David Douglas. *The Author of Waverly: A Critical Study of Walter Scott*. London: Palgrave Macmillan, 1971.
Dickson, Vernon Guy. "Truth, Wonder, and Exemplarity in Aphra Behn's Oroonoko." *SEL: Studies in English Literature, 1500–1900* 47, no. 3 (2007): 573–94.
Dixon, Dennis. "Godden v Hales Revisited – James II and the Dispensing Power." *The Journal of Legal History* 27, no. 2 (2006): 129–52.
The Doctrine of Passive Obedience and Nonresistance, as Established in the Church of England. London, 1710.
Dolan, Francis. *Whores of Babylon: Catholicism, Gender, and Seventeenth-Century Print Culture*. Ithaca, NY: Cornell University Press, 1999.
Don Sebastian, King of Portugal: An Historical Novel in Four Parts. London: Printed for R. Bentley and S. Magnes, 1683.
Doody, Margaret Anne. *The Daring Muse: Augustan Poetry Reconsidered*. Cambridge: Cambridge University Press, 1985.
Doyle, Laura. *Freedom's Empire: Race and the Rise of the Novel in Atlantic Modernity, 1640–1940*. Durham, NC: Duke University Press, 2008.
Dryden, John. "Don Sebastian." In *The Works of John Dryden*, edited by Earl Miner and George R. Guffey, vol. 15, *Plays: Albion and Albanius, Don Sebastian, Amphitryon*. Berkeley: University of California, 1976: 57–220.
 The Works of John Dryden. Vol. 3, *Poems, 1685–1692*. Edited by Earl Miner and Vinton Dearing. Berkeley: University of California, 1969.
Duncan, Ian. *Modern Romance and Transformations of the Novel*. Cambridge: Cambridge University Press, 1992.
Dunn, Allen. "The Precarious Integrity of the Postsecular." *boundary 2* 37, no. 3 (2010): 91–99.

During, Simon. *Against Democracy: Literary Experience in the Era of Emancipation*. New York: Fordham University Press, 2012.

Dworkin, Ronald. *Religion without God*. Cambridge, MA: Harvard University Press, 2013.

"What Is a Good Life." *The New Review*, October 11, 2011.

Ellenzweig, Sarah, and John H. Zammito, eds. Introduction to *The New Politics of Materialism: History, Philosophy, Science*, 14–27. Oxfordshire: Routledge, 2017.

Ellesby, James. *The Doctrine of Passive Obedience*. London, 1685.

English Currant: From Friday Dec. 21 to Wednesday Dec. 26, 1688, no. 5. London, 1688. *17th–18th Century Burney Collection Newspapers*.

Equiano, Olaudah. *The Interesting Narrative of the Life of Olaudah Equiano*. Peterborough: Broadview, 2001.

Erskine-Hill, Howard. *Poetry of Opposition and Revolution: Dryden to Wordsworth*. Oxford; New York: Clarendon Press, 1996.

Esposito, Robert. *Bios: Biopolitics and Philosophy*. Translated by Timothy Campbell. Minneapolis: University of Minnesota Press, 2008.

Etherege, George. *The Letterbook of Sir George Etherege (1928)*. Edited by Sybil Rosenfeld. Oxford: Oxford University Press, 1928. Quoted in James Kinsley and Helen Kinsley, eds., *Dryden: The Critical Heritage*. London: Routledge, 1971.

Ferguson, Frances. "Philology, Literature, Style." *ELH* 80, no. 2 (2013): 323–41.

"Romantic Memory." *Studies in Romanticism* 35, no. 4 (1996): 509–33.

Ferguson, Margaret W. "Juggling the Categories of Race, Class, and Gender." *Women's Studies* 19, no. 2 (1991): 159–81.

Ferguson, Moira. "Oroonoko: Birth of a Paradigm." *New Literary History* 23, no. 2 (1992): 339–59.

Ferris, Ina. *The Achievement of Literary Authority: Gender, History, and the Waverly Novels*. Ithaca, NY: Cornell University Press, 1991.

Fessenden, Tracy. *Culture and Redemption: Religion, the Secular, and American Literature* (Princeton, NJ: Princeton University Press, 2007).

Fielding, Henry. *The History of Tom Jones, a Foundling*. London, 1749.

Figgis, John Neville. *The Divine Right of Kings*, 2nd ed. Cambridge: Cambridge University Press, 1914.

Figlerowicz, Marta. "'Frightful Spectacles of a Mangled King': Aphra Behn's Oroonoko and Narration through Theater." *New Literary History* 39, no. 2 (2008): 321–34.

Filmer, Robert. *Patriarcha: Or, the Natural Power of Kings*. London, 1680.

Fitzmaurice, James. "Fancy and the Family: Self-Characterizations of Margaret Cavendish." *The Huntington Library Quarterly* 53, no. 3 (1990): 199–209.

Fletcher, Angus. *Allegory, the Theory of a Symbolic Mode*. Princeton, NJ: Princeton University Press, 2012. First published 1964 by Cornell University Press, Ithaca, NY.

Fludernik, Monika. "The Fiction of the Rise of Fictionality." *Poetics Today* 39, no. 1 (February 1, 2018): 67–92.

Frei, Hans W. *The Eclipse of Biblical Narrative: A Study in Eighteenth and Nineteenth Century Hermeneutics*, revised ed. New Haven, CT: Yale University Press, 1980.
Fuller, Francis. *A Treatise of Faith and Repentance*. London, 1684.
Gallagher, Catherine. "Embracing the Absolute: The Politics of the Female Subject in Seventeenth-Century England." *Genders* 1 (March 1988): 24–29.
 "The Rise of Fictionality." In *The Novel: Volume 1: History, Geography, and Culture*, edited by Franco Moretti, 336–63. Princeton, NJ: Princeton University Press, 2006.
 Telling It Like It Wasn't: The Counterfactual Imagination in History and Fiction. Chicago: University of Chicago, 2018.
Gamer, Michael. "Waverly and the Object of (Literary) History." *Modern Language Quarterly* 70, no. 4 (December 1, 2009): 495–525.
Gardiner, Ann Barbeau. "Division in Communication: Symbols of Transubstantiation in Donne, Milton, and Dryden." In *Religion in the Age of Reason: A Transatlantic Study of the Long Eighteenth Century*, edited by Kathryn Duncan, 1–17. New York: AMS Press, 2009.
Gelber, Michael Worth. "Dryden's Theory of Comedy." *Eighteenth-Century Studies* 26, no. 2 (Winter 1992): 261–83.
Gill, Anthony. *The Political Origins of Religious Liberty*. Cambridge: Cambridge University Press, 2007.
Gillespie, Katharine. *Domesticity and Dissent in the Seventeenth-Century*. Cambridge: Cambridge University Press, 2004.
Goldie, Mark. "The Revolution of 1689 and the Structure of Political Argument." *Bulletin of Research in the Humanities* 83 (1980): 473–564.
Goodman, Kevis. "Romantic Poetry and the Science of Nostalgia." In *The Cambridge Companion to British Romantic Poetry*, edited by James Chandler and Maureen N. McLane, 195–216. Cambridge: Cambridge University Press, 2008.
 "'Uncertain Disease': Nostalgia, Pathologies of Motion, Practices of Reading." *Studies in Romanticism* 49, no. 2 (2010): 197–227.
Gordon, Avery. *Ghostly Matters: Haunting and the Sociological Imagination*. Minneapolis: University of Minnesota Press, 2008.
 "Some Thoughts on Haunting and Futurity." *Borderlands* 10, no. 2 (2011): 1–21.
Gordon, Scott Paul. *The Power of the Passive Self in English Literature, 1640–1770*. Cambridge: Cambridge University Press, 2002.
Gottlieb, Evan. *Feeling British: Sympathy and National Identity in Scottish and English Writing, 1707–1832*. Lewisburg: Bucknell University Press, 2007.
Greaves, Richard L. "Concepts of Political Obedience in Late Tudor England." *Journal of British Studies* 22, no. 1 (1982): 23–34.
Grell, Ole Peter, Jonathan I. Israel, and Nicholas Tyacke, eds. *From Persecution to Toleration: The Glorious Revolution and Religion in England*. Oxford: Oxford University Press, 1991.

Griffiths, Paul J., and Reinhard Hütter, eds. *Reason and the Reasons of Faith*. New York: Bloomsbury, 2005.
Guffey, George. "Aphra Behn's Oroonoko: Occasion and Accomplishment." In *Two English Novelists: Aphra Behn and Anthony Trollope*, 1–41. Los Angeles: William Andrews Clark Memorial Library, UCLA, 1975.
Habermas, Jürgen. *An Awareness of What Is Missing: Faith and Reason in a Post-Secular Age*. Cambridge: Polity, 2010.
———. *The Structural Transformation of the Public Sphere: An Inquiry into a Category of Bourgeois Society*. Cambridge, MA: MIT Press, 1989.
Hahn, Scott, and Benjamin Wiker. *Politicizing the Bible: The Roots of Historical Criticism and the Secularization of Scripture, 1300–1700*. Chicago: Crossroad, 2017.
Hanlon, Aaron R. "Margaret Cavendish's Anthropocene Worlds." *New Literary History* 47, no. 1 (2016): 49–66.
Hanson, Elizabeth. "Torture and Truth in Renaissance England." *Representations* 34 (Spring 1991): 53–84.
Harmon, Graham. "Levinas and the Triple Critique of Heidegger." *Philosophy Today* 53, no. 4 (2009): 407–13.
———. "The Well-Wrought Broken Hammer: Object-Oriented Literary Criticism." *New Literary History* 43, no. 2 (2012): 183–203.
Harol, Corrinne. *Enlightened Virginity in Eighteenth-Century Literature*. New York: Palgrave, 2006.
———. "Misconceiving the Heir: Mind and Matter in the Warming Pan Propaganda." In *Vital Matters*, edited by Helen Deutsch and Mary Terrell, 130–46. Toronto: University of Toronto Press, 2012.
———. "Whig Ballads and the Past Passive Jacobite." *Journal for Eighteenth-Century Studies* 35, no. 4 (2012): 581–95.
Harris, Tim. *Revolution: The Great Crisis of the British Monarchy, 1685–1720*. London: Penguin, 2007.
Harth, Phillip. *Pen for a Party: Dryden's Tory Propaganda in Its Contexts*. Princeton, NJ: Princeton University Press, 2015.
Hartman, Saidiya. "The Time of Slavery." *South Atlantic Quarterly* 101, no. 4 (Fall 2002): 757–77.
Haydon, Colin. *Anti-Catholicism in Eighteenth-Century England, c. 1714–80: A Political and Social Study*. Manchester, NY: Manchester University Press, 1993.
Hayot, Eric. *On Literary Worlds*. Oxford: Oxford University Press, 2012.
Hazlitt, William Carew. *The Spirit of the Age; or, Contemporary Portraits*. London: G. Bell & Sons, 1886.
Heidegger, Martin. "The Origin of the Work of Art." In *Poetry, Language, Thought*, translated by Albert Hofstader, 15–73. New York: Harper & Row, 1971.
Hensley, Nathan. "Armadale and the Logic of Liberalism." *Victorian Studies* 51, no. 4 (2009): 607–32.
———. *Forms of Empire: The Poetics of Victorian Sovereignty*. Oxford: Oxford University Press, 2016.
Hertzler, James R. "Who Dubbed It 'The Glorious Revolution?'" *Albion* 19, no. 4 (1987): 579–85.

Hesse, Barnor. "Escaping Liberty: Western Hegemony, Black Fugitivity." *Political Theory* 42, no. 3 (2014): 288–313.
Hickes, George. *Jovian, or, an Answer to Julian the Apostate by a Minister of London*. London, 1683.
    The Judgement of an Anonymous Writer Concerning ... I. A Law for Disabling a Papist to Inherit the Crown, II. The Execution of Penal Laws against Protestant Dissenters, III. A Bill of Comprehension: All Briefly Discussed in a Letter Sent from beyond the Seas to a Dissenter Ten Years Ago. London: Printed by T. B. for Robert Clavel to be sold by Randolph Taylor, 1684.
    A Sermon Preach'd before the Honourable House of Commons. London, 1692.
Hickman, Jared. *Black Prometheus: Race and Radicalism in the Age of Atlantic Slavery*. Oxford: Oxford University Press, 2017.
Hill, Christopher. *The Century of Revolution, 1603–1714*. New York; London: Routledge, 2014.
Hobbes, Thomas. *Leviathan*. Edited by J. C. A. Gaskin. Oxford: Oxford University Press, 1996.
Hobby, Elaine. "Introduction: Prose of the Long Restoration (1650–1737)." *Prose Studies* 29, no. 1 (2007): 1–3.
    Virtue of Necessity: English Women's Writing, 1646–1688. Ann Arbor: University of Michigan Press, 1989.
Hoeveler, Diane Long. "Anti-Catholicism and the Gothic Imaginary: The Historical and Literary Contexts." *Religion in the Age of Enlightenment* 3 (2012): 1–31.
Hofer, Johannes. "Medical Dissertation on Nostalgia." Translated by C. K. Anspach, *Bulletin of the History of Medicine* 2, no. 6 (1934): 376–91.
Holmesland, Oddvar. *Utopian Negotiation: Aphra Behn and Margaret Cavendish*. Syracuse, NY: Syracuse University Press, 2013.
Holyday, Barten. *Of the Nature of Faith: A Sermon*. London, 1654.
Hooke, Robert. *Micrographia, or, Some Physiological Descriptions of Minute Bodies Made by Magnifying Glasses: With Observations and Inquiries Thereupon*. London: Printed by J. Martyn and J. Allestry, 1665.
Horowitz, James. "Partisan Bodies: John Dryden, Jacobite Camp, and the Queering of 1688." *Restoration: Studies in English Literary Culture, 1660–1700* 39, no. 1 (November 10, 2015): 17–60.
Hoxby, Blair, and Ann Baynes Coiro, eds. *Milton in the Long Restoration*. Oxford: Oxford University Press, 2016.
Hughes, Derek. "Dryden's Don Sebastian and the Literature of Heroism." *Yearbook of English Studies* 12 (1982): 72–90.
    "Race, Gender, and Scholarly Practice: Aphra Behn's Oroonoko." *Essays in Criticism* 52, no. 1 (January 2002): 1–22.
Hughes, Jason. *Learning to Smoke: Tobacco Use in the West*. Chicago: University of Chicago Press, 2003.
Hume, David. *Enquiries Concerning the Human Understanding and Concerning the Principles of Morals*. Edited by L. A. Selby-Bigge, 2nd ed. Oxford: Clarendon Press, 1902/1963.

Further Letters of David Hume. Edited by Felix Waldmann. Edinburgh: Edinburgh Bibliographical Society, 2014.

History of England: From the Invasion of Julius Caesar to the Revolution of 1688. Foreword by William B. Todd. 6 vols. Indianapolis, IN: Liberty Fund, 1985.

"Of the Liberty of the Press." In *The Complete Works and Correspondence of David Hume, Electronic Edition, Essays Moral, Political, and Literary*, Part 1, edited by T. H. Green, T. H. Grose, and Norman Kemp Smith, ebook. Charlottesville, VA: InteLex, 2000.

"Of National Character." In *Essays Moral, Political, Literary (LF ed.)*. Liberty Fund, 1777.

A Treatise of Human Nature. 3 vols. London, 1739–40.

A Treatise of Human Nature. Edited by L. A. Selby-Bigge and P. H. Nidditch, 2nd ed. Oxford: Oxford University Press, 1978.

Hutchinson, C. *Of the Authority of Councils and the Rule of Faith.* London: Printed for R. Clavel, W. Rogers, and S. Smith, 1687.

Iser, Wolfgang. "Fiction – The Filter of History." In *New Perspectives in German Literary Criticism*, edited by Richard E Amacher and Victor Lange, 86–104. Princeton, NJ: Princeton University Press, 2015.

Israel, Jonathan. Introduction to *The Anglo-Dutch Moment: Essays on the Glorious Revolution and Its World Impact*, 1–46. Cambridge: Cambridge University Press, 2003.

"William III and Toleration." In *From Persecution to Toleration: The Glorious Revolution and Religion in England*, edited by Ole Peter Grell, Jonathan I. Israel, and Nicholas Tyacke, 129–70. Oxford: Oxford University Press, 1991.

[Jackson, William]. *Of the rule of faith a sermon at the visitation of the Right Reverend Father in God, William Lord Bishop of Lincolne, holden at Bedford August 5, 1674.* Cambridge, 1675.

Jager, Colin. "Common Quiet: Tolerance around 1688." *ELH* 79, no. 3 (2012): 569–96.

James, Susan. *Passion and Action: The Emotions in Seventeenth-Century Philosophy.* Oxford: Oxford University Press, 1997.

James II, King of England. *A Declaration of His Most Sacred Majesty, King James II to All His Loving Subjects in the Kingdom of England.* London, 1689.

King of England. *King James the Second His Gracious Declaration to All His Loving Subjects for Liberty of Conscience* [April 4, 1687]. Quoted in J. P. Kenyon, *The Stuart Constitution.* Cambridge: Cambridge University Press, 1986.

King of England. *Scottish Declaration of Toleration*, February 12, 1687.

King of England. Speech by James II to an assembly of lords and privy councilors, reported in BPL, Ms AM. 1502 7, no. 49, October 23, 1688. Quoted in Scott Sowerby, *Making Toleration: The Repealers and the Glorious Revolution.* Cambridge, MA: Harvard University Press, 2013, 290 n.3.

Jameson, Fredric. *The Political Unconscious: Narrative as a Socially Symbolic Act.* Ithaca, NY: Cornell University Press, 1982.

Postmodernism, or, the Cultural Logic of Late Capitalism. Durham, NC: Duke University Press, 1991.
Preface to *The Historical Novel*, by György Lukács. Translated by Hannah Mitchell and Stanley Mitchell. Lincoln: University of Nebraska Press, 1983.
Jardine, Lisa. *Going Dutch: How England Plundered Holland's Glory.* Reprint edition. New York: Harper Perennial, 2009.
Jarrells, Anthony S. *Britain's Bloodless Revolutions: 1688 and the Romantic Reform of Literature.* New York: Palgrave Macmillan, 2005.
Jasper, David, and Daniel Anlezark. "Biblical Hermeneutics and Literary Theory." In *The Blackwell Companion to the Bible in English Literature*, edited by Rebecca Lemon, Emma Mason, Jonathan Roberts, and Christopher Rowland. Hoboken, NJ: Wiley Online Books, 2010. https://doi.org/10.1002/9781444324174.ch3.
Johnson, Amanda Louise. "Thomas Jefferson's Ossianic Romance." *Studies in Eighteenth-Century Culture* 45 (2016): 19–35.
Johnson, Samuel. *An Answer to the History of Passive Obedience.* London, 1709/10.
"Dryden." In *Lives of the Poets*, edited by Roger Lonsdale, 121–217. Oxford: Oxford University Press, 2006.
Julian the Apostate. London, 1682.
The Lives of the Poets a Selection. Oxford: Oxford University Press, 2009.
"Personification." In *A Dictionary of the English Language in Which the Words Are Deduced from Their Originals, and Illustrated in Their Different Significations by Examples from the Best Writers*, 4th ed., revised by author. Dublin: Printed for Thomas Ewing, 1775.
Jolley, Nicholas. "Leibniz on Hobbes, Locke's Two Treatises and Sherlock's Case of Allegiance." *The Historical Journal* 18, no. 1 (1975): 21–35.
Jones, J. R., ed. *Liberty Secured? Britain before and after 1688.* Stanford, CA: Stanford University Press, 1992.
Kahn, Victoria. *The Trouble with Literature.* Oxford: Oxford University Press, 2020.
The Future of Illusion: Political Theology and Early Modern Texts. Chicago: University of Chicago Press, 2014.
Wayward Contracts: The Crisis of Political Obligation in England, 1640–1674. Princeton, NJ: Princeton University Press, 2004/2009.
Kant, Immanuel. *An Answer to the Question: "What Is Enlightenment?".* London: Penguin UK, 2013.
"An Answer to the Question: What Is Enlightenment?" In *What Is Enlightenment?: Eighteenth-Century Answers and Twentieth-Century Questions*, translated and edited by James Schmidt, 58–64. Berkeley: University of California Press, 1996.
Critique of Pure Reason. Translated by Paul Guyer and Allen Wood. Cambridge: Cambridge University Press, 1997.
Religion within the Boundaries of Mere Reason. Translated by Allen Wood and George Di Giovanni. Cambridge: Cambridge University Press, 1997.
Kaplan, Benjamin. *Divided by Faith: Religious Conflict and the Practice of Toleration in Early Modern Europe.* Cambridge, MA: Harvard University Press, 2007.

Kaufmann, Michael. "Locating the Postsecular." *Religion & Literature* 41, no. 2 (2009): 67–73.

Kegl, Rosemary. "The World I Have Made: Margaret Cavendish, Feminism, and the Blazing World." In *Feminist Readings of Early Modern Culture: Emerging Subjects*, edited by Valerie Traub, M. Lindsay Kaplan, and Dympna Callaghan, 119–41. Cambridge: Cambridge University Press, 1996.

Keller, Eve. "Producing Petty Gods: Margaret Cavendish's Critique of Experimental Science." *ELH* 64, no. 2 (1997): 447–71.

Kemerling, Garth. "Baruch Spinoza: Life and Works." *Brewminate*, November 12, 2011, https://brewminate.com/early-modern-philosophy-spinoza-and-leibniz/.

Kendall, R. T. *Calvin and English Calvinism to 1649*, revised ed. Eugene, OR: Wipf & Stock, 2011.

Kent, Eddy, and Terri Tomsky. *Negative Cosmopolitanism*. Montreal: McGill-Queen's University Press, 2017.

Kenyon, J. P. *Revolution Principles: The Politics of Party, 1689–1720*. Cambridge: Cambridge University Press, 1977.

Kettlewell, John. *Christianity, a Doctrine of the Cross: Or, Passive Obedience*. London, 1695.

Kidd, Colin. "Race, Empire, and the Limits of Nineteenth-Century Scottish Nationhood." *The Historical Journal* 46, no. 4 (2003): 873–92.

Kinsley, James, and Helen Kinsley, eds. *Dryden: The Critical Heritage*. London: Routledge, 1971.

Knights, Mark. *Representation and Misrepresentation*. Oxford: Oxford University Press, 2005.

Koselleck, Reinhardt. *Futures Past: On the Semantics of Historical Time*. Translated by Keith Tribe. Cambridge, MA: MIT Press, 1990.

Kramnick, Jonathan Brody. "Locke's Desire." *The Yale Journal of Criticism* 12, no. 2 (October 1, 1999): 189–208.

Kraynak, Robert P. "John Locke: From Absolutism to Toleration." *American Political Science Review* 74, no. 1 (1980): 53–69.

Kroll, Richard. "The Double Logic of Don Sebastian." In *John Dryden: A Tercentenary Miscellany*, edited by Steven N. Zwicker, 47–69. San Marino, CA: Huntington Library, 2001.

———. "'Tales of Love and Gallantry': The Politics of Oroonoko." *Huntington Library Quarterly* 67, no. 4 (2004): 573–605.

Lakoff, George. *Moral Politics: How Liberals and Conservatives Think*, 3rd ed. Chicago: University of Chicago Press, 2016.

Lamb, Johnathan. "Imagination, Conjecture, and Disorder." *Eighteenth-Century Studies* 45, no. 1 (October 14, 2011): 53–69.

Latour, Bruno. *We Have Never Been Modern*. Cambridge, MA: Harvard University Press, 1993.

Leibniz, Gottfried Wilhelm. *New Essays on Human Understanding*. Translated and edited by Peter Remnant and Jonathan Bennett. Cambridge: Cambridge University Press, 1981.

Leibniz, Gottfried Wilhelm. "Reflexions on the Work that Mr. Hobbes Published in English on 'Freedom, Necessity, and Chance." In *Theodicy: Essays on the Goodness of God, the Freedom of Man, and the Origin of Evil*, edited by Austin Farrer, translated by E. M. Huggard, 393–404. New Haven, CT: Yale University Press, 1952.

Theodicy: Essays on the Goodness of God, the Freedom of Man, and the Origin of Evil. Edited by Austin Farrer, translated by E. M. Huggard. New Haven, CT: Yale University Press, 1952.

Levenson, Jon Douglas. *The Hebrew Bible, the Old Testament, and Historical Criticism: Jews and Christians in Biblical Studies*. Louisville, KY: Westminster/John Knox Press, 1993.

Levinas, Emmanuel. *Totality and Infinity: An Essay on Exteriority*. Translated by Alphonso Lingis. Dordrecht: Kluwer, 1991.

Levine, George. *The Realistic Imagination: English Fiction from Frankenstein to Lady Chatterly*. Chicago: University of Chicago Press, 1981.

Levitt, Laura. "What Is Religion, Anyway? Rereading the Postsecular from an American Jewish Perspective." *Religion & Literature* 41, no. 3 (2009): 107–18.

Lewis, C. S. "Shelly, Dryden, and Mr. Eliot." In *Selected Literary Essays*. Cambridge: Cambridge University Press, 2013: 187–208.

Lewis, Jayne. *The English Fable: Aesop and Literary Culture, 1651–1740*. Cambridge: Cambridge University Press, 2006.

Lincoln, Andrew. *Walter Scott and Modernity*. Edinburgh: Edinburgh University Press, 2007.

Lipking, Joanna, ed. *Oroonoko: A Norton Critical Edition*. By Aphra Behn. New York: Norton, 1997.

Lipking, Joanna. "'Others', Slaves, and Colonists in Oroonoko." In *The Cambridge Companion to Aphra Behn*, edited by Derek Hughes and Janet Todd, 166–87. Cambridge: Cambridge University Press, 2004.

Livingston, Donald W. "Hume's Historical Conception of Liberty." In *Liberty in Hume's History of England*, edited by Nicholas Capaldi and Donald W. Livingston, 102–53. Dordrecht: Springer Netherlands, 1990.

Lloyd, Howell A. Conclusion to *European Political Thought 1450–1700: Religion, Law and Philosophy*, 498–509. Edited by Howell A. Lloyd, Glenn Burgess, and Simon Hodson. New Haven, CT: Yale University Press, 2007.

Locke, John. "Civil and Ecclesiastical Power." In *Locke: Political Essays*, edited by Mark Goldie, 216–20. Cambridge: Cambridge University Press, 1997.

The Clarendon Edition of the Works of John Locke: The Reasonableness of Christianity: As Delivered in the Scriptures. Edited by John C. Higgins-Biddle. New York: Oxford University Press, 2000.

An Essay Concerning Human Understanding, 4th ed. Edited by P. H. Nidditch. Oxford: Oxford University Press, 1975.

An Essay Concerning Human Understanding. Oxford: Oxford University Press, 2008.

"A Letter Concerning Toleration." In *Second Treatise of Government and a Letter Concerning Toleration*, edited by Mark Goldie, 121–68. Oxford: Oxford University Press, 2016.

[Locke, John]. *Second Treatise on Government*. London, 1689/90.
Two Treatises of Government and a Letter Concerning Toleration. Edited by Ian Shapiro. New Haven, CT: Yale University Press, 2003.
Long, Thomas. *The Historian Unmask'd*. London, 1689.
Lowenthal, David. *The Past Is a Foreign Country*. Cambridge: Cambridge University Press, 1985.
Lukács, György. *The Historical Novel*. Translated by Hannah Mitchell and Stanley Mitchell. Lincoln: University of Nebraska Press, 1983.
The Theory of the Novel. Translated by Anna Bosock. Berlin: Merlin Press, 1971.
Luther, Martin. *Martin Luther's Ninety-Five Theses*. Translated by Timothy Wengert. Minneapolis, MN: Fortress Press, 2015.
"Secular Authority: To What Extent It Should Be obeyed." In *Martin Luther: Selections from His Writings*, edited by John Dillenberger, 363–402. Garden City, NJ: Anchor/Doubleday, 1961.
Macaulay, Thomas Babington. "Art. I – The Poetical Works of John Dryden." *The Edinburgh Review* 93 (January 1828): 1–36.
The History of England from the Accession of James II. Vol. 1. New York: Harper, 1849.
Macaulay, Thomas Babington, and C. H. Firth. *The History of England from the Accession of James II*. London: Folio Press, 1985.
MacCormick, Neil. "Legal Right and Social Democracy." *Queens Quarterly; Kingston, Ont.* 89, no. 2 (Summer 1982): 290–304.
Mack, Ruth. *Literary Historicity: Literature and Historical Experience in Eighteenth-Century Britain*. Stanford, CA: Stanford University Press, 2009.
MacPherson, Sandra. *Harm's Way: Tragic Responsibility and the Novel Form*. Baltimore: Johns Hopkins University Press, 2010.
Mahmood, Saba. *Pious Formations: The Islamic Revival and the Subject of Feminism*. Princeton, NJ: Princeton University Press, 2004.
Politics of Piety: The Islamic Revival and the Feminist Subject. Princeton, NJ: Princeton University Press, 2011.
"Secularism, Hermeneutics, and Empire: The Politics of Islamic Reformation." *Public Culture* 18, no. 2 (2006): 323–47.
Makdesi, Sari. "Colonial Space and the Colonization of Time in Scott's Waverly." *Studies in Romanticism* 34, no. 2 (Summer 1995): 155–87.
Mannheim, Karl. "Conservative Thought." In *From Karl Mannheim*, edited by Kurt H. Wolff, 260–350. New York: Oxford University Press, 1971.
"The Problem of Generations." In *Karl Mannheim Essays*, edited by Paul Kecskemeti, 276–322. London: Routledge, 1972.
Maurer, A. E. Wallace. "The Form of Dryden's Absalom and Achitophel, Once More." *Papers on Language and Literature* 27, no. 3 (1991): 320–37.
McGann, Jerome. "Philology in a New Key." *Critical Inquiry* 39, no. 2 (2013): 327–46.
McGee, J. S. "Conversion and the Imitation of Christ in Anglican and Puritan Writing." *Journal of British Studies* 15, no. 2 (1976): 21–39.

McGirr, Elaine. *Heroic Mode and Political Crisis, 1660–1745*. Plainsboro Township, NJ: Associated University Press, 2009.
McKeon, Michael. "Genre Theory." In *Theory of the Novel: A Historical Approach*, edited by Michael McKeon, 1–4. Baltimore: Johns Hopkins University Press, 2000.
"Historicizing Absalom and Achitophel." In *The New Eighteenth Century: Theory, Politics, English Literature*, edited by Felicity Nussbaum and Laura Brown, 23–40. New York: Methuen, 1987.
"Historicizing Patriarchy: The Emergence of Gender Difference in England, 1660–1760." *Eighteenth-Century Studies* 28, no. 3 (Spring 1995): 295–322.
The Origins of the English Novel, 1600–1740. Baltimore: John Hopkins University Press, 1987/2002.
"Paradise Lost, Poem of the Restoration Period." *Eighteenth-Century Life* 41, no. 2 (2017): 9–27.
Politics and Poetry in Restoration England: The Case of Dryden's Annus Mirabilis. Cambridge, MA: Harvard University Press, 1975.
"The Politics of Pastoral Retreat: Dryden's Poem to His Cousin." In *Enchanted Ground: Reimagining John Dryden*, edited by Jayne Lewis and Maximillian Novak, 91–110. Toronto: University of Toronto Press, 2004.
Mendelson, Sara Heller. *The Mental World of Stuart Women: Three Studies*. Amherst: University of Massachusetts Press, 1987.
Mendus, Susan. Introduction to *Justifying Toleration: Conceptual and Historical Perspectives*, 1–20. Cambridge: Cambridge University Press, 1988.
Mercer, M. J. "Fuller, Francis (1636?–1701)." In *Oxford Dictionary of National Biography*. Oxford: Oxford University Press, September 23, 2004. https://doi.org/10.1093/ref:odnb/10228.
Meyers, William. *Dryden*. London: Hutchinson, 1973.
Miles, Tia. *Tales of the Haunted South: Dark Tourism and Memories of Slavery from the Civil War Era*. Chapel Hill: University of North Carolina Press, 2015.
Mill, John Stuart. *On Liberty and Other Essays*. Edited by Mark Philp and Frederick Rosen. Oxford: Oxford University Press, 2015.
"Review of Brodie, *History of the British Empire*." *The West Minster Review* 2 (1824): 34. Cited in Donald W. Livingston. "Hume's Historical Conception of Liberty." In *Liberty in Hume's History of England*, edited by Nicholas Capaldi and Donald W. Livingston, 105–53. Dordrecht: Springer Netherlands, 1990. 152 n.1.
Millgate, Jane. *Walter Scott: The Making of the Novelist*. Toronto: University of Toronto Press, 1984.
Mills, Charles. *Black Rights/White Wrongs: The Critique of Racial Liberalism*. Oxford: Oxford University Press, 2017.
Racial Contract. Ithaca, NY: Cornell University Press, 2014.
Milton, John. "Tetrachordon." In *The Essential Prose of John Milton*. Edited by Wiliam Kerrigan, John Rumrich, and Stephen M. Fallon. New York: Random House Publishing Group, 2013.

A Treatise of Civil Power in Ecclesiastical Causes Shewing That It Is Not Lawfull for Any Power on Earth to Compell in Matters of Religion. London: Printed by Tho. Newcomb, 1659.

Miner, Earl. "Dryden and the Issue of Human Progress." *Philological Quarterly* 40, no. 1 (January 1961): 120–29.

——— "Introduction: Borrowed Plumage, Varied Umbrage." In *Literary Transmission and Authority: Dryden and Other Writers*, edited by Jennifer Brady and Earl Roy Miner, 1–26. Cambridge: Cambridge University Press, 1993.

——— "Ovid Reformed: Fable, Morals and the Second Epic?" In *Literary Transmission and Authority: Dryden and Other Writers*, edited by Jennifer Brady and Earl Roy Miner, 79–120. Cambridge: Cambridge University Press, 1993.

Miner, Earl, and Jennifer Brady, eds. *Literary Transmission and Authority: Dryden and Other Writers*. Cambridge: Cambridge University Press, 1993.

Mintz, Samuel I. "The Duchess of Newcastle's Visit to the Royal Society." *Journal of English and Germanic Philology* 51, no.2 (April 1952): 168–76.

Mitchell, Joshua. "Hobbes and the Equality of All under the One." *Political Theory* 21, no. 1 (1993): 78–100.

Mohamed, Feisel G. *Milton and the Post-Secular Present: Ethics, Politics, Terrorism*. Stanford, CA: Stanford University Press, 2011.

Molesworth, William. *The English Works of Thomas Hobbes*. London: Longman, Brown, Green, and Longmans, 1845.

Morrison, Toni. *Beloved*. New York: Plume, 1987.

Morrissey, Lee. "Literature and the Postsecular: Paradise Lost?" *Religion & Literature* 41, no. 3 (2009): 98–106.

Mufti, Amir. *Forget English!: Orientalisms and World Literature*. Cambridge, MA: Harvard University Press, 2016.

Murphy, Andrew R. *Conscience and Community: Revisiting Toleration and Religious Dissent in Early Modern England and America*. University Park: Pennsylvania State University Press, 2001.

Murray, Molly. *The Poetics of Conversion in Early Modern English Literature: Verse and Change from Donne to Dryden*. Cambridge: Cambridge University Press, 2009.

Myers, William. "Politics in *The Hind and the Panther*." *Essays in Criticism* 19, no. 1 (January 1969): 19–34.

Nenner, Howard. *The Right to Be King: The Succession to the Crown of England, 1603–1714*. Chapel Hill: University of North Carolina, 1995.

Neocleous, Mark. "Staging Power: Marx, Hobbes and the Personification of Capital." *Law and Critique* 14, no. 2 (2003): 147–65.

Nord, Philip. Introduction to *Formations of Belief: Historical Approaches to Religion and the Secular*. Edited by Philip Nord, Katja Guenther, and Max Weiss, 1–10. Princeton, NJ: Princeton University Press, 2019.

Norton, John. *A Discussion of that Great Point in Divinity, the Sufferings of Christ: And the Questions about His Righteousnesse Active, Passive*. London, 1653.

Novak, Maximillian. "John Dryden's Politics: The Rabble and Sovereignty." In *John Dryden (1631–1700): His Politics, His Play, and His Poets*, edited by

Claude Rawson and Aaron Santessa, 86–105. Newark: University of Delaware, 2003.
O'Connell, Lisa. "Literary Sentimentalism and Post-Secular Virtue." *Eighteenth-Century Life* 41, no. 2 (2017): 28–42.
O'Donnell, Mary Ann. *Aphra Behn: An Annotated Bibliography of Primary and Secondary Sources*. New York: Garland, 1986.
  "Private Jottings, Public Utterances: Aphra Behn's Published Writings and Her Commonplace Book." In *Aphra Behn Studies*, edited by Janet Todd, 285–309. Cambridge: Cambridge University Press, 1996.
Ogg, David. *England in the Reigns of James II and William III*. Oxford: Clarendon, 1957.
Parliament of England. An Act to Retain Queen's Majesty's Subjects in Their Due Obedience, 1580/81. 23 Eliz. I. c.1.
Passive Obedience in Actual Resistance. London, 1691.
Pateman, Carole. *The Sexual Contract*. Cambridge: Polity, 1988.
Pateman, Carole, and Charles Mills. *Contract and Domination*. Cambridge: Polity, 2007.
Paulson, Ronald. *The Fictions of Satire*. Baltimore: Johns Hopkins University Press, 1967.
Pepys, Samuel. *The Diary of Samuel Pepys. Vol. 9, 1668–1669*. Edited by Robert Lathan and William Matthews. London: G. Bell & Sons, 1970.
Pérez-Ramos, Antonio. *Francis Bacon's Idea of Science and the Maker's Knowledge Tradition*. Oxford: Oxford University Press, 1988.
Pfaller, Robert. *On the Pleasure Principle in Culture: Illusions Without Owners*. London: Verso, 2014.
Pierce, Thomas. *A Prophylactick from Disloyalty in These Perilous Times*. London, 1688.
Pincus, Steve. *1688: The First Modern Revolution*. New Haven, CT: Yale University Press, 2009.
Pinkham, Lucile. *William III and the Respectable Revolution*. Cambridge, MA: Harvard University Press, 1954.
Pino, Melissa. "Translating toward Eternity: Dryden's Final Aspiration." *Philological Quarterly* 84, no. 1 (Winter 2005): 49–75.
Pittock, Murray. *The Invention of Scotland: The Stuart Myth and the Scottish Identity, 1638 to the Present*. London: Routledge, 2014.
  Poetry and Jacobite Politics in Eighteenth-Century Britain and Ireland. Cambridge: Cambridge University Press, 2006.
Plank, Geoffrey. *Rebellion and Savagery: The Jacobite Rising of 1745 and the British Empire*. Philadelphia: University of Pennsylvania Press, 2005.
Plumb, J. H. *The Origins of Political Stability, England, 1675–1725*. Boston: Houghton Mifflin, 1967.
Pocock, J. G. A. *The Ancient Constitution and the Feudal Law: A Study of English Historical Thought in the Seventeenth Century*, 2nd rev. ed. Cambridge; New York: Cambridge University Press, 1987.

The Machiavellian Moment: Florentine Political Thought and the Atlantic Republican Tradition, revised ed. Princeton, NJ: Princeton University Press, 2016.

Three British Revolutions, 1641, 1688, 1776. Princeton, NJ: Princeton University Press, 1980.

Porter, Gerald. "'Who Talks of My Nation?' The Role of Wales, Scotland, and Ireland in Constructing 'Englishness.'" In *Imagined States: Nationalism, Utopia, and Longing in Oral Cultures*, edited by Luisa Del Guidice and Gerald Porter, 101–35. Logan: Utah State University Press, 2001.

Price, Fiona. "The Uses of History: The Historical Novel in the Post-French Revolution Debate and Ellis Cornelia Knight's Marcus Flaminius (1792)." In *Reading Historical Fiction: The Revenant and Remembered Past*, edited by Kate Mitchell and Nicola Parsons, 187–203. New York: Palgrave Macmillan, 2013.

Priestley, Joseph. *An Essay on the First Principles of Government*. Dublin, 1768.

Prior, Matthew, and Charles Montagu. *The Hind and the Panther, Transvers'd to the Story of the Country Mouse and the City-Mouse*. London, 1687.

Rancière, Jacques. *Politics of Literature*. Translated by Jacqueline Rose. Cambridge: Polity Press, 2011.

"Writing, Repetition, Displacement: An Interview with Jacques Rancière." *Novel* 47, no. 2 (2014): 301–10.

Rawson, Claude Julien. *Satire and Sentiment, 1660–1830*. Cambridge: Cambridge University Press, 1994.

Reverend, Cedric. "Dryden and the Canon: Absorbing and Rejecting the Burden of the Past." In *Enchanted Ground: Reimagining John Dryden*, edited by Jayne Lewis and Maximillian Novak, 203–25. Toronto: University of Toronto Press, 2004.

Richardson, Samuel. *Clarissa: Or the History of a Young Lady*, reprint ed. Edited by Angus Ross. New York: Penguin, 1986.

Richetti, John. "The Public Sphere and the Eighteenth-Century Novel: Social Criticism and Narrative Enactment." *Eighteenth-Century Life* 16, no. 3 (1992): 114–29.

Rivero, Albert J. "Aphra Behn's Oroonoko and the 'Blank Spaces' of Colonial Fictions." *SEL Studies in English Literature, 1500–1900* 39, no. 3 (1999): 443–62.

Robbins, Corey. *Reactionary Mind: Conservatism from Edmond Burke to Sarah Palin*. Oxford: Oxford University Press, 2011.

Robertson, Fiona. *Legitimate Histories: Scott, Gothic, and the Authorities of Fiction*. Oxford: Clarendon, 1994.

Rogers, John. *The Doctrine of Faith: Wherein Are Practically Handled Ten Principall Points, Which Explain the Nature and Vse of It*. London, 1627.

The Matter of Revolution: Science, Poetry, and Politics in the Age of Milton. Ithaca, NY: Cornell University Press, 1998.

Rosaldo, Renato. *Culture & Truth: The Remaking of Social Analysis: With a New Introduction*. Boston: Beacon Press, 1993.

Rose, Jacqueline. *Godly Kingship in Restoration England: The Politics of the Royal Supremacy, 1660–1688*. Cambridge: Cambridge University Press, 2011.
Rosenthal, Laura J. "Oroonoko: Reception, Ideology, and Narrative Strategy." In *The Cambridge Companion to Aphra Behn*, edited by Derek Hughes and Janet Todd, 151–65. Cambridge: Cambridge University Press, 2004.
Roth, Michael S. "The Time of Nostalgia: Medicine, History and Normality in 19th-Century France." *Time & Society* 1, no. 2 (1992): 271–86.
Russo, Elena. "How to Handle the Intolerant: The Education of Pierre Bayle." In *Imagining Religious Toleration: A Literary History of an Idea, 1600–1830*, edited by Alison Conway and David Alvarez, 119–35. Toronto: University of Toronto Press, 2019.
Ryan, Alan. "Hobbes, Toleration, and the Inner Life." In *The Nature of Political Theory*, edited by David Miller and Larry Siendentop, 197–218. Oxford: Clarendon, 1983.
Sacheverell, Henry. *Perils of False Brethren*. London, 1709.
Sarasohn, Lisa. *The Natural Philosophy of Margaret Cavendish: Reason and Fancy during the Scientific Revolution*. Baltimore: Johns Hopkins University Press, 2010.
Schilling, Bernard. *Dryden and the Conservative Myth: A Reading of Absalom and Achitophel*. New Haven, CT: Yale University Press, 1961.
Schmitt, Carl, and George Schwab. *Political Theology: Four Chapters on the Concept of Sovereignty*. Chicago: University of Chicago Press, 1985.
Schochet, Gordon. "John Locke and Religious Toleration." In *The Revolution of 1688–89: Changing Perspectives*, edited by Lois G. Schwoerer, 147–64. Cambridge: Cambridge University Press, 1992.
Schwoerer, Lois G., ed. *The Revolution of 1688–1689: Changing Perspectives*. Cambridge: Cambridge University Press, 1992.
Scott, Joan. *Sex and Secularism*. Princeton, NJ: Princeton University Press, 2018.
Scott, Walter. *Waverly: Or, 'Tis Sixty Years Since*. London: Penguin 1985.
Scruton, Roger. *How to Be a Conservative*, reprint ed. London: Bloomsbury Continuum, 2015.
Sebastiani, Silvia. *The Scottish Enlightenment: Race, Gender, and the Limits of Progress*. Translated by Jeremy Carden. New York: Palgrave Macmillan, 2013.
Sedgwick, Eve Kosofsky. "Paranoid Reading and Reparative Reading, or, You're So Paranoid, You Probably Think This Essay Is About You." In *Touching Feeling*, 123–52. Durham, NC: Duke University Press, 2003.
Seidel, Kevin. *Rethinking the Secular Origins of the Novel: The Bible in English Fiction 1678–1767*. Cambridge: Cambridge University Press, 2021.
Seidel, Michael. *Satiric Inheritance: Rabelais to Sterne*. Princeton, NJ: Princeton University Press, 1979.
Seller, Abednego. *A Defence of Dr. Sacherverell. Or, Passive-Obedience Prov'd to Be the Doctrine of the Church of England*. London, 1710.
———. *The History of Self-Defense*. London: Printed for Theodore Johnson, 1689.

Sensabaugh, George F. "Milton and the Doctrine of Passive Obedience." *Huntington Library Quarterly* 13, no. 1 (1939): 19–54.
Shaffern, Robert W. "Images, Jurisdiction, and the Treasury of Merit." *Journal of Medieval History* 22, no. 3 (January 1, 1996): 237–47.
Sharpe, Kevin. *Rebranding Rule: The Restoration and Revolution Monarchy, 1660–1714*. New Haven, CT: Yale University Press, 2013.
Shell, Alison. "Popish Plots: The Feign'd Curtizans in Context." In *Aphra Behn Studies*, edited by Janet Todd, 31–49. Cambridge: Cambridge University Press, 1996.
Shields, Juliet. *Sentimental Literature and Anglo-Scottish Identity, 1745–1820*. Cambridge: Cambridge University Press, 2010.
Siegfried, B. R. "The City of Chance, or, Margaret Cavendish's Theory of Radical Symmetry." *Early Modern Literary Studies*, Special Issue 9 (May 2004): 1–29.
Sikorski, Wade. "Toleration and Shamanism." *New Political Science* 13, no. 1 (1993): 3–20.
Sills, Adam. "Surveying 'The Map of Slavery' in Aphra Behn's Oroonoko." *Journal of Narrative Theory* 36, no. 3 (2006): 314–40.
Simpson, Kenneth. *The Protean Scot: The Crisis of Identity in Eighteenth Century Scottish Literature*. Aberdeen: Aberdeen University Press, 1988.
Sisken, Clifford. "Personification and Community: Literary Change in the Mid- and Late Eighteenth Century." *Eighteenth-Century Studies* 15, no. 4 (1982): 371–401.
Skinner, Quentin. "Hobbes and the Purely Artificial Person of the State." *Journal of Political Philosophy* 7, no. 1 (March 1999): 1–29.
Slaughter, Thomas P. "'Abdicate' and 'Contract' in the Glorious Revolution." *The Historical Journal* 24, no. 2 (June 1981): 323–37.
Slotkin, Richard. "Fiction for the Purposes of History." *Rethinking History* 9, nos. 2–3 (June 1, 2005): 221–36.
Smith, Kimberly K. "Mere Nostalgia: Notes on a Progressive Paratheory." *Rhetoric & Public Affairs* 3, no. 4 (2000): 505–27.
Soni, Vivasvan. *Mourning Happiness*. Ithaca, NY: Cornell University Press, 2010.
Southgate, Beverly. "Sergeant, John (1623–1707)." In *Oxford Dictionary of National Biography*. Oxford: Oxford University Press, September 23, 2004. https://doi.org/10.1093/ref:odnb/25095.
Sowerby, Scott. *Making Toleration: The Repealers and the Glorious Revolution*. Cambridge, MA: Harvard University Press, 2013.
Speck, W. A. *Reluctant Revolutionaries: Englishmen and the Revolution of 1688*. Oxford; New York: Oxford University Press, 1988.
Speed, John. *The History of Great Britaine*. London, 1614. Quoted in Jacqueline Rose, *Godly Kingship in Restoration England: The Politics of the Royal Supremacy, 1660–1688*. Cambridge: Cambridge University Press, 2011, 93n14.
Spengemann, William C. "The Earliest American Novel: Aphra Behn's Oroonoko." *Nineteenth-Century Fiction* 38, no. 4 (1984): 384–414.

Spinoza, Benedictus de. *Ethics, Part 3: The Collected Works of Spinoza*. Vol. 1, edited and translated by Edwin Curley. Princeton, NJ: Princeton University Press, 1985.
Spivak, Gayatri. "Rethinking-Comparativism." *New Literary History* 40, no. 3 (2009): 609–26.
Stafford, William. *Socialism, Radicalism, and Nostalgia: Social Criticism in Britain, 1775–1830*. Cambridge: Cambridge University Press, 1987.
Stalnaker, Joanna. "Description and the Nonhuman View of Nature." *Representations* 135, no. 1 (2016):72–88.
Starobinski, Jean, and William S. Kemp. "The Idea of Nostalgia." *Diogenes* 14, no. 54 (June 1966): 81–103.
Starr, Gabrielle. "Cavendish, Aesthetics, and the Anti-Platonic Line." *Eighteenth-Century Studies* 39, no. 3 (Spring 2006): 295–308.
Staves, Susan. *Players' Scepters: Fictions of Authority in the Restoration*. Omaha: University of Nebraska Press, 1979.
Stein, Jordan Alexander Stein. "Angels in (Mexican) America." *American Literature: A Journal of Literary History, Criticism, and Bibliography* 86, no. 4 (2014): 683–711.
Stewart, Susan. *On Longing: Narratives of the Miniature, the Gigantic, the Souvenir, the Collection*. Durham, NC: Duke University Press, 1992.
Stoeckl, Kristina. "Defining the Postsecular." Paper presented at the seminar of Prof. Khoruzhij at the Academy of Sciences in Moscow in February 2011, viewed May 5, 2022, from Stoeckl_enpostsecular.pdf.
Stroh, Silke. *Gaelic Scotland in the Colonial Imagination: Anglophone Writing from 1600 to 1900*. Chicago: Northwestern University Press, 2017.
Su, John J. *Ethics and Nostalgia in the Contemporary Novel*. Cambridge: Cambridge University Press, 2005.
Sussman, Charlotte. "The Other Problem with Women: Reproduction and Slave Culture in Aphra Behn's Oroonoko." In *Rereading Aphra Behn: History, Theory, Criticism*, edited by Heidi Hutner, 212–33. Charlottesville: University Press of Virginia, 1993.
Swanson, R. N. *Indulgences in Late Medieval England: Passports to Paradise?* Cambridge: Cambridge University Press, 2007.
Promissory Notes on the Treasury of Merits: Indulgences in Late Medieval Europe. Leiden: Brill, 2006.
Taylor, Charles. "Nationalism and Modernity." In *Theorizing Nationalism*, edited by Ronald Beiner, 219–45. Albany: State University of New York Press, 1999.
A Secular Age. Cambridge, MA: Harvard University Press, 2007.
A Secular Age. Princeton, NJ: Princeton University Press, 2008.
Taylor, Jeremy. *The Rule and Exercises of Holy Living*. London, 1650.
Teixeira, José. *The True Historie of the Late and Lamentable Aduentures of Don Sebastian King of Portugall after His Imprisonment in Naples, Vntill This Present Day, Being Now in Spaine at Saint Lucar de Barrameda*. London, 1602.
Teskey, Gordon. *Allegory and Violence*. Ithaca, NY: Cornell University Press, 1996.

Thell, Anne. "'[A]s Lightly as Two Thoughts': Motion, Materialism, and Cavendish's Blazing World." *Configurations* 23, no. 1 (2015): 1–33.

Thomas, Roger. "Comprehension and Indulgence." In *From Uniformity to Unity, 1662–1962*, edited by Geoffrey F. Nuttall and Owen Chadwick, 191–253. London, 1962.

Till, Barry. "Stillingfleet, Edward (1635–1699)." In *Oxford Dictionary of National Biography*. Oxford: Oxford University Press, published September 23, 2004; last modified January 3, 2008). https://doi.org/10.1093/ref:odnb/26526.

Tillotson, John. *THE Rule of Faith, Or, an ANSWER to the TREATISE of Mr. I.S. Entituled, Sure-Footing, &c. by JOHN TILLOTSON ... ; to which is Adjoined A REPLY TO Mr. I.S. His 3d APPENDIX, &c, by EDW. STILLINGFLEET*, 2nd ed. London: Printed by H.C. for Sa. Gellibrand, at the Golden-Ball in St. Paul's Church-yard, 1676.

Tocqueville, Alexis de. *The Old Regime and the French Revolution. Translated by Stuart Gilbert*. Garden City, NJ: Doubleday Anchor, 1955.

Toland, John. *Mr. Toland's Reflections on Dr. Sacheverells Sermon*. London, 1710.

Tønder, Lars. *Tolerance: A Sensorial Orientation to Politics*. Oxford: Oxford University Press, 2013.

Torrance, Ian. "Hamilton, Patrick (1504–1528)." In *Oxford Dictionary of National Biography*. Oxford: Oxford University Press, September 23, 2004. https://doi.org/10.1093/ref:odnb/12116.

Trevelyan, George Macaulay. *The English Revolution, 1688–1689*. London: Oxford University Press, 1938.

Trevor-Roper, Hugh. *The Invention of Tradition*. Cambridge: Cambridge University Press, 2015.

Trubowitz, Rachel. "The Reenchantment of Utopia and the Female Monarchical Self." *Tulsa Studies in Women's Literature* 11, no. 2 (1992): 229–45.

Trumpener, Katie. *Bardic Nationalism: The Romantic Novel and the British Empire*. Princeton, NJ: Princeton University Press, 1997.

Tumbleson, Raymond D. *Catholicism in the English Protestant Imagination: Nationalism, Religion, and Literature, 1660–1745*. Cambridge: Cambridge University Press, 1998.

Turner, Francis. *Sermon Preached before the King on the 30/1 of January 1680/1*. London, 1681.

Turner, Henry S. "Lessons from Literature for the Historian of Science (and Vice Versa)." *ISIS: Journal of the History of Science in Society* 101, no. 3 (September 2010): 578–89.

Tyacke, Nicholas. "The 'Rise of Puritanism' and the Legalizing of Dissent, 1571–1719." In *From Persecution to Toleration: The Glorious Revolution and Religion in England*, edited by Ole Peter Grell, Jonathan I. Israel, and Nicholas Tyacke, 17–49. Oxford: Oxford University Press, 1991.

Tyerman, Christopher. *God's War: A New History of the Crusades*. Cambridge, MA: Belknap Press of Harvard University Press, 2006.

Urban II. An Act to Retain Queen's Majesty's Subjects in Their Due Obedience, 1580/81.

Van Sant, Ann Jessie. *Eighteenth-Century Sensibility and the Novel: The Senses in Social Contact*. Cambridge: Cambridge University Press, 2004.

Vickery, Amanda. *The Gentleman's Daughter: Women's Lives in Georgian England*. New Haven, CT: Yale University Press, 1998.

Viswanathan, Gauri. "Secularism in the Framework of Heterodoxy." *PMLA* 123, no. 2 (2008): 466–76.

Vox Populi, Vox Dei. London, 1709.

Wagner, Geraldine. "Romancing Multiplicity: Female Subjectivity and the Body Divisible in Margaret Cavendish's Blazing World." *Early Modern Literary Studies* 9, no. 1 (2003): 1–59.

Walker, John. *The Antidote: Or, a Seasonable Discourse on Rom. 13.1*. London, 1684.

Walker, William. "Force, Metaphor, and Persuasion in Locke's *A Letter Concerning Toleration*." In *Difference & Dissent: Theories of Tolerance in Medieval and Early Modern Europe*, edited by Cary J. Nederman and John Christian Laursen, 205–29. Lanham, MD: Rowman & Littlefield, 1996.

Wall, Cynthia. *The Prose of Things*. Chicago: University of Chicago Press, 2014.

Ward, Ann, ed. *Matter and Form: From Natural Science to Political Philosophy*. Lanham, MD: Rowman & Littlefield, 2009.

Ward, Graham. *True Religion*. Malden: Blackwell, 2003.

Warner, Michael. "Publics and Counterpublics." *Public Culture* 14, no. 1 (2002): 49–90.

Warner, William B. "Licensed by the Market: Behn's Love Letters as Serial Entertainment." In his *Licensing Entertainment: The Elevation of Novel Reading in Britain, 1684–1750*, 45–87. Berkeley: University of California Press, 1998.

Wasserman, Earl. "The Inherent Values of Eighteenth-Century Personification." *PMLA* 65, no. 4 (1950): 435–63.

The Subtler Language: Critical Readings of Neoclassic and Romantic Poems. Baltimore: Johns Hopkins University Press, 1968.

Watt, Ian. *The Rise of the Novel*. Berkeley: University of California Press, 1967.

Weber, Max. *The Protestant Ethic and the Spirit of Capitalism*. Translated by Talcott Parsons. New York: Charles Scribner's Sons, 1958.

Weinbrot, Howard D. *Eighteenth-Century Satire: Essays on Text and Context from Dryden to Peter Pindar*. Cambridge: Cambridge University Press, 1988.

Welwiller, W. J. *To peace and truth. Obedience Active and Passive Due to the Supream Povver*. London, 1643.

White, Hayden. "Introduction: Historical Fiction, Fictional History, and Historical Reality." *Rethinking History* 9, nos. 2–3 (June 1, 2005): 147–57.

Wickman, Matthew. *The Ruins of Experience: Scotland's "Romantic" Highlands and the Birth of the Modern Witness*. Philadelphia: University of Pennsylvania Press, 2007.

Williams, Abigail. *Poetry and the Creation of a Whig Literary Culture 1681–1714*. Oxford: Oxford University Press, 2005.

Williams, Raymond. *Keywords: A Vocabulary of Culture and Society*. New York; Oxford: Oxford University Press, 1985.
Wilson, Kathleen. "Inventing Revolution: 1688 and Eighteenth-Century Popular Politic." *Journal of British Studies* 28, no. 4 (1989): 349–86.
Wilt, Judith. *Secret Leaves: The Novels of Walter Scott*. Chicago: University of Chicago Press, 1985.
Wolfson, Adam. *Persecution or Toleration: An Explication of the Locke-Proast Quarrel, 1689–1704*. Lanham, MD: Lexington Books, 2010.
Wolin, Sheldon. *Politics and Vision: Continuity and Innovation in Western Political Thought*. Princeton, NJ: Princeton University Press, 2009.
Worden, Blair. "Toleration and the Cromwellian Protectorate." In *Persecution and Toleration*, edited by W. J. Sheils, 199–233. Oxford: Blackwell, 1984.
Wright, Stephen. "Rogers, John (1610–1680)." In *Oxford Dictionary of National Biography*. Oxford: Oxford University Press, September 23, 2004. https://doi.org/10.1093/ref:odnb/23984.
Yang, Chi-ming. "Asia out of Place: The Aesthetics of Incorruptibility in Behn's Oroonoko." *Eighteenth-Century Studies* 42, no. 2 (2009): 235–53.
Young, Hershini Bhana. *Haunting Capital: Memory, Text and the Black Diasporic Body*. Hanover, NH: University Press of New England, 2006.
Zagorin, Perez. *Hobbes and the Law of Nature*. Princeton, NJ: Princeton University Press, 2009.
Zetterberg Gjerlevsen, Simona. "A Novel History of Fictionality." *Narrative* 24, no. 2 (May 2016): 174–89.
Zimbardo, Rose. "The Late Seventeenth-Century Dilemma in Discourse: Dryden's Don Sebastian and Behn's Oroonoko." In *Rhetorics of Order/Ordering Rhetorics in English Neoclassical Literature*, edited by Clifford Earl Ramsey, 46–67. Newark: University of Delaware Press, 1989.
Žižek, Slavoj. *On Belief*. London; New York: Routledge, 2003.
Zook, Melinda S. "Early Whig Ideology, Ancient Constitutionalism, and the Reverend Samuel Johnson." *Journal of British Studies* 32, no. 2 (1993): 139–65.
  Radical Whigs and Conspiratorial Politics in Late Stuart England. University Park: Pennsylvania State University Press, 1999.
Zwicker, Laura. "The Politics of Toleration: The Establishment Clause and the Act of Toleration Examined." *Indiana Law Journal* 66, no. 3 (1991): 773–99.
Zwicker, Steven N. *The Cambridge Companion to John Dryden*. Cambridge: Cambridge University Press, 2004.
  Dryden's Political Poetry: The Typology of King and Nation. Providence, RI: University Press of New England, 1972.
  Lines of Authority: Politics and English Literary Culture, 1649–1689. Ithaca, NY: Cornell University Press, 1993.

Index

1688–89
  glorious revolution, 5, 214, 219
  history, 1–3, 5–7, 67, 69, 77, 135, 183
  impact, 82, 178, 212–16, 219, 225, 235
  literature, 1–2, 6–9, 37, 76–77, 80–81, 123, 144–47, 162, 182, 184, 187, 189, 201, 212–14, 218, 225–28
  politics, 73, 82, 180, 187, 195, 212
  secularization, 29, 67, 127
abdication
  in fiction, 145, 147, 149, 151–52, 154, 218
  and revolution, 5
  Stuart, 145, 160, 211, 218
absolutism, 69, 78, 90, 106, 109, 128
  versus liberty, 214
  Stuart, 68, 75, 219
aesthetics
  baroque, 45–46, 49, 52, 184–85, 190, 192–96, 198–99
  neoclassical, 153, 162, 192–93, 195
afterlife, 182
agency, 150–51
  liberal, 179, 199–200, 218, 243–45
  narrative, 48
  and obedience, 198–99
  personal, 8, 11, 36, 46, 48–49, 55, 103, 123, 177, 186, 193–95, 197, 200, 217, 221, 227, 231
  political, 5, 17, 103, 124, 146, 151, 177, 182, 189, 194–96, 213, 216, 221
  revolutionary, 218–19, 231–32
  and temporality, 135, 155, 157–58
allegory. *See also* personification
  and allegoresis, 16, 135, 138, 154–55, 162
  baroque, 193, 195
  for faith, 53
  in fiction, 15, 17, 47, 50, 52–53, 116, 135–38, 142, 155, 157, 196, 199, 213
  forms, 9, 135, 146, 157–58, 162, 192, 194–95, 213
  for history, 18

  literary, 147, 171
  political, 8–9, 48, 55, 136–37, 145, 149, 184, 195, 199–200, 225
  religious, 139, 142, 184
analogy
  analogue, 120
  metaphor, 14, 40, 50, 76, 83, 88, 113, 146, 149–51
  simile, 50, 105, 113, 116, 120, 124, 151
apostolic, 40, 136, 141–44, 146–47, 156, 158, 164, 168, 213
Arendt, Hannah, 215, 217
Asad, Talal, 3, 161
authority
  authorization, 81, 200
  communal, 13
  community, 118
  divine, 144
  familial, 84
  gendered, 84
  government, 2, 70–71, 75–79, 81–82, 84–85
  innate, 142–43
  institutional, 41
  and obedience, 39
  papal, 36, 95, 183
  patriarchal, 82, 225, 228
  personal, 41, 187
  political, 41, 178, 191
  and politics, 39, 41, 68–69, 73, 75, 144, 151
  religious, 41, 82, 118
  secular, 181, 183
  sovereign, 77, 81–82
  state, 40, 43–44, 84
  transcendent, 190
  unjust, 218

Bainbrigg, Thomas, 181–82
Baker, J. Wayne, 58, 60
Bayle, Pierre, 106
Behn, Aphra
  conservatism, 1, 9, 54–55, 90, 178, 196, 199

275

Behn, Aphra (cont.)
  Love Letters, 15, 29, 44–54, 200
  Oroonoko, 9, 177–79, 183–201, 209, 213
  prose, 14, 29, 38, 47, 65, 83, 156, 192, 225
  as writer, 53, 160, 182, 225, 233
belief
  and action, 113, 178, 189, 215, 231–32
  versus action, 189, 198
  versus culture, 8
  dis-, 33
  and epistemology, 37
  versus faith, 30, 32–33, 35–38, 41–42, 55, 190, 243
  in fiction, 51, 148, 150
  historical, 34, 240–41
  and indulgence, 75, 78
  philosophical, 117
  political, 107
  Protestant, 34
  religious, 27–28, 38–39, 47, 53, 70–71, 114, 160, 202
  spiritual, 154
  and tolerance, 67, 70, 114
Bible, the. *See also* scripture
  faith, 30–32, 34
  New Testament, 31, 59, 62, 141, 183
  Old Testament, 59, 62, 136, 182
  reading, 31, 141, 153, 161
  typology, 136–37, 194
  verse, 31, 169, 182
Breda, Declaration of, 68, 106
Brown, Laura, 159
Burke, Edmund, 13, 15, 90
  indulgence, 84–89
  politics, 12, 211
  slavery, 86–88, 96–97
Burnet, Gilbert, 211–12

capitalism
  and colonialism, 88
  global, 119, 132
  and politics, 11, 90, 196, 215, 224, 246
  property, 96, 185–86
Catholicism
  1688–89, 1, 3, 8, 219, 223
  and anti-Catholicism, 182
  and the Church, 76, 137–39, 142–43
  and indulgence, 68, 73, 76, 82–83, 85
  and monarchs, 67, 178, 183
  pope, 35, 181, 183
  priesthood, 141
  and Protestantism, 35, 37, 104, 142, 182
  reading practice, 17
  and ritual, 45, 103, 162
  and sex, 28
  and toleration, 71, 92, 106, 127, 129, 132
  and transubstantiation, 42, 71
  treason, 72
  writers, 1, 37, 134–35, 139, 160, 162, 178
causation
  versus description, 111
  in fiction, 149, 153–55, 194
  and history, 135–36, 146, 168
  and indulgence, 79
  and slavery, 150
  and temporality, 135, 157–58, 216–17
Cavendish, Margaret, 1, 9, 103, 107–9, 160, 177, 213
  Blazing World, The, 104–6, 109, 111, 113–17, 120–22, 124, 213
  conservatism, 104, 106, 124
  Observations on Experimental Philosophy, 105, 111–12, 124
  Orations of Divers Sorts, 117
Cheah, Pheng, 119–20, 132
Church of England, 32, 37, 67, 73, *See also* religion
Cibber, Colley
  The Nonjuror, 222
colonization, 17–18, 89, 185, 210, *See also* imperialism
community, 114, 136, 198, 233
  attachment to, 220–21
  continuity, 220
  and displacement, 220
  experimentalist, 111
  forming, 118, 125, 177
  island, 110
  political, 10
  reader, 160
conformity, 34
  mandated, 67, 117
  non-, 34, 93
  religious, 67–68, 73, 114–15, 117
conscience
  and freedom, 60, 89, 106, 108–9, 117, 198
  and obedience, 179–80, 183, 191, 194
  and politics, 60
  private, 207
  religious, 181, 192, 194
  Stuart, 70–72
conservatism, 85
  versus abstraction, 72, 149, 152, 244
  as anti-foundational, 89
  as anti-revolution, 14, 177, 234, 243
  as antitheoretical, 23, 81, 116, 244
  and authority, 191
  and liberalism, 12, 16–17, 81, 90, 104, 121, 151, 196, 199, 215, 220–22, 233–34, 243

literary, 2–3, 7, 9–17, 29, 47, 53–55, 84, 89–90, 104, 116, 122, 134, 137, 142, 151, 157–61, 177, 186, 199, 212–13, 216, 222, 227, 232–34
   political, 143, 215, 231
   and revolution, 148, 218
   and temporality, 214–18, 227–30, 232
   versus traditionalism, 156, 215
contract, 97
   versus honor, 189–90
   and lying, 191
   and obedience, 178
   personal, 48
   political, 15, 52
   religious, 30, 32, 34, 76
   social, 15, 44, 55, 82
   theory, 82
conversion
   to Catholicism, 72, 134–35, 158–60, 162
   literary, 16
   narrative, 45, 51, 114–15, 148, 160

Deleuze, Gilles, and Feliz Guttari, 118–19
Derrida, Jacques, 64, 118
diversity, 106–7, 121, 127
   biological, 109
   and liberalism, 16, 104, 123
   in literature, 31, 107, 113, 122, 184, 213
   in nature, 111
   of opinion, 31, 112, 117, 122, 132
Dryden, John
   Absalom and Achitophel, 135–37, 139, 143–44, 146, 155
   allegory, 135, 149, 162, 225
   Catholicism, 158–60, 163
   conservatism, 1, 9, 157–59, 233
   critique, 57, 163, 166–68, 170, 172
   Don Sebastian, 6, 9, 135, 144–57, 161, 169, 171, 213, 225
   Hind and the Panther, the, 135, 137–44, 146, 153, 155, 161, 167
   reading methods, 103, 168, 171, 177
   reason, 28
   religion, 134

economy, 232
   colonial, 89, 185
   global, 123
   prosperity, 3, 214
   slave, 213
   spiritual, 72
   traditionalist, 215
embodied
   experience, 40, 138, 161
   faith, 46, 136, 143, 162

passivity, 196
past, 135–36, 146
practice, 16, 136, 155, 230
sovereignty, 40, 92
Enlightenment, the, 11, 27, 219, *See* also reason
   epistemology, 36
   history of, 23
   and modernity, 27
   and secularism, 28, 30, 37
   Scottish, 230
   theories, 107, 129, 216, 230
   writers during, 107, 161
epistemology
   and faith, 27–38, 41, 51, 69–71
   and indulgence, 75
   and secularization, 4, 11, 14–15, 42
epitsemology. *See* also truth
Equiano, Olaudah, 15, 87, 89–90
ethics
   and action, 149, 156, 177, 184, 220, 230
   in fiction, 45, 154–56, 197
   conservative, 17
   and feeling, 161
   human, 123, 178
   Hume, David, 75
   liberal, 129, 190
   morals, 27, 33, 35–36, 55, 71, 76, 88, 106, 112, 138–39, 154–56, 178, 181–82, 188–89, 192, 197–200, 229–31, 233
   and politics, 17, 42, 111, 189
   and responsibility, 229, 241
exception, 196
   abstraction, 72
   exceptionality, 185, 195–97, 199
   human exceptionality, 107–8
   sovereign exceptionality, 157
Exclusion Crisis, 54–55, 135–36

fable
   Dryden, John, 135, 137, 139, 144, 157, 170
   form, 135, 138, 140, 158
   Hobbes, Thomas, 40
   Leibniz, Gottfried Wilhelm, 122, 127, 130
faith. *See* also fidelity, belief, religion
   bad, 86
   Catholic, 142
   civil, 36
   conservative, 54
   crisis of, 29, 31, 35, 39, 45–47
   domains of, 30–31, 36, 46–47, 51
   embodied, 46
   evidence of, 194
   in fiction, 14–15, 46, 53–56, 103, 138, 141, 148, 190, 195, 213, 232–33
   fictional, 52

faith. (cont.)
    lack of, 15, 40, 47–48, 50–51
    literary, 47
    meaning of, 27–35, 39, 41–44, 58
    nature of, 37, 90
    political, 30, 42–43, 232
    producing, 43
    purposes of, 37, 41, 59, 90, 243
    romantic, 46
    rule of, 37–38
    and secularization, 2, 42
family
    collective, 85, 218
    hierarchy, 82
    name, 226
    relations, 64, 83, 87, 229
    royal, 218
    structure, 55
    values, 55, 227–28
feelings
    affect, 3, 17, 31–32, 34–35, 42, 45, 47–48, 71–72, 74, 151–54, 161–62, 193, 216, 230
    affection, 84–86, 187
    and causation, 43, 161, 170, 216
    human, 2, 216
    individual, 48, 162
    and indulgence, 90
    negative, 72
    physical, 48
    reason and, 82–83
    repression, 72
    romantic, 44, 54, 146, 149, 151, 154
    secular, 161
    sentiment, 135, 195
    sovereign, 71
    unsaid, 72, 187
Ferguson, Frances, 161, 229
feudalism, 157
fiction
    faith, 45–47, 51–53, 55–56, 90
    form, 103, 145, 149, 225, 243
    gothic, 222
    historical, 3, 18, 154, 177, 216–17, 224–25, 227–33, 243
    imagination, 115
    politics, 211–14, 224, 230, 247
    prose, 6, 14, 29, 38, 83, 104, 192, 198, 201
    romance, 185
    worlds, 105
fidelity
    in-, 37, 46, 50
    lack of, 43
    narrative, 51
    romantic, 46–47, 55
    sexual, 27, 29–31, 49, 54

Fielding, Henry
    Tom Jones, 222, 224
freedom, 86, *See* also liberty
    academic, 109, 117
    balancing, 111
    of conscience, 89, 106, 109
    female, 83
    individual, 35, 123
    and indulgence, 88
    of interpretation, 161
    lack of, 75
    liberal, 13, 38, 68, 83, 90, 121, 151, 199–200
    limitations of, 244
    mental, 15, 67, 79, 82, 88, 233
    personal, 85, 214
    physical, 15
    political, 15, 82, 84, 107, 151, 244
    potential, 191–92
    of religion, 3, 5, 12, 15, 67–69, 72–73, 76, 91–93, 106, 117
    and slavery, 17
    of speech, 15, 68–69, 77, 89
friendship, 149, 152, 229
    and faith, 33
    practice of, 152
Fuller, Francis, 34, 36

Gallagher, Catherine, 55–56, 90, 99, 128, 198, 209
gender
    distinctions, 152
    and government, 116
    inequality, 67, 200
    in literary criticism, 184
    and race, 68, 179, 184, 199–200
    women, 10, 15, 82–84, 108, 115, 124, 162, 179, 184, 193, 199–200, 239, 243
genre, 7–8, 14, 45, 108, 162, 173, 245, *See* also novel
    historical fiction, 228, 230, 232, 241
    roman à clef, 48
    romance, 56, 144, 149, 178, 185, 187–93, 199, 232, 239
    tragicomedy, 135, 146, 157–58, 168
geography, 131, 162
    in fiction, 110, 113, 189–91, 228
    global, 195, 213
    new world, 17, 104, 190, 199, 207
government, 43, 89, 106, 116, 118, 180–81
    and authority, 81–82, 84–85
    versus business, 86
    Christian commonwealth, 41, 44
    ecclesiastical, 77
    fictional, 39, 114–15, 121
    mixed, 75, 77, 79, 81, 244

monarchy, 69, 77, 150
  and science, 109, 113
  tyranny, 148

Hayot, Eric, 119–20, 132
Heidegger, Martin, 118
hero
  heroism, 188, 192–93, 197, 226
  Jacobite, 83
  passive, 178, 202–5
  Protestant, 67
  reader, 154, 156, 159
  romantic, 185, 187, 192
historicity, 90, 135, 214, 220, 233
  critical methods, 143, 159, 161
history
  biblical, 136–37, 146
  British, 219, 223
  English, 5, 75
  faith, 14, 29–30, 38, 54–55
  in fiction, 145, 154, 191, 197
  interpretations of, 178, 180, 184, 195, 211, 214, 217, 227, 232
  Jacobite, 221, 223–24, 228
  of indulgence, 73–75
  literary, 3, 6–10, 16–18, 52–53, 89, 103, 108, 125, 134, 139, 142, 144, 146, 157–59, 162, 184, 213, 223, 225, 233–34, 243, 245–46
  political, 55, 69, 72, 77, 106, 136–37, 158, 178, 214, 216, 219
  religious, 3, 34, 182–83
  secular, 162
  or temporality, 16
  theory, 230, 232
  of toleration, 106
Hobbes, Thomas
  conservatism, 54–55, 90
  faith, 28, 39, 56
  influence, 55, 107–8, 129
  Leviathan, 3, 15, 29, 39–44, 112, 123
  politics, 29, 213
Holyday, Barten, 32, 34–36
honor, 192
  code of, 190
  versus contract, 189–91
  versus love, 152
  military, 192
  in romance, 189
humanity, 49, 88–89, 137, 141, 143–44, 193, 195–96
Hume, David, 15, 84, 90
  Enquiries, 79
  History of England, The, 75–79
  indulgence, 15, 75–82, 89, 233, 244
  Liberty of the Press, 76

racism, 15, 75, 88
slavery, 88–89
Treatise of Human Nature, A, 79–81
Hume, David indulgence, 78, 80–81

ideology, 6, 8, 11, 152, 159
  political, 3, 7, 17, 215, 218
  secular, 12, 216
imagination, 45, 75, 78, 113, 147, 215, 223, 229
  and faith, 39
  female, 106
  fictional, 3, 16, 104–5, 107, 109, 115–18, 121–23, 145, 211–12, 233, 243
  human, 39, 103, 108, 118, 121, 124
  individual, 117
  literary, 16, 38, 55, 103–6, 109, 116, 120–25, 213, 216, 233, 245
  and nostalgia, 220, 230, 233, 237
  political, 6, 8, 29, 40, 43, 79–81, 89, 106, 120, 124, 211–12, 214–15, 219, 224, 233
  potential of, 90, 120
  and readers, 145, 154–55, 162, 177, 225
  and reason, 116
  theories of, 2
  utopian, 9, 119
imperialism, 150, 223–24, 230, 238
individuality, 13, 92, 123, 199
  versus collective, 109, 120, 122, 124, 157
  and interpretation, 135, 148, 153, 180
  liberal, 13, 17
  political, 49, 72, 78, 177, 195, 217–18, 220–21, 225–28, 230–31
Indulgence, Declarations of
  Charles II, 68, 71–72, 77, 93, 127
  James II, 68–69, 71, 75, 78, 81–82, 93, 127, 165, 196
  Stuart, 15, 67, 70–76, 84
  Urban II, 74
interiority, 179, 192–95
Ireland, 67, 69, 85
irony
  and David Hume, 88
  and *The Hind and the Panther*, 160
  and indulgence, 68, 77, 86–89
  and the Jacobite, 18, 217, 219, 222, 224, 233
  in literary history, 53, 134, 183, 216, 224
  and *Love Letters*, 45, 52
  and *Oroonoko*, 17, 183, 186, 194
  rhetoric, 87
  and *Waverly*, 233

Jackson, William, 34, 36
Jacobite, 218, 233
  cause, 213, 222, 230, 233
  depictions of, 226

Jacobite (cont.)
　experience, 13
　figure, 18, 83, 177, 216–17, 219, 221–25, 233, 237
　history of, 228
　and nostalgia, 18, 216, 221, 223–26, 228, 230, 234
　as revolutionary, 18, 216, 218–19, 222, 225–28, 230
　uprisings, 214, 223, 227
James II, King of England, 46
　Catholicism, 67, 183
　perception of, 12, 78, 81–82, 178, 182, 211, 215, 218
　reign, 31, 68–69, 136, 146, 155
　religious freedom, 67, 69
　as sovereign, 71, 75, 196, 199, 227
Johnson, Samuel (1649–1703), 180, 182–83, 203–4
Johnson, Samuel (1709-1784), 49, 134, 138, 163, 167, 171

Kahn, Victoria, 55, 187, 244
Kant, Immanuel, 56, 72, 130, 219, 230
　religion, 27

Lacan, Jacques, 32
Lamb, Jonathan, 55
law
　and authority, 75, 78, 180
　civil, 71
　Clarendon Code, 68
　common, 14, 85, 143
　divine, 144, 181
　English, 195, 212, 218
　exceptions, 72, 89, 196
　versus faith, 29, 31–34, 42, 70, 179
　freedom from, 244
　function of, 77
　Godden v. Hales, 68
　human, 70, 137
　interpretation of, 73
　natural, 16, 39, 70, 122, 124, 128, 186, 189, 196, 208
　penal, 67–68, 71, 85, 91
　physical, 200
　and punishment, 43
　secular, 33, 181
　sovereign, 72, 179
　suspension, 69
Leibniz, Gottfried Wilhelm,
　fiction, 123–24
　Theodicy, 122
Levinas, Emmanuel, 118

liberalism, 7–8, 10–16, 68–69, 71–72, 82–83, 90, 162–63, 199–201, 215–16, 243–46
　and abstraction, 14, 72, 197, 200, 245
　and action, 221
　and conservatism, 233–34
　critique of, 17
　and diversity, 16, 104, 106, 113, 122–23, 159
　and freedom, 121
　history of, 1–2
　and literature, 151, 222–23
　modern, 38, 69, 78
　and progress, 220, 227
　and racism, 213
　and revolution, 214, 220, 224, 232
　and rights, 76, 95, 196
　and secularization, 2–6, 103
　and slavery, 87–90, 210
　and values, 55
　and violence, 88–90, 132, 179, 200, 212
liberty. *See also* freedom
　desire for, 214
　force of, 75
　human, 38
　of conscience, 108, 117, 198
　political, 5, 74, 77, 79, 180, 218
　principle of, 75–76
　religious, 15, 35, 67–69, 74, 76, 113
　and slavery, 88–89, 196
　theory of, 75–76
literary
　abstraction, 156, 233
　experimentation, 7–8, 11–14, 47, 49, 90, 104–5, 109, 111, 116, 123, 125, 135, 137, 142, 157, 162, 199, 213–14, 246
　form, 2–4, 8–9, 13–15, 17, 47, 52, 55, 103–4, 108, 116, 119, 125, 135, 138, 145–46, 154, 156–60, 177, 195, 197–99, 201, 213, 216–17, 225, 231–32, 234, 243–46
　history, 3, 6–10, 16–18, 52–53, 103, 108, 125, 134, 139, 142–44, 146, 157, 159, 162, 213, 223, 225, 233–34, 243, 245
　imagination, 2–3, 8, 16, 38, 43, 55, 89, 103–5, 107, 109, 116, 119–25, 212–13, 216, 233, 245
　relation to politics, 8–9
literary criticism, 10, 118–19, 147, 159
1688–9, 2, 6–8, 162, 182
eighteenth century, 28
Blazing World, 106
deconstruction, 159
hermeneutic, 16–17, 135, 139, 141, 143–44, 146, 152, 158, 161–62
Jacobitism, 234
John Dryden, 134–35, 139, 142, 158–59
Leviathan, 39

Margaret Cavendish, 111, 124
Oroonoko, 184, 189, 197
passive obedience, 180–81, 183
personification, 49, 65
philology, 139, 161
politics, 10
post-critical, 17
post-hermeneutic, 161–62
postsecular, 2–4, 6, 8, 11–12, 18, 38, 44, 52, 54, 75, 91, 103–4, 135–36, 147, 154–55, 158–59, 161–62, 200, 245
secular, 3, 44, 52–53, 55, 161
The Blazing World, 108, 124
Waverly, 226, 229, 231
Locke, John, 56, 106, 130, 178
Letter Concerning Toleration, 67, 69
liberty, 216
religion, 27, 37, 71
Second Treatise on Government, 82
loyalist, 46–47, 54, 179, 181–84, 195, 224
Lukács, György, 232
Luther, Martin, 73
language, 76

Mack, Ruth, 146, 155, 164, 168, 170
Mahmood, Saba, 161–62
Mannheim, Karl, 13, 23, 126, 156, 227, 233
marriage. *See also* family
as event, 108
and faith, 150
and fidelity, 30, 153
monogamy, 169
and pleasure, 140
and politics, 151
representations of, 151
as response, 141
and women, 83
Marxism, 214
historians, 6
Whig/Marxist debate, 6–7
McGann, Jerome, 161
McKeon, Michael, 7, 12, 52, 162, 165
mentation, 2, 13
literary, 14, 89, 104, 243
Mill, John Stuart, 88, 223
Miner, Earl, 134, 164

narration, 5, 47, 52–53, 177, 187, 200
limited, 177
literary, 9, 14, 29, 213
narrator, 3, 17, 44–46, 50–53, 91, 110, 113, 143, 156, 178–79, 186, 188–91, 194, 196–200, 225
novelistic, 9, 17, 85, 177, 179, 243
omniscient, 15, 50–51

third-person, 209
nation, 68, 107, 121, 224, 230
political, 6
sovereign, 107, 120
-state, 123
nature
cultural, 108
human, 136, 149, 183, 186, 199, 214
and humanity, 39, 195
law of, 43, 103, 107, 121, 124, 178, 199
limits of, 187
literary, 214
parts and wholes of, 110–13
political, 108, 231
state of, 55, 190
theories of, 107
nostalgia, 2, 13, 17, 228, 232, 243
British, 221, 225
conservative, 224
critique of, 219–21
disease of, 221
English, 222, 224
and fiction, 216
fictional, 220
history, 18, 216, 219, 223, 225, 229
Jacobite, 216, 219, 221–26, 228, 230, 234
logic of, 18, 223
political, 233
and revolution, 216, 219–21, 225, 227, 229–30, 232–34, 243
and romantic memory, 230
novel, 56, 220, 230
epistolary, 15, 48, 52
form, 15, 17, 48, 55, 83, 156, 177, 192, 195, 197–99, 225–27, 234
genre, 52, 227
gothic, 222
historical, 216, 225, 230–32, 234
history, 6, 8, 10–11, 15, 17, 45, 47, 52–53, 184, 187, 189, 193, 195, 199, 222, 225–26, 230
narrator, 3, 9, 17, 45, 85, 177, 179, 243
novelization, 156, 225
realist, 178

obedience, 35, 85, 185
active, 77, 178–79
dis-, 17, 42, 178–81, 184, 187–88, 193
versus faith, 29, 31
female, 83
to law, 33
passive, 2, 17, 177–84, 186–91, 195, 197–99, 213, 222
political, 28, 41, 178, 182, 215, 219
religious, 28

obedience (cont.)
  rules of, 123, 180
  theories of, 180, 195

passivity, 177–89, 193, 200, 243
  and the body, 194–95, 197
  of the body, 181, 194–95
  law of, 178, 186, 196, 200
  and lying, 190–91, 193, 207
  moral, 188, 192
  in narration, 9, 161, 177–78, 186–87, 192, 194, 196–200, 218, 226
  and nature, 195
  and obedience, 2, 17, 177–84, 186–91, 195, 197–99, 213, 222
  political, 185–86, 192, 226
  politics of, 183
  and readers, 161
  and witnessing, 178, 199–200
patriarchy, 82
peace, 106–7
  and diversity, 109–10
  enforcing, 107, 114–15, 185
  versus happiness, 140
  inherent, 118
  and nature, 111–12
  political, 106, 114, 211
  producing, 117–20, 124
  and prosperity, 68
personification, 29, 39, 48–50, 120
philosophy, 89
  enlightenment, 220
  and faith, 28, 42
  and indulgence, 79, 81
  materialist, 40–43, 107–8, 120, 128–29, 195, 232
  monist, 40, 103, 107, 113, 124
  natural, 109, 112
  of worlds, 118, 120
  versus philology, 161
  philosophers, 80, 115, 119
  political, 29, 40, 107
  practical, 154
  skeptical, 79
  and truth, 105, 116, 207
  vitalist, 103, 108–9, 111–13, 121, 124, 129
Pincus, Steve, 215
Pocock, J. G. A., 14, 167
poetry, 153
  didactic, 136
  Dryden, John, 159–60
  ecopoetics, 49
  occasional, 8, 17, 143, 155
  political, 47, 136–37, 178

political
  action, 10, 17, 48, 136, 145, 154, 182–83, 189, 191–92, 196–97, 217, 224, 228, 230–31, 244
  party, 135, 182, 233
postsecular, 146, 234
  baroque, 52
  conservatism, 14, 81, 90, 104, 121, 158, 233, 243
  critique, 161–62, 200
  culture, 3, 8, 245
  England, 147
  ethos, 2
  faith, 53–54, 233
  narrative, 45
  perspective, 1–2, 20, 54, 74
  reading practice, 135, 147, 154–57, 163
  revolution, 218
privacy, 149, 162
  and faith, 28–29, 38
  and happiness, 140, 153
  and judgement, 36
  privatization of religion, 1, 28
  and property, 185
  versus public, 2, 6, 78, 117, 153
  and reading, 153–56
  of subjectivity, 33
progress
  belief in, 232
  of civilization, 75, 78, 219, 221, 230
  denial of, 232
  enlightened, 233
  liberal, 227, 233
  narrative, 5, 11
  political, 137, 215, 217
  and revolution, 225
  scientific, 214
  secular, 217

race, 179, 193, 199, 223
  conceptions of, 88, 109, 213
  and enslavement, 89, 200
  and gender, 67, 179, 184, 199–200
  and liberalism, 89, 200, 213
  in literary criticism, 184
  and myth, 213
  and racialization, 224–25
  and racism, 88
  whiteness, 89, 227
Rancière, Jacques, 10–11
reading, 125, 140, 151, 225, 227
  ethic, 152
  methods, 2, 9, 12, 103, 135, 145
  model, 135
  modes, 103, 160–61, 243

practice, 14, 16–17, 53, 55, 134–36, 139, 141–42, 147, 152–62
scripture, 31, 38, 135, 141, 143–44, 153, 161
theory, 16, 147, 160, 162
realism, 195, 199–200
  baroque, 195
  and contract, 189
  literary, 153, 184, 199
reason, 82, 103, 116
  and authority, 79, 81
  enlightened, 223
  and faith, 36
  human, 37–38, 41, 70–71, 103, 146, 158, 180
  modes, 27–28, 148
  and philosophy, 79
  skeptical, 75
  versus superstition, 3
  theoretical, 13
rebellion, 8, 17, See also revolution
  biblical, 136
  cause, 43, 137, 227
  colonial, 213–14, 223, 226
  consequence, 229
  and fidelity, 46, 49, 54, 137
  Jacobite, 216, 225
  political, 49, 54
  prohibition of, 180–81, 212, 221, 224
  Protestant, 224
  right to, 81, 178, 183, 218, 230
  slave, 193, 199–200
Reformation, 74, 235
  event, 32, 74, 217
  spirituality, 162
  theologians, 14, 34–36
  tradition, 32
  writers, 31, 33, 75–76, 80, 86
religion, 50, 52, See also Catholicism
  1688–9, 1, 37, 74, 82
  Anglican, 4, 35, 37, 69, 73, 138, 142, 148, 152, 165, 179, 181–83
  Calvinism, 3, 34–35
  Catholicism, 137
  and conservatism, 54
  and faith, 27–35, 39–42, 45–47, 51, 55
  freedom of, 3, 5, 12, 15, 67–69, 72–76, 106, 117
  as institution, 158
  Islam, 147, 162
  Lutheran, 33, 35
  monism, 113
  political theology, 14, 17, 29, 31, 33, 38, 41–42, 45, 103, 200, 233
  versus politics, 4, 40, 42, 52, 54, 73, 106, 118, 159, 179, 243

Protestant, 3, 8, 28, 31, 33–38, 45, 67, 74, 76, 179, 182, 224
and revolution, 217
and science, 109, 112
studies of, 28
and superstition, 223
theology, 14, 29, 31, 33–39, 52–54, 74, 76, 107, 138, 140, 218
as truth, 27, 31, 35, 53, 114–15, 137–38
responsibility, 229
  individual, 70, 228
  legal, 43, 229
  political, 85, 107, 145, 231
Restoration, 4
  literature, 1–2, 6–9, 12, 17, 28, 30–31, 45, 54, 134, 144, 151, 160, 213, 245
  period, 5, 73, 82, 104, 106, 123, 134, 183, 245
  politics, 6, 13–15, 54, 233–34
  religion, 37, 67, 69, 153, 181
  violence, 107
revolution, 2, 220–21, 225, See also rebellion
  1688–9, 5, 7, 9, 17–18, 74, 81, 137, 147, 211–16, 218–19, 225, 227–28, 233
  anti-, 9, 14, 136, 147, 156, 177, 199, 212–13, 232, 234, 243, 245
  as allegory, 149
  cause, 158
  civil war, 67–68, 70, 106–7, 181
  etymology, 214
  French, 12, 212
  political, 6
  Protestant, 219
  Puritan, 5, 54, 67, 218
  and secularity, 5, 217–18
  slave, 200, 213, 233
  and temporality, 16–17, 157–58, 215, 227, 232–33
Richardson, Samuel, 15
  Clarissa, 83, 90, 225
rights, 69, 75, 198, 214
  civil, 82
  democratic, 67
  divine, 45, 178, 181
  heritable, 81, 83, 85
  inalienable, 76, 157
  individual, 41, 72
  language of, 76–77
  legal, 123
  liberal, 13, 38, 69, 76, 83, 90, 196, 200
  logic of, 82
  origin of, 84, 88, 195
  political, 77, 85, 189
  to rebel, 81, 178, 218, 230
  royal, 78

rights (cont.)
  sovereign, 68, 70
Rights, Bill of, 69, 73
ritual, 193, 196
  cultural, 8
  reading practice, 17, 53, 155, 162
  religious, 45, 103, 114–15, 162
Rogers, John, 34
Romance. *See* genre
romanticism, 7
royalty
  in fiction, 150–53, 178, 185–86, 188, 195–96, 199
  and indulgence, 67, 69, 77, 80
  and liberalism, 243
  royalism, 49, 104, 108, 142
  and toleration, 69

satire, 8, 108, 137, 143
  baroque, 194
science, 28, 121, 160, 214
  as art, 111
  experimental, 110
  and literature, 105, 109, 112
  natural, 16, 104, 107
  new, 108
  and opinion, 115
  parts and wholes, 115, 123
  phenomena, 105
  political, 55, 107
  and politics, 111, 113
  and religion, 53, 55, 109, 111
Scotland, 33, 69, 219, 222–23, 233, 238
  Highlander, 222–23
Scott, Walter, 9
  Waverly, 3, 18, 216, 225–33
scripture, 31, *See* also Bible, the
  reading, 31, 38, 135, 141, 143–44, 158
  rules of, 37–38
secular, 105, 139, 141, 143, 157, 217
  authority, 181, 183
  Christianity, 3, 41, 44, 71
  church and state, 4, 27, 33
  critique, 139, 161
  culture, 11, 16, 52–53, 103, 123, 245
  defining, 154
  enlightenment, 37
  epistemology, 14
  ethos, 3
  history, 55
  ideals, 1, 17, 52, 106, 162, 177, 217
  infidelity, 50
  law, 33, 181
  liberalism, 4–7, 15, 37–38, 109, 121, 148, 177, 216, 218, 221, 243

modernity, 51, 55
nationalism, 16
politics, 138, 141
progress, 217, 225
reading practice, 135, 161
relations, 33
Restoration, 153
revolution, 217
sovereign, 39–40
temporality, 144, 216
theology, 200
time, 154, 158, 216–18, 243
view, 90, 134, 137
secularization, 105, 137, 217, 223, 233
  Anglican, 148
  critique, 4, 39, 141
  and critique, 8, 12, 49, 103, 158, 161
  defining, 3
  history of, 45, 53, 67
  impact, 2, 4–6, 8, 12, 28, 243
  modern, 147
  narrative, 3–5, 11, 39, 53
  of faith, 14–15, 27–29, 31, 35–36, 38, 41–42, 46–47, 53–55
  process of, 1, 55
  project, 38, 90, 109
  reading and, 17
  and reading, 200
  response to, 3–5, 13, 54, 158, 160
  theories, 33
  thesis, 27–28, 39, 41, 52, 55, 123
skepticism, 4, 15, 75, 79, 88–89
slavery, 74, 82, 86, 90, 243
  chattel, 88–89, 200
  and colonization, 84, 177, 221, 233
  in fiction, 145, 150, 178, 183–86, 188, 190–99
  as metaphor, 48, 86–88
  modern, 195
  new world, 199
  and racism, 15, 17, 88, 200, 213
  Surinam, 213
sola fide, 31, 33–35, 58, 61
sovereignty, 48, 72, 152, 154
  absence of, 47
  and agency, 218
  British, 233
  Christian, 44
  English, 36
  expectation, 123, 149
  of God, 33, 46
  imperial, 113, 115
  and invasion, 109
  political, 39–41, 43–44, 46, 49, 71, 107, 114, 121, 123

royal, 67, 72–73, 82, 149, 187
and the state, 43
subjects, 40, 43, 83, 91, 106, 116, 179
theory, 116, 196
and violence, 104
speculation, 89, 91
Spinoza, Benedict, 63, 119, 123, 127
religion, 28
Sterne, Laurence
Tristram Shandy, 222
Stillingfleet, Edward, 37–38, 62
Stuart Monarchy
anti-, 136
Declarations, 15, 67–69, 71–74, 196
kings, 67, 71, 84, 136
politics, 6, 45, 67, 71, 73–75, 160, 179, 181, 196, 224
representations, 8, 219
response to, 76–77, 216
subjectivity, 4, 189, *See also* individuality, interiority
individual, 11
liberal, 190
political, 179, 181–82, 184, 199, 215, 218–21, 224
religious, 27–28, 33–35, 38
suffering, 50, 122, 178, 188, 195–97, 226
body, 195–97
Jesus, 34, 181, 183
nostalgia, 221
and obedience, 179, 181–83, 188
symbolism, 32, 45, 50, 121, 143, 149, 183, 185, 223

Taylor, Charles, 217–18
temporality
and agency, 231–32
chronology, 135, 189–91, 216–17, 219
cyclical, 135, 214, 217, 219
in fiction, 138, 150, 154–55, 230
generations, 152, 223, 227–28, 232–33
literary, 16–17, 103, 119, 135, 144, 146, 190, 222
memory, 145, 155, 227, 229–31, 233
and nostalgia, 219, 223, 232
revolutionary, 214, 216, 218, 228
theory, 16, 158, 216–17, 243
Teskey, Gordon, 195–96
Tillotson, John, 37–38
tolerance
liberal, 16
toleration, 70
etymology, 118
in-, 78, 117, 124
and indulgence, 15, 67–75, 78–79, 82, 85, 90, 114, 243
liberal, 15, 69, 71–72, 104, 106, 109, 122
politics, 107, 109, 112, 118
process, 70–72
religious, 1, 15, 69–71, 106
repression, 71
right, 69
of science, 55
and secularization, 12, 71, 109, 117
theory, 107
and violence, 105–6, 124
virtue, 78
Toleration, Act of, 70, 72–73, 93, *See also* freedom, religion
William, 69, 78, 127
Tory, 77, 225
satirists, 7–8
tradition, 84, 141, 148
Catholic, 76
English, 76, 81
faith and, 30
and faith, 32
Highland, 224
importance of, 152
literary, 146, 162
oral, 37
philosophical, 118
political, 77, 108, 157, 186, 215, 233
postsecular, 12
Reformation, 32
structures, 55
traditionalism, 54, 84, 104, 156, 196
Tragicomedy. *See* genre
translation
Dryden, John, 135, 157–58, 160
religious texts, 135, 194
secular, 143
truth, 110, 143, 195, *See also* epistemology, faith
and contract, 189
eternal, 146
and faith, 29, 34–37, 42, 90, 141
and feelings, 140, 187, 216
human, 137, 217
and indulgence, 79, 89, 91
as judge, 120
of law, 70
moral, 154, 206
and Nature, 111
and oaths, 189
objective, 51
philosophical, 116
religious, 27–28, 31, 53, 70, 114–15, 137–39
scientific, 105, 111
subjective, 189

truth (cont.)
    and toleration, 70, 73
    transcendent, 194
    and trust, 32–33, 35–36, 38

violence, 122
    animal, 138
    authorized, 118
    fleeing, 122
    and imagination, 106
    inevitable, 124, 197
    and infidelity, 50
    inherent, 109, 118, 124
    justification for, 123
    physical, 140
    political, 107, 142, 144, 197, 212
    rape, 83, 169
    sexual, 197
    sovereign, 16, 104, 107
    state, 8, 105–6, 109, 122, 124

Watt, Ian, 52–53

Weber, Max, 3, 35, 61
Whig
    in fiction, 222
    history, 137, 211
    influence, 8
    party, 77, 182, 225, 233
    perspective, 1, 3, 5–7, 68, 136, 178, 180, 182–84, 189–90, 194, 211–12, 214, 218
worlds, 114, 243
    and conflict, 119–20, 123–24
    connecting, 104, 117–20, 122, 124
    creation of, 105, 117, 119–20, 125, 133
    fictional, 16, 103–5, 112, 116, 119, 121–24, 138, 214, 243
    and gods, 118
    and governance, 115, 118
    interpretations of, 118
    plurality, 105, 107, 114–15, 118–19, 121, 123
    possible, 122, 124, 177
Žižek, Slavoj, 32

Zwicker, Steven, 136, 159–60

Milton Keynes UK
Ingram Content Group UK Ltd.
UKHW031445290224
438476UK00003B/7